THE MAKING OF A SYRIAN IDENTITY

SOCIAL, ECONOMIC AND POLITICAL STUDIES OF THE MIDDLE EAST AND ASIA

(S.E.P.S.M.E.A.)

(Founding editor: C.A.O. van Nieuwenhuijze)

VOLUME 98

THE MAKING OF A SYRIAN IDENTITY

Intellectuals and Merchants in Nineteenth Century Beirut

BY

FRUMA ZACHS

BRILL
LEIDEN · BOSTON
2005

This book is printed on acid-free paper.

Library of Congress Cataloging-in-Publication Data

Zachs, Fruma.
The making of a Syrian identity : intellectuals and merchants in nineteenth century Beirut / by Fruma Zachs.
p. cm.
Includes bibliographical references and index.
ISBN 90-04-14169-3 (alk. paper)
1. Beirut (Lebanon)—Intellectual life—19th century. 2. Syrians—Lebanon—Beirut. 3. National characteristics, Syrian. 4. Beirut (Lebanon)—History—19th century. I. Title.

DS89.B4Z33 2005
305.892'75691056925'09034—dc22

2004066041

ISSN 1385-3376
ISBN 90 04 14169 3

PRINTED IN THE NETHERLANDS

To Noam, Offir, and Inbar

CONTENTS

LIST OF ILLUSTRATIONS

Figures

Map

PREFACE

As long as I can remember myself as a thinking individual, I have been preoccupied with the fundamental question of my own identity, that is, who am I? This question has been the essence of my reality, since I am half Ashkenazi (descendents of Jews from Central and Eastern Europe) and half Sephardic (descendents of "Eastern" or "Oriental" Jews, principally from the Middle East). When I later became a researcher in the field of Middle Eastern history, this topic quickly found its way into my own lines of investigation. This understanding came to me only towards the end of my writing.

Gradually, as I grew familiar with the heterogeneous society of Syria in the nineteenth century, I felt that researching the Christian Arabs constituted a special challenge in the pursuit of understanding their multifaceted identity. Delving into their cultural duality (West and East), might enable me to better understand my own duality. The Christian Arabs were caught in a multi-cultural world, as I am, although the pertinent societies and cultures differ. Yet, the fundamental question remains similar: how should they, and I, define ourselves?

In 1997, I submitted a doctoral thesis on this subject to the University of Haifa, yet I felt that there was still much to be done. I was fortunate to receive the Israeli Junior fellowship awarded by St. Antony's College (Oxford) and thus was able to expand and deepen my knowledge and prepare future research for this book. Throughout my academic studies, Professor Butrus Abu-Manneh kindled my interest in this subject, inspired me and stimulated my mind with his helpful remarks. I am most grateful to him for all of his assistance, particularly in helping me through the periods when I truly believed that this book would remain only in spirit. My deep thanks, as well, to Professor Gad Gilbar, who encouraged me through all the years I spent working on this book. His fascination with the topic of merchants in the Middle East and our conversations influenced and inspired my own research.

During the preparation of this study I consulted a number of friends and colleagues, whose critiques I sought. Each one of them supported and encouraged me in his or her own unique way, and I am deeply grateful to them all: Professor Ami Ayalon, Dr. Basilius

Bawardi, Dr. Eyal Ginio, Dr. Michael Eppel, Mrs. Nicole Khayat, Dr. Uri Kupferschmidt, Miss Yafit Marom, Mr. Amir Mubarky, Professor Reuven Snir, Dr. Ruth Roded and Dr. Itzchak Weismann. My sincere thanks go to all of them, but, as usually, sole responsibility lies with the author.

I also feel indebted to the late Professor Panayotis J. Vatikiotis. I had the opportunity to attend his dynamic courses when he came to teach in Haifa some years ago. He often explained to me that we should treat questions in history not as complicated issues remote from reality but as part of our actual daily life. I hope that I managed to bring forth this outlook.

I would also like to thank the Truman Institute in Jerusalem, for granting a scholarship that aided me in publishing this book. To Ms. Marsha Brown who exerted much effort to improve the English text. I would also like to thank Brill Academic Publishers, especially Professor Reinhard Schulze, for whose helpful remarks I am thankful. I likewise thank Mrs. Trudy Kamperveen for her devoted help in the publication of this book.

Finally, for me the most important debt is the one to my family. To my husband Noam, who helped and encouraged me in every possible way to bring to fruition this endeavour, which had been maturing in my mind for several years; and to my two daughters, Offir and Inbar, who helped me grow into the writing of history.

Haifa, August 2004
F. Z.

NOTE ON TRANSLITERATION

For the most part, Arabic terms have been used throughout this book, transliterated in accordance with the *International Journal of Middle East Studies*. In the case of names of individuals or families I have chosen the name most commonly used by these individuals or families themselves. In the case of places, proper names commonly found in Western literature appear in their familiar Latinised form, and were not transliterated. Yet, whenever a place appeared that I thought was less familiar in Western literature, the name was transliterated.

Throughout the book (but especially in Chapter Three), in most cases I have used modern Turkish orthography for names (rarely) and for administrative terms in Ottoman Turkish, again in keeping with the *International Journal of Middle East Studies*.

"Tā' marbūṭa" is written as 'a' and not 'ah.' Mostly, a roman 's' has been added to make Arabic words plural. I have also transliterated the word "history" in Arabic as "tārīkh" and not "ta'rīkh" (meaning the writing of history or historiography), which has come into common use by historians.

Finally, during the period covered by the book, the word "Syria" appeared in Arabic (and still does) in two forms—it either ends with a "long 'a'," or ends with a "tā' marbūṭa." In the case of the former, I chose to transliterate it as "Sūriyā." In the case of the latter, I use the form "Sūriyya."

LIST OF ABBREVIATIONS

ABCFM	American Board of Commissioners for Foreign Missions
AUB	American University of Beirut
FO	Public Record Office, London, Foreign Office
HL	Houghton Library, Harvard University, Cambridge, Mass.
NA	National Archives, Washington D.C.
PRO	Public Record Office, London
PRONI	Public Record Office Northern Ireland, Belfast
SAC	St. Antony's College, Oxford
SPC	Syrian Protestant College

INTRODUCTION

In political terms, the modern Middle East is generally seen as the outcome of agreements made before, during, and immediately after the First World War, when France and Britain divided the former Arab provinces of the Ottoman Empire into their own spheres of influence. Under the Mandate system of the newly created states, Iraq and Palestine came under the tutelage of Britain; Lebanon and Syria under that of France. Similarly, when in socio-cultural terms we speak today of an "Iraqi identity" or a "Syrian identity," the general assumption of much of contemporary research is that these identities first came into existence in the twentieth century, namely under the Mandates.

After researching the formation of the Syrian identity, I claim that not only should we locate its roots during the course of the nineteenth century, but that we should also view its emergence initially and largely as due to indigenous factors. As Schölch wrote regarding Palestine, ". . . when the borders of the mandate zone were drawn, they were not the arbitrary, artificial, drawing-board product of the colonial powers. Rather, "Palestine" [in our case Syria] had slowly taken shape in the course of the nineteenth and early twentieth centuries in the consciousness of both its inhabitants and its central government."[1]

This book is not about nationalism. Rather, it deals with the process of what can be interpreted as "proto-nationalism." In recent years, books have been published which analyse the emergence of a national identity in some of the countries in the Middle East, but none of them focuses entirely on the crucial phase of proto-national identity. In order to understand the role of this stage in formulating identity in the Middle East, the present book examines this process in the case of Syria, as it is reflected in the activities of the Christian-Arab intellectuals,[2] mainly Greek Orthodox and Protestants, particularly

---

[1] Alexander Schölch, *Palestine in Transformation, 1856–1882*, trans. by William C. Young and Michael C. Gerrity (Washington DC, 1993), p. 10.

[2] Following Sharabi, I use the term Christian "in a broad sense to signify social and psychological traits rather than religious affiliation." As he elaborates, "Christian intellectualism as a mental outlook was the product of a social and psychological process peculiar to the experience of certain Christian social strata in Syria (including Lebanon and Palestine). It was in large part the result of the transformation of

in Beirut but also in Tripoli. As such, the book concentrates on the emergence of the Syrian identity or Syrian patriotism (*waṭaniyya*) in this population. Examined are the origins, influences, stages of evolution and components of the emerging Syrian identity and patriotic sensibility. The development of this identity is described as the product of both local and external developments.

Proto-nationalism as an historical descriptive concept probably came into use as early as the 1960s. It has mostly been applied to the struggle between the colonial administration and local elites in the late nineteenth and early twentieth centuries.[3] Nevertheless, when referring to the term "proto-nationalism" in the book, I mean the initial phase of self-definition that led to self-identity or cultural identity of these Christian-Arab intellectuals under the political umbrella of the Ottoman Empire. This stage did not incorporate a struggle against the "colonial administration," since Ottoman rule was generally accepted by these intellectuals.

This process of constructing self-identity could also be thought of as a prerequisite for eventually creating a national identity. I define the latter as the phase which politicises this self or cultural identity and in which the political struggle for independence begins to take place not only among the educated elite but also among larger sectors of society. Thus, Proto-nationalism in the Syrian case is the stage at which certain variants in the identity of groups of people began to coalesce. These changes were mainly a means of cultural identity, motivated by economic and social changes and the desire

---

Christian education in the nineteenth century and of economic and social change which the Christians pioneered." Hisham Sharabi, *Arab Intellectuals and the West: The Formative Years, 1875–1914* (Baltimore, 1970), p. ix. Throughout the book, I use the term "intellectual" as a general definition for people who engaged in activity requiring the creative use of the intellect and who where socially and culturally involved. An Arabic term of similar connotation is *muthaqqaf*. For a sub-group occupied mainly with literary activity, I sometimes prefer the use of "literati."

[3] See, for example, Shelton Stromquist, "The Communist Uprising of 1926–1927 in Indonesia: A Re-Interpretation," *Journal of Southeast Asian History*, Vol. 7 (1967), pp. 189–200; Bela Kiraly, "Prussian Diplomatic Adventure with Poland and the Feudal Revolt in Hungary in 1790," *Polish Review*, Vol. 12 (1967), pp. 3–11; Nikki R. Keddie, "Pan-Islam as Proto-Nationalism," *The Journal of Modern* History, Vol. 4 (1969), pp. 17–28; "Popular Proto-Nationalism," Eric. J. Hobsbawm, *Nations and Nationalism since 1780—Programme, Myth, Reality*, 2nd ed. (Cambridge, 1999), pp. 46–79. In some ways, part of the work of Antony Smith can be seen as tracking the development of proto-nationalism.

of certain groups of people to build their self-identity or to re-define the one which they already possessed, rather than manifestations of aspirations for political self-determination.

On the other hand, by using the term "proto-nationalism" we imply that the development of the Syrian identity in the nineteenth century eventually carried into the twentieth century and led to the development of Syrian nationalism. Although it seems that this is indeed the case with the Syrian region and is in fact the reasoning behind my perception of this phase as proto-nationalism, this assumption requires further research, which is not within the purview of this book. In light of this, I minimise the use of the term "proto-nationalism" and mainly emphasise terms such as "notion," "idea" and "concept" for describing the initial roots and stages of this evolving self-identity. Only in reference to the stages after this self-image had been moulded and had become part of a growing and defined identity, do I introduce the term "Syrian identity."

* * *

One of the important conceptual changes among Christian-Arab intellectuals during the nineteenth century was the transformation of their communal into a territorial identity. From the beginning of the Muslim conquest to about the second half of the nineteenth century, the concept of *Bilād al-Shām* was paramount. The term *Bilād al-Shām*, which was the Arabic designation for the lands between the eastern coastal area of the Mediterranean and the Syrian Desert, was largely a regional and cultural referent. Neither boundaries nor a clearly defined territory were designated; the term was devoid of any national connotation. Rather, Islamic criteria—religious, sectarian and communal identities—were the elements defining it.

However, even before the middle of the nineteenth century, and in parallel to this concept, a "Syrian identity" had begun to develop. By the term "Syria" I refer to generally defined boundaries that encompass the region of Greater Syria, namely the three Ottoman provinces (*eyalets*) of Aleppo, Sidon and Damascus. This region more or less encompassed the same area of today's Syria, Lebanon, Jordan and Palestine/Israel. It also encapsulates historical and cultural characteristics dating back to pre-Islamic times. As part of this identity, the region of Syria was considered one territorial entity and homeland for its inhabitants, who were conceived of as being Syrians with an Arab culture. The identity was essentially a secular, territorial and cultural one, aimed at blurring the multi-sectarian and communal identities that prevailed in this region.[4]

Even though this identity was intended to include the entire population (meaning Muslims as well as Christians), it was essentially a Christian-Arab identity. The majority of the Muslims did not adopt this identity until towards the end of the nineteenth century. When they did so, the Muslims emphasised different aspects and characteristics from those held by the Christians, while maintaining others as the Christians had articulated them.

The development of the Christian Arabs' self-image as Syrians evolved during a period of transformation that took place throughout Ottoman society, influencing Muslims and non-Muslims alike. Yet, other narratives, which are beyond the scope of this book but nonetheless apparently influenced or have been influenced by this evolution, both directly and indirectly, are also important for understanding the development of this Syrian identity. Two major examples of other narratives are the shifts in self-identity that took place among the Christian Catholics, namely the Lebanese/Phoenician narrative[5] in the region of Syria, and the shift that occurred within the

[4] Simultaneously with the transformation from the term "*Bilād al-Shām*" to "Syria" and from the second half of the nineteenth century, i.e. before Kemal Atatürk assumed the rule in modern Turkey, we find that in Istanbul and in Anatolia educated Ottomans began defining themselves as Turks. This shift from Ottoman identity (based on religious, not ethnic background) to Turkish identity marked (as in the Syrian case) the transfer from a primary identification with Islam to one with the modern nation. In fact, and again like the Syrian case, this new Turkish identity came to replace the Ottoman or Islamic one. See Bernard Lewis, *The Emergence of Modern Turkey*, 2nd ed. (London, 1961), pp. 320–348; Keddie, "Pan-Islam as Proto-Nationalism," p. 17.

[5] Regarding the Lebanese/Phoenician narrative, see the recent works of Asher Kaufman, e.g. Asher Kaufman, "Phoenicianism: The Formation of an Identity in Lebanon in 1920," *Middle Eastern Studies*, Vol. 37 (2001), pp. 173–194; Asher Kaufman, *Reviving Phoenicia: The Search for Identity in Lebanon* (London, 2004). The book follows the social, intellectual and political development of the Phoenician myth of origin in Lebanon from the mid-nineteenth to the end of the twentieth century. This Lebanese/Phoenician narrative prevailed mainly among the Catholics, especially the Maronites, but developed after the emergence of the Syrian narrative. Some of its characteristics can be uncovered within the pages of the newspaper *al-Mashriq*. In fact, some parameters of the Syrian narrative (such as the Phoenician heritage) were later adopted, and eventually adapted, by Lebanese nationalists. See also the recent book of Kais Firro, *Inventing Lebanon: Nationalism and the State under the Mandate* (London, 2002), which deals, among other things, with the connection between the Lebanese idea and the Maronite Church. Also the works of Basīliyūs Bawārdī, *Bayna al-Ṣaḥrāʾ*

Muslim population.[6] In this regard, the Syrian narrative of the Beiruti middle stratum,[7] which is of a minority, combined with other narratives that have been examined extensively are, in the final analysis, what eventually influenced, among other things, the growth of the Syrian identity and perhaps the Syrian national identity as well. Still, the Syrian narrative predates these other competing regional narratives. As the main purpose of this book is to explore the Syrian narrative which until now has not been thoroughly analysed,[8] I chose not to compare it with these other narratives that developed after its emergence and have already enjoyed the attention of previous research.

Research dealing with the identity of the Christian-Arab population in the region of Syria has focused primarily on the transformation of their economic and social status, or their contributions to Lebanese identity, Arab identity and the Arab National Movement.[9] Their role in the revival of the Arabic language and culture, which is known as the *Nahḍa*, is also emphasised. Furthermore, much has been written on Arab identity, the Egyptian, the Palestinian or the Lebanese identities, but until now no research has focused on the rise of the Syrian one as an independent topic, nor have its background and roots been analysed.

---

wal-Baḥr: Baḥth fī Ta'thīr al-Qawmiyyatayn al-Lubnāniyya—al-Fīnīqiyya wal-Sūriyya ʿalā al-Adab al-ʿArabī al-Muʿāṣir, unpublished M. A. Thesis, University of Haifa, 1998; Basīliyūs Bawārdī, "Adab al-Qawmiyya al-Lubnāniyya al-Fīnīqiyya: al-Taṣwīnī Awwal Riwāya bil-Lugha al-Lubnāniyya Kanamūdhaj Nassī," *al-Karmil Abḥāth fī al-Lugha wal-Adab*, Vol. 20–21 (2000–2001), pp. 7–79.

[6] See, for example, the recently published book by Itzchak Weismann, *Taste of Modernity: Sufism, Salafiyya and Arabism in Late Ottoman Damascus* (Leiden, 2001). The book focuses on the Muslim narrative during the late nineteenth century. It shows that developments towards modernisation among the Muslims of Damascus existed, and examines, among other things, the relationship between the modernisation of Muslim society and the rise of Arab nationalism.

[7] I will enlarge on this term in Chapter One.

[8] There is, for example, an article by Itamar Rabinovich which gives a general overview of this issue. Itamar Rabinovich "Syria and the Syrian Land: The 19th Century Roots of the 20th Century Development" in Thomas Philipp (ed.), *The Syrian Land in the 18th and 19th Century* (Stuttgart, 1992), pp. 43–53.

[9] Many of these studies focus on the Christian Catholics. See for example, Robert Haddad, *Syrian Christians in Muslim Society: An Interpretation* (Princeton, 1970); Bruce Masters, *Christians and Jews in the Ottoman Arab World: The Roots of Sectarianism* (Cambridge, 2001). The latter focuses on the Catholics in Aleppo from the sixteenth to the nineteenth centuries. In fact, this book describes the social and economic background of the Christians' activities in Beirut, which replaced Aleppo as their most important centre in the region. In addition, see: Firro, *Inventing Lebanon.*

Some research has explored the cultural contribution of the Christian Arabs to the development of Syrian patriotism during the nineteenth century, but it is primarily limited to an examination of the activities of Buṭrus al-Bustānī, a prominent Christian intellectual of this period. The emergence of a Syrian identity was taken for granted in that research; its fundamental assumption was that Syrian patriotism evolved following the civil war of 1860. This traumatic event, according to this research, sharpened the need for a new identity among Christian Arabs in order to re-define their status within a predominantly Muslim society.

In contrast, this book sets out to demonstrate that the formation of a Syrian identity began before 1860. The economic, social and intellectual backgrounds to this process, and the stratum of the population that promoted it, are examined and explained. The focus of this study is primarily to pursue the "indigenous voice,"[10] since its principal object is to analyse the Syrian identity through the eyes and voices of the Christian-Arab intellectuals. Hence, the Arabic writings of these intellectuals comprise most of the sources used. These are contained in local Arabic documents, many of which have barely been considered to date from this perspective, viz., nineteenth-century Arab newspapers and periodicals, chronicles, historical novels and short stories (*uqṣūṣa*), and the literary products of the many cultural societies that flourished during the period (lectures, books, etc.).

In our case, the term "indigenous" refers to local Arabs, particularly to the voice of the intellectuals. Their exposure to the West does not detract from the locality of their voice; still, it was influenced by other actors on the "local" scene such as Ottoman bureaucrats and American missionaries. Thus the resulting voice may be considered an indigenous one. In this Syrian narrative it is difficult to draw a dividing line between "foreign" and "indigenous" voices. Eventually, the Syrian narrative, as will be shown, was played out by several performers and its "voice" was sounded by each of them (not necessarily in harmony).[11]

As to non-local sources, most previous studies concerning these Christian Arabs have principally relied on European sources and documentation, especially on the French archives, while others con-

[10] Masters, *Christians and Jews in the Ottoman Arab World*, p. 13.

[11] I would like to thank Professor Reinhard Schulze for his thoughts on this issue.

centrated on Ottoman archives. In the preparation of this book, the non-local sources most extensively utilised were American archives. Indeed, the encounter of the locals with American missionaries receives special attention within the book.

Christian Arabs were not simply passive in the process of their encounter with the West or their modernisation. In reality they were very active. This fact, along with the methods they used to cope with the changes, tailoring them to their own needs and society, and encompassing their own authentic view in the process, is examined here. The relationship with the West was problematic not only for the Muslim population but also for the Christians, who were also part of Ottoman society.

The attitude of the local Christians towards the West was ambivalent. On the one hand, they admired Western achievements. On the other hand, they were strongly aware of having been made, in a sense, "victims," as well as beneficiaries, of Western penetration into the Ottoman Empire. For perhaps the first time, Christian Arabs whose families had lived as recognised and integral parts of the Ottoman Empire were seen more clearly as "the other" by the Muslim majority. Somewhat threatened by their encounter with the more technologically advanced West, the Muslims increasingly saw the Christian minority within their society as having special links with these Western—all Christian—powers. The Christians, for their part, welcomed their co-religionists, but also suddenly found themselves more distanced and isolated from their surroundings. Note that throughout the history of the Ottoman Empire, the autonomy of minority groups was recognised. Christians (as well as Jews) were granted communal, social and religious autonomy, within the larger Muslim society. Hence, in their self-identification, they saw themselves first and foremost as Arabs and only then as Westerners or even as Christians. In this sense they preferred to become "proud Arabs" and not "imperfect Europeans."

The development of the Syrian identity is analysed from the modernist approach which envisions nationalism, or in our case proto-nationalism, as a modern phenomenon and as a composite artefact, composed of different cultural sources. This development is considered a constructed, an imagined or an invented tradition.[12] My point

[12] Anthony Smith, *Myths and Memories of the Nation* (Oxford and New York, 1999),

of departure is that identities are flexible, and change according to the needs of their society. Thus, the Syrian identity is presented here as these intellectuals developed it during the nineteenth century.

Generally, as Edward Said emphasised, the construction of identity "involves establishing opposites and 'others' whose actuality is always subject to the continuous interpretation and re-interpretation of their differences from 'us.'"[13] In the case of the Christian Arabs who tried to construct a multi-cultural identity, the principal purpose of their evolving self was to construct new limits to their identities or to change the ones that already existed within the local population. The constructing of their self-identity can be seen not only as opposite to the "others" which in many cases were the Muslims, but more importantly, as an effort to build their identity together with that of the "other." The aim was to create a new self or a collective self that would encompass the region's entire population, be it Muslim or Christian. They saw themselves as part of the "other" and from that perspective, tried to construct the inter-relationships in a new way, one that would both follow and preserve the transformations that their society was undergoing. Finally, in the case of the Christian Arabs, the West was another manifestation of their definition of the "other." Eventually, these two "others" would create the dichotomy inherent in the Christian Arab's identity.

This book deals primarily with two questions: What were the reasons and circumstances leading to the development of this Syrian identity? And, in what way was this identity shaped? The first two chapters analyse the economic, social and cultural developments germane to this process. In this regard, two stages were discerned. The first stage, on which the first chapter focuses, originated in Mount Lebanon and lasted from the late eighteenth century until the first half of the nineteenth century. Certain distinct economic, social and cultural developments towards the end of the eighteenth century, highlighting the beginning of the rise of a discrete Christian-Arab middle stratum under Amīr Bashīr II (1788–1840), proved crucial for the inception of the formative process of constructing the Syrian

---

pp. 163–186; Hobsbawm, *Nations and Nationalism Since 1780*, pp. 1–13; Eric Hobsbawm and Terence Ranger (eds.), *The Invention of Tradition* (London, 1983), pp. 1–2; Ernest Gellner, *Nations and Nationalism* (Ithaca, 1983), pp. 48–49; Benedict Anderson, *Imagined Communities*, 2nd ed. (London, 1991).

[13] Edward Said, *Orientalism*, (London, 1995), p. 332.

identity. The second stage, described in the second chapter, took place throughout the rest of the nineteenth century, when the centre of development shifted from the Mountain to Beirut and Tripoli, and a middle stratum arose in these cities. Attention in this chapter focuses on the connection existing between the accelerated urbanisation of Beirut and the consequent social changes in that city, on one hand, and the emergence of the Syrian identity on the other.

The third chapter examines the contribution of the Ottoman Empire to the creation of this identity, particularly as inspired by the *Tanẓīmāt* policy of reforms promulgated between the years 1856–1876. The fourth chapter explores the contribution of certain American Protestant missionaries who were active in the region from the early decades of the nineteenth century, to the development of this identity. As far as I know, this is the first such interpretation of the effect of the American Protestant missionaries. Until now, their contribution was viewed as relating to the *Nahḍa* or to the Arab National Movement.

The fifth and last chapter enlarges on the way that the Christian Arabs shaped this multicultural identity and defined its characteristics through three new genres of their writings: newspapers, historiography and historical novels. Finally, a brief epilogue evaluates this identity under Sultan Abdül Hamid II and describes its effect on Arab identity at the beginning of the twentieth century.

CHAPTER ONE

FIRST NOTIONS OF A "SYRIAN VISION": THE PERIOD OF AMĪR BASHĪR II

Three developments which occurred during the reign of Amīr Bashīr II, ruler of Mount Lebanon between the years 1788–1840, were important for the initial steps in the formation of the Syrian identity.[1] The first was the rise of Mount Lebanon as the economic centre for the whole Syrian region. This process had already begun during the second half of the eighteenth century, but it was only under the rule of Amīr Bashīr II that it reached its zenith. The second development was the rising status of the Shihābī Emirate and the growing centralisation of its government and institutions. The third and last was the appearance of an educated Christian middle stratum,[2] which included mainly merchants and intelligentsia.

Through these developments, this period provided the first impetus towards building a new concept, namely a Syrian vision. By this term it is meant that during this stage, as part of their growing awareness, the middle stratum in the Mountain began to envision the region of Syria as a single territorial entity. Mount Lebanon was perceived as an integral and central part of this territorial entity, with its own Arab heritage and culture.

---

[1] For further details on Amīr Bashīr see: Asad Rustum, *Bashīr Bayna al-Sulṭān wal-ʿAzīz, 1804–1841* (Beirut, 1966); Gabriel Enkiri, *Aux Origines du Liban Contemporain: Le Regne de Bechir II* (Beirut, 1973); Charles H. Churchill, *Mount Lebanon: A Ten Year's Residence, 1842–1852* (London, 1853); Kamal S. Salibi, *The Modern History of Lebanon* (London, 1965); David Urquhart, *The Lebanon: A History and Diary*, Vol. 1 (London, 1860), pp. 91, 138; Salīm Khaṭṭār al-Daḥdāḥ, "al-Amīr Bashīr al-Kabīr al-Maʿrūf bil-Malṭī," *al-Mashriq*, Vol. 22, 1924, pp. 566–577, 696–702.

[2] I chose to define this group, both in the case of the Mountain and later in Beirut, using the general and somewhat flexible term—"middle stratum." In contrast to the terms "bourgeoisie" or "class" which developed in the historical and social reality of the West, "middle stratum" allows for an almost culture free affinity. In Chapters One and Two it is used to encompass a number of sub-groups. As we shall see, the Mountain middle stratum and the Beiruti middle stratum differ from each other but had some overlapping sub-groups.

First Phase: The Rise of the Mountain Middle Stratum

The period of Bashīr II's rule was a turning point in the history of the Christian Arabs in Syria in general and in Mount Lebanon in particular. Bashīr was a local Muslim ruler from the Shihābī house who was the strong ruler of Mount Lebanon for more than fifty years. At first, local forces prevented the young Shihābī Amīr from augmenting and enhancing his power. One of them was the strong and influential *vali*, Aḥmad Pāshā al-Jazzār, who ruled from 1776 to 1804, and who, on several occasions, became the *vali* of both the Sidon (Acre) and the Damascus provinces.[3] Both the Mountain and Bashīr were subordinate to his rule. After the death of al-Jazzār in 1804, Bashīr was able to gradually aggrandise power, and he became the central figure of authority in the region.

In fact, from 1804 until 1841, Bashīr's control and influence encompassed a far greater area than the region which he formally ruled—namely not just the Mountain, but the bulk of greater Syria. The extent of his influence is illustrated by the fact that the *vali*s of Sidon during his time, Sulaymān Pāshā (1805–1819) and later on ʿAbdallāh Pāshā (1819–1832), occasionally depended on his support, military strength and influence. Whenever a major feud developed between the *vali* of Sidon and one of his neighbouring rivals (usually the *vali* of Damascus), Bashīr's assistance was sought. The armies of most *vali*s of Syria were mercenaries and had to be paid. Thus, the *vali*s were unable to field large armies for long periods of time. In contrast, Bashīr chose to recruit his army from amongst the peasants of the Mountain. General mobilisation in the Mountain could raise an army of twelve thousand or more soldiers; that army was also more obedient than the Pāshās' mercenary armies. This fact helps to explain why the *vali*s of Syria often depended on the good offices of Bashīr. His army also served another purpose: it was essential in helping the *vali*s to collect taxes. Sidon's *vali* also called upon Bashīr, as his official *Muḥaṣṣil* (tax collector) in Mount Lebanon, to collect

[3] On al-Jazzār see: Aḥmad Ḥaydar al-Shihāb, *Tārīkh Aḥmad Pāshā al-Jazzār* (Beirut, 1955); Ibrāhīm al-ʿAwra, *Tārīkh Wilāyat Sulaymān Bāshā al-ʿĀdil 1804–1819* (Sidon, 1936), pp. 84, 203, 205, 290, 310; Amnon Cohen, *Palestine in the 18th Century* (Jerusalem, 1973), pp. 92–111; Muḥammad Kurd ʿAlī, *Khiṭaṭ al-Shām*, Vol. 2 (Beirut, 1969–1972), pp. 200–202; Thomas Philipp, *Acre: The Rise and the Fall of a Palestinian City, 1730–1831* (New-York, 2001), pp. 48–78.

his taxes even though the *valī*'s lands lay outside Bashīr's formal territory. Similarly, the *vali* requested Bashīr's assistance in any uprising in the latter's *vilâyet* or even outside it.

Under Sulaymān Pāshā, Bashīr's power flourished, especially from 1810 when he and Sulaymān conquered Damascus together. With that conquest, Sulaymān Pāshā was appointed as the *vali* of the two provinces, Sidon and Damascus, and became the ruler of the whole region, from just south of Aleppo in the north to the northern border of the province of Sinai in the south. Amīr Bashīr II, as the right-hand man of the ruler of the entire region of Syria, became much more powerful, even though Sulaymān's appointment over the two provinces lasted only about a year.[4]

Later, in the early 1820s, ʿAbdallāh Pāshā attempted to get rid of Amīr Bashīr, but ʿAbdallāh soon recognised that Bashīr was indispensable, and restored him to his post. In 1831, when Ibrāhīm Pāshā conquered the area, Bashīr's position as a key figure in the region was undermined. Finally, after Ibrāhīm Pāshā was forced to abandon Syria, the Porte exiled Bashīr to Malta in 1840 for co-operating with Ibrāhīm Pāshā.

During his reign, Amīr Bashīr managed to strengthen his power also inside Mount Lebanon. In order to do so he had to deal with the Druze *muqāṭaʿjī*s (landlords). In fact, under his rule, and prior to it as well, Mount Lebanon could be characterised as "pseudo-feudal"[5] with a traditional social structure, based on a tax-farming system, the *muqāṭaʿa*. In general, the *muqāṭaʿjī*s themselves selected the Mountain's Amīr, who was then "officially appointed" by the Ottoman governor of Sidon in exchange for fixed annual taxes. In order to consolidate

[4] For more details see: Fruma Zachs, "Mīkhāʾīl Mishāqa—The First Historian of Modern Syria," *British Journal of Middle Eastern Studies*, Vol. 28, no. 1 (2001), p. 75.

[5] The term "pseudo-feudalism" is used in order to avoid the term "feudalism" which is not appropriate for Middle Eastern society. Still, the form of government in Mount Lebanon had several elements similar to the basic classic pattern of feudal society in Western Europe in the Middle Ages. In both cases, a wealthy stratum owned the land, passed it on by inheritance, and dwelt among the people who worked the land. However, differences existed between the two societies, for example, in terminology. In Europe, the landowning class was called the aristocracy; in Mount Lebanon the landlords were called *muqāṭaʿjī*s; those who worked the land in Europe were called serfs and had no freedom; in Mount Lebanon they were called *fallāḥs* and they were free. The similarity of the social structure to feudalism was great in the Mount Lebanon area, but was absent in other parts of the Ottoman Empire, where the landowners did not always live in the district where their land was located and the land could not be passed on by inheritance.

most of the power in his own hands, Bashīr II strove to limit the "feudal" system prevailing in Mount Lebanon. To accomplish this, he had to undermine the power of the Druze *muqāṭaʿjīs*, who were greater in number and wealth than the Christians *muqāṭaʿjīs*.

And indeed, from the very outset of Bashīr's rule, he made inroads against the *muqāṭaʿjīs*' positions and authority, stirred up trouble among their leaders, seized their lands, often transferring these to Christian ownership at low prices. Some *muqāṭaʿjīs* were even exiled. The culmination of this process came after 1825, when Bashīr crushed the power of the Druze leader Bashīr Junblāṭ, and became the unrivalled leading figure in the Mountain.[6] Thus, from his position of authority as a sort of paramount arbitrator and manager of local affairs, he became an unconstrained despot. Despite this, the basic social structure of family ties in the Mountain was not greatly affected. However, Bashīr now transferred the emphasis from loyalty among families to loyalty between them and himself, temporarily associating most of the client networks more closely to his person, utilising a variety of methods to do so, as described below. In addition, towards the end of the eighteenth century, it appears that Amīr Bashīr converted from Islam to Christianity.[7] This partly explains his policy towards Christians. While the Druze *muqāṭaʿjīs* and others suffered from Bashīr's policies, the Christian population of the Mountain benefited by them, especially from Bashīr's economic policies which encouraged trade between the Mountain and the Syrian hinterland, particularly the silk-trade.

Even before the period of Amīr Bashīr II, silk had become the main product of the Mountain, and Christians and Druze began to accumulate some wealth in its trade.[8] When Amīr Bashīr became the ruler of Mount Lebanon, he was aware of the commercial potential of the silk trade and of the growing power of the middle stratum

---

[6] Carol Hakim-Dowek, *The Origins of the Lebanese National Idea 1840–1914*, D. Phil. Dissertation, St. Antony's College, Oxford, 1997, pp. 39–40; Ṭannūs al-Shidyāq, *Akhbār al-Aʿyān fī Jabal Lubnān*, 2 vols., ed. Buṭrus al-Bustānī (Beirut, 1954), pp. 278–281; ʿAbbās Abū Sāliḥ, *al-Tārīkh al-Siyāsī lil-Imāra al-Shihābiyya fī Jabal Lubnān 1697–1842* (Beirut, 1984).

[7] Apparently, the Shihābī family began to convert to Christianity in the middle of the eighteenth century. For more details, see: Iliya. F. Harik, *Politics and Change in a Traditional Society: Lebanon 1711–1845* (Princeton, 1968), pp. 155–160.

[8] Richard Van Leeuwen, "Monastic Estates and Agricultural Transformation in Mount Lebanon in the 18th Century," *International Journal of Middle East Studies*, Vol. 23 (1991), p. 602; William. R. Polk, *The Opening of South Lebanon, 1788–1840* (Cambridge, Mass., 1963), p. 77.

which profited from it. During his reign, he knew how to use these developments to further strengthen the economic status of the Mountain and of course his own. He especially encouraged Christians to plant and cultivate mulberry orchards and to deal in silk,[9] a product that was intended for export to the region of Syria as well as to Europe. Thus, even though silk commerce in the Mountain had already begun in the seventeenth century and increased in the middle of the eighteenth century, it was mainly during Bashīr's time that this commerce reached its peak. Subsequently, Christian merchants who dealt in this material along with other commodities became wealthier and more influential; their overall status improved and they became leading figures first in the Mountain and then in the entire region of Syria as well. Some of them were powerful prior to Bashīr's period of rule, but managed to further improve their economic and social status under him. In several cases, their prosperity lasted even after the Shihābī Emirate came to an end.

The growing importance of the Christian merchants can also be explained by the commercial needs of the foreign merchants in the region who appointed local *wakīls* (representative/agent), quite naturally from among the Christians. Eventually, the local Christian families managed to earn more than did the Druze *muqāṭaʿjīs* and began to take their places, not just economically but socially and politically as well.

Bashīr also promoted the Christians in administrative positions. For the first time in local history, Christian families almost monopolised the highest clerical positions. Their health improved with access to better services, and their lives became safer. They took advantage of the new economic opportunities available, and by the beginning of the nineteenth century had become a sizeable majority of the Mountain population.

Other improvements resulted from this situation. Before the period of Amīr Bashīr, the "traditional" agrarian society of the Mountain had been divided into two principal groups, the landowners and the land cultivators, with no social mobility between them. The traditional

[9] The Shihābī family itself was involved in silk commerce. For example, Amīr Ḥasan, the brother of Amīr Bashīr, the *vali* of Kisrawān and the rest of the family were engaged in the silk trade. Amīr Ḥasan established shops in the port of Jūnya. He placed merchants in these shops in order to sell silk and other merchandise. Also, Amīr Bashīr II, encouraged their engagement in the silk trade and gave them incentives to do so. Manṣūr al-Ḥatūnī, *Nabdha Tārīkhiyya fī al-Muqāṭaʿa al-Kisrawāniyya* (Beirut, 1887), p. 219.

elite was composed of the landowners—the *muqāṭaʿjīs*, the amīrs and the *aʿyān*. The majority of the population was made up of *fallāḥs* who cultivated the land. Under Bashīr, this traditional structure began to undergo a transformation. A new middle stratum composed mainly of Christian merchants as well as some *muqāṭaʿjīs* and *fallāḥs* joined the existing two groups. This stratum was dynamic in character and included several sub-groups with various functions. Some members of this new middle stratum were commercial intermediaries between the Mountain and the hinterland of Syria, while others were active traders with Europe, mainly in silk but also in grain, tobacco, cotton and additional goods.[10] Other members were *fallāḥs* who had entered into commerce and had accumulated wealth, as well as landowners who began to trade and try-out other commercial activities. Finally, this new stratum also included members of the intelligentsia or literati who constituted a component of the court of Amīr Bashīr.[11] Together they represented the very essence of social and economic life in the Emirate and thus provided it with its source of stability and power. Several of its members eventually turned into social elite of kind.

Gradually, this new middle stratum became the foundation for economic activities in the Mountain; later, during Bashīr's reign, it evolved into the main economic factor in the entire region of Greater Syria. This was partly due to its share in the growing commerce conducted between the Mountain and the Syrian hinterland, which made both the merchants of the stratum and Bashīr quite wealthy. In contrast to al-Jazzār, who monopolised commercial activities and collected high taxes from the merchants, occasionally even confiscating their merchandise,[12] Bashīr promoted their activities but knew how to take advantage of them as well.[13] His own fortune was steadily growing. By comparison, at the beginning of the nineteenth century

[10] I. M. Smilanskaya, "From Subsistence to Market Economy—1850's," in Charles Issawi, (ed.) *The Economic History of the Middle East, 1800–1914* (Chicago, 1961), pp. 236–240; Ghastūn, Dūkūssū, "Tārīkh al-Ḥarīr fī Bilād al-Shām," *al-Mashriq*, Vol. 15, 1912, pp. 374–380; Abū Ṣāliḥ, *al-Tārīkh al-Siyāsī lil-Imāra al-Shihābiyya*, pp. 72–73.

[11] A more detailed discussion of this group can be found later in this chapter.

[12] Families such as Anḥūrī and Mishāqa, who suffered economically under al-Jazzār Pāshā, re-established their position under Amīr Bashīr II. Mīkhāʾil Mishāqa, *Kitāb Mashhad al-ʿAyān bi Ḥawādith Sūriyā wa- Lubnān*, ed. Kh. ʿAbdu, and A. H. Shakhāshīrī (Cairo, 1908), pp. 7, 144.

[13] Amīr Bashīr encouraged commerce, especially under Sulaymān Pāshā. The same process occurred in Nablus. Beshara Doumani, *Rediscovering Palestine: Merchants and Peasants in Jabal Nablus, 1700–1900* (Berkeley, 1995), pp. 100–102.

Bashīr Junblāṭ was considered the richest man in the Mountain, his annual income in 1810 being estimated at one million *qurūsh*; but Amīr Bashīr's income by the end of his reign was nine million *qurūsh* (about 83,000 pounds).[14]

Moreover, during Amīr Bashīr's period the nascent "Emirate institutions" that he established, and the fact that he managed to use and further strengthen the Emirate institutions that had existed before his time, allowed this stratum to accumulate power. Of significance in stabilising the economic status of the Emirate was the security and stability which he enforced. In contrast to the past, when the *muqāṭaʿjīs* conducted their business by themselves, Bashīr now headed several systems in the Emirate, including the administrative bureaucracy, tax collection, treasury and so on, which in many cases helped promote local economic activity. These Emirate institutions became central to the life of the local population in general and the merchants in particular and can be thus seen as "state institutions" in the process of formation.

The economic, social and political developments created a new balance of power in the Emirate. It was natural that Amīr Bashīr, who weakened the power of the *muqāṭaʿjīs*, would become dependent on this growing Christian middle stratum, which was partly his own creation. Bashīr nurtured them as a loyal group that would personally owe him their commercial, social and political prestige, a group that he could rely on. He wanted to eliminate the *muqāṭaʿjīs* as a political, social and economic power and turn the Emirate into a centralised system run by a bureaucracy which he appointed and which was accountable to him. In other words, Bashīr sought to strengthen his rule by subordinating all the sects and positioning himself above their ruling families, i.e. the *muqāṭaʿjīs*.

Bashīr was aware of the growing potential of the economic and social status of the Christian middle stratum, and in a sense he became their protector and representative. Yet his economic success was a by-product of the economic changes in the Mountain and not vice versa. He did not create this process; rather, he rode the wave, catalysing and accelerating a process that was already in motion. In this sense, the circumstances created Bashīr and not the other way around. However, this was only one aspect of the situation.

[14] Abū Ṣāliḥ, *al-Tārīkh al-Siyāsī lil-Imāra al-Shihābiyya*, p. 325.

The interwoven relationship between Amīr Bashīr and the small but growing Christian middle stratum was a complex one. Even though great power became concentrated in the hands of the Amīr, it was not absolute power. On the one hand, the Christian middle stratum apparently depended on him, especially since he offered them both status and stability, which had not been their lot in the past. On the other hand, the growth of this middle stratum made Bashīr dependent on them as well, since their commerce ensured his prosperity and that of his reign. Most of the Amīr's income came directly or indirectly from this commerce. Thus, the merchants needed Bashīr for his protective policy, and he needed their support of his reign. The resulting bilateral relationship produced a more mobile society in which initiative could advance one's economic standing, and eventually one's social status; the merchants in particular benefited from these changes. This development contrasted with the Mountain's past traditional, pseudo-feudal, and hierarchical society.[15]

Zahle and Deir al-Qamar were two towns in the Mountain, which grew and prospered under these circumstances. They both can serve as prototypes for the above-mentioned developments and can illustrate the growing power and importance of the Christian middle stratum. Their history will reveal the two-sided relationship between this social middle stratum and Amīr Bashīr II, and demonstrate the establishment of an indigenous economic network throughout the Syrian interior. Later, during the nineteenth century, this network would play an important role in the growing economic ties of the whole region of Syria with Europe.[16]

Zahle and Deir al-Qamar had already begun to flourish from the mid-eighteenth century; as early as the 1840s they became important economic centres in and for the Mountain. At the same time,

---

[15] Dominique Chevallier, *La Société du Mont Liban: A l'Epoque de la Révolution Industrielle en Europe* (Paris, 1971), p. 102.

[16] Beshara Doumani emphasised that "In Greater Syria during most of the Ottoman period, local and regional commerce was every bit as important, if not more so in terms of daily life, as trade with Europe." and he rightfully added that "These [economic] networks [that were being built locally] also connected the interior regions to each other and, in the process, made it possible for European businessmen and the Ottoman government to gain access to the surplus of these regions." Thus, the local network was a very important phase in the economic activity of the region that would be strengthened with the penetration of the Western Powers. Beshara Doumani, *Rediscovering Palestine*, see introduction, especially, p. 5; Roger Owen, *The Middle East in the World Economy, 1800–1914* (London, 1982), pp. 52–53.

they were also active in the economic trade with the entire region of Syria. By the end of the 1850s, the Christian population in these two towns was larger than that of the Druze. They were both heavily involved with commerce in silk but also engaged in newly emerging economic fields. These towns represented two distinct economic processes that took shape under Amīr Bashīr's rule. Locally, they conducted trade with the entire region of Syria and neither with a particular city nor region/district. Globally, their trade began to be part of the international economy.[17]

From the 1790s until the mid-nineteenth century, Zahle was in the process of turning into one of the most important economic centres of the Mountain. According to ʿĪsā Iskandar al-Maʿlūf, a member of a prominent family in Zahle, this prosperous town had grown, albeit slowly, from 1750 to 1800, reaching a population of almost a thousand inhabitants by the end of the eighteenth century. Under Bashīr, who ruled from 1788 to 1840, that population growth accelerated ten-fold, and by the late 1850s Zahle's population had jumped to some 10–12,000 people[18] and was referred to as "the capital city of Lebanon."[19]

---

[17] Alixa Naff, *A Social History of Zahle, the Principal Market Town in Nineteenth Century Lebanon*, Ph.D. dissertation, University of California, Los Angeles, 1972, Vol. 1, pp. 206–212. We cannot understand the development of Zahle and Deir al-Qamar without paying attention to the changes that took place in *Bilād al-Shām* in the seventeenth and eighteenth centuries. The most important phenomenon that is conspicuous in the life of the cities in *Bilād al-Shām* in the eighteenth century and the beginning of the nineteenth century is that the city's role as a centre of commerce and craftsmen was reinforced. The same process took place in small towns such as Deir al-Qamar and Zahle. Īrīnā Smīlīyānskāyā, *al-Bunā al-Iqtiṣādiyya wal-Ijtimāʿiyya fī al-Mashriq al-ʿArabī ʿalī Mashārif al-ʿAṣr al-Ḥadīth*, translated from Russian (Beirut, 1989), pp. 137–182.

[18] Leila Fawaz, *An Occasion For War: Civil Conflict in Lebanon and Damascus in 1860* (London, 1994), p. 34. In 1810 the population of Zahle was 800–900 houses. Before 1860, the population was 12,000. In 1887 it was 18,000. In 1907–1908 the population of Zahle was 35,000; ʿĪsā Iskandar al-Maʿlūf, *Tārīkh Zaḥla* (Beirut, 1984), pp. 217–218; ʿĪsā Iskandar al-Maʿlūf, *Dawānī al-Quṭūf fī Tārīkh Banī Maʿlūf* (Beirut, 1907–1908), p. 117; John L. Burckhardt, *Travels in Syria and the Holy Land*, Vol. 1, translated by Fuat Sezgin (London, 1822) pp. 4–5; Hinrī Abū Khāṭir, *Jumhūriyyat Zaḥla—Awwal Jumhūriyya fī Sharq Bayrūt* (Beirut, 1978), pp. 165–168. In order to stress this considerable growth of Zahle, it is important to compare it with other growing towns in the region. For example, in 1851 the population of Jerusalem was 15,000. In 1854 the population of Acre was estimated at 10,000 and the population of Jaffa was estimated at nearly 5,000 people. Yehoshua Ben-Arieh, "The Population of the Large Towns in Palestine during the First Eighty Years of the Nineteenth Century, According to Western Sources," in Moshe Maʿoz (ed.), *Studies on Palestine during the Ottoman Period* (Jerusalem, 1975), pp. 52, 54–5, 57.

[19] Abū Khāṭir, *Jumhūriyyat Zaḥla*, p. 5.

During the first years of his reign, the residents of Zahle did not co-operate with Bashīr. However, starting in 1805, the Druze became increasingly interested in the town. In response, its inhabitants, most of whom were Greek Catholics, sought the Amīr's support and found a way to use his power against the Druze. Trade was a natural outgrowth of Zahle's strategic location on the western edge of the Biqāʿ, which lies between the Lebanon and anti-Lebanon mountain ranges and the Syrian hinterland, between the grain production areas of the Biqāʿ and Ḥawrān valleys and the livestock breeding pastures of Mount Lebanon. As the Mountain grew more and more mulberry trees for the silk industry which Bashīr encouraged, it was unable to supply its own grain needs. Naturally, Zahle was the classic candidate to fulfill this deficiency. Due to its location close to the Biqāʿ and Baʿalbek plains, Zahle became the commercial centre for grain, its residents buying it cheaply from the plains and transporting it to the Mountain. With their virtual monopoly on grain, the people of Zahle managed to become very wealthy.[20]

However, the link between the plains and the Mountain was not Zahle's only source of profit. Its merchants bought grain and flock from Syria's hinterland as well, trading with cities such as Homs and Aleppo. A large number of Zahle's residents were merchants and entrepreneurs who traded with and/or employed itinerant peddlers, exchanged goods with other districts and speculated in grain. With increasing capital at their disposal, some of them sold and bought land. Many traded with the traveling merchants plying their trade between the Syrian coast and the interior. By the mid-1760s, Zahle had started trading; the impetus it received under Bashīr turned it into a centre that linked the Mountain, the plains and Damascus with the Syrian coast. Astride the trade route from Aleppo and Damascus to Beirut and Europe beyond, Zahle saw a constant flow of goods and merchants passing in both directions. The Maʿlūf family is a typical example of the growing economic and even political activities of the Greek-Catholic merchants of Zahle. The Maʿlūfs traded in silk, tobacco and livestock. Their far-reaching trade connections included Damascus, the Mountain, the plains of what are

---

[20] Naff, *A Social History of Zahle*, Vol. 1, p. 5; al-Maʿlūf, *Tārīkh Zaḥla*, pp. 132–133; Leila T. Fawaz, "Zahleh and Dayr al-Qamar—Two Market Towns of Mount Lebanon During the Civil War of 1860," in Nadim Shehadi and Dana H. Milles (eds.), *Lebanon: A History of Conflict and Consensus* (London, 1988), pp. 50–52.

now Lebanon and Syria, and Europe. The family held much property in the Biqāʿ and Baʿalbek valleys.[21] Ighnātius al-Maʿlūf, who was the Bishop of Diyār Bakr and also became the Bishop of Zahle and the Biqāʿ in 1816, traded mainly in livestock. As ʿĪsā Iskandar Maʿlūf tells us, the commerce of Zahle under Ighnātius "extended to Aleppo and to other places [in the Syrian hinterland]."[22] Ighnātius was very close to Amīr Bashīr and on several occasions assisted him with the affairs of the Emirate. An example from the following generation of the family is Nuʿmān al-Maʿlūf (b. 1831). He was active after the reign of Amīr Bashīr II, not only in the region of Syria but also, in later years, in other regions. Nevertheless, it is reasonable to assume that his family fortune and success derived, among other things, from the achievements that his family had already attained during the period of Amīr Bashīr, not only in Mount Lebanon but in the entire region of Syria and beyond, even after the Amīr was long gone. Nuʿmān's main business was in livestock and crops. He also rented out several villages and bought property in Baʿalbek and the Biqāʿ. He was a very well known figure among the merchants, clerks and consuls of his time. In 1863 he earned 200,000 *qurūsh* a month solely from his trade in livestock. In later years his economic activities extended to Damascus and Beirut, trading in wheat in Damascus, and engaging in large scale economic enterprises from the 1860s to the 1880s in Beirut. He entered into partnerships with leading merchant families in this city including the Bustrus, Sursuq and Mudawwar families, who will be discussed in the second chapter. Nuʿmān's economic activities, especially his trade in livestock, extended as far as Alexandria, Iraq and Anatolia.[23]

The growth and development of Zahle and the success of its merchants soon depended on the entire region. Commerce inside Zahle was diverse. Some merchants dealt with livestock, tobacco, crops or alcohol, establishing and operating processing plants in the town. Also, the silk from hundreds of looms was sent as merchandise to Zahle.

Zahle was also an important military centre for Amīr Bashīr. Whenever Bashīr needed troops, he could rely on the people of Zahle, and

[21] For information on al-Maʿlūf see Albert Hourani, "Historians of Lebanon," in Bernard Lewis and Peter M. Holt (eds.), *Historians of the Middle East* (London, 1962), pp. 234–235; al-Maʿlūf, *Dawānī al-Quṭūf*, pp. 256, 313, 323–327, 389–390, 514, 580–581; Naff, *A Social History of Zahle*, Vol. 1, p. 132.

[22] Al-Maʿlūf, *Dawānī al-Quṭūf*, p. 387.

[23] *Ibid.*, pp. 389–391.

in fact, a considerable portion of Bashīr's army consisted of soldiers from Zahle. In most cases, they were the spearhead of his army.[24] In 1810, when Amīr Bashīr supported the *vali* of Sidon against the *vali* of Damascus, he took with him 400 armed men from Zahle alone.[25]

In summary, we can say that local economic development in Zahle, which went back as far as the mid-eighteenth century, caught the attention of Amīr Bashīr II. He contributed to its further development and transformation into a market town which played a crucial role in the growing economy of the entire region of Syria. The Emirate depended on Zahle to supply its main needs. Bashīr himself emphasised its usefulness by saying that "[in Zahle] the merchants supply the money whenever there is a need for it and the men serve whenever there is a war."[26]

A similar process began at Deir al-Qamar. Its transformation into the most prosperous centre in the Mountain had already begun in the eighteenth century. As in the case of Zahle, it reached its zenith under Amīr Bashīr. In 1843, Rose, the British Consul in Beirut during the 1840s, wrote that the policy of the Amīr was to make Deir al-Qamar "the focus of Christian industry and Christian physical force."[27] Bashīr would thus also have at hand a force to oppose the Druze chiefs. Rose added that "His [Bashīr's] actions changed the small capital of the Druze into the most thriving commercial town in the Mountain, with the Christian population five or six times larger than that of the Druze."[28]

Zahle was very important to Amīr Bashīr, but Deir al-Qamar became his main focus. Indeed, Deir al-Qamar was growing into a market town serving the Emirate and the entire region of Syria. At the beginning of the nineteenth century it housed 4,000 people; by the late 1850s, its population reached over 7,000.[29] The majority of

---

[24] William G. Browne, *Travels in Africa, Egypt and Syria from the Year 1792 to 1798* (London, 1806), p. 469.

[25] Burkchardt, *Travels in Syria*, Vol. 1, p. 7; al-Maʿlūf, *Tārīkh Zaḥla*, pp. 120–121, 177; al-Maʿlūf, *Dawānī al-Quṭūf*, p. 232.

[26] Rustum Bāz, *Mudhakkirāt Rustum Bāz*, ed. Fu'ād Afrām al-Bustānī (Beirut, 1955), p. 112.

[27] FO 226/83 Rose to Stratford Canning, 30 April 1843.

[28] *Ibid.*; Charles H. Churchill, *The Druzes and the Maronites Under Turkish Rule from 1840–1860*, 2nd Impression (New York, 1973), p. 104.

[29] Fawaz, *An Occasion for War*, p. 38; Shukrī al-Bustānī estimates the population of Deir al-Qamar before 1900 at 15,000 people. See: Shukrī al-Bustānī, *Dayr al-Qamar fī Ākhir al-Qarn al-Tāsiʿ ʿAshar—Muḥāwala Tārīkhiyya Ijtimāʿiyya wa Iqtiṣādiyya*

the town's population was Christian, most of who were Greek Catholics and Maronites.[30] As the capital of the Emirate and as an administrative centre, the town was extremely important.[31] In contrast to Zahle, Deir al-Qamar is located on the opposite side of the Mountain, facing the coast. This geographic location naturally led to its status as a commercial centre, linking the coastal regions, Mount Lebanon, Damascus, and the Syrian hinterland. As an export centre for silk, soap, tobacco, cotton and grain, and the site of a large livestock market, by the mid-nineteenth century Deir al-Qamar was a leading trade centre in the region and the richest town in the Mountain. In particular, it was the heart of the silk trade for the entire region, and this became its main source of wealth. As the wholesale centre for the silk trade, middlemen from Deir al-Qamar collected most of the silk from the Mountain and sold it to entrepreneurs in Sidon and Beirut; or to Syrian traders in Damascus, Aleppo, Homs, and Hama. To meet the demand for silk cloth, Deir al-Qamar eventually became a main centre for manufacturing this material.

The dual role of Deir al-Qamar as a commercial town and as an administrative centre enhanced the growth of a strong Christian middle stratum which enjoyed many privileges under Bashīr. He gave his capital, Deir al-Qamar, special attention, constructing buildings, repairing old roads and building new ones, which in turn enabled the flourishing commerce to expand even more. Bashīr exempted the merchants from taxes; in turn, they lent him money.[32] Very soon, the population displayed their wealth in grand houses and elegant clothing, mostly made of silk.[33] Shops offering European merchandise were opened. A growing number of clever businessmen became familiar with the West, and occasionally traveled abroad. The town enjoyed a thriving economy, bustling with shops and production facilities. Deir al-Qamar's 300 looms and 60 shops gained fame and became known by the quality of their merchandise throughout the region of Syria.[34]

(Beirut, 1969), p. 13. In 1880 the population was estimated at 7,000–8,000 people. Laurence Oliphant, *The Land of Gilead with Excursions in the Lebanon* (London, 1880), pp. 353–361.

[30] Andrew A. Paton, *Modern Syrians* (London, 1844), pp. 66–82.

[31] Even though Bashīr moved his seat of government from Deir al-Qamar to Bayt al-Din, he continued to retain Deir al-Qamar as his political centre.

[32] Chevallier, *La Société du Mont Liban*, p. 99.

[33] On the clothing habits in the Mountain, see Bāz, *Mudhakkirāt*, pp. 132–135.

[34] *Ibid.*, p. 112.

Under such conditions, the town became attractive to many people. Seeking stability or new opportunities, they came to the town from all over the Mountain, from the entire region of Syria, including the cities of Aleppo and Damascus, and even as far as Istanbul itself.[35]

The growing wealth of the town in general and of the merchants in particular brought money into Bashīr's treasury and supported his court as well. In comparison to Zahle, Deir al-Qamar was more urbanised, more open to the outside world, and gradually became more intricately connected to the market economy.

In 1898, Rustum Bāz (1819–1902) from the prominent Bāz family in Deir al-Qamar wrote his memoirs. Rustum himself was raised in Bashīr's court and was very close to him. When the Amīr was exiled to Malta, Rustum accompanied him. After the Amīr's death, Rustum settled in Beirut and engaged in commerce between the Mountain and Istanbul. His memoirs are an important source, revealing new details on the economic activities of Amīr Bashīr, his relationship with the middle stratum and the growing importance of Deir al-Qamar as the economic centre of the Mountain.

As Rustum describes in his memoirs, most of the economic life of the Emirate centred in the *qayṣariyya* of Deir al-Qamar. The *qayṣariyya*, a kind of a covered market or bazaar building, was surrounded by shops (*maghāliq*) and stores.[36] It functioned as the main centre for silk in the Mountain, which arrived there and was handed over to the wholesalers (*samāsira*), who weighed it and then sold it to the merchants. The merchants sold the silk in the interior regions of Syria in cities such as Homs, Damascus and Aleppo. Some of the silk went to owners of looms in Deir al-Qamar and was processed into cloth, women's scarves, and other woven products.

In short, the merchants and the wholesalers had the right to buy and sell the silk freely, apparently without the control of Bashīr, and thus managed to accumulate much wealth. However, despite the Amīr's apparent *laissez-faire* policies, the truth is that Bashīr was deeply involved in the commerce of the *qayṣariyya*. Rustum noted

[35] ʿĪsā Iskandar al-Maʿlūf, "Dayr al-Qamar ʿalā ʿAhd al-Amīr," extracts from an article in Manāra, rep. in *al-Mashriq*, 1931, p. 302. In this article, al-Maʿlūf quotes several pages from the memoirs of Rustum Bāz. See, Bāz, *Mudhakkirāt*, p. 112.

[36] In his memoirs Rustum used the word *qaysāriyya* which was probably confused with the word *qayṣariyya*. These buildings were built by the Amīrs and the *muqāṭaʿjīs* of the Mountain. See, J. G. Hava, *al-Farāʾid* (Beirut, 1986), p. 609. See also the remarks of al-Maʿlūf in "Dayr al-Qamar ʿalā ʿAhd al-Amīr," p. 302.

that most of the buildings, shops and warehouses in the *qayṣariyya* were owned by Bashīr, who would rent them to members of the leading merchant families in Deir al-Qamar. He also owned the measuring and weighing devices and rented them out to these families. The high prices the merchants paid Bashīr are some indication of the extent of their income, since rent fees were naturally only a portion of their profits.[37] Thus, even more than Zahle, Deir al-Qamar provided Bashīr with the economic fuel that moved the wheels of the Emirate.

These merchant families from Deir al-Qamar were engaged in a range of economic spheres, with commercial links stretching across Syria. The Mishāqas dealt in silk and tobacco; the Ṣūṣās traded in silk, tobacco and sheep; the Thābit family owned mulberry trees and silk worms; the Dūmānī family dealt in sesame seeds and oil, olives, grapes and silk; al-Bustānī family[38] traded grain, sheep, tobacco and silk; while the Shidyāqs concentrated on livestock. Others families, while retaining their mercantile interests, also served in Bashīr's bureaucracy, like the Daḥdāḥs,[39] most of whom were employed in the bureaucracy and administration under Bashīr, but retained their commercial interests in the silk trade as well.

Members of the middle stratum from Deir al-Qamar and Zahle quickly realised, just as Amīr Bashīr had, that the existing pseudo-feudal system was indeed limiting and an obstacle to their own interests. Their successful efforts to neutralise the *muqāṭaʿjīs*, with Bashīr having more power, and the middle stratum accumulating more wealth than the *muqāṭaʿjīs*, transformed their towns into the hub of a wider region, expanding their activities as their prospering commercial enterprises grew. They understood that their commercial success was the source of their power, and strove to preserve and enhance their new status. They grew wealthier, even though Bashīr sometimes demanded high taxes[40] and requested huge loans, which he frequently

37 For example, the soap factory was rented to the Shūʿā family for 1,225 *qurūsh* a year. The slaughter-house for cattle was rented to Abū-Mārūn for 1,030 *qurūsh* a year and so on. Bāz, *Mudhakkirāt*, pp. 113–114; Fruma Zachs, "Commerce and Merchants under Amīr Bashīr II: From Market Town to Commercial Centre." Forthcoming.

38 Shukrī al-Bustānī, *Dayr al-Qamar fī Ākhir*, pp. 20–77; al-Maʿlūf, *Dawānī al-Quṭūf*, pp. 310, 390.

39 Salīm Khaṭṭār al-Daḥdāḥ, "al-Kūnt Rashīd al-Daḥdāḥ wa-Usratuhu," *al-Mashriq*, Vol. 4, 1901, 381–396, 452–461, 489–498. See also: al-Ḥatūnī, *Nabdha Tārīkhiyya*, pp. 260–263; See also: Anṭūniyūs Abū Khaṭṭār al-ʿAynṭūrīnī, *Mukhtaṣar Tārīkh Jabal Lubnān*, ed. Ilyās Qaṭṭār (Beirut, 1983), pp. 64–65.

40 Al-Maʿlūf, *Dawānī al-Quṭūf*, pp. 117–122. For example, Bashīr imposed high

omitted to return. Despite their power, these merchants were unable to challenge Bashīr,[41] especially since he controlled a large portion of the economic activities in the Mountain. Nevertheless, they profited from this situation, gaining more than they lost; by fulfilling their obligations towards Bashīr, they enjoyed special privileges and authority.

For example, in the case of Zahle, Bashīr reduced their transport taxes, especially those between the Mountain and the plains. In several cases the Amīr transferred the right to collect the *mīrī* (taxes) from the *muqāṭaʿjīs* to the leading merchant families. Bashīr also improved and built bridges and roads in the vicinity of both towns. This middle stratum was aware that they depended on Bashīr in order to protect their own commerce. As long as Bashīr's rule was firm and steady, conditions remained stable and their commercial enterprises would prosper. As individuals, they could promote their interests and manoeuvre the situation to their advantage, to a degree that they had been unable to achieve in the past.

When Bashīr was exiled in 1840, most of the merchants who could manage to make the transfer did so, leaving Deir al-Qamar for Beirut or other coastal cities. One such merchant family was the Ṣūṣās, a rich family from Deir al-Qamar. In fact, this family, along with twenty or thirty other merchants from Deir al-Qamar, decided not to return after the exile of Bashīr, no matter what form of government would be established. When events calmed down, they planned to collect their credits back in Deir al-Qamar, sell their property and settle in Beirut, Sidon or elsewhere. After the exile of their patron, they did not see returning to Deir al-Qamar as a reasonable option.[42]

Of course, the growing importance and wealth of the stratum enabled it to further expand its field of operations. Deir al-Qamar and Zahle gained importance not only for the Emirate but also in the eyes of the entire region. A good example that illustrates this point is the fact that when Ibrāhīm Pāshā conquered *Bilād al-Shām*

---

taxes upon them. In 1790, Zahle paid the Amīr 15 purses which amounted to 7,500 piasters. He took 800 piasters from some families and when that was not enough, he took another 15 purses. Naff, *A Social History of Zahle*, Vol. 1, p. 212.

[41] Aḥmad Ḥaydar al-Shihāb, *Lubnān fī ʿAhd al-Umarāʾ al-Shihābiyyīn*, Vol. 3, eds., Asad Rustum and Afrām al-Bustānī, (Beirut, 1933), p. 776. It is important to emphasise that on many occasions Bashīr enforced his control over this stratum. Such was the case with the Daḥdāḥ family. In 1793, Bashīr called upon Salīm al-Daḥdāḥ and his brother to come and serve him and threatened them that if they did not do so he would destroy their houses. Al-Ḥatūnī, *Nabdha Tārīkhiyya*, p. 213.

[42] FO 226/83, Rose to Stratford Canning, 30 April 1843.

in 1831–1832, one of his first acts was to send a messenger to Deir al-Qamar to ask the Amīr to join him.[43] He also sent half of his military force to Zahle and turned it into one of the region's main military centres; as noted, Zahle was famous for its soldiers and Ibrāhīm could use it as a buffer city because of its strategic location.

Under Bashīr, the entire region of Syria surrounding the Mountain became the field of economic activities for these merchants, with the Mountain as its centre. Thus, they perceived not only the Mountain but the entire expanse of Syria as one region; it would be natural for them to imagine it as a whole and identify with it as their territorial and economic sphere of activity. Naff wrote, regarding Zahle, that ". . . the ambitions of its members drove them to play a more active role not only in the affairs of their community, but in the region as well, and to court the attention of Bashīr."[44] Smilanskaya wrote that

> Towns played the role of regional commercial centres (as may be observed, for example, in Damascus, Beirut, and Zahleh). The development of commercial relations (. . . the impact of growing industrial production on the development of the domestic market) suggests the evolution toward a common market, which for the time being was confined to Syria, Lebanon, and Palestine. *The "guiding spirit" of this movement was the emerging national commercial bourgeoisie . . .*[45]

This description leads us to ask another question. Were the growing economic activities of these merchants, inter-connected as they were with a wider region, accompanied by a gradual increase in "political" aspirations beyond the borders of the Mountain? In most cases, it is difficult to discern the views of the merchants (most of them did not usually write about such issues). But in the case of Mount Lebanon, many merchants were also members of the intelligentsia. By examining the writings of this group, mainly of those who were active in Deir al-Qamar, we will also be able to get a glimpse into the state of mind of the merchants, as well as that of the middle stratum as a whole.

---

[43] For more details on Ibrāhīm Pāshā see: Polk, *The Opening of South Lebanon*, pp. 83–106; Asad Rustum, *Bashīr Bayna al-Sulṭān wal-ʿAzīz, 1804–1841* (Beirut, 1956–1957).

[44] Naff, *A Social History of Zahle*, Vol. 1, p. 217. See also: pp. 142–143.

[45] See: Smilanskaya, "From Subsistence to Market Economy," p. 231. The last sentence is set in italic for emphasis.

The Literary Circle

Under the rule of Amīr Bashīr II Deir al-Qamar, the capital of the Mountain, was not only its administrative and political centre but a cultural one as well. Bashīr is usually described as a strong and ruthless leader who crushed his enemies and struggled to fortify his power. Yet he had another side, which was to encourage the educational and cultural life of the Emirate.[46] It cannot be claimed that intellectual life developed only thanks to him. Rather, circumstances themselves, namely the increasing wealth of Christian towns under the Emirate (and especially Deir al-Qamar), the expanding opportunities provided by the economic prosperity of the town, the exposure to other cultures by people who could afford to travel, the knowledge of languages and openness to new ideas, all created a fertile basis for fostering culture, and the growth of an educated stratum.

This atmosphere of cultural activity allowed Bashīr to skillfully surround himself with educated administrators and literati, personally loyal to him, to help him govern the Emirate. As with the merchants, they and Bashīr were mutually dependent on each other. This intelligentsia, especially in Deir al-Qamar, will be referred to here as the literary circle. It was comprised of several groups, including bureaucrats and administrators, poets and literati (who sometimes served as administrators as well), and finally and most important for the development of the notion of Syria—court historians. A closer look at each group reveals two processes (which are in fact two aspects of the same development) that had already evolved at this stage. These would later grow in strength during the nineteenth century, in several cases by the same families or even by the same people. The first of the two processes is the *Nahḍa*, the revival of Arabic language and culture during the nineteenth century, while the second is the emergence of the Syrian idea.

As previously mentioned, the administrative and bureaucratic circles were very important to Bashīr. In many cases, he, who was aware of the importance of education to the Emirate, gave several members of the merchant families positions in his court, or encouraged them to go to Egypt and other places to expand their knowledge, knowing that they would contribute to his Emirate after their return.

---

[46] Al-Daḥdāḥ, "al-Amīr Bashīr al-Kabīr al-Maʿrūf bil-Malṭī," pp. 574–577, 697–698.

He did this with families such as the Mishāqas, the Daḥdāḥs,[47] the Ma'lūfs from Zahle and the Ṣfayrs, as well as other families whose main activity was in the fields of administration and bureaucracy, such as the Zalzals, Bāzs, Shāwīshs, Shaḥādas, Far'ūns and the Ẓamalūtīs. Since these members of merchant families held bureaucratic positions in Bashīr's court, they were able to translate their economic power into political influence and thus gain greater economic and social status.

In time, the court and its members became a cultural circle within the Emirate, creating its own court poetry and literature which, later in the nineteenth century, would influence the entire region of Syria. After 1825, when Bashīr had crushed Junblāṭ's power, he was able to concentrate greater efforts on enhancing culture during his administration.[48] He promoted science (especially medicine), literature and poetry. Poets and other intellectuals visited him and were guests in his palace.

Furthermore, especially from the beginning of the nineteenth century, a literary circle of Arab writers and poets existed in Bashīr's court; this circle produced many books including collections of poetry, some of which are well-known and read until this very day. A number of these writers were educated in schools that were established in the Mountain during Bashīr's reign[49] and thus had acquired knowledge

---

[47] A good example is the Daḥdāḥ family, who dealt with silk and gradually became very close to the Amīr. They acted as his advisors and arbitrators in conflicts between Amīrs of the Mountain. They were also part of Bashīr's *dīwān* and collected the *mīrī* taxes. Some members of this family also held the position of *mudabbir* (the highest position in the administration of the Emirate) for 58 years. A few of the positions were hereditary, passed on from father to son, and in this way the family became more influential and wealthy, especially since Bashīr gave them lands and property in gratitude for their loyalty. Butrus F. Sāfir al-Khūrī, *al-Amīr Bashīr al-Shihābī* (Beirut, 1950), p. 96; Mīkhā'īl Mishāqa, *al-Jawāb 'alā Iqtirāḥ al-Aḥbāb*, (Beirut, 1874), p. 69; Salīm Khaṭṭār al-Daḥdāḥ, "al-Kūnt Rashīd," pp. 381–395; al-Ḥatūnī, *Nabdha Tārīkhiyya*, pp. 260–263. On the term *mudabbir* see: Harik, *Politics and Change in a Traditional Society, Lebanon 1711–1845* (Princeton, 1968), pp. 168–172; Chevallier, *La Société du Mont Liban*, p. 88; Bāz, *Mudhakkirāt*, p. 127.

[48] Travel books seldom described this atmosphere in Deir al-Qamar. See: Laurence Oliphant, *The Land of Gilead with Excursions in the Lebanon* (London, 1880); Francis Egerton, *A Tour in the Holy Land in May and June 1840* (London, 1841), pp. 353–361; S. S. Hill, *Travels in Egypt and Syria* (London, 1866), pp. 380–381; al-Daḥdāḥ, "al-Amīr Bashīr," pp. 561–577.

[49] I am referring to schools that were conducted in the same manner but established after 'Ayn Waraqa, such as Madrasat Mār 'Abdā, which was established in 1831 and Mār Yūḥannā, which was established in 1812. See: al-Khūrī, *al-Amīr Bashīr*, pp. 99–100.

of Arabic as well as other languages. The most prominent among these schools was ʿAyn Waraqa, the Maronite college that opened its doors in 1789, only one year after Bashīr became the ruler of the Mountain. Classes were held in Arabic, and Arabic itself was taught as a subject.

Fāris al-Shidyāq (1804–1877) and Buṭrus al-Bustānī (1819–1883) were only two of several well-known Arabic literati who received their Arabic education there and would later have a strong influence on the development of the *Nahḍa*. Al-Bustānī was also destined to become a leading figure in promoting Syrian patriotism during the nineteenth century.[50]

ʿAyn Waraqa was distinctive in that it taught Arabic not only as part of its religious studies, as was customary until then, but also as part of its "secular" curriculum and non-religious subjects. In general, the school taught Arabic language and literature, history, foreign languages, science, algebra and so on. This range of subjects contrasted with the existing school systems among Muslims, which were highly traditional (consisting mainly of Quranic studies) and which considered non-religious books and studies a luxury, or rejected them entirely as unsuitable to the traditional curriculum.[51]

In this atmosphere, Bashīr could gradually surround himself with *udabāʾ* (literati) who were well versed in Arabic. His awareness of the importance of education for the prosperity of the Emirate was one reason for encouraging the growth of an educated middle stratum with a leading intellectual elite that would help him cultivate the heritage of his Emirate. In order to preserve this heritage of Arabic language and culture, they wrote Arabic poetry and prose, especially during the 1820s and the 1830s; much of it was written to glorify Amīr Bashīr.[52] In turn, Bashīr supported and encouraged them, by

---

[50] On ʿAyn Waraqa see: Yūsuf al-Dibs, *al-Jāmiʿ al-Mufaṣṣal fī Tārīkh al-Mawārina al-Muʾaṣṣal* (Beirut, 1987), pp. 378–379; Hariq, *Politics and Change*, p. 169; w. n, "Buṭrus al-Bustānī," *al-Hilāl*, Vol. 4, 1895, pp. 362–363.

[51] The Maronite interest in the Arabic language increased during the eighteenth century, especially since they sang psalms in Arabic (*mazāmīr ʿArabiyya*) in their monasteries. Also, during this period, the first book on Arabic grammar was written, entitled *Baḥth al-Maṭālib* by Jirmānūs Farḥāt. Most of Buṭrus al-Bustānī's generation was taught from this book. In fact, later on Buṭrus al-Bustānī re-published it.

[52] Fruma Zachs, "Towards a Proto-Nationalist Concept of Syria? Revisiting the American Presbyterian Missionaries in the Nineteenth-Century Levant," *Die Welt Des Islams*, Vol. 41 (2001), pp. 168–171.

giving them positions in his court as letter writers or tutors for his children, inviting them to feasts held in his palace, etc.[53]

Some members of these families became famous throughout the region in the fields of Arabic literature and poetry and finally, in the second half of the nineteenth century, as promoters of Syrian Arab patriotism.[54] The circle included several outstanding scholarly figures of the region, such as Nāṣif al-Yāzijī (1800–1871), who for 12 years served as the Amīr's secretary. He rapidly became one of the leading scholars of Arabic in all of Syria.[55] In fact, during his lifetime he served either directly or indirectly as a teacher to most of the region's authors of Arabic literature in the nineteenth century.

A further example is Buṭrus Karāma (1774–1850), who was a poet and linguist, proficient in Arabic and Turkish. In 1810 he was invited to Amīr Bashīr's court in order to teach his children. He also served the court as the Secretary of Foreign Affairs and was Bashīr's *mudabbir* (the highest position in the administration of the Emirate).[56] Another example is Niqūlā al-Turk (1763–1827), who was the Amīr's private poet and wrote the book entitled *Majmūʿat Ḥawādith al-ʿArab* (Collection of Arab Events). He also tutored the Amīr's sons and, as in the case of other intellectuals, he served the Amīr as adviser in political issues and held an administrative post. In this case, Niqūlā al-Turk was the head of the treasury. Over the years he became so important and close to Amīr Bashīr that he was responsible for most issues of the Emirate. Al-Turk can also be taken as an example of the close ties between the intellectuals and the merchants. His daughter Warda, a poet herself, was married to one of the leading merchants in Deir al-Qamar, Jirjis Andrāwus al-Ṣūṣā.[57] In one of his songs from

[53] The question as to why Amīr Bashīr II encouraged Arabic language and culture is very difficult to answer. One assumption is that it originated with the Maronites who began to find interest in Arabic as a language of expression. It is also connected with the Jesuit missionaries who actively cultivated the Arabic language. Bashīr was probably part of this trend.

[54] Amīr Bashīr fed 2,000 people every day in his palace; Hill, *Travels in Egypt*, pp. 380–381; George Robinson, *Three Years in the East* (London, 1837), pp. 25–30.

[55] For more details on Yāzijī see: Jurjī Zaydān, *Tārīkh Ādāb al-Lugha al-ʿArabiyya*, Vol. 4 (Cairo, 1957), pp. 240–241; Yūsuf al-Dibs, *Tārīkh Sūriyya*, Vol. 8 (Beirut, 1905), pp. 691–693.

[56] Yūsuf Sarkīs, *Muʿjam al-Maṭbūʿāt al-ʿArabiyya wal-Muʿarraba*, Vol. 1 (Cairo, 1929), p. 1550; Niqūlā Ziyāda, *Abʿād al-Tārīkh al-Lubnānī al-Ḥadīth* (Beirut, 1972), pp. 172–182; Albert Hourani, *Arabic Thought in the Liberal Age 1798–1939* (London, 1962), p. 95.

[57] Al-Maʿlūf, *Dawānī al-Quṭūf*, p. 390; See: Shukrī al-Bustānī, *Dayr al-Qamar fī*

1809, al-Turk wrote that Arabs and non-Arabs worshipped Bashīr.[58]

The growing interest and awareness by the intellectuals of their Arab language and culture reflects the fact that this group was in the process of defining its self-image. Furthermore, while it had the encouragement and blessing of Bashīr, it is difficult to discern whether the establishment of the *Nahḍa* was the deliberate intention of the Amīr, or the result of an unplanned process. By this time, Deir al-Qamar and Zahle had become fertile ground for new ideas. They had been transformed from little villages with local markets to central towns with cultural influence over other places throughout the region. The importance of this stratum and of these cities sharpened the Christian Arab's self-identity and these intellectuals quickly became a regional source of intellectual ideas and influences.

Tracing the origins of this Syrian vision (which cannot yet be characterised as an identity) is difficult, although a crystallisation of cultural awareness that would later herald the Syrian notion can be found during Bashīr's time. An analysis of the poetry and literature of the intelligentsia naturally reveals a strong affinity with the merchants. Most poets wrote not only to glorify the Amīr, but also in praise of their fellow intellectuals, friends or merchants from their own stratum. Their writing shows that they formed a close circle around Bashīr, focused on the latter, the Emirate and their own daily interests. Their literary work rarely dealt with social or economic issues which may have concerned the rest of the population in the Mountain.[59]

This tendency is partly shared by another group in the court, the court historians, especially those who wrote during the second half of the nineteenth century. Even though they wrote not only on polit-

---

Ākhir, p. 14. Other figures from this group are the poets Ilyās Iddih, Yūsuf Shalfūn, Iskandar Abkāryūs and members of the al-Khūrī family, some of whom were sent by Bashīr to Tripoli and Sidon to learn *fiqh* and sciences. Mīkhā'īl Sabbāgh participated in the cultural activities of the *Nahḍa*. The poet Naṣīf bnu Ilyās Munʿim al-Maʿlūf (1823–1865). Al-Maʿlūf, *Dawānī al-Quṭūf*, p. 314. Mishāqa, *Kitāb Mashhad al-Aʿyān*, p. 75.

[58] Niqūlā al-Turk, *Dīwān al-Muʿallim Niqūlā al-Turk*, Vol. 1, ed. Fu'ād Afrām al-Bustānī (Beirut, 1970), p. 260; Lūwīs Shīkhū, *Tārīkh al-Ādāb al-ʿArabiyya, 1800–1925* (Beirut, 1991), p. 59.

[59] Turk wrote in honour of the Daḥdāḥs and others. In addition, the terms that are used to describe the borders of the Emirate are: *aqṭār bilādinā, quṭur*. Turk, *Diwān al-Muʿallim Niqūlā al-Turk*, Vol. 1, pp. 43–44, 64–66, 115, 173; Vol. 2, pp. 237, 253, 255, 257.

ical issues but also on social and economic ones, they mainly focused on the Mountain's middle stratum. In the writings of these historians, who recorded the local history of the region, we can also distinguish the early expressions of the Syrian idea. They related the history of the Emirate as witnessed through their own eyes and minds.

Moreover, their books reveal the chronological development, dynamics and characteristics of the notion of a Syrian identity, which was to evolve over the course of the century. Naturally, these historians were called upon to glorify their ruler, as were the poets. Some of them wrote their books during the period of Bashīr's rule, while others probably wrote under its influence, but after his reign had ended.[60] Their true motivations and the elements that influenced them cannot be clearly determined at this distance of time.

Four historians who had direct or indirect ties with the Emirate can offer us some answers. The first of these, chronologically, is Amīr Ḥaydar Aḥmad al-Shihāb (1761–1835), a nephew of Amīr Bashīr II, and his close contemporary. He was responsible for administration and military missions under Bashīr. In the 1830s, whilst Bashīr was still in power, Amīr Ḥaydar wrote the book[61] entitled *al-Ghurar al-Ḥisān fī Akhbār Abnā' al-Zamān* (freely translated as The Most Outstanding News of the Time), in order to glorify his uncle. This book was later edited by Asad Rustum, who discarded the first part of the book concerning the pre-Shihābī time and renamed it *Lubnān fī ʿAhd al-Umarā' al-Shihābiyyīn* (Lebanon under the Period of the Shihābī Princes).[62] It included three volumes, covering the period beginning with the rise of the Shihābī Emirate (1697) and ending with the beginning of Egyptian rule in *Bilād al-Shām*.

The second author is the Maronite Ṭannūs al-Shidyāq (1791–1861), brother of Fāris and Asʿad al-Shidyāq, who belonged to a family that served Amīr Bashīr II. Ṭannūs was educated in ʿAyn Waraqa and was frequently employed on political missions by the Amīr, and occasionally dealt in commerce as well.[63]

In 1859, about two decades after the Shihābī Emirate came to an end, al-Shidyāq's book was edited by another intellectual from the

---

[60] I will concentrate on some of the books in this chapter, especially on those that were written closer to the period of Bashīr. I will discuss other books in the last chapter, in order to trace the developments of the idea through the nineteenth century.
[61] The book was probably completed in 1833.
[62] Aḥmad Ḥaydar al-Shihāb, *Lubnān fī ʿAhd al-Umarā' al-Shihābiyyīn*, Vol. 3.
[63] Buṭrus al-Bustānī, *Dā'irat al-Maʿārif*, Vol. 10, pp. 428–430.

Mountain—Buṭrus al-Bustānī, who published it in two volumes entitled *Akhbār al-Aʿyān fī Jabal Lubnān* (Information About the Distinguished People of Mt. Lebanon).[64] In contrast to Ḥaydar, he included the history of the Emirate during the Egyptian occupation.

One more example was the book *al-Jawāb ʿalā Iqtirāḥ al-Aḥbāb* (The Answer to the Request of the Beloved), completed in 1873 by Mīkhāʾīl Mishāqa (1800–1888), who admired Bashīr from childhood onward.[65] Born in Deir al-Qamar, Mishāqa settled in Damascus when he was in his forties. He followed in his father's footsteps by working at the court of Amīr Bashīr II, representing him and collecting Bashīr's taxes from the Mountain.[66] The Mishāqa family, which got its first impetus under the rule of Amīr Bashīr II, became a prominent one in Mount Lebanon and later in Damascus; it also had influence in Beirut. Mīkhāʾīl was a Catholic who converted to Protestantism in 1848. His book describes the history of *Bilād al-Shām* from the mid-eighteenth century until the 1870s, through the history of the Mishāqa family in general and that of Mīkhāʾīl in particular. Last but not least is the book *Dawānī al-Quṭūf fī Tārīkh Banī Maʿlūf*, (Available Information on the History of al-Maʿlūf Family), another Mountain family biography, this time by a member of the Maʿlūf family, ʿĪsā Iskandar al-Maʿlūf, who published his book in 1907 or in 1908, even later than Mishāqa did.[67]

---

[64] Shidyāq, *Akhbār al-Aʿyān*. Ṭannūs al-Shidyāq spoke of "Syria" when referring to pre-Islamic times and of *al-Shām* when dealing with Islamic history.

[65] There are other versions of this book. Mīkhāʾīl Mishāqa, *Muntakhabāt min al-Jawāb ʿalā Iqtirāḥ al-Aḥbāb*, ed. A. Rustum and S. Abū-Shaqrā (Beirut, 1955). For an English translation see: Mikhāyil Mishāqa, *Murder, Mayhem, Pillage, and Plunder—The History of Lebanon in the 18th and 19th Centuries*, trans. by Wheeler M. Thackston, Jr. (Albany, 1988).

[66] Mishāqa, *Kitāb Mashhad al-Aʿyān*, p. 11. Since Mīkhāʾīl's book was written in the 1870s, his importance in shaping the last phase of Syrian identity will be delved into in the final chapter. I am referring to his book at this stage since he belonged to the literary circle at the court. He spent many years in close proximity to Bashīr, and certainly would have begun to shape and solidify his feelings and opinions during his years of service under the Amīr.

[67] I am aware that this is a problematical idea, since the last two books were written so long after the end of the Emirate and could have emerged from other processes and circumstances. What I want to emphasise is that the beginning of these processes went back to the period of Amīr Bashīr II and to the notions that were being formulated then. In retrospect, this period was the beginning of the process. Thus, it is not accidental that the same ideas developed later under the second and third generations of the same families which had served in the court of Amīr Bashīr II or were close to him.

In each book, one can find the first basic parameters of a vision for Syria that would develop and serve as the core for additional ideas, becoming a more cohesive concept in later years and throughout the nineteenth century. One such characteristic is the notion of the Emirate as a peak period in the history of the region of Syria. The books position the rule of Amīr Bashīr II as a turning point in regional history. Apparently, the authors perceive his reign as having been blissful and prosperous not just for the Mountain but for the whole region. Mishāqa even went further, and wrote that it was a pity that Amīr Bashīr II did not succeed in preserving the Mountain's autonomy, because later on his dynasty might have ruled in Syria in the same way that Muḥammad ʿAlī's dynasty ruled Egypt.[68]

From the geographical point of view, these books did not focus mainly on Mount Lebanon but refer to the whole area of Syria as well—especially mentioning the *Vilâyet*s of Damascus and Sidon.[69] These territorial borders are also emphasised as being within Amīr Bashīr's sphere of influence, intimating that his authority stretched way beyond his formal area of rule—namely not just the Mountain, but Greater Syria. Bashīr is described as a strong and influential ruler who played a pivotal role in the eyes of the Ottoman *vali*s across the Syrian region. The authors of these books seem to believe that Amīr Bashīr was the one who had the ability to control the problematical areas of Syria.[70] This view is strongly emphasised in

---

[68] Mishāqa, *Kitāb Mashhad al-Aʿyān*, p. 133. It is important to emphasise that these sentences are the speculation of Shakhāshīrī.

[69] For example, even though al-Maʿlūf focused on Zahle, he wrote a chapter on "The origin of the inhabitants of Syria" as a point of departure for his book. The components on which Syrian identity is based would develop later in the second half of the nineteenth century. Al-Maʿlūf referred to the pre-Islamic period and began to talk about the Greeks and the Romans and the Arab elements, saying that in the past the Christian Arab tribes mixed with the Syrian population. He emphasised the fact that when we look at the inhabitants of Syria we see that the Maronites and the Syrians are the most ancient, since they trace their antecedents to "*al-sulāla al-Sūriyya al-aṣliyya*." In another place al-Maʿlūf described the Shihābs and named them "al-Umarāʾ al-Sūriyyūn." See: al-Maʿlūf, *Dawānī al-Quṭūf*, pp. 136–137, 263, 288. The same notion is evident in the other books. See especially, Shidyāq, *Akhbār al-Aʿyān*, Vol. 1, pp. 12–13; Vol. 2, pp. 129–131; Ḥaydar al-Shihāb, *Lubnān Fī ʿAhd*, Vol. 3, pp. 558–561; Hourani, "Historians of Lebanon," pp. 230–233; Zachs, "Mīkhāʾīl Mishāqa," pp. 79–83.

[70] To emphasize that this attitude did not exist among writers not affiliated with the court see, for example, the case of Ḥanāniyya al-Munayyir (1756–1823), a Maronite priest from the Mountain. His book focuses only on a limited area, in this case the Shūf. He also chose the Shihābī Emirate as his main topic, but did

the first three books. They describe the incident of 1810, in which Yūsuf Pāshā, the *vali* of Damascus, came to realise that he would not be able to prevent the Wahhābīs from infiltrating his *vilâyet*. He then turned to Sulaymān Pāshā, the *vali* of Sidon, and requested his assistance. The latter did not hesitate in his response, asking Amīr Bashīr to send his forces as well. The writers imply that Sulaymān Pāshā, the *vali*, knew that this was the only way to recruit a large army in a relatively short time. When Amīr Bashīr joined Sulaymān's army and succeeded in conquering Damascus, the impression made—by connation—in all three books is that this incident decisively established the status of Bashīr throughout the entire Syrian region.[71]

Finally, it is important to note that even though the last two books were written following a substantial number of changes in the region from the time of the Emirate, they still highlight the same notions but more clearly and consistently. For example, the first two do not reveal as clear a vision as does Mishāqa's book, which will be discussed in the last chapter of this study.[72]

Thus, in the context and reality of this "secular" Christian middle stratum, the authors depicted Amīr Bashīr II as the most important figure in the whole region, since this was the impression held at that time. This view, as we saw in Mishāqa's book, appealed to their imagination and gave them the inspiration for the notion of a wider region than the Mountain, i.e. the region of Syria. In time, this developed in parallel with the economic notion of a broad hinterland that also suited the interests of the merchants, a group that belonged to a common background of social and political realities, had interrelated families and were interconnected socially and commercially.

Hobsbawm stated that "concepts, of course, are not part of free-

---

not consider Bashīr II as having influenced the whole region. Ḥanāniyya al-Munayyir, *al-Durr al-Marṣūf fī Tārīkh al- Shūf* (Beirut, 1984). See also another nineteenth-century chronicle, Manṣūr al-Ḥattūnī, *Nabdha Tārīkhiyya*.

[71] See, for further details, Zachs, "Mīkhā'īl Mishāqa," especially pp. 75, 79–83; Mishāqa, *al-Jawāb*, p. 102; Ḥaydar al-Shihāb, *Lubnān fī 'Ahd*, Vol. 3, pp. 556–561; Shidyāq, *Akhbār al-A'yān*, Vol. 2, pp. 129–131.

[72] These different phases of the notion will be elaborated on later. One of them is the semiotic transformation of words, especially in our case, terms that describe the region's borders. The transformation from *Bilād al-Shām* to Syria was crucial in creating a new identity, the Syrian identity. For example, Ḥaydar uses the word *Bilād al-Shām*. Shidyāq already used the word "Syria" and Mishāqa wrote phrases such as, *sukkān Sūriyya, Sūriyyūn, rijāl Sūriyya*. See: Shidyāq, *Akhbār al-A'yān*, Vol. 1, pp. 12–13; Mishāqa, *al-Jawāb*, pp. 295, 304, 315.

floating philosophical discourse, but socially, historically and locally rooted, and must be explained in terms of these realities."[73] Indeed, the realities in the daily life of these writers influenced their thoughts and ideas, i.e. their economic reality and how they conceived their ruler and his region politically, or how they wanted the rest of society (the "other") to conceive it. Historians such as Mishāqa began to outline the first steps in the construction of a Syrian idea and marked the first description of its initial characteristics. These historians began to see the Emirate as part of the heritage of Mount Lebanon. Later on, they also grasped it as part of the heritage of the region of Syria. Accordingly, the outstanding characteristic of the idea of Syria during Bashīr's period was the embryonic image that began to form among Bashīr's circle, that the region of Syria constituted one entity. This received even further significance under Ibrāhīm Pāshā. Therefore, we can say that the period of Amīr Bashīr II probably had a tremendous impact on the history of the Christian Arabs and the way in which they conceived themselves in the long run. His influence and the effect of his era would leave its mark on the imagined heritage of the middle stratum onward until the end of the nineteenth century.

Also, the Christian court historians of the middle stratum engaged in secular and political writing, the main focus of which was the struggle for the Mountain's economic and political status. Some of them were also the vanguard of the language movement that would arise in the second half of the nineteenth century. This correlation between Arab language and culture on one hand and the region of Syria on the other would be another key characteristic in the development of a Syrian identity in later years. In addition, this "secular" attitude would develop alongside another well-known notion—that of Lebanese identity, although this was developed by the Maronite church and included a limited region, i.e. the Mountain.

Thus, in addition to the thesis that the Emirate was the basis for Lebanese identity, this chapter has shown that, alongside this self image, another kind of awareness evolved, that of a Syrian notion.

As to the question of what stood behind these ideas, we can assume that Amīr Bashīr II and the court intelligentsia strove to justify and preserve their status and the Emirate's status as a legitimate autonomous

[73] Hobsbawm, *Nations and Nationalism*, p. 9.

entity directly subordinate to Istanbul, with no intermediate bureaucrats. The entire region of Syria and all of its sects were subsumed in this entity, with one ruler and cultural heritage. Their vision conceived of the region of Syria as a unity with the Mountain as its centre. Nevertheless, it would take nearly twenty years before these ideas again came to the fore.

The above description makes us wonder whether some of the ideas and notions that developed among the Christian middle stratum in the Mountain also evolved independently in later years, or did the end of the Emirate bring about the end of these concepts as well? Did this idea belong to limited groups, or was it the basis for a continuous process serving the first quest for a Christian-Arab self-concept? These questions will be examined in depth in the following chapter.

CHAPTER TWO

BEIRUT AND THE EMERGENCE OF A "SYRIAN IDENTITY": CHRISTIAN ARABS AS AGENTS OF CHANGE[1]

In many ways, the emergence of a Christian middle stratum in the region of Syria and the evolvement of its identity was a two-stage process. The first stage occurred under Amīr Bashīr II in Mount Lebanon from the end of the eighteenth century until the first half of the nineteenth century. The second stage took place in Beirut, particularly from the second half of the nineteenth century. Following local events, many members of the Mountain's middle stratum, above all the Christians of al-Shūf, migrated to Beirut, thereby making substantial contributions to that city, both economic and cultural. This stratum, as we shall see, integrated into the social and economic fabric of Beirut and its own middle stratum, already in the process of evolving. Together, they composed the new Beiruti middle stratum. Under the city's prevailing conditions, this stratum adapted and developed its identity—as a Syrian one, springing from its growing "political" awareness.

In Beirut, new circumstances and parameters re-shaped the concept of this growing Christian middle stratum and moulded its self-image. During this phase, however, the Syrian notion was transformed into a more defined and consolidated Christian-Arab identity than it had been in the Mountain. In other words, concepts or ideas which first appeared in the Syrian periphery (the Mountain in our case), would later be re-shaped and further developed in the atmosphere of a larger urban economic centre, such as Beirut. The development of Beirut as the central city in the region of Syria during the nineteenth century constituted a crucial stage in shaping the self-image of the Christian Arabs. In this respect, I will focus on why and to what extent some of the notions of "Syria," which began to evolve in the Mountain, were strengthened and actually accelerated

[1] In contrast with the common term "agents of the West."

among the Beiruti middle stratum. I will also describe and classify the social groups that advanced these ideas and will try to explicate their interests in doing so, the complex dynamics of the city itself and the interactions among its heterogeneous groups, on the route to creating a wider non-sectarian identity.

This development of the city will be presented using the three-circle model, i.e. economic, social and cultural circles, similar to the model used to describe the period of Amīr Bashīr II. These three circles shaped the self-identity of one group vis-à-vis the other or, as in the case of the Syrian identity, as part of the other. In other words, these parameters helped a particular minority group (the Christian Arabs) to distinguish itself from the other (the Muslim society), but at the same time, and perhaps even more importantly, to become part of that society as well. As will become evident in the case of the Christian Arabs, the effort to become part of a larger community, a process that would eventually reshape that larger community, was as strong as their search for a unique self-identity.

Beirut as an Economic and Cultural Centre of Syria

Toward the end of the Emirate and under the influence of the occupation of Ibrāhīm Pāshā, the region of Syria had already accumulated some economic experience with the West. Ibrāhīm's rule, and the Emirate itself, hastened the imbalance between the Muslim and the Christian communities to the point where, in certain respects, the Christians were better off than were the Muslims. The rule of Ibrāhīm Pāshā over Syria only reinforced the developments that took place under Amīr Bashīr. Ibrāhīm's social policies were marked by tolerance towards the non-Muslim population, and his economic policies allowed freer activity of foreigners (Western merchants, diplomats, and missionaries) than had been the case previously.[2] As a result of this policy, commercial ties between Beirut and markets in Europe strengthened.

[2] On Ibrāhīm, see: William R. Polk and Richard L. Chambers (eds.), *Beginnings of Modernization in the Middle East—The Nineteenth Century* (Chicago, 1966), pp. 160–175; Shimon Shamir, "Egyptian Rule (1832–1840) and the Beginning of the Modern Period in the History of Palestine," in A. Cohen (ed.), *Egypt and Palestine* (Jerusalem, 1984), pp. 214–231.

Due to administrative changes he introduced, the region was united for the first time under a central governor (*Hükümdar*) located in Damascus.[3] The old division of the region into *eyalet*s was abolished and the region became one administrative entity, ruled by a single governor. However, Ibrāhīm's rule in Syria was that of an Egyptian ruler, a foreigner, and it ended after ten years.

In order to understand the growing economic importance of the region in general and of Beirut in particular, they must be viewed in the context of the wider economic changes occurring at the time under the Ottomans, which affected the city as well. Most influential among these were the growing penetration of the West into the region and the continually increasing entwining of the local market into the world economy. The 1838 signing of the Balta-Liman agreement between Sultan Maḥmud II and the British can be perceived as the apex of this process. This agreement allowed the West to penetrate the Porte's economy by organising and reducing taxation. The penetration became even more aggressive and intensive, especially since the West was continuously trying to find new markets for its goods as the industrial revolution in Europe expanded.[4]

Gradually, a dynamic import-export trade developed between the region of Syria and the West; Syria's markets grew concomitantly.[5] Opportunities in international commerce were opening for local traders and merchants. At the same time, however, Muslim merchants who dealt primarily with local crafts and products suffered the greatest loss, since they could not compete with the newly imported, mass-produced European goods. By contrast, those who dealt in import and export, both foreign and local merchants, were the principal beneficiaries of this situation, and these were mainly Christians (of course, some Muslims were included in this group as well). The purchase of goods produced in West European countries,

---

[3] Asad Rustum (ed.), *al-Uṣūl al-ʿArabiyya li-Tārīkh Sūriyya fī ʿAhd Muḥammad ʿAlī Bāshā*, 2nd ed. (Beirut, 1987), pp. 50–51; Sulaymān Abū ʿIzz al-Dīn, *Ibrāhīm Bāshā fī Sūriyā* (Beirut, 1929).

[4] FO 195/221, Black to Rose (Consul General of Beirut), 4 May 1843; Jacob C. Hurewitz, *The Middle East and North Africa in World Politics*, Vol. 1 (London, 1975), pp. 265–266; Charles Issawi, *The Economic History of the Middle East, 1800–1914* (Chicago, 1966), pp. 38–40; Rustum, *Bashīr Bayna al-Sulṭān*, pp. 117–143.

[5] FO 78/715, Moore, Review of the British Trade with Syria During 1846; Lewis J. Farley *The Massacres in Syria* (London, 1861), pp. 194–195; John Bowring, *Report on the Commercial Statistics of Syria* (London, 1840).

their transport to the region of Syria, and the export of products from the Syrian regional network via the local markets to European countries had a direct impact on the spiralling foreign activity in the area. As commerce increased, entrepreneurs, agents, and moneylenders took on roles of increasing importance; the presence of consuls became necessary. Missionaries usually followed, promoting foreign activity in the area even more. The policies of the Porte from 1856 on, manifested by the *Tanẓīmāt* reforms and the concept of *Osmanlılık*, described in greater detail in the next chapter, further strengthened the status of Christians throughout the Empire.[6]

An outcome of this economic growth was that a large portion of the commerce was now conducted by sea. On the one hand, this adversely affected the caravan trade along land routes and to internal cities.[7] On the other hand, coastal towns like Beirut benefited from these dynamics. Indeed, in light of these developments, Beirut was transformed into an important urban and economic city centre and one of the foremost harbours for the whole region of Syria.[8] If in the first half of the nineteenth century Beirut was engaged in fierce competition with other port cities, by the end of the century it had succeeded in outstripping them all.

Already in 1813, traders became aware of the advantages of Beirut. Simultaneously, towns such as Sidon, important principally for the Christian merchants, were declining in importance. Observing the transport of British goods to the city and the rise of local wealth in Beirut, the French, too, began to evince interest in the city, especially in the constant growth of the silk trade in the Mountain. This was one of the reasons which eventually brought the French to decide to place a consul there.

The essence of the economic rise of Beirut stemmed from an array

---

[6] I will enlarge on these terms in Chapter Three. The *Tanẓīmāt* reforms refer principally to the *Hatt-ı Hümayun* of 1856, which granted Christians equal civil rights.

[7] US/NA (National Archives), Commercial Report of American vice Consul Barclay to Washington, 30 August 1858; US/NA, Johnson, Trade Report of Damascus, 1864; Leila Fawaz, "The Changing Balance of Forces between Beirut and Damascus in the Nineteenth and Twentieth Centuries," *Revue de Monde Musulman et de la Mediterranee* (1990), pp. 208–214; Linda Schatkowski-Schilcher, *The Islamic Maqased of Beirut—A Case Study of Modernization in Lebanon*, M.A. Thesis, American University of Beirut, 1969, pp. 60–63.

[8] Other ports such as Alexandria, and in some measure Alexandretta and Tripoli, developed rapidly, and became a central axis around which commercial activity progressed. Inland cities such as Baghdad, Damascus, Aleppo, and Hama, which traded with countries such as Egypt, Turkey, Persia, and India, accordingly suffered.

of factors, which ultimately concentrated the Syrian interaction with the foreign trade in Beirut. Foreign and local merchants during that period moved from town to town, each person seeking greater profit. These translocations influenced the situation in general, and involved capital, expertise, and trade ties. The merchants' mobility and choices tipped the scales in favour of Beirut.[9]

Precisely determining the beginning of this process is difficult. In the 1820s there was still no sign that the town was to become an important centre of Syria. Tripoli and Sidon were indeed larger in population and trade turnover.[10] Significant development seems to have occurred chiefly in the 1830s and 1840s (corresponding to the reign of Ibrāhīm Pāshā and the end of the Emirate). This perception is reinforced by the words of Guys, the French Consul in Beirut from the mid-1840s to the late 1850s, who noted that already in the 1830s Beirut was the most important commercial centre among the coastal cities.[11] Nor did this transformation escape the eyes of local Christian Arabs. Buṭrus al-Bustānī, who compiled his encyclopedia *Dā'irat al-Maʿārif* (Encyclopedia of Knowledge) in the 1870s, wrote under the entry "Beirut" that "its progress has no equal in any place in Europe."[12] Likewise, the growth of the city's population attests to this trend. At the beginning of the nineteenth century, the population of Beirut numbered about 6,000. Towards the century's end it was approximately 120,000, an astounding 20-fold increase.[13]

---

[9] Eyup Y. Özveren, *The Making and Unmaking of an Ottoman Port City: Nineteenth Century Beirut, its Hinterland, and the World Economy*. Ph.D. Dissertation, University of New York, 1990, pp. 73–84.

[10] Marwan Buheiry, *Beirut's Role in the Political Economy of the French Mandate, 1919–1939*. Papers on Lebanon, Centre for Lebanese Studies (Oxford, 1986), pp. 1–3.

[11] Henri Guys, *Beyrout et le Liban* (Paris, 1850), p. 8.

[12] Buṭrus al-Bustānī (ed.), "Beirut," *Dā'irat al-Maʿārif*, Vol. 5, p. 750.

[13] For other figures and estimations of the population in Beirut during the nineteenth century, see: Leila T. Fawaz, *Merchants and Migrants in Nineteenth Century Beirut* (London, 1983), p. 1; Michael Johnson, *Class and Client in Beirut—the Sunni-Muslim Community and the Lebanese State, 1840–1985* (London, 1986), p. 12; Lūwīs Shīkhū, *Bayrūt—Tārīkhuhā wa-Āthāruhā* (Beirut, 1925), p. 94. The American missionaries reported that in 1824 Beirut's population was estimated at 14–15,000 people. Other sources mention only 5,000 people. Eli Smith, an active missionary in Beirut, wrote that when he came to the city in 1826 the population, including the suburbs, figured 5,000 but had increased to 15,000 in 1839 and to 30,000 in 1856. See: *The Missionary Herald*, Vol. XX, No. 4, Fisk and King, April 1824; *The Missionary Herald*, Vol. XX, No. 7, Goodel, 24 June 1824; US/NA, M. Johnson to A. Johnson, 31 December 1869. Henry S. Osborn, *The Holy Land Past and Present* (London, 1868), p. 60. In 1906 the population in Beirut was 150,000, composed of 100,000 Christians and 50,000 Muslims. US/NA, T367, Roll 23, Vol. 23, Allen Bargnloz to Secretary of

The main impetus came particularly during the second half of the nineteenth century. Beirut's successful accession to the position of Aleppo, which had been a major centre of trade and production in geographical Syria during the seventeenth and eighteenth centuries, was the climax of this process.[14]

Lord Dufferin (the British representative at the Beirut Conference following the civil war of 1860) commented in 1861 that Beirut had grown, and had turned into "the principal trading port of Syria." He added that its commercial ties with the neighbourhoods of the Mountain and with the city of Damascus were becoming very important.[15] Other European sources tended to describe it as a European city. Isabel Burton, for example, wrote in the 1870s that "Beirut is a demy-civilized, semi-Christianized, demy-semi-Europeanized town, with a certain amount of comfort and European manners and customs: it enjoys perfect safety . . . it has free communication with Europe by post and telegraph—in fact it is somewhat more European, or rather, Levantine, than Oriental."[16] Others named it "the queen of the Levant."

It was not long before the economic developments led to social changes in the region. The rapid transformation of Beirut was attracting many migrants from within Syria, especially from Mount Lebanon, as well as from other port cities. Beirut itself, like the region of Syria as a whole, was populated by a plethora of communities and minorities, all locked in a chronic conflict. But changes were yet to come. From the 1840s, mass migrations to the city turned its Christian population into its leading community, numerically and economically. In addition, the city became the area's main port, serving the entire region of Syria. A careful look at the "push and the pull" factors of the city will explain why these changes occurred.

State, 16 July 1906. Additional estimates taken from the *Salname* under Rāshid Pāshā, the first *Salname* conducted in the *vilâyet.* This source provide lower estimates of the Beirut population for 1871; according to that, Beirut had 4,886 households, evidently not including the suburbs, but only the city itself. The average family size in those days was considered to have 4–5 people; so the population was between 19,500 and 24,450. These figures probably undercount children, women and foreign residents. See: *Salname-yi Vilâyet-i Suriye*, 1288AH/1871.

[14] US/NA, Calhoun, W. Eddy, W. Bird, D. Bliss, R. G. Dodge, C. Van Dyck to Cass, 19 November 1858; F. A. Neale, *Eight Years in Syria, Palestine and Asia Minor from 1842–1850.* Vol. 1 (London, 1851), p. 208; Anonymous, *Ḥasr al-Lithām ʿan Nakabāt al-Shām* (Cairo, 1895), p. 12.

[15] FO 195/659, Dufferin to Bulwer, 25 April 1861.

[16] Isabel Burton, *The Inner Life of Syria, Palestine, and the Holy Land*, Vol. 1 (London, 1875), p. 18.

Immigration to Beirut

"Push" Factors

The first major movement to the city began already at the time of Ibrāhīm Pāshā's conquest. Many Christians who had fled to the Mountain under the regime of al-Jazzār (late eighteenth century) took the opportunity under the tolerant Ibrāhīm Pāshā to return to the city of Beirut, re-establishing their businesses and dealing in foreign trade. Another series of events during the nineteenth century constituted an ongoing process that pushed the Christian population to Beirut. From 1841 through 1842, and then in 1845, animosities between Muslims, Christians and Druze erupted, followed by a massive migration from rural areas to Syrian cities in general, and to Beirut in particular. The peak of this process was the civil war in Mount Lebanon and Damascus in 1860, which became a milestone in the history of Syria in general and in the history of the Christian Arabs in particular.

In 1840, when Bashīr II was exiled to Malta and Ibrāhīm Pāshā left Syria, the Druze *muqāṭaʿjī*s began to return to Mount Lebanon and to demand their lands which were now in the hands of Christian merchants and *fallāḥūn*. This process was one of the important factors aggravating existing inter-communal discord; it sparked the civil war of 1841. The Christian middle stratum, which had developed during the reign of Bashīr II and which enjoyed his protection, was now left with no guardian, and its members began to flee from the Mountain and migrate mainly to Beirut, which was already central to their economic and social life. These migrants included many middle stratum members from Zahle and Deir al-Qamar, as well as other places in the Mountain. Most of them tried not only to preserve and to revive their economic and social status, but to utilise their knowledge and experience and develop them further under the new opportunities that Beirut had to offer. After all, the profitable relationship between the Mountain and Beirut was already well known to them. The only difference was that now they would be conducting their business from this city. In some instances, branches of some families already lived in Beirut.[17]

---

[17] See: Fawaz, "Zahle and Deir al-Qamar," pp. 55–56; Churchill, *The Druzes*, p. 34. In many cases it was the second and third generation of these families who

Shortly after their arrival in the city, some of them (especially second or third generation migrants) became central figures in certain fields, such as silk export from the city to the West. Although estimating how many families from the Mountain lived in Beirut is difficult, we do know that the same families from the Mountain emerged in many economic and cultural activities of the city. It is important to point out that the Mountain middle stratum integrated into an economic development that already existed in Beirut and eventually became an integral part of the local Beiruti middle stratum. It did not initiate the economic boom in Beirut but rather catalysed and perhaps strengthened a process which was already taking place.

Then in the 1850s, an economic crisis in the silk industry caused many more Christians to flee the Mountain, since its economy was based mainly on production of silk. They fled to Beirut. After 1860, the number of migrants steadily increased. This time, the flow was mainly from the Mountain, from Aleppo and from Damascus; people fled to safer places such as Beirut and even as far as Egypt.[18] As the population in these places declined, artisans had smaller markets. They in turn left the inland towns and cities, seeking better livelihoods in the coastal city.

The migratory movements occurring between the 1840s and the 1860s wrought a significant demographic and social change on the population of Beirut in favour of the Christians. After 1860, Beirut became the first city in the region of Syria with a Christian majority.[19]

---

had a leading economic and social status in Beirut. The Maʿlūfs from Zahle and some of its members are a prototypical family, who transferred their success to Beirut. Some of its members integrated into the economy of the city. The Maʿlūfs had ties with leading Beiruti merchant families such as the Sursuqs and the Mudawwars, trading in sheep and wheat. Another family was the Ṣūṣās, from Deir al-Qamar, who also became active in Beirut. One of its members, ʿAbdallāh Afandī, was one of the big money changers in Beirut. The family had strong commercial ties with another leading merchant family from Beirut, Bustrus, dealing in sheep. Members of other families, such as the Shalfūns, Shidyāqs, Ṣfyres, Thābits, Zalzals, al-Bustānīs, and Daḥdāḥs, immigrated to Beirut and merged into its economic and cultural life. See: al-Maʿlūf, *Dawānī al-Quṭūf*, pp. 314–316, 389–391, 465–469.

[18] Fawaz, *Merchants and Migrants*, p. 122; Thomas Philipp, *The Syrians in Egypt* (Stuttgart, 1985), pp. 78ff.

[19] In the opinion of Fawaz, until 1845 the number of Muslims and Christians in Beirut was equal, about 9000 in each community. Then the number of Muslims rose, but the number of Christians rose even more. In 1858 two thirds of the population was Christian. In the 1860s, after the civil war, there were 18,000 Muslims and 28,000 Christians in the city. In 1875 the respective figures were 20,000 and 35,000. Between 1840 and 1875 the number of Muslims doubled, but the number of Christians increased almost four-fold. See: Fawaz, *Merchants and Migrants*, p. 45.

These circumstances, among others, made the city a magnet for thousands more Christian refugees.

"Pull" Factors

The Christian migration to Beirut was not accidental. Several external and local reasons constituted catalysts pulling the Christians specifically into this city. As noted, by the 1840s Beirut had become safer than the Mountain, and large waves of migration flowed into it. More than a few reasons stood behind this process. Naturally, the rise in commercial activity in all the coastal towns gave Beirut an important role in the region. From the beginning of the century, Beirut's import and export with Europe constantly expanded. Between 1827 and 1862 trade through Beirut's port increased eight-fold.[20] Beirut exported silk, olive oil, tobacco, fruit, almonds and more.[21] For the most part, the city imported cotton and silk cloths, sugar, leather, coffee, iron, copper and tea.[22] The majority of the commerce was with France (the silk trade), Britain (cotton cloths) and the United States (cotton cloths).[23] During that period, especially following the inauguration of the direct route via steamships (by French, Austrian, and Russian companies), most of the trade to Beirut was carried out by European vessels.[24]

---

[20] Johnson, *Class and Client*, p. 13. Import and export figures of Beirut's port show the central position of trade with the West. During the nineteenth century Beirut became the chief port for all of Syria. An illustration of this rise is the total value of goods imported and exported through the port during that century. For example, in 1825 the value of exports from Beirut was 3,995,645 French francs. The value of imports was 5,907,873 francs. By contrast, in 1857 the respective figures were 40,339,900 francs (ten fold) and 40,457,990 francs (almost seven fold).

[21] US/NA, Johnson to Seward, 30 September 1861.

[22] Johnson stated, for example, that in 1862 Beirut imported goods totalling 46,521,000 French francs in value. Exports were worth 31,279,000 francs, i.e. the total trade volume was almost 78 million francs [about $15.5 million at the current exchange rate]. In 1867, income from imports was $9.8 million, and from exports about $6.8 million.

[23] US/NA, Report on the Trade in Beirut, Johnson to Seward, 30 September 1863; A. Johnson to Seward, 30 December 1863; US/NA, Trade Report of Beirut, 1869; Dominique Chevallier, "Western Development and Eastern Crises in the Mid-Nineteenth Century—Syria Confronted with the European Economy," in William R. Polk and Richard L. Chambers (eds.), *Beginnings of Modernization in the Middle East—The Nineteenth Century*, p. 206.

[24] US/NA, The Trade of Syria, Beirut, 28 December 1864.

In addition, the manufacture of silk and other goods in Mount Lebanon and the Beirut area drew Western merchants to the region. They began to settle in Beirut, and to invest in the establishment of enterprises and in the technical development needed to streamline commerce. Consequently, import and export expanded still more.[25]

The appearance of many foreigners entailed a further development. The European powers began to set up consulates and legations in Beirut, among other reasons to protect the merchants and entrepreneurs active on their behalf in the area.[26] The consular presence and the rise in the number of foreign residents made Beirut safer and more convenient for Christian migrants. Merchants and agents, who became the chief players in Beirut's financial circle, became the main beneficiaries of the city's growth.

Another parameter throughout the century was the transformation of Beirut into an important administrative centre for the region. This tendency already began under Ibrāhīm Pāshā, whose policy was to intensify European involvement and penetration and strengthen the economic links with Europe. During his reign the status of the Christians in Beirut became both established and consolidated. Even missionary activity was permitted, including the opening of educational institutions in the area. One of Ibrāhīm's goals was to encourage the development and activity of the ports in the coastal cities. He regarded Beirut as the port of Damascus. Therefore, as early as 1833, about half of Syrian exports passed through the Beirut port.[27] Due to the growing importance of the city, Ibrāhīm moved the administrative centre of the central coast to Beirut, a measure that gave it further advantages over other port cities. The administrative significance of Beirut increased even further after Ibrāhīm's departure.

In 1840, Beirut underwent a number of administrative changes. Following the withdrawal of the Egyptians and the restoration of Ottoman rule, Syria was divided into three provinces (*eyalet* or *paşalık*), namely Aleppo, Damascus, and Sidon. Beirut was made capital of the Sidon *vilâyet*. Accordingly, the administrative representative of the central government resided there. The business dealings of the mer-

[25] FO 195/221, Black to Moore, 30 July 1841; Buṭrus al-Bustānī (ed.), "Ḥarīr," *Dāʾirat al-Maʿārif*, Vol. 7, pp. 15–16; *al-Jinān*, Vol. 1, No. 12, 1870, pp. 243–244.

[26] See also, Nabil Saleh (ed.), *The Qadi and the Fortune Teller* (London, 1996), pp. 69–70.

[27] Özveren, *The Making and Unmaking*, p. 87.

chants and entrepreneurs in the city increased as it was now easier for them to obtain licenses and approval for economic agreements by the government when its offices were nearby. They were saved the need for costly and lengthy journeys to other centres.[28]

The administrative status of Beirut suffered somewhat from the reorganisation of the region under the *Vilâyet* Law in 1864; the law brought about the establishment of the *Vilâyet* of Syria a year after that. Under this reorganisation, Beirut was demoted to a *sancak* of Syria under Damascus, the administrative centre of the *vilâyet*. Twenty-three years later, in 1888, the central government recognised its pivotal position and restored Beirut to its former status. Now it served as the government's centre. Similarly, it became the regional capital of the *Vilâyet* of Beirut, which consisted of five *sancaks*: Latakia, Tripoli, Beirut, Acre, and Nablus.

Local infrastructure improvements, particularly in transportation, made the city even more attractive. In the 1840s and 1850s regular maritime routes became established between the ports of the West and Beirut, and towards the end of the century additional steamship lines developed, plying regular, scheduled routes between Alexandria, Beirut, Istanbul, Marseilles, and other European cities. New land routes were opened and inaugurated in the region. In 1858, work began on the Beirut-Damascus road. With its completion in 1863, the transport of goods from the coast to Damascus was facilitated, and the link between Beirut and the Syrian interior improved. Furthermore, between 1851 and 1861 the French opened good-quality roads between Beirut and Deir al-Qamar.

By the middle of the century the city was also an important financial centre. In 1857 the British set up the first European bank in Beirut. In 1863 a telegraph functioned there, connecting the city with Europe. Six years later the Suez Canal opened a factor that intensified Western interest in the region even more. Western businessmen increased their investments, and Western involvement in Beirut expanded constantly.

Towards the end of the century the port was so busy that a new quay had to be built in 1887. These developments made the Syrian hinterland ever more dependent on Beirut's port. Accordingly, the tight bonds with the hinterland enhanced the city's development; the region's interior served as the field of economic activity for Beirut's

[28] Issawi (ed.) *The Economic History of the Middle East*, p. 13.

port. Beirut's ties with the Syrian region were more substantial than those of the other port cities on the Syrian coast. The city provided not only trade but also security (mainly consular) and varied opportunities for employment. In contrast to the past when Christian merchants (such as the Bustrus family) and Muslim merchants (such as the Bayhum family) who operated in the city had been obliged to flee in times of hardship, as early as the 1830s the Christian families began to feel far safer there and staked their futures on the city.

Thus, during the nineteenth century, Beirut grew from a harbour town of scant importance into the most advanced urban and commercial centre on the eastern Mediterranean seaboard. In contrast to the past, when it had served only as the port of Mount Lebanon, it now functioned as the port city for Damascus and other cities in the region. Trade networks traversed the region, linking merchants from Beirut, Jaffa, Nablus, Damascus and Aleppo. Later on, this trend mushroomed when a rail system, completed in the last decade of the nineteenth century, connected coastal cities with cities in the interior and cities in the interior with their hinterlands, creating the so-called "emergent national political economy" process.[29]

Did these economic developments affect the local Christian Arabs socially, to the point that they began to re-define their identity? Did they see the city as described by the Western writers? Or perhaps they saw it and themselves in another light? The description of the next phase will try to offer some answers.

Second Phase[30]*—The Emergence of the Beiruti Middle Stratum and its Characteristics*

In 1868 the American Consul in Beirut wrote "Everyone in Syria prefers to be a merchant [rather] than a farmer or a manufacturer."[31] And indeed, the economic development of Beirut influenced the city's social structure by creating a new social group that had not existed previously. Prior to the connection with the world market, the main

[29] James L. Gelvin, *Divided Loyalties—Nationalism and Mass Politics in Syria at the Close of Empire* (Los Angeles, 1998), p. 159.

[30] The term "second phase" is in relation to the "first phase" mentioned in Chapter One. The Beiruti middle stratum completed the crystallisation of this new identity during this phase.

[31] US/NA, Trade Report of Beirut, 30 September 1868.

social groups in the city included the higher stratum, which consisted mainly of government or army officials, Muslim notables and *ʿulamāʾ*. The majority of the population belonged to the lowest stratum, consisting of workers who earned wages only on a daily basis, and the unemployed. A small portion of this stratum had become craftsmen, shopkeepers and small merchants, although little evidence exists concerning this group and their influence on the city. In all likelihood, some of its members took advantage of the new economic opportunities available, and became part of the rising middle stratum.

The new economic structure, which was now based mainly on commerce, enterprise, and middlemen, produced a strong Beiruti middle stratum,[32] composed mainly of Christian Arabs. Some of its members were Beiruti residents of long standing, while others were families who had migrated to the city, especially from the Mountain but also from coastal cities such as Tripoli and from some cities in the interior. Roughly classified, the Mountain middle stratum emerged from the end of the eighteenth century towards the end of the Emirate, while the Beiruti middle stratum emerged mainly from the 1820s until the 1880s.

In contrast to the middle stratum of the Emirate, which was more "traditional" in its outlook, its Beiruti counterpart was an urban stratum, more exposed to the education, culture and hence the ideas of the West. And yet, as mentioned, after the end of the Emirate, a portion of the middle stratum from the Mountain interlaced with the Beiruti middle stratum and thus can be perceived to have become part of the latter.[33] Indeed, the ties and expertise of more than half a century, which the members of the Mountain middle stratum carried with them to Beirut, were assimilated into the growing experience of the Beiruti middle stratum. Eventually, the Mountain middle stratum catalysed and assisted in the growth of the Beiruti middle

[32] Other researchers, such as Leila T. Fawaz, Dominique Chevallier, Fatma M. Göçek and Irena Smilanskaya, tended also to use the term "bourgeoisie" in order to define this Beiruti middle stratum. See: Smilanskaya, "From Subsistence to Market Economy," pp. 235–236, 240, 244; Fawaz, *Merchants and Migrants*, p. 65; Chevallier, *La Societe du Mont Liban*, pp. 202–209. See also Fatma M. Göçek, *Rise of the Bourgeoisie, Demise of Empire—Ottoman Westernization and Social Change* (New York, 1996), especially p. 89; Sharabi, *Arab Intellectuals and the West*, p. 2.

[33] See footnote no. 17 that emphasises how families from the Mountain integrated into the city, becoming part of this sub-stratum and establishing ties with Beiruti families.

stratum, not only from the financial point of view, but also in cultural aspects and in how they perceived themselves. These concepts would shape the Christian Arabs' growing sense of self during the nineteenth century, moulding its future form. Thus, the Beiruti stratum can be grasped in part as a new and yet a continuous phase in the emergence of a Christian middle stratum in the region of Syria.

A detailed study of the families comprising the Beiruti middle stratum helps reveal its characteristics. The families and individuals whom I researched in order to demonstrate the paradigm of this chapter are taken from lists of members of cultural societies in Beirut, such as *al-Jamʿiyya al-Sūriyya li-Iktisāb al-ʿUlūm wal-Funūn* (The Syrian Society for the Acquisition of Sciences) (1847–1852) and *al-Jamʿiyya al-ʿIlmiyya al-Sūriyya* (The Syrian Scientific Society) (1858–1860, 1868–1869).[34] The idea that this middle stratum was the source of the Syrian notion surfaces immediately upon observing that the societies included the name "Syria" in their titles and identified with it; this occurred even prior to the creation of the *Vilâyet* of Syria. They focused their interest on issues connected with Syria as a country, took an interest in Arab culture, and wished to broaden the public's knowledge of these topics. In the following pages we will see who were the people who supported these societies and why did they choose to define themselves as "Syrian" societies. Scrutinising the background of the families whose members participated in these societies helps to reveal some answers. This examination also indicates the basis for the model of the middle stratum which stood behind and encouraged this "Syrian identity."

A study of some of the members of these societies, which encompassed 36 families and 125 individuals,[35] leads to the conclusion that this middle stratum may be regarded as having been divided into two sub-strata: upper-middle and lower-middle. The first sub-stratum described—the upper-middle, was comprised primarily of the city's merchants. This group consisted of long-standing Beiruti residents, who took advantage of the city's growth to accumulate even

---

[34] See: ʿAbd al-Karīm Gharāyiba, *Sūriyya fī al-Qarn al-Tāsiʿ ʿAshar, 1840–1876* (Cairo, 1961), pp. 219–220, 242–244; Buṭrus al-Bustānī, *al-Jamʿiyya al-Sūriyya lil-ʿUlūm wal-Funūn 1847–1852*. ed. Yūsuf Quzmā Khūrī (Beirut, 1990), pp. 17–18.

[35] It's important to note that many leading families from the middle stratum (from Mount Lebanon—Zahle and Deir al-Qamar) took part in these cultural activities. Some families are the Shalfūns, the Thābits, the Daḥdāḥs, the Shidyāqs, and the Khūrīs. For more details on these families see: Appendix I, pp. 219–244.

more wealth, as well as newly-arrived, rich merchants and entrepreneurs, who participated in the growing trade with Europe. Some of these newcomers had already accumulated their wealth in Mount Lebanon, where they engaged in the silk industry. They managed to highly benefit from the new circumstances in Beirut, displaying great acumen in mediating between the families in the Mountain and the foreign merchants frequenting the city. The links forged by the newcomers with these foreign merchants increased and expanded. In time, the newcomers managed to learn the foreigners' methods, take over their networks and eventually even a portion of their activities.

The second sub-stratum—the lower-middle, can be described as a "petit-bourgeoisie," and included intelligentsia, writers and members of the liberal professions. Members of this group were products of the new educational institutions of the city as well as educated newcomers attracted by the employment opportunities of Beirut. It is important to emphasise that the distinction between these two substrata is somewhat artificial and is introduced mainly in order to explain the stratum's dynamics. In many cases the borders between the two sub-strata were quite indistinct. Members of the middle stratum could easily belong to both sub-strata. In some cases, members of the same family belonged to the intelligentsia, while others to the entrepreneurial and merchant sub-stratum.[36]

The city's merchants were the first to grasp the significance of the changes taking place and were able to parlay this knowledge into financial prosperity. They moved astutely into import and export, and made good use of their social connections. Soon they became very rich and possessed lands throughout the region of Syria. They began to invest in economic and cultural projects in Beirut.

Some of these were merchant families originally from the Mountain, such as the Daḥdāḥs, Mishāqas, Zalzals, Thābits, Bustānīs, Maʿlūfs and the Ṣūṣās. For example, in the 1840s the Daḥdāḥ family had a company in Beirut, which was called *Sharīkat Daḥdāḥ*, which had ties with Marseilles and London.[37] The focus of this chapter, however,

---

[36] As James Bill emphasised, the social pyramid of societies is not clear-cut. The layers of society do not stand apart. On the contrary, each layer could also be part of another layer or stratum. James Bill, "Class Analysis and the Dialectics of Modernization in the Middle East," *International Journal of Middle East Studies*, Vol. 3 (1972), pp. 417–434.

[37] Chevallier, *La Société du Mont Liban*, p. 88.

is primarily the families of Beiruti origin, who have not been mentioned until now. A good example is the Sursuq family, of Christian Orthodox origin. Their economic activities were diverse, and included shipping, silk, and wheat transport to London and to Cyprus. The family included bankers, who invested in projects such as the Suez Canal, the Beirut-Damascus highway, and the Beirut Harbour Company. During the nineteenth century, the Sursuq family become the wealthiest Christian family in the Ashrafiyya quarter. Toward the end of the century, they purchased vast tracts of lands from the Ottoman Empire, totalling over a quarter of a million *dūnams*. The family's income from its properties in 1883 was $200,000.[38]

Other examples of merchant families were the Misks, Abkāryūs, the Ṭrāds and the Yannīs; the Mudawwars, who were Greek Catholics, and dealt mainly in silk manufacture; and the Bustrus family, which was of Greek Orthodox origin and engaged in import and export of agricultural goods, chiefly wheat. They also acted as shipping agents for steamers operating out of Liverpool.[39] They were in partnership with a Muslim family, the Bayhums, importers-exporters in Beirut. The Bayhums traded in agricultural goods such as silk, wool, and cotton, and the like.[40]

In short, this sub-stratum included many "big" merchants. The Muslims among them were also considered as notables. Accordingly, a number of its members, especially the Muslims, were recognised as part of the city's elite. However, in general, most of the group represented the middle stratum.

A number of factors enabled the merchants to become so rich and over time, establish and strengthen their economic and social status. Apart from their financial ties with Europe, one of the major reasons for their prosperity was the development of the silk manufacturing industry. This, as we have seen, had already existed in Mount

---

[38] On the Sursuqs see: Fawaz, *Merchants and Migrants*, pp. 91–93; Ḥasan Ḥallāq, *al-Tārīkh al-Ijtimā'ī wal-Iqtiṣādī wal-Siyāsī fī Bayrūt wal-Wilāyāt al-ʿUthmāniyya fī al-Qarn al-Tasiʿ Ashar- Sijillāt al-Maḥkama al-Shrʿiyya fī Bayrūt* (Beirut, 1987), p. 205; Rashid Khalidi, *Palestinian Identity—The Construction of Modern National Consciousness* (New-York, 1997), p. 107.

[39] On the silk commerce see: Ghastūn Dūkūssū, "Tārīkh al-Ḥarīr fī Bilād al-Shām," *al-Mashriq*, Vol. 15, 1912, pp. 374–380. On these families see: Ḥasan Ḥallāq, *Bayrūt al-Maḥrūsa fī 'Ahd al-ʿUthmānī* (Beirut, 1987), p. 271; Jurjī Zaydān, *Tarājim Mashāhīr al-Sharq fī al-Qarn al-Tāsiʿ 'Ashar*, Vol. 1 (Cairo, 1922), pp. 145–147; Vol. 2, pp. 320–321; FO 195/1113, Eldridge to Elliot, 6 June 1876.

[40] Johnson, *Class and Client*, pp. 14, 60–67.

Lebanon, but continued to develop between the 1840s and the 1880s, to the point that silk became one of the principal exports from Beirut's port. In fact, even though the Mountain was the centre for manufacturing silk, it was the Christian merchants of Beirut who became its main marketers, and thus in time the ones who earned the most from this industry. They acted as successful middlemen between the Lebanese cocoon producers and the Western fabric traders, who were for the most part French. Some of the silk was sold on European markets and brought in considerable income for those trading in it.[41] Only a tiny fraction of this money reached the hands of the farmers and cocoon producers themselves, or the workers who actually spun the silk. Most of the money remained in the hands of the Beirut and Tripoli merchants who served as brokers between the manufacturers-farmers and the businessmen of Marseilles and Lyons.[42]

As demonstrated, this system harmed not only the farmers, but also the traditional *muqāṭaʿjīs*, who were weakened by the changing economy. Concomitant with the decline of the *muqāṭaʿjīs*,[43] the Christian middle stratum in the city steadily established itself. The silk trade and the construction of the local spinning mills starting in the 1840s contributed further to this collapse, and gave added impetus to the rise of the Beiruti middle stratum, eventually bestowing on the Christians economic supremacy along the coast and throughout much of the region of Syria. More than that, the Western consulates and missions established in the city assisted them on their road to success. Many members of this stratum had been educated at mission schools which had been widely established as early as the 1820s. Hence, Western culture was not foreign to them. Speaking several European languages and becoming familiar with the habits of the foreign merchants, the Beiruti Christians were able to forge close, profitable ties with their foreign counterparts. These relationships exposed them to new ideas and enhanced their ability to adapt to change.

The Beiruti Christians skilfully exploited the special rights granted by the Ottomans to the foreign consulates and saw the economic

[41] Kais Firro, "Silk and Agrarian Changes in Lebanon, 1864–1914," *International Journal of Middle East Studies*, Vol. 22 (1990), p. 79; Owen, *The Middle East in the World Economy*, pp. 154, 160.

[42] Smilanskaya, "From Subsistence to Market Economy," p. 231; Firro, "Silk and Agrarian Changes," p. 161.

[43] Chevallier, *La Société du Mont Liban*, p. 196.

potential inherent in their gaining consular protection.[44] Accordingly, they sought any possible means of strengthening their ties to the consulates.[45] In this manner, they were able to bypass the restraints of Ottoman legislation and enjoy consular sponsorship. Many succeeded in acting as dragomans for the consulates. First they offered their services as interpreters gratis. They also stepped forward as mediators between the consulate and local people, assisted with the translation of administrative matters, mediated between European wholesalers and local retailers, and provided assistance to European investors.[46]

In this way, as time passed, the native Christians were able to become consular clerks and obtain complete consular protection. They could handle their business through the consulates, receiving from them convenient and profitable economic and legal benefits. The latter in turn encouraged foreign companies from various countries to hire the local Christian merchants as their representatives, thus providing the merchants an advantage in winning tenders for proposals. The scope of the ties between the merchants and the consuls was extensive. On the other hand, the local commercial families did not hesitate to move from the service of one consulate to another or to be attached to several consulates at once, according to their needs. For their part, the consulates found it useful to employ the local families, given their skills; the fact that the merchants were local residents and were familiar with the culture and language of the inhabitants was of great benefit to the consuls. Utilising their attributes, the local merchants were able to function as suitable mediators between the consular representatives and the local population.[47] Soon, the merchants began to request fees for the services that they had hitherto provided free of charge, and they skilfully utilised their

---

[44] The British representative in Beirut reported that the Zalzal brothers, local merchants, sought British protection to facilitate their dealings. They set up a business in Manchester, and declared themselves a British company. Other local merchants similarly tried to obtain consular protection. FO 195/806, Rogers to Logie, 29 April 1867.

[45] Arnon Groiss, *Religious Particularism and National Integration: Changing Perceptions of the Political Self-Identity among the Greek-Orthodox Christians*. Ph.D. dissertation, Princeton University, 1986, p. 12.

[46] Chevallier, *La Société du Mont Liban*, pp. 206–207; Edmunde Burke, "Rural Collective Action and the Emergence of Modern Lebanon—A Comparative Historical Perspective," in Nadim Shehadi and Dana Haffar Milles (eds.) *Lebanon: A History of Conflict and Consensus* (London, 1988), pp. 18–19.

[47] Göçek, *Rise of the Bourgeoisie*, pp. 92–97.

contacts and employment to further improve their economic status. The Mishāqa family, for example, is known to have worked for the British consulate and to have made use of these ties to consolidate its links with Western merchants. Other examples are the Mudawwar family, whose revenues were mostly from commerce but whose family members also worked at the French consulate as interpreters and clerks. The family produced smart operators, adept at finding new ways of making profits. The Thābit family found employment at the American consulate and members of the Bustrus family acted as dragomans at the French consulate.[48] As noted above, some families were linked to more than one consulate. Members of the Yannī family, for example, worked with the Belgian and the American consulates in Tripoli. The Kātsifilīs of Tripoli acted as vice-consuls and as consular agents for the British, Dutch, Spanish Austrian, and Hungarian consuls.[49] As a result, and in contrast to the situation in other port cities that were developing at that time (e.g. Alexandria), where the control of the city's economy was largely in the hands of foreigners, in Beirut the native Christian middle stratum held the reigns of financial power.

While they set up local firms and enterprises in partnership with the foreigners, in a fairly short period of time, the local Christians acquired some of the Europeans' businesses and ran them by themselves. Among these, the Christian Greek Orthodox were the most prominent.[50] Thus, starting as middlemen they became manufacturers

---

[48] *Ḥadīqat al-Akhbār*, No. 31, 1858.

[49] For further details on members of these families and others see: FO 195/274, Moore to Rose, 13 February 1847; FO 195/806, Rogers to Stuart, 22 November 1864; FO 195/787, Eldridge, 23 December 1864; FO 195/274, Rose, 27 May 1847; FO 195/965, Burton to Barron, 5 January 1870; FO 195/1047, Green to Elliot, 10 November 1874; FO 195/187, Rose to Bankhead, 28 December, 1841; St. Antony's College (SAC), Tibawi Papers, box 3, file 1, A. Yenni to Smith, 6 November 1861; 'Abdallāh Ḥabīb Nawfal, *Tarājim 'Ulamā' Ṭarāblus wa-Udabā'uhā*, 2nd ed. (Tripoli, 1984), pp. 78–81, 149–152, 187–186; Yūsuf Dāghir, *Al-Aṣūl al-'Arabiyya lil-Dirāsāt al-Lubnāniyya* (Beirut, 1982), p. 366; Salīm Salām, *Mudhakkirāt Salīm 'Alī Salām*, ed. Ḥasan Ḥallāq (Beirut, 1982), p. 136; US/NA, Hay to Brown, 20 November 1871; Houghton Library (HL) ABC: 50, box 1, Tabet to Smith, 15 August 1841.

[50] In 1895, of 120,000 residents only 4,320 were foreigners. By contrast, in Alexandria the number of foreigners doubled between 1846 and 1882, and they came to constitute more than 20 percent of its population. Özveren, *The Making and Unmaking*, pp. 153, 159; Harris Exertzoglou, "The Development of a Greek Ottoman Bourgeoisie: Investment Patterns in the Ottoman Empire, 1850–1914," in Dimitri Gondicas and Charles Issawi (eds.), *Ottoman Greeks in the Age of Nationalism:*

and established factories of their own. The European enterprises found it difficult to compete, a fact which depleted the number of foreign silk producers.[51] This atmosphere strengthened the merchants' indigenous roots in the city. As a result, they invested in it, supporting various projects in the fields of education and cultural societies to the point that they grasped it as their own *waṭan*. Thus, in contrast to other coastal cities, where investment and profit were largely in foreign hands, in Beirut the local merchants were capable of exploiting the city's rapid economic development, and they accumulated great wealth, some of which they re-invested in the city.

Economic interests in the city also led to social associations and relationships with Muslim merchants who were members of this stratum. Even though for the most part, the Muslim merchants did not possess a similar social background (education and mastery of languages) or the social connections with the West, as the Christians did, they were an important link in the growing commerce in the region and they wisely assimilated into it.[52] Most of the activity of the Christian Arabs was in the coastal regions, but the imported goods had to be transferred from the coast to the hinterland while raw materials as well as manufactured goods had to be brought from the interior to the coast for shipment to the West. In order to preserve this route, the Christian Arabs needed the assistance of the Muslim merchants, who were familiar with commerce in the region's interior. In this sense, the Christian and the Muslim merchants cooperated together and kept alive a mutual interest. In addition to the Bayhums, mentioned above, one can recall the ʿArafāts, a Nabulsī family that dealt with textile and acted as middlemen merchants for

Politics, Economy and Society in the 19th Century (Princeton, 1999), pp. 89–107; See also, May Davie, "Pouvoir Rural, Pouvoir Urbain: l'Èchec de l'État au Liban," *Cahiers de la Mediterranee*, No, 46/47 (1993), pp. 263–264. See for important Greek Orthodox families in Beirut, May Davie, "Les Familles Grecques Orthodoxes de la Ville de Beyrouth—à Travers les Cahiers du Badal ʿAskariyyat (1876–1895)," *Annales d'Histoire et d'Archeologie*, Vol. 5 (1986), pp. 32–43.

[51] The presence of foreigners in the city did indeed reach its peak between the years of the Egyptian occupation and mid-century, but it declined throughout the nineteenth century, especially during the last third of the century. Fawaz, *Merchants and Migrants*, pp. 86–87. US/NA, Eldridge to Leampbell, 24 October 1876.

[52] For further details see: Alfred Bonne, *The Economic Development of the Middle East* (New York, 1945), pp. 10–11; Philip K. Hitti, "The Impact of the West on Syria and Lebanon in the Nineteenth Century," *Cahiers d'Histoire Mondial*, Vol. 2 (1955), p. 622.

powerful trade houses in Beirut. By the end of the nineteenth century, some members of the ʿArafāt family were the first in Nablus to join the ranks of the emerging professional middle stratum in Greater Syria. They traded both in Beirut and in Damascus.[53]

More examples of such co-operation may be seen in the economic partnership between the Bustrus' and the Bayhums. Still another is that of the Christian Asʿad Khayyāṭ, who in 1847 wrote about his commercial co-operation with a Muslim merchant named Ḥājj ʿAbdallāh.[54] In this environment, a financial network began to form between the coast and the interior and also in and between the hinterland's centres of commerce.[55]

The other half of the evolving middle stratum, i.e. the second sub-stratum, was composed of the intelligentsia, mainly writers and white-collar workers. Much like the merchants, many of them worked for the foreign consulates as translators and clerks, had attended the Catholic or Protestant missionary schools in the city, and had acquired fairly broad educations. Among this group were doctors, teachers, lawyers, authors, journalists, engineers, linguists and so forth. In economic terms they possessed fewer financial means than did the merchants.

This sub-stratum included people such as Buṭrus al-Bustānī and his son Salīm, (1846–1884) who both engaged in journalism, literature, and linguistics; Khalīl al-Khūrī (1836–1907), a translator and journalist, writer, and civil servant; Salīm Dyāb (b. 1848) and Asʿad Ḥaddād, (1853–1920) both physicians; the Yāzijīs, a family of civil servants, who produced linguists such as Naṣīf (1800–1871) and poets such as Ibrāhīm (1846–1906); and the Nawfals.[56] Also included are the Muslim Yūsuf al-Asīr (1815–1889) and the Qabbānī family, whose members were an amalgamation of merchants and intellectuals. Members of all the above families participated in the cultural and

---

[53] Doumani, *Rediscovering Palestine*, p. 6.

[54] Asʿad Y. Khayyāṭ, *Voice of Lebanon* (London, 1847), p. 40.

[55] See also, Mahmoud Haddad, "The City, the Coast, the Mountain, and the Hinterland: Beirut's Commercial and Political Rivalries in the 19th and Early 20th Centuries," in Thomas Philipp and Birgit Scheabler (eds.), *The Syrian Land: Processes, Integration and Fragmentation* (Stuttgart, 1998), p. 152.

[56] For further details see: ʿĪsā Iskandar Maʿlūf, "Khalīl al-Khūrī al-Lubnānī," *al-Muqtaṭaf*, Vol. 34, 1909, pp. 12–14; Nawfal, *Tarājim ʿUlamāʾ*, pp. 193–195; Mīshāl Jiḥā, *Ibrāhīm al-Yāzijī* (London, 1992); Zaydān, *Tārīkh Ādāb al-Lugha al-ʿArabiyya*, Vol. 4, p. 69; US/NA, without reference, 13 April 1859.

educational activities of Beirut side by side, especially following the civil war of 1860.[57]

Most Muslims did not attend the missionary schools and instead received a traditional Muslim education. However, in light of the circumstances prevailing in the city, some of them came into contact with the American missionaries and took part in the cultural activities that the latter organised. A typical example is the abovementioned Yūsuf al-Asīr. He studied at al-Azhar University, specialising in Muslim theology and Arabic literature. Later on he was employed as a judge in Tripoli and served as the Muftī of Acre. Al-Asīr helped the American missionaries to translate the Bible into Arabic. Eventually he settled in Beirut, and became the first Muslim to work with missionaries. Other examples are the Ṣulḥ family, who served as civil servants and as army officers; Ibrāhīm al-Aḥdab, (1826–1891) whose pursuit was literature and poetry, and who was the editor of the first Muslim journal in the region, *Thamarāt al-Funūn* (Fruits of Knowledge), published in Beirut. Al-Aḥdab was also a member of the *vilâyet*'s Education Committee. Another prominent Muslim family were the Qabbānīs, in particular ʿAbd al-Qādir al-Qabbānī, a journalist and author, who established *Thamarāt al-Funūn.*[58]

Members of the intelligentsia held various occupations during their lifetime, often in a number of fields, shifting between a money-oriented profession or commercial activity and a purely scholarly one. Familiar with the needs of the society and the city in which they lived, they adapted readily to the changes around them. For example, Mīkhāʾīl Mishāqa, a physician, writer and translator, is known to have dealt in trade and commerce (namely the silk industry) several times during his lifetime, alongside his scholarly and professional work. In the 1840s he reinforced his links with the American consulate so that, as he himself attested, it might help him strengthen his ties with European merchants. Mishāqa explained that his liveli-

---

[57] Other Christian families from this sub-stratum are: Ṣābūnjī, ʿArmān, Ḥabālīn and the Muslim Danā family. Abdul Latif Tibawi, *American Interests in Syria, 1800–1901* (Oxford, 1966), pp. 83, 163, 214; Salām, *Mudhakkirāt Salīm*, p. 112; SAC, ABC: 50, box 1, 1856.

[58] Jurjī Zaydān, *Tarājim Mashāhīr al-Sharq*, pp. 164–166; Ḥasan, Ḥallāq, *Awqāf al-Muslimīn fī Bayrūt fī al-ʿAhd al-ʿUthmānī—Sijillāt al-Maḥkama al-Sharʿiyya fī Bayrūt* (Beirut, 1988), p. 155; Fīlīb dī Ṭarrāzī, *Tārīkh al-Ṣiḥāfa al-ʿArabiyya*, Vol. 2 (Beirut, 1913–1924), pp. 101–104; ʿĪsā Mārūn Khūrī, *Malāmiḥ min al-Ḥarakāt al-Thaqāfiyya fī Ṭarāblus khilāl al-Tāsiʿ ʿAshar* (Tripoli, 1982), p. 12.

hood from study and medicine was inadequate, and he required additional sources of income.[59]

Similar arguments can describe Buṭrus al-Bustānī, who is known to have been one of the leading literati of his time but was also a very sharp-witted businessman. During his lifetime he expanded his business dealings as writer and publisher of books not only for the sake of literary interest (which was probably his main concern), but quite naturally also for his own livelihood. For example, for publishing the first volume of the Arabic encyclopedia *Dāʿirat al-Maʿārif* he received payment from Ismaʿīl Pāshā. The latter ordered a thousand copies of the first volume. Al-Bustānī's close friend and longtime acquaintance, the American missionary Eli Smith, shed additional light on this facet of al-Bustānī's endeavours. In a letter that Smith wrote in 1851 to Rufus Anderson, the secretary of the "Board" in Boston, he explained that certain members of the mission wished to terminate al-Bustānī's work as a translator so that he might enter the clergy. However, he writes, he himself advised al-Bustānī not to do so for several reasons. One of them was that this pursuit would not provide al-Bustānī with enough money to live on, and he would have to find another fixed source of income before becoming a clergyman. Smith offered him a position as dragoman at the American consulate. Al-Bustānī turned him down, disappointed at the low wage that was suggested. In the end, al-Bustānī decided for the time being to devote several hours of each day to translation for the missionaries and combine it with work at the printing house. In this way, he was able to double his salary.[60] In a letter written just four years later, in 1855, Smith explained to al-Bustānī why in his opinion he was not suited for the cloth. His first reason was that al-Bustānī made his acceptance of the calling conditional on his being provided with a living and an income. His second reason stemmed from al-Bustānī's character. He had become, Smith wrote, "a man of the book and not a man of the spirit." Smith continues to explain that al-Bustānī was known as an intelligent man, canny in business affairs, and a sharp operator in transactions.[61] From these and other examples a

[59] Mīkhā'īl Mishāqa, *Muntakhabāt min al-Jawāb ʿalā Iqtirāḥ al-Aḥbāb*. eds. A. Rustum and Ṣ. Abū-Shaqrā (Beirut, 1955), p. h.

[60] HL, ABC: 60, box 2, Smith to Anderson, 17 June 1851.

[61] HL, ABC: 60, box 2, Smith to al-Bustani, March 1855.

tendency becomes noticeable among the people of the middle stratum, i.e. that economic interests dominated, sometimes even supplanted, the cultural ones. Little wonder that sometimes these two elements merged in the activities of members associated with this stratum.

Indeed, alongside the economic growth, education became very central in the middle stratum's life as the city grew. The development of the local intelligentsia in Beirut did not occur *ex nihilo*. Beirut was not only an economic centre for Syria but an important educational and cultural one as well. One side of this was the growth of "Western" education in the city, that began developing from the 1830s. The rapid development of the city and its relative safety attracted many missionaries. For them, especially for the American Protestant missionaries, the city's large Christian population was fertile soil for propagation of the Gospel. The missionaries planned to make Beirut a religious and educational centre for all Syria. They believed that the city contained many elements that would foster spiritual growth.[62] Already during the reign of Ibrāhīm Pāshā, several missionary schools were established in the region. These served as bases, enabling the missionaries to expand their range of activities thereafter throughout the nineteenth century. The American missionaries founded an infrastructure of elementary and secondary schools (most of them in Beirut and throughout Mount Lebanon) during that period. The crowning glory of this effort was the inauguration of the Syrian Protestant College (SPC) in Beirut in 1866. In addition, they translated many books into Arabic, printed them and distributed them among the population.

In 1834, they moved their press from Malta to Beirut. This measure was of great importance in the development of education in Beirut. Although the missionaries' chief goal was to distribute religious documents, the fact that they wrote textbooks and translated them into Arabic increased the number of distributed books, and made the written word more accessible to the majority of the population. Similarly, they helped to pave the way for the publication of journals and books edited and written by local talent. The missionaries depended on the local intelligentsia in more than one sense. In fact, ties had existed between the American missionaries and the local intelligentsia ever since the days of the Emirate, especially with

[62] HL, ABC: 16.8.1, Vol. 16, Annual Report of the Beirut Station, 1862.

those who were literate in Arabic (e.g. those who had been educated in ʿAyn Waraqa); the missionaries learned the local language from them, so as to become closer to the local population. Later, these natives became teachers in the missionaries' schools. The reaction of the Catholic and the Jesuit missionaries was not long in coming. Sensitive to the successes of the Protestant missionaries, they too began to establish their own educational infrastructure.[63]

In general, most of the missionaries' educational institutions in the region were concentrated in Beirut itself. In fact, the only two colleges (later to become universities) in the region were established there and thus most members of the middle stratum were able to get their education locally. Hence, one can safely say that the city was able to supply most demands the intelligentsia might have had for advanced education.

Accompanying these expanded educational opportunities, quite naturally, was increased exposure to the West and its ways. Daily contact with Westerners, Western thought and behaviour brought several of the Christians belonging to this stratum to imitate the West in cultural and material aspects. Members of this group gradually began to adopt some of the Western fashions, habits, and other cultural characteristics. However, this was not a monolithic response; many intellectuals were aware of the result of this approach and purposely took pains to preserve their own traditional way of life and heritage. Nevertheless, alongside these developments, from the mid-nineteenth century on, economic ties with the West exposed the stratum to the styles, fashion and nuances of daily Western life. On top of this, the wealthy Christian merchants, whose activities enjoyed consular protection, no longer suffered as before from the many restrictions of the government. Now, in view of the fact that the Empire sought to improve it's standing with the Western Powers, the native Christians benefited from greater freedom of expression and could flaunt their acquisitions without fear of the jaundiced eye of the regime. And yet, even though they could showcase their achievements more than had been possible in the past, they chose not to dress completely in Western fashion but wore a mixture of Western and local traditional fashion. From the *sijill* of Beirut we can identify this combination. It appears that most male residents

[63] The Catholic missionaries established the Saint Joseph College in Beirut in 1875.

(Muslim and Christian) donned a traditional *sharwal* and some sort of men's gown open at the front (*qumbāz*). They also wore cashmere waistcoats and shoes known as *lāstīq* (especially the rich) and a *tarbush* on their heads. In fact, the *sijill* emphasises that intellectual groups from various communities became somewhat Westernised (*tafarnaja*) in their habits and dress, increasingly so towards the end of the nineteenth century. They wore European suits (*bidhla*), but were careful to retain traditional headgear. Thus, the habits in Beirut (as exhibited by the Christians), the *sijill* demonstrates, vacillated between a clear duality, East and West. This duality would become the essence characterising this stratum.[64] Such vacillation also reflected the confusion among this middle stratum in regard to their self-identity, at this stage.

In contrast to the picture presented in the *sijill*, Western sources underscore the influence of Western fashions more vividly.[65] They indicate that the local Christians embraced Western culture, trying to replace their own with it. These sources tend to put more emphasis on the changes occurring within this Christian middle stratum as a result of Western influence, than on the elements that it preserved from its own heritage. Neale, a British traveller who stayed in the area from 1842 to 1850, wrote in his book that the people of Beirut were growing richer and were becoming interested in European fashions. Many of them went to school, knew Italian, and used foreign languages in regular daily intercourse.[66] Another traveller, Paton, observed in 1841 that Syrian women wore clothes imported from Britain.[67] He stressed that changes occurring in other fields of life also revealed Western taste. For example, homes were now furnished in Italian and French style. Paton comments that this feature was particularly evident in the residences of civil servants and well-to-do merchants.

The city itself took on a European appearance, and many of its buildings were of Western character (in contrast to the traditional inland cities, built in the Muslim style). Towards the end of the century a European lifestyle developed, mainly among the wealthier

[64] Ḥallāq, *al-Tārīkh al-Ijtimāʿī*, pp. 17, 21.

[65] In the 1850s there were about 100 European families in Beirut. Neale, *Eight Years in Syria*, Vol. 1, p. 209.

[66] *Ibid.*, pp. 210–211; Harriet Rattray, *Country Life in Syria* (London, 1876).

[67] Paton, *The Modern Syrians*, p. 14.

classes. Indeed, Muslim and Christian merchants, such as the Sursuqs, the Bustruses, the Ṭrāds, and the Bayhums, steadily moved out to new suburbs and lived according to European standards. The city itself began to have flat-roofed houses, with white painted walls and blue-green or red external lattices. In general, the new suburban houses of the wealthy Beiruti merchants were exuberant with numerous large windows, balconies and galleries looking onto the surrounding gardens and neighbouring streets. They were ". . . often decorated with marble, stone and stucco elements in the historicist styles of a European kind."[68] Some of the townspeople began to use products that had not existed in the region before. They drank tea and smoked cigarettes.[69]

Ties among the literati and merchants from this middle stratum were close and they acted together for a common cause—the advancement of Beirut. They were careful to marry among themselves. For example, the Yannī and Kāstifilīs families and the Khlāṭ and the Naḥḥās families were connected by marriage, as were others. Cooperation was also evident in the establishment of joint projects. As an illustration, when Nasīm Khlāṭ, a merchant and writer, wished to found an Orthodox school, he was aided by Alexander Kāstifilīs (member of a merchant family), by the Nawfal family (merchants and intellectuals), and by Jurjī Yannī (a writer), all of whom helped fund the project.[70] Merchants who accumulated great wealth invested in cultural as well as economic projects. Often, a rich merchant sponsored an intellectual whose means were limited. For example, Mīkhā'īl Mudawwar (b. 1822) helped Khalīl al-Khūrī to finance and establish the journal *Ḥadīqat al-Akhbār* (Garden of News).[71] Al-Khūrī, who appreciated this support, acknowledged it in print in the fifth issue of the journal. He explained to his readers the significance of the funding metaphorically by stating that thanks to Mīkhā'īl, the journal "flows in the gardens of *al-Shām* and waters the sons of the *waṭan* (i.e. Syria)."[72]

---

68 See, Ralph Bodenstein, "Housing the Foreign—A European's Exotic Home in Late Nineteenth-Century Beirut," in Jens Hanssen, Thomas Philipp and Stefan Weber (eds.), *The Empire in the City—Arab Provincial Capitals in the Late Ottoman Empire* (Beirut, 2002), pp. 106–107.

69 Buheiry, *Beirut's Role*, pp. 1–3; W. M. Thomson, *The Land and the Book* (London, 1888), p. 60.

70 Nawfal, *Tarājim 'Ulamā'*, pp. 131–132.

71 Ṭarrāzī, *Tārīkh al-Ṣiḥāfa*, Vol. 2, p. 112.

72 *Ḥadīqat al-Akhbār*, No. 1, 1 January 1858.

The economic ties that existed in the city between Muslims and Christians have already been mentioned. At the same time, the city began to develop a joint social and cultural life, which found expression in the formation of many cultural societies. Their aim was to nurture and expand the intellectual horizons of their members in the region of Syria. In some of these groups, Christians were active alongside Muslims. This was the case in 1858 when *al-Jamʿiyya al-ʿIlmiyya al-Sūriyya* was founded. It ceased operations in 1860, and renewed them in 1868. Another example was the establishment in 1860 of *al-ʿUmda al-Adabiyya li-Ishhār al-Kutub al-ʿArabiyya* (The Cultural Society for the Publication of Arabic Books). Christians as well as Muslims were also active in this association.[73] Mutual cultural work is evident in other fields as well, such as the newspaper *Thamarāt al-Funūn*, the editorial staff of which included both Christians and Muslims.[74]

Hence, not only economic activities in the city but cultural activities as well, served to expand social ties amongst the city's residents. Whether the social ties led to commercial ones or vice versa is difficult to determine. In any event, the two evidently co-existed, and were mutually beneficial.

The consequence of this kind of activity was very obvious in the civil war of 1860. Naturally, the reaction of some Muslims to the improved status of the Christians was not late in appearing, and it manifested itself in various places throughout Syria. That geographically widespread reaction constituted one of the causes of the civil war in 1860.[75] Still, it is important to note that the civil war, which occurred in Mount Lebanon and Damascus, passed Beirut by. Nor were the other coastal cities: Tripoli, Sidon or Jaffa involved. Moreover, during the animosities there were instances of Beiruti Muslims helping Christians in their distress. Apparently, the good relations and

---

[73] This type of ties between Muslims and Christians continued throughout the nineteenth and the twentieth centuries. For example, the primary formal goal of *Jamʿiyat Tahdhīb al-Shabība al-Sūriyya* (Education Association of Syrian Youth, established in 1903), was to serve the country. Partly sponsored by Muḥammad Bayhum, it had 230 members. From the time of its establishment, it financed 91 students. Other goals of this society were educational and patriotic, such as to advance the "*nahḍa al-waṭaniyya and maḥabbat al-istiqlāl*." (patriotic awakening and love of independence). *Al-Kuliyya*, Vol. 5, March 1914, pp. 154–161.

[74] *Thamarāt al-Funūn*, No. 1, 20 April 1875.

[75] L. Schatkowski-Schilcher, *The Islamic Maqaṣed of Beirut*, pp. 18–19 and James A. Reilly. "Damascus Merchants and Trade in the Transition to Capitalism," *Canadian Journal of History*, Vol. 27 (1992), pp. 1–27.

mutual co-operation that developed between the two communities in Beirut withstood this trial of violence.[76]

From the above description of the nature of the economic, social and cultural ties of the city, further insights and greater understanding of the middle stratum can be gleaned. The city created a network of relations between the Christian community and the educated Muslim community on an economic and cultural basis, not quite a purely social one. The entire population in the region of Syria cannot be characterised as eager for relations of this kind, but from a study of the middle stratum it is quite clear that a range of circumstances made co-operation possible between the two groups.

Muslim merchants were also responsible for cultural projects, but mainly towards the end of the nineteenth century. In 1878 *al-Maqāṣid al-Khayriyya al-Islāmiyya* (The Good Intentions Society) was established. All of its participants were members of the leading Sunni merchant families. The society tried to hold cultural activities among the Muslim population (similar to the Christians before them) and to found an educational infrastructure by building schools.

The growing educational activity, created in its wake extensive cultural activity, in which most of the city's middle stratum participated, whether they were merchants, literati, Muslims or Christians.

World View of the Beiruti Middle Stratum: The Concept of Tamaddun

As Beirut became the foundation for the economic and cultural life of the Beiruti middle stratum, it also became a central parameter in their outlook. They perceived Beirut as the economic centre of all Syria and as a bridge between the Syrian interior and the outside world. Members of the stratum also deemed Beirut to be the social and cultural centre of the region of Syria, to the point that they referred to the city as a "*firdaws arḍī ṣaghīr*" (small paradise on earth).[77]

---

[76] Kamal S. Salibi, "The 1860 Upheaval in Damascus as Seen by al-Sayyid Muhammed Abu'l-Suʿud al-Hasibi, Notable and Later Naqib al-Ashraf of the City," in William R. Polk and Richard L. Chambers (eds.), *Beginnings of Modernization in the Middle East—The Nineteenth Century* (Chicago, 1966), pp. 185–202.

[77] Salīm al-Bustānī, "Madīnat Bayrūt wa-Iḥtiyājātuhā," *al-Jinān*, Vol. 15, No. 16, 1884, p. 481.

In light of their new situation and their exposure to Western education, along with their need to preserve their own local heritage, the Christian middle stratum felt that they should redefine themselves to further contribute to the advancement of the city. They did this by re-educating their society, reiterating and re-emphasising the virtues of the city. Thus, Buṭrus al-Bustānī, along with many other intellectuals, began to call for the city's "progress" as the primary concern of intellectual energies. The stratum believed that if this process would succeed in Beirut, it would radiate outwards to the entire region of Syria.

This centrality of the city found expression in the writings of the intellectuals until the end of the nineteenth century. For example, in al-Bustānī's encyclopedia *Dāʾirat al-Maʿārif*, he wrote under the entry "Beirut," with uncharacteristic subjectivity and vigour, "it has remained the centre of the connection of Syria and Mount Lebanon to Europe" and that "it is the first city in the empire," describing it as "the centre for economic activity for the entire coastal region . . . and an economic centre of the *vilâyet*"[78] (i.e., the *Vilâyet* of Syria that was established in 1865).

On another occasion, in 1869, al-Bustānī delivered a lecture before *al-Jamʾiyya al-ʿIlmiyya al-Sūriyya* entitled "On Human Society and the Encounter between Arab and Western Customs" (*Khiṭāb fī al-Hayʾa al-ʿIjtimāʿiyya wal-Muqābala bayna al-ʿAwāʾid al-ʿArabiyya wal-Ifranjiyya*).[79] Although this lecture focused on the point at which the customs of the East and West came into contact, a central theme in the thought of these intellectuals, its content reveals al-Bustānī's cosmopolitan perspective and the centrality of the city in his views. While reviewing some of al-Bustānī's criticisms of the city, it also described Beirut as a prototype in microcosm for an "ideal society," to be achieved within a heterogenic society. Through the lecture we can catch a glimpse of this stratum's social perception and its attitudes towards the environment in which it lived and functioned. Al-Bustānī explained that it was hardly possible to find, anywhere in the world, one city that could supply the complete natural, intellectual, cultural, and religious needs of an entire society, but Beirut is such a city.

---

[78] Al-Bustānī, "Beirut," p. 752.

[79] Buṭrus al-Bustānī, *Khiṭāb fī al-Hayʾa al-ʿIjtimāʿiyya wal-Muqābala bayna al-ʿAwāʾid al-ʿArabiyya wal-Ifranjiyya* (Beirut, 1869).

He described Beirut as "our dwelling place and our motherland,"[80] and treated it as an important centre for its inhabitants, for Syria, and for the ties with foreign countries. His deep connection to the city is stressed when he defined it as "homeland" (*waṭan*), while he named Syria his "country" (*bilād*).[81] He refers to its population as *mutamaddinūn* (civilised) in the sense that they are urban and educated. Al-Bustānī argued that Beirut was not only an economic bridge to the West but also the link connecting the people to the cultures of both the East and the West. Indeed, the intelligentsia grasped the city as merging these two cultures. They understood the advantages that the city offered and its unique nature, and they wished to make use of these attributes to establish a cohesive and active society. They strove for a "progressive" society with the means for broadening education and cultural activities, seeing it as extending beyond the personal interests of its members and clear of religious conflict.

Everyday life naturally became part of the outlook of the Beiruti middle stratum. This outlook in turn had other ramifications. The economic and social developments also stressed the need of the stratum to redefine its self-identity. Daily life mirrored a dichotomy that was the essence of the Christian middle stratum's identity and its realities, already evident in the way they dressed. As a minority trying to live peacefully and in prosperity in the midst of a Muslim majority, the stratum saw itself as an integral part of local society. On the other hand, they were Christians, and in many ways saw themselves as influenced by Western culture, striving to adopt Western "cultural ideas" and become more cosmopolitan in their outlook.

One should bear in mind that the encounter with the West was traumatic, not only for the Muslims but sometimes for the Christian Arabs themselves, who perceived themselves as part of the Ottoman society but suddenly were viewed by others as part of the West. This was the source of a growing conflict that would be at the centre of the intellectual thought of Christian Arabs in Syria throughout the nineteenth century. They continued to see themselves as part of the Ottoman society but at the same time were to some extent drawn to the culture of the West. This encounter, particularly strong in a city such as Beirut, suddenly placed the Christian population in the

---

80 *Ibid.*, pp. 7–8.
81 *Ibid.*, p. 8.

spotlight of events and in a new position, constituting yet another reason for requiring self-definition. Suddenly, they were "even more Christian" and thus "less local"—outsiders, in the eyes of the Muslim population. Their wealth and advancement in society just added to the tensions that were nourishing the growing frustrations on the part of the Muslim community. Now, the Christians had to deal with this new state of affairs.

Members of the stratum did not see any contradiction in associating themselves with both sides, i.e. the indigenous and the foreign. As the process continued and their self-awareness shaped itself, it came almost naturally for them to believe that the only way to combine the two aspects of their perspective was to merge them into their identity, as two dimensions completing the whole. This process was somewhat akin to what was already known to them from their daily occupation and economic activities. As mediators transferring goods from Syria to the West and vice versa, and as mediators between two cultures, they later encapsulated these two sides in their own identity.

Gradually, this identity evolved into a combination of Arab and Syrian parameters, which would ultimately define the duality of their identity, as will be explicated in the last chapter of this book. These parameters, as we have already seen, began to develop during Amīr Bashīr II's rule. A more thorough and comprehensive process occurred among the middle stratum in Beirut, especially in light of the growing tension between Muslims and Christians in the region, which reached its peak in a series of violent conflicts. By combining these two parameters, the Christian middle stratum could redefine themselves and the other, preserving the legitimacy of every dimension of their lives in the framework of the new circumstances. In most cases, members of the stratum preferred to see themselves as more closely connected to the indigenous community among which they had lived for centuries and to which their family and activities were tied. Thus, they acted in a manner as to belong and be part of the surrounding majority community. In other words, they struggled to define their "unique" selves, but only in the framework of the general, vis-à-vis the other, and under no circumstances as outsiders of the Ottoman Empire, which they also felt part of. In this sense they saw themselves not as agents of the West but as agents for themselves and their local society. They perceived themselves as agents of "modernisation," or as agents of change in their society, not by transforming it into a Western one but by using the West as a tool to advance aspects of their society.

Naturally, intellectual interest in the West and the imitation of its customs and fashions entailed exposure to the Western way of thinking and its ideas. As a result, the stratum developed a dialogue with the West which reveals that its attitude toward it was ambivalent; they were far from accepting the West's culture and influence without examining the effect on local society or on themselves. Members of the stratum scrutinised the weaknesses and the potential benefits to be derived from any such adoption. In general, they believed that a link should exist among all the peoples of the world and they should form one great family. As they saw themselves in a period of transition, their primary ambition was to emerge from their "traditional" society, and to reshape it as a more "open" or "advanced" society in which all of its members could be equal. In this perspective, they did not want their society to be similar or imitate the West, but rather to reflect the culture and civilisation of the East, evolving vis-à-vis the West. They believed that the East had in the past served as a source of influence for the West and that now in the nineteenth century it should strive to rekindle its magnificent past and bring its people to what Khalīl al-Khūrī and other intellectuals called "the new era" (*al-ʿaṣr al-jadīd*) or "the generation of light and knowledge."[82] At this point, the main question that must be raised is not whether this stratum tried to become "Westernised," i.e. become part of Western culture, as was sometimes claimed, but rather to what extent did this stratum want to adopt Western mores and morals.

An intense debate regarding this issue, which was also part of the changing identity of the Christian Arabs, was apparent in the writings of the intellectuals during the second half of the nineteenth century. The debate ran the gamut between those who desired to accept the culture of the West in as many aspects as possible, and those who advocated adopting elements of its influence in a selective way, as long as the local heritage was preserved and respected. What

[82] This attitude is strongly emphasised in Khalīl al-Khūrī's writing. See: Khalīl al-Khūrī, *al-ʿAṣr al-Jadīd* (Beirut, 1863), pp. 28–31; see also: Buṭrus al-Bustānī, "Khuṭba fī Ādāb al-ʿArab," in Buṭrus al-Bustānī, *al-Jamʿiyya al-Sūriyya lil-ʿUlūm wal-Funūn*, p. 117.

stands out from an examination of these writings is that the leading intellectuals belonging to the Beiruti middle stratum chose the second way. Their views, reflected in their writings, shows that their primary interest lay in the struggle to transform their society from a "traditional society" built on the codes of religion (Christianity or Islam) to a "modern and civilised society." Or, as al-Bustānī expressed it in his famous lecture *Khuṭba fī Ādāb al-ʿArab* (Lecture on the Arab Culture) "from the rule of the *fiqh* to the rule of *ādāb*" (culture), i.e. culture rather than religious law should prevail.[83] Along these lines, they believed that they could live peacefully.

In this respect, they saw themselves as *mutamaddinūn*. In many cases they interpreted *tamaddun* as the opposite of being savage barbarians (*Khushūna*). For them, *tamaddun* was defined in many cases in the sense of being civilised (*mutaḥaḍḍir*), or being part of an urban society, not in the sense of becoming Westernised by adopting blindly from the West, without selection or filtering. They believed in synthesising elements of both, primarily preserving their local cultural heritage, adapting and modifying it with Western values that could be helpful in maintaining and furthering their status in society.

Thus, the construction of their self-identity was part of the process of their "modernisation." For years, one of the main discourses among the Beiruti middle stratum continued to be the meaning of the term *tamaddun*. The writing on this subject was especially intense in the periodical *al-Jinān* (Gardens), where it was the main issue addressed in short stories and articles published there.[84] What is revealed in these writings is that this term, as an element of the emerging Christian identity, was flexible or rather problematic to define with precision.[85]

For example, the Christian intellectuals conceived patriotism as one of the parameters of *tamaddun*.[86] So, if someone wished to become *mutamaddin*—a man of civilisation and culture, he must invest in his

---

[83] *Ibid.*

[84] Most of the short stories published in *al-Jinān* concentrate on criticising the behaviour of the local society, and in particular, in many cases, the manner in which they adopted Western culture. Through these stories, the intellectuals tried to illustrate the importance of *tamaddun* and the preferable ways of achieving it. See: Salīm al-Bustānī, "Najīb wa-Laṭīfa," *al-Jinān*, Vol. 3, No. 6, 1872, pp. 201–204; Salīm al-Bustānī, "Ẓifāf Farīd," *al-Jinān*, Vol. 2, No. 13, 1871, pp. 447–452.

[85] See: Buṭrus al-Bustānī (ed.), "*tamaddun*," *Dā'irat al-Maʿārif*, Vol. 6, pp. 213–215.

[86] Aḥmad Wahabī, "al-ʿAwā'id," *al-Jinān*, Vol. 4, No. 4, 1873, pp. 474–476.

local patriotism and love his country and its people, regardless of their different religious backgrounds. To be *mutamaddin*, they wrote, is not a self-investment in the way you dress, talk and behave, but the investment you put into your *waṭan*. Through their literature, they tried to teach their readers, both women and men, and to explain to them how they could strive to become part of "a true civilised society." They indicated two ways to become civilised. The positive way was to reform society from the inside (*tamaddun dākhilī*) by returning to its roots and its true heritage. The negative way for society to become civilised lied in adopting foreign manners or material artifacts from another culture or civilisation (*tamaddun khārijī*), meaning the West.[87]

They were also among the first to call for gender equality and the need to understand the importance of women's role in society; the woman was the one who educated the new generation of the *waṭan*. They believed that if one wanted to measure *tamaddun* in a society, he should examine the status of the women in it. Thus, in the process of building a new identity, the position and figure of the woman came to mirror the extent of modernisation in the Syrian society. Women were often recruited for the process of modernisation, as they were the ones who defined or symbolised the local culture. Often, as Yuval-Davis suggested, they had to carry the "burden of representation" since they were perceived as the symbolic bearers of identity and honour, both personally and collectively.[88]

The issue of how women and men should become *mutamaddin* or *mutamaddina* is reflected in the short stories of Salīm al-Bustānī. For example, in the story *Bint al-ʿAṣr* (The Woman of the Age), published in 1875 in the journal *al-Jinān*, Salīm described the social life of men and women in the Beiruti middle stratum, illustrating it through the lives of two couples—Jamīla and Anīs, whom Salīm criticised as an example of the negative side of Westernisation; and Rīma and Mājid, whom Salīm portrayed as role models for the stratum members in this matter. In general (but not as a rule), the social life in Beirut is represented in the stories as hierarchal, full of rivalry, hypocritical and capitalistic. The Beiruti middle stratum is described as always in pursuit of acquiring money and status.

---

[87] Salīm al-Bustānī, "Asmā," *al-Jinān*, Vol. 4, No. 23, 1873, pp. 826–827.
[88] Nira Yuval-Davis, *Gender and Nation* (London, 1997), p. 45.

Jamīla represents this negative side of the city's population (she is *mar'a ghayr mutamaddina*). Her character is somewhat grotesque and ridiculous. She takes as much as she can from the West, in her dress, manners and language, and particularly in materialistic features; but she lacks intellect. Her fickle mind is illustrated by her admiration for and blind imitation of Western culture: when asked if Western dance is amusing, she replies "but of course, it comes from the West."[89] Anīs is the same. He is described as looking after his economic interests but doing nothing for the sake of the city and its education.

Meanwhile, through the figure of Mājid, Salīm illustrates the other side of the debate, his own point of view regarding how the Beiruti stratum should define its attitude towards the West. Mājid is quoted as saying that society should not take everything from Western culture, since not everything in it is suitable. Mājid declared that adopting from the West should be a selective process. His ideas are seen once again in a discussion with Jamīla in which he claims that Western dance is not fitting for local society. He does not like the way that women dress nor their manner of conversing freely with male strangers. Mājid says that the West should not discontinue these customs but that the local society should avoid allowing this style of dance to penetrate local codes of conduct. Then he asked, with a tinge of bitterness, why Europeans preserve their customs and we (the Beiruti society) do not. Jamīla, who was surprised by Mājid's views, thought to herself with disbelief "and I thought that he is a *mutamaddin*, but he is far from this, since he challenges the European customs."[90]

Mājid, of course, was in love with Rīma, Jamīla's sister, whose attitude towards the West is opposed to Jamīla's, but close to his own. She is the example of *al-mar'a al-mutamaddina*—knowledgeable about both the West and her own heritage. She is familiar with foreign languages but is also well educated in her own Arabic language. Although dressing in "a modern way" and European in appearance, Rīma does not allow European thinking to influence her thoughts. She remembers her responsibilities to her society and is aware of its future and needs.[91] Again, this time through Rīma, the preservation

---

[89] Salīm al-Bustānī, "Bint al-ʿAṣr," *al-Jinān*, Vol. 6, No. 2, 1875, p. 67.
[90] *Ibid.*, No. 2, p. 68.
[91] *Ibid.*, especially No. 1, pp. 30–32, No. 2, pp. 66–70, No. 3, pp. 103–105.

of the indigenous is stressed as imperative. In this respect, women had to carry or preserve society's traditions, but at the same time they symbolised modernity in society.

The issue of the role of the women in the *waṭan* is mainly emphasised in historical novels, as will be described in detail in the fifth chapter. Yet, the two roles are interconnected, since a woman who considered herself as being cultural was exhorted to invest in and contribute to her homeland.

Christian intellectuals criticised the rapid Westernisation of the people of Beirut and described this as a false *tamaddun*. They depicted it as "a body without a head, or a head without a body, or a man without hands."[92] They were aware of the possibility that this kind of Westernisation made them look like "fools" in the eyes of the West, and rejected the West as an ideal culture that could automatically fit their world. Sometimes they even mocked Western manners or dress and presented them as the "fools," as figure 2.1 shows.

Beiruti Christian Arabs interpreted the term *tamaddun* in accordance with their own concepts of self identity and in line with their interests in regards to status in their society which they frequently called the society of the *Sharq* (East).[93] In some ways perhaps, they even perceived the West and its culture as a threat to their own culture. Salīm al-Bustānī presented this attitude in 1882, whilst the British occupied Egypt, in an article appearing in his journal *al-Jinān*. In it, he hinted that the true intentions of the West were cloaked by its offer of civilisation (*lābisa athwāb tamadduniyya*) and this was intended, so he insinuated to his readers, to eventually dominate the East.[94] Once again their duality, this time in relationship with the West, influenced the way that the Christian intellectuals perceived themselves and their society.

[92] Salīm al-Bustānī, "Asbāb Taqaddum Bayrūt wa-Numuwwuhā al-Sarīʿ," *al-Jinān*, Vol. 15, No. 15, 1884, pp. 449–451; see also, Salīm al-Bustānī, "Madīnat Bayrūt," *al-Jinān*, Vol. 15, No. 16, 1884, pp. 481–483.

[93] Fransīs Marrāsh, "Fī Tarbiyat al-Nisāʾ," *al-Jinān*, Vol. 3, No. 22, 1872, pp. 768–770; Fransīs Marrāsh, "al-Mar'a bayna al-Khushūna wal-Tamaddun," *al-Jinān*, Vol. 3, No. 17, 1872, pp. 586–588; Wadīʿ al-Khūrī, "al- Nisāʾ," *al-Jinān*, Vol. 16, No. 6, 1885, pp. 178–181 and No. 7, pp. 210–214; Khalīl Maʿādī, "Ta'akhkhur Bilādinā wa-Taqaddumuhā," *al-Jinān*, Vol. 10, No. 7, 1879, pp. 232–238; Yaʿqūb Nawfal, "Ḥaqīqat al-Musāwa," *al-Jinān*, Vol. 14, No. 14, 1883, pp. 431–432.

[94] Salīm al-Bustānī, "Mudākhalāt al-Ajnabiyya wal-Ḥuqūq al-Waṭaniyya," *al-Jinān*, Vol. 13, No. 3, 1882, pp. 65–67.

Fig. 2.1 "The new fashion"—a mockery of Western dress code
["Mulaḥ," *al-Jinān*, Vol. 16, 1885, p. 702.]

Another important point that should be noted is that this stratum was self-aware of its role as the representative of its local society and culture in the eyes of the West. They conceived themselves as mediating between the new ideas of the West and their own local culture. Members of this stratum believed that the task of selectively choosing Western ideas and transferring them to the local population in their own language and discourse lay upon their shoulders. In order to fulfil this task and fit in with the rest of the community, they would often take terms that were part of the heritage of the local majority, the Muslim community, and reinterpret them to suit their needs.

The process was also utilised in the other direction: Salīm's father, Buṭrus al-Bustānī, interpreted "Western" terms, by sometimes giving them new "adjusted" meanings. Examples are his definitions of terms such as "*dīmuqrāṭiyya*" (democracy) and "*jumhūriyya*" (not in the sense of "republic" but "community") appearing in his Arabic encyclopedia *Dā'irat al-maʿārif*, which was attuned to the local context. Al-Bustānī wrote that "*dīmuqrāṭiyya*" meant that "the reins of government are in the hands of the people and their notables (*aʿyān*)."[95] Further on he wrote that in a democracy, government is not conducted by any one group within the nation (*al-umma*) but that each and every individual fulfils his desire.[96]

Thus, we can say that the middle stratum's stance was not monolithic or static in its attitude towards the West. In contrast, the way they perceived Beirut and its importance to the region in general, and to themselves in particular, was monolithic. Beirut was a microcosm and prototype for the life they wanted. Believing as they did that Beirut represented the commercial and cultural centre of the entire Syrian region, they wanted to constantly find ways for it to flourish and bring tranquillity and prosperity to all the people of this "small *waṭan*." The Beiruti middle stratum's point of view in general, and its city in particular, soon became the basis for a wider concept of regional identity and self-awareness. The content and parameters of this self-awareness would also reveal and reflect the way that Christian Arabs in the region of Syria re-organised and defended their identity as a Syrian one.

The Beiruti Middle Stratum and the Syrian Identity

It was in Beirut, that important centre for the whole region of Syria, that the groundwork was laid for a fresh outlook regarding Syria, namely that it was a single region with a progressive population sharing common interests. The good cultural and economic ties between the different communities may have stemmed in part, as elucidated above, from the common economic interests of the inhabitants, who grasped the commercial potential inherent in full co-operation. At a time when the axis of a city's social development is economic, the unifying factor among society's members (mainly the merchants) is

---

95 Buṭrus al-Bustānī (ed.), "Dīmuqrāṭiyya," *Dā'irat al-Maʿārif*, Vol. 8, p. 232.
96 Buṭrus al-Bustānī (ed.), "Jumhūriyya," *Dā'irat al-Maʿārif*, Vol. 6, pp. 533–534.

naturally economic and commercial. Such indeed was the issue closest to the hearts of the Beiruti merchants, and it apparently served to bridge the gaps of religion and ethnicity. The opportunities created in the city as a result of the economic growth were capable of breaking down inter-communal boundaries, replacing them with socio-economic ties.[97] Those merchants with greater money-making interests, tended to act with more tolerance towards members of the other community. In the absence of such a connection, only rivalry and envy remained, which at times escalated into actual hostility, culminating in violence, as happened in other places at the time.

As a rule, members of the new stratum were closely attached to the city with what can be coined as "urban patriotism." For them, Beirut symbolised the cultural and economic centre of the entire region—Greater Syria. They believed that if they wished to develop the city's economy and bring about progress, it was best for peace and quiet to prevail among its population, providing a stable and safe environment. In this manner they would be able to transact their business efficiently, and the city would attract foreign merchants. Cultural life, too, would expand and attract an increasing number of participants.

Why then did the merchants link Beirut to the entire Syrian region? The answer, it seems, is that the merchants in particular had an economic interest in seeing Syria as a single entity, as this tied Beirut (their place of operation) with the Syrian hinterland, on which they depended economically. They set up their offices in Beirut as here was the port at which the goods they traded in arrived and where the local merchants who came to buy from them gathered.

At the same time, a Syrian framework could provide a wide domain for their activities. The new roads[98] allowed them to market their goods efficiently in areas with which they were familiar and in which

---

[97] See for further details, Iliya F. Harik, "The Impact of the Domestic Market on Rural-Urban Relations in the Middle East," in Richard Antoun and Iliya F. Harik (eds.), *Rural Politics and Social Change in the Middle East* (London, 1972), pp. 337–363.

[98] Fawaz notes that several historians regard the Beirut-Damascus road as the most important factor in turning Beirut into the leading port on the Syrian coast. Evidence of the importance of this highway can be seen in the large profits of the company that controlled it and in the fact that most of the silk spinning mills in the 1860s were built along it. See: Fawaz, *Merchants and Migrants*, p. 69.

they could promote their businesses. Apparently, their interest also stemmed from their desire to expand their commerce in the hinterland, beyond Beirut.[99]

In all likelihood, the economic activities and aspirations of the Beiruti merchants contributed to viewing the Syrian region as a single entity, with its centre at Beirut. The merchants' membership in the cultural societies that formed in Beirut, which defined it as "Syrian" and desired, among other things, to see all Syria as a single region, affirms this assumption. The semantic transition from "*Bilād al-Shām*" to "Syria" is critical as well, since it indicates a change in the perception of the Christian-Arab self, as will be discussed thoroughly in the last chapter.

As members of this sub-stratum hardly discussed the topic in question in their writing, it is difficult to gauge their mindset and to

[99] Comparison of the volumes of import and export through this port and others in the region proves the superior importance of Beirut and its centrality for transporting goods between the Syrian hinterland and Western Europe. Most of the data for Beirut concerns its own import and export trade with the West. Additional figures for the transport of goods to and from the Syrian ports and the inland cities are hard to come by. Such figures are needed to prove that Beirut indeed served as the main port for the region and that it mediated between Western Europe and the inland cities of Syria. Such proof would verify that the Beiruti merchants had a motive for regarding the Syrian region as one whole, with Beirut at its centre. Bowring points out the centrality of Beirut. He states in his report for 1840 that "Beirut is the most flourishing port in Syria," John Bowring, *Report on the Commercial Statistics of Syria* (London, 1840), p. 52. The figures he provides show that commerce with France was the most prosperous during that period. When this trade in various Syrian ports is analysed, it becomes clear that Beirut had much more traffic than did other ports. For example: in 1835, 3,405 tons passed through Beirut, 3,882 tons through Alexandretta, 1,952 tons through Latakia, and 1,787 tons through Tripoli. In 1836 the figures were 10,768 tons through Beirut, 600 tons through Alexandretta, 2,991 tons through Latakia, and 2,340 tons through Tripoli. In 1837 16,242 tons went through Beirut, 1,904 tons through Alexandretta, 2,700 tons though Latakia and 1,521 tons through Tripoli. Bowring, pp. 55, 71–76. On the basis of these figures one may conclude that most of the commerce to and from the Syrian inland region and on to the West passed through Beirut during the period. Elsewhere in the report, Bowring briefly surveys the ports along the Syrian coast. He states that the ports of Jaffa, Tyre, and Sidon were choked and inconvenient for anchorage; Tartus' port was safe only for single ships; Tripoli's port was small and usable only in summer. This left only the ports of Alexandretta and Beirut. Regarding Alexandretta, Bowring notes that this port had first-class conditions, but the city itself lay in a swamp, a factor that kept visitors away. The port served mainly for Antioch, Aleppo, and northern Syria. Hence, Beirut port, which served Damascus and Palestine [sic], was the leading and most flourishing port of the Syrian region. Bowring, pp. 51–52. This portrayal, as presented by Bowring, became increasingly true over the course of the century.

prove their direct attachment to the Syrian concept. Still, it is noteworthy that they had the financial means to support members of the intelligentsia who did endorse this concept. In this way they could preserve their growing economic and social status in the framework with which they were familiar. Thus, it is evident, as Hobsbawm stated, that "the role of economies defined by state frontiers was large."[100] Such was the case in the region of Syria. The interaction in Beirut between the intellectuals and merchants was crucial for the building of their local identity. It demonstrates as well that merchants cannot be seen only in light of their economic function, as their activities encompassed much more. Directly and indirectly, they were also partly responsible for shaping new ideas and identities. Accordingly, in the middle of the nineteenth century, the focal point from which the Christian middle stratum viewed the wider region of Syria shifted from the Mountain, where it had been during the period of Amīr Bashīr II, to the port city of Beirut.[101] In both cases, centres of economic and cultural activities became the focus of the concept and identity of the region's Christian middle stratum.

Members of the intelligentsia also attached themselves to the Syrian concept, partly for the economic interests mentioned, but also because the interaction between them and the merchants strengthened and fulfilled a variety of needs that went beyond simple economic intercourse. Unlike the merchants, this sub-stratum looked further ahead rather than being concerned for the immediate welfare of the city, and mainly stressed their apprehension for the future of the entire region. They, too, wanted the city to develop and society to flourish, but they were also anxious to ensure that the heterogeneous structure of Beirut's society would still facilitate their living as Christians within a Muslim society. They were concerned about their personal safety and the future of society as a whole, in case communal conflict

[100] Hobsbawm, *Nations and Nationalism*, p. 25.

[101] The tie between the inhabitants of the Mountain and the concept of Syria can be seen through the "Syrian Scientific Society" (1868) which acted to promote this concept. Participation of many members from the Mountain middle stratum in the activities of the society in Beirut is evident. Two examples are the Maʿlūf family and the Shalfūns. For example, Yūsuf ibn Khūrī al-Shalfūn, whose father was close to Amīr Bashīr, worked for Khalīl al-Khūrī in his newspaper. The newspaper promoted ideas regarding Syria. Other families are: the Thābits, Daḥdāḥs, Zalzals, Khūrīs, Shidyāqs and so forth. Gharāyiba, *Sūriyya fī al-Qarn al-Tāsiʿ Ashar*, pp. 242–244; al-Maʿlūf, *Dawānī al-Quṭūf*, pp. 466, 582, 588.

erupted. Throughout the century, they invested a great deal of efforts to define and highlight common features of the two religions, particularly after the civil war in 1860, but also prior to that. These events vindicated their fears that society in Beirut and in Syria as a whole was liable to disorder, and that steps had to be taken to correct the situation. Their concern was social, cultural, and also ideological. They sought to provide a secular and territorial cure for the maladies of the society in which they lived, and it took the form of the Syrian concept. Viewing the whole region (not only the city) as an entire political entity rather than just an economic one, they envisaged Syria as a single region with a unified population having its own unique culture and heritage. Beirut, therefore, could not be a separate unit detached from the region; it had to be seen as an integral part of it. As was the case in other trade and manufacturing towns around the world with strong links to their hinterland, Beirut implanted in the middle stratum a very strong sense of regional identification and perhaps an almost exaggerated pride in the social practices that the middle stratum believed to be unique to their city.

In contrast to the merchants, the intelligentsia expressed their ideas widely in the press, in books, in historical novels and through learned societies. Accordingly, this sub-stratum was responsible for formulating, writing, and distributing the ideas that created the proper background for the emergence of the Syrian concept. Meanwhile, the merchants' contribution often concentrated on financing this activity of the writers, and occasionally even taking an active part in it. Earlier, we saw the example of Mīkhā'īl Mudawwar, who financed and helped in the establishment of the journal *Ḥadiqāt al-Akhbār*, the first journal to embrace the Syrian concept.[102]

The intelligentsia's vision of the region of Syria as a single entity is also verified in a report by Colonel Fraser (Lord Dufferin's replacement in the investigation of the disturbances in Mount Lebanon and Damascus of 1861). Fraser reported that at the Beirut Conference it was decided to establish an autonomous *mutaṣarrifiyya* of Lebanon, namely to separate it administratively from the Syrian region. He noted that many people were pleased that this agreement had been

[102] See Fruma Zachs, "Building a Cultural Identity: The Case of Khalīl al-Khūri," in Thomas Philipp and Christoph Schumann (eds.), *From the Syrian Land to the States of Syria and Lebanon* (Beirut, 2004), pp. 27–39.

reached a year after the events, but general disappointment was still felt among the Europeans and the local intellectuals that no comprehensive solution for all Syria had been found.[103]

The conception of the Syrian region as one whole served the interests of both sub-strata, whose thinking at this point merged to strive for the same goal. Each group had its own interests. The mutual interaction between the merchants and the intelligentsia also sprang from the general outlook of the middle stratum, which believed that economic growth would eventually bring cultural development. This was one of the reasons that, later on, they pointed to the Phoenician period as exemplifying the pinnacle of the region's economic and cultural achievements.[104]

Their perception of the region as one entity also reveals dimensions of the evolving identity of the Beiruti middle stratum. The way in which they reorganised their identity in regard to their region and the other can thus be discerned. In other words, the concept of Syria reflected the manner in which the middle stratum moulded its identity.

Under the circumstances, it was natural for members of the Beiruti middle stratum to aspire to some kind of autonomy that could further facilitate its general activities without the direct interference of the Ottoman Empire. However, in order to receive this autonomy, they needed to demonstrate to the Ottomans that they did not constitute a political threat to the Porte and that they did not want to dissociate themselves from the Ottoman Empire, but rather to redefine their status within its framework. Since the Beiruti middle stratum saw itself connected to local society and as an integral part of the Ottoman society, especially from 1856 on, when the Ottomans began improving the conditions of the Christians, they strove to remain under Ottoman rule.

[103] PRONI (Public Record Office of Northern Ireland), MD&A, mic. 22, reel 12, Vol. 13, Fraser to Dufferin, 7 July 1861.

[104] This idea was also part of the influence of the American missionaries, as will be discussed in Chapter Four. It is repeated in the writings of the second generation of these families, who received their education from the missionaries at the Syrian Protestant College. For example, see: Daud Qurbān on "The Importance of Studying Economics," *al-Kuliyya*, June 1912, No. 8, Vol. 3, pp. 217–222; Tawfīq Qandalaft, "Inna Aḥwāl al-Bilād al-Ṭabī'iyya wal-Iqtiṣādiyya Ashadd Ta'thīr fī Qiyām al-Umam wa-Suquṭuhā min al-Aḥwāl al-Adabiyya wal-Akhlāqiyya," *al-Kuliyya*, June 1912, No. 8, Vol. 3, pp. 221–223.

Despite their apparent contentment, members of the stratum desired to change some of the existing inter-relations with the region's Muslim society and also with the centre, i.e. the Porte. Thus, as already mentioned, they constructed their identity on two levels. They strove to maintain their status as an integral part of the local society. In this sense, they defined themselves as Arabs. On the other hand, they attempted to redefine a new framework for their society under the influence of Western ideas. In this sense they defined themselves as Syrian.

I also mentioned the duality existing in the thinking of these Christian Arabs and the natural tendency to combine this dichotomy into an integrated whole in their identity. This combination took the shape of the construction of the Syrian identity with an Arab culture at its centre.

The insistence of the Christian-Arab middle stratum on its membership in the indigenous society is clear from some of their personal decisions. Some of them had the opportunity to receive foreign citizenships, but preferred to spend only temporary periods outside the Empire, returning to live under Ottoman rule in their native society. The majority, for the most part, did not attempt to attain European passports but many did place themselves under the protection of various European consuls. This behaviour allowed them to gain more power while they enjoyed the best of both worlds—they were faithful Ottoman subjects and yet benefited from unique privileges provided by the West. In this way, their mediating role was preserved. Later, this role would be portrayed in their own self-constructed identity. Perhaps this can also help to explain why no clear evidence exists that this stratum aspired to create a territorial entity under the West and thus disconnect themselves from the Empire.

There is little doubt that sometimes the middle stratum saw the European merchants as their rivals. Economically, they both competed for the same market. In fact, they strove to preserve their local cultural heritage despite foreign influence. Thus, and in contrast to the "dependency theory" (which often describes the middle stratum in Syria as an almost static social stratum with a predefined character, dependent upon European capitalism and serving its interests, without any intention of becoming an active local middle stratum),[105]

[105] A similar process occurred among the Greek Orthodox. Exertzoglue, "The Development of the Greek Ottoman Bourgeoisie," pp. 90–91.

the Beiruti middle stratum was an active one, which invested in the city and in its people and defined its own identity. This conclusion also stands in clear contrast to research suggesting that members of this stratum merely paved the way for the penetration of the West.

Aware of its own important role as cultural and economic mediator between the indigenous and the foreign, it was natural for members of the Beiruti middle stratum to preserve their status as key figures for both sides. If they joined the West they would most probably have lost their status in the eyes of the Ottomans; if they identified themselves completely with and loyal to local society, they would not be trusted as much by the West. Their position ensured them that the West would need them as arbitrators with the Ottomans and the Syrian region. At the same time, they could connect the interior hinterland with the coastal region, playing a local role within society. Beirut was the perfect environment to make them believe that this could be done, as long as they could maintain equilibrium between the two dimensions of their role.

In summary, the development of the Syrian identity was not only due to the impact of the West. Indigenous roots had an effect as well, going back to the time of Bashīr II. The developments in Beirut, coming as they did on the foundation created under Bashīr, produced a desire for an imagined autonomic entity among the Beiruti middle stratum, i.e.—Syria. Therefore, the development of the Syrian identity began even prior to the period of the French Mandate in the early twentieth century.

Beirut of the nineteenth century encompassed both a powerful merchant stratum and an intelligentsia, who nurtured a vision as well as "political" motivation. This middle stratum boosted and vitalised the building of the Syrian identity through the growing need to define its members, a minority living among a Muslim majority. Although they were a minority within the Ottoman society, they saw it as the only society they sought to belong to. Their growing social and economic success increased their belief that an amalgam including them and the rest of the population was possible, and they directed their efforts to attain this fusion. The attempt to achieve such a blend between their identity and that of the other would eventually ignite a process of inventing a new concept—the Syrian identity.

Thus, the evolution of the Christian Arabs' identity and their need to re-define their position in society led, in many ways, to the construction of the Syrian concept or vice versa. In fact, constructing the concept of Syria and their own identity were actually two sides of the same coin. We cannot understand the growth of the concept without tracking the development of the Christian Arabs' identity. We can also conclude that without the developments in the Mountain, the Syrian notion could not have received its initial impetus, and without developments in Beirut it could not have continued to grow. These two phases were both necessary for formulating and moulding the Syrian identity in its first stages.

Up until now, we have examined the indigenous developments that contributed to the creation of a Syrian identity. The following two chapters will describe the external factors that served as additional catalysts for constructing this identity during the nineteenth century. Further changes arising from modifications in the imperial central government, highlighted in the next chapter, brought this sub-stratum another step nearer to fashioning their identity, this time by the legitimisation which the middle stratum received from the Porte.

CHAPTER THREE

RE-ENFORCING AN IDENTITY: THE *TANẒĪMĀT* REFORMS

As the Christian Arabs strove to redefine their self-image in Beirut through their relationship with the Muslim population, the Porte itself, starting in 1856, made an effort to reorganise interrelationships among its population by promoting a collective identity for all the inhabitants of the Empire, namely what is known as the principle of Ottomanism. This principle was included in the measures promulgated by the Porte between the years 1856–1876, known as the late *Tanẓīmāt* reforms, which were undertaken to modernise and Westernise the Empire. These reforms and Ottoman policies regarding the Syrian region during that time eventually became one of the important catalysts contributing to the construction of the Christian Arabs' identity. As Masters wrote:

> The bureaucrats in the capital were not unaware of the transitions that were occurring in the realm they administered. Their actions often played a decisive role in determining the fate of the empire's religious minorities and in formulating their political identities. The construction of the social community was very much a product of an ongoing interaction between the Ottoman bureaucrats, representing the Sultan, and his subjects, Muslim and non-Muslim alike.[1]

A Turning Point—Hatt-ı Hümayun

In 1831–1832, Ibrāhīm Pāshā's army occupied the region of Syria. His conquest of the area created an international crisis and raised Western political interest in the region. As a result, the fears of the Ottomans regarding the future of the Syrian region increased and they began to do everything in their power to retain it within their dominions.

[1] Masters, *Christian and Jews in the Ottoman Arab World*, pp. 13–14.

In the meantime, the Western Powers made increasingly vociferous and frequent demands to improve the condition of non-Muslims in the Empire, especially after the Crimean War (1854–1856). Having successfully defended the Ottoman Empire against Russian aggression in this war, France and England were in a position to ensure that Mahmud II accede to their demands. Understanding that they had to foster the sympathy of the West, the Ottomans introduced reforms regarding the status of the non-Muslim population. In 1855 they abolished the *jizya* (poll tax) imposed on all non-Muslims; thereafter, the status of the non-Muslims improved, and they were obliged to serve in the military. The culmination of this process was the publication of the *Hatt-ı Hümayun* in 1856, the result of pressure by the British, French and Austrian ambassadors. The decree was a turning point in the Ottoman Empire vis-à-vis most of the issues concerning non-Muslims. The *Hatt-ı Hümayun* and the reforms contained in it were key elements in the policies of the Foreign Minister, Fuʿād Pāshā, and the Grand Vizier, ʿAlī Pāshā. The two leading Ottoman statesmen were architects of the late *Tanẓīmāt* reforms, and saw these reforms as a means of maintaining political stability of the Porte.

The main idea of the *Hatt-ı Hümayun* was to establish equality between Muslims and non-Muslims. It consciously paved the way for better integration of Christians within the Empire, a step in which the Christian population was interested, but which contradicted Muslim tradition. The decree granted equal civil rights to non-Muslims, and strove to abolish aspects of their humiliating status. Their status prior to these reforms was inferior, and they were perceived by the ruling authorities and by the population in general as "second-class subjects." Accordingly, they were obliged to dress in a distinctive way; they could not be appointed to high office; they were forced to pay the *jizya*; and their evidence in the *sharīʿa* court against a Muslim was not considered valid.

The decree purported to change this situation. In its very first sentence, the Sultan stated his desire to improve the condition of all his Muslim and non-Muslim subjects and stressed equality among the different communities. This equality was declared in many spheres: military service, administration, law, public schools, public employment, and social standing. One of the important laws incorporated into the decree was that members of any religion could be appointed to government administrative posts; training and ability would henceforth be the criteria for employment. As for conscription, the non-Muslims as well as the Muslims could make a one time payment, the *badal*, in exchange for release from military recruitment. Another law, enacted later, established that a foreigner had the right to buy real estate within the Empire. The decree also stated that no person would be forcibly converted to another religion. A few additional examples can help to sharpen understanding of the decree and its effects. For instance, all taxes and imposts on members of the Christian faith would be abolished; the movable goods and real estate of the Christians would not be touched, and so on.[2] The *Hatt-ı Hümayun* introduced a new form of government administration, based on principles of equality and justice for all inhabitants and granting them equal status.

Christians of the region of Syria welcomed this changed attitude. As a result, the basis for Christian-Arab intellectual activity and for social and economic advancement was gradually enlarged; Christian Arabs began to acquire administrative positions and improved their status. They were also granted more freedom to express their opinions. As a result, they started to openly declare their ideas regarding their new Syrian identity and soon made their voices heard in the local press and publications.[3]

Already in 1858, only two years after the proclamation of the edict, the weekly newspaper *Ḥadīqat al-Akhbār* appeared. This newspaper managed to be published for more than fifty years.[4] The first Arabic newspaper in Beirut, it served as a medium for distributing ideas of Syrian patriotism and identity.[5] Its editor was a Christian Arab from the Beiruti middle stratum by the name of Khalīl al-Khūrī who from 1860 on was under the patronage of Fu'ād Pāshā, the Ottoman foreign minister at that time.

This tendency to publicly advance the ideas of Syrian *waṭaniyya* increased after the events of 1860, when Christian intellectuals became

---

[2] See: Roderic H. Davison, *Reform in the Ottoman Empire 1856–1876* (Princeton, 1963), pp. 81–113. For the translation of the decree into English, see: Jacob C. Hurewitz, *The Middle East and North Africa in World Politics*, Vol. 1 (London, 1975), pp. 315–318.

[3] Roderic H. Davison, "Turkish Attitudes Concerning Christian Muslim Equality in the Nineteenth Century," *American Historical Review*, Vol. 59, No. 4 (1954), pp. 844–864.

[4] Only copies of the first ten years (1858–1868) are available in the Bodleian Library, Oxford.

[5] Fruma Zachs, "Building a Cultural Identity: The Case of Khalīl al-Khūrī," pp. 31–36.

more active, calling openly for a non-communal and secular identity, for unity and tolerance within the population in the Syrian region, for the love of their beloved homeland—Syria, and for loyalty to the secular Arab heritage. This development of a local identity seemed to be the perfect solution for the Beiruti middle stratum, enabling them to preserve and even increase their prosperity in the region, while at the same time, maintaining their delicate balance with the Muslim population and remaining part of Ottoman society.

The timing was also important, since the intellectuals saw in the *Tanẓīmat* reforms a new era of opportunities for them. They used the 1856 edict as a stepping-stone to strengthen their evolving local identity. Newspapers, which were established by Buṭrus al-Bustānī in the period after the promulgation of the edict, such as *Nafīr Sūriyya* (Clarion of Syria), a series of bulletins published between 1860–1861, *al-Jinān*, which was published between 1870–1886, and *al-Janna* (Garden or Paradise), published between 1870–1884, also dealt openly with this new identity.

As the intellectuals began to realise the potential of this decree, they tried to disseminate its ideas among the educated local population. A closer look at the writings of Christian intellectuals during this period reveals their ardent support for the decree and its ideas. An attempt was made to put aside communal differences. The principles of the edict were affirmed and conveyed mainly through the medium of the press. The periodical *al-Jinān*, for example, published articles maintaining that there is no difference between the various communities constituting the Syrian population, and equality among them was emphasised.[6] Others such as *Nafīr Sūriyya* and *Ḥadīqat al-Akhbār* stressed similar themes.[7] Buṭrus al-Bustānī even printed some of the points of the decree in his *Nafīr Sūriyya*, and called for its principles to be respected.[8] According to his words ". . . the people of the homeland have rights that they receive from the homeland, just as they have duties towards it. . . . Among these are the basic

[6] Salīm al-Bustānī, "Limādhā Naḥnu fī Ta'akhkhur," *al-Jinān*, Vol. 1, No. 6, 1870, pp. 161–163; Salīm al-Bustānī, "al-Ulfa wal-Ittiḥād," *al-Jinān*, Vol. 1, No. 12, 1870, pp. 243–244; See also, *Nafīr Sūriyya*, 14 January 1861.

[7] *Ḥadīqat al-Akhbār*, No. 117, 8 August 1861; *Nafīr Sūriyya*, 14 January 1861.

[8] *Nafīr Sūriyya*, 22 February 1861. For more details, see: Stephen Paul Sheehi, "Inscribing the Arab Self: Buṭrus al-Bustani and Paradigms of Subjective Reform," *British Journal of Middle Eastern Studies*, Vol. 27 (2000), pp. 7–24.

rights to defend their blood, honour and right for freedom."[9] Al-Bustānī, who did not see any contradiction between Ottomanism and the Syrian identity, truly believed that under this new era of reforms the local population could develop its own self.[10] Only against this setting is it possible to understand the activities of Christian intellectuals in the region, such as Buṭrus and Salīm al-Bustānī, Khalīl al-Khūrī, Mīkhā'īl Mishāqa and others, who encouraged Syrian identity during these years, particularly until the rise of Abdül Hamid II in 1876.

This Ottoman policy, important to all minorities in the Empire, influenced the Christians in Syria as well. Since the concentration of Christian Arabs was greater in Beirut than anywhere else in the Empire, the effect of the edict of 1856 on this large group of people was particularly marked. The conceptual basis created among the Christians, calling for unity and homogeneity among all minorities in Syria, was now easier to propagate. Obviously, the Ottomans, as promoters of this policy, did not hinder but rather encouraged the trend to build a local Syrian identity within the framework of the Ottoman Empire. This was the reason why Christian intellectuals could write about and disseminate these ideas in the first place.

The Osmanlılık *Principle*

The *Hatt-ı Hümayun* heralded the first step in the advancement of a larger idea of ʿAlī Pāshā and Fu'ād Pāshā, i.e. the principle of Ottomanism. According to it, as Abu-Manneh writes:

> . . . the subjects of the Sultan (*raʿiyet*) came to be regarded as citizens of the Ottoman state who enjoyed equal political and civil rights. Moreover, by virtue of inhabiting the Ottoman lands, their identity was defined as Ottomans. Thus the concept of Ottomanism was based on a territorial, and not on a communal identity, as had been the case

[9] Towards the end of the nineteenth century we can find similar ideas in the first Muslim journal published in Beirut, *Thamarāt al-Funūn*, which contained an article entitled "Freedom," stating that this term meant equal rights among citizens. It held that every person in the country had to have freedom of speech and action. See: *Thamarāt al-Funūn*, No. 3, 4 March 1875; see also, *Nafīr Sūriyya*, 25 October 1860.

[10] Butrus Abu-Manneh, "The Christians Between Ottomanism and Syrian Nationalism: The Ideas of Butrus al-Bustani," *International Journal of Middle East Studies*, Vol. 11 (1980), p. 297; See also, *al-Jinān*, Vol. 1, No. 10, 1870, p. 675.

> formerly. Both concepts: the principle of equality and territorial identity of the "citizen" were, according to the *Shariʿa*, innovations. As such they form fundamental changes in the structure of the Muslim state.[11]

Thus, the professed aim of this principle was to remove the barriers dividing the various communities (*millets*) in the Empire and to create one civil identity among Ottoman subjects. The idea embraced equality (mainly political), between subjects-citizens, as was the case of the decree of 1856, and the notion of a common nationality—*Osmanlılık*. This perception and its concepts were far from the Islamic one, whereby the rights, status, and duties of the individual were derived from his place in the religious community. The new perception was Western and secular in its approach, whereby the rights and status of the citizen stemmed from his very citizenship in the Empire and his loyalty to its government.

Prior to the period under consideration, the Empire rarely made an attempt to create a basis for unity among its different communities. Accordingly, it was difficult to create inter-communal solidarity and social integration in Ottoman society. Until the nineteenth century, the Sunni community had dominated, while every other non-Muslim or non-Sunni community was marginal, especially in its political power. This system had been inherited from earlier Muslim states, and it served the Porte for a long time. As early as the sixteenth century, Ottoman rule in the region was restricted to measures for maintaining Ottoman supremacy, manifested by maintaining the balance of power among the various forces in the provinces and preserving the status quo in other spheres. Daily life and current matters in society were left in the hands of the subjects themselves and their own institutions.[12]

This situation began to change, due to the new economic and social reality that developed over the course of the nineteenth century, both inside and outside the Empire. European penetration of the Empire increased and posed new challenges for the government in Istanbul. Fuʾād and ʿAlī were afraid that, in the future, the Christian population would attempt to detach itself from the Porte.

---

[11] Butrus Abu-Manneh, *Studies on Islam and the Ottoman Empire in the 19th Century 1826–1876* (Istanbul, 2001), p. 128. See also, pp. 115–124.

[12] Moshe Maʿoz, *Ottoman Reform in Syria and Palestine, 1840–1861* (Oxford, 1968), p. 4.

By creating the principle of Ottomanism, they believed that they could strengthen and centralise the Empire, reduce the separatist tendencies of certain population groups, and invigorate the loyalty of the subjects. They held that the adoption of several Western tenets would help them to reinforce the Porte and create a strong Ottoman political community. It was natural that their point of departure would be the non-Muslim population.

Fu'ād and ʿAlī believed that through Ottomanism, they could pave the way to a further goal they strove for, namely integration of all the minorities in the Empire within the socio-political framework of the Ottoman State. In doing so, their main objective (between 1856–1871) was to create a new political community that would encompass the entire population of the Empire, and likewise form within it a new identity based on equal rights among its people, who would recognise the Empire as their homeland. In this way they hoped to deflect the loyalty of the non-Muslims from their local community and direct it to the Empire, making them regard it as their state.

The timing was important here as well, since this new policy and its new political concept were evolving in parallel with the emerging Syrian identity in Beirut. Only by thoroughly understanding the parameters of Ottomanism will it be possible to understand the fertile basis that eventually made the emergence of the Syrian idea possible. In other words, the policy of Fu'ād Pāshā and ʿAlī Pāshā helped accelerate the evolution of a local identity among the Beiruti middle stratum, which seemed as if it was going to develop over time in any case.

Between the years 1856 and 1869, the idea of Ottomanism was manifested in the enactment of three laws. Coincidentally, each of these laws also served as a catalyst and influenced the development of Syrian identity.

An examination of the first law, the Land Law of 1858, finds that it allows the parameters of local and secular identity to be formed. Originally it was intended to restore to the Empire those territories that, over the years, had in one way or another slipped out of its control. It also aimed to gradually broaden and strengthen usage and ownership rights over the land. One result of the law was that it gradually strengthened the attachment of the individual to his land by official registration, with formal documentation of ownership (*ṭābū*). Land, if its ownership was proved, could be traded or bequeathed.[13] This law constituted an important phase in the development of the Syrian patriotic idea in later years.

Fu'ād Pāshā and ʿAlī Pāshā went further, reorganising the Ottoman provinces under a decentralised system, although within each province the administration was centralised. They accomplished this through the second law, the *Vilâyet* Law (*Vilâyet Nizamnamesi*) of 1864, which was designed to create larger administrative units from the existing provinces in the Empire. These were to be ruled by talented and experienced governors (*valis*) selected by merit. The *valis* were given a wide margin for independent action particularly in matters connected with law, economy, administration and politics, and were required to consult with the Porte only on matters of prime importance. They oversaw the implementation of decisions of the Administrative Council and of those emanating from Istanbul, supervised tax collection and were responsible for law and order. There were certain limitations to their authority. For example, the *vali* was subordinate to the Ministry of the Interior in Istanbul and had no jurisdiction over the army in the *vilâyet*. Beside him there was a bureaucracy of officials, as in Istanbul, who observed his moves.[14] Nevertheless, as a result of this law the Syrian *vali* became more powerful than before, and had a great deal of influence over the policies of the province.

The law also represented the first general extension of the elective and representative principles down to the lower divisions of the new provinces. This was achieved through the establishment of a general council (*Majlis ʿUmūmī*), to be assembled annually, in every new province. In this way, the notables (Muslims and non-Muslims) who were elected to these councils or had low- or medium-level positions in the administration became more involved in the local government, which probably increased their identification with their

[13] Lewis, *The Emergence of Modern Turkey*, pp. 116–117; Ruth M. Roded, *Tradition and Change in Syria during the Last Decades of Ottoman Rule: The Urban Elite of Damascus, Aleppo, Homs and Hama, 1876–1918*, Ph.D. dissertation, University of Denver, 1984, pp. 117–119; Stanford J. Shaw and Ezel K. Shaw, *History of the Ottoman Empire and Modern Turkey*, Vol. 2 (Cambridge, 1977), p. 88; Haim Gerber, *The Social Origins of the Modern Middle East* (Boulder, 1987), pp. 67–72.

[14] For further details on this changing status of the *vali*, see: FO 195/1153, Jago to Jocelyn, Damascus, 4 March 1877; FO 195/1306, Jago to Layard, 16 December 1884; FO 195/ 1480, Dickson to Syndham, Damascus, 16 December 1884.

province;[15] perhaps it also encouraged some of them to gradually develop notions of local patriotism.

The third law was the Law of Ottoman Nationality of 1869, which granted Ottoman nationality to all the inhabitants of the Empire, regarding them as "Imperial subjects" or "subjects of the Ottoman State." The law applied to all its inhabitants (including non-Muslims) and stipulated that every individual of the Empire would be deemed an Ottoman citizen. Non-Ottoman Europeans who lived in the Empire for more than five years were eligible to become Ottoman citizens. Consequently, a person was no longer defined as a subject but as a citizen in the Western sense of the word. The law's broader significance was that, once again, individual identity was now legally determined according to the territory in which one lived and not by one's religious affiliation.[16]

The *Osmanlılık* principle and the three laws mentioned above created the basis for the development of Ottoman identity, but also generated motifs or interpretations that conceptually could encourage the construction of a local identity among elements of the population. This kind of identity could be seen as a partial by-product of the ideas of Ottomanism.

As Ottomanism sought to weaken the communal structure of Ottoman society, the Christian Arabs increased their ambitious efforts toward the same goal. They realised that the integration of Syrian society was essential for tranquillity in the region and for the creation of common interests between themselves and the Muslims.[17] The ethnic mosaic of Syrian society with a Muslim majority and twelve other minority communities, with their own primordial notions, made this kind of policy necessary. Each of the minority communities was centred on its own religious hierarchy and leaders, and each had a different degree of awareness of its internal solidarity. The communities were separate from each other and distinct from the Muslim Sunni majority; integration was difficult, although Ottomanism aimed to achieve just that.

---

[15] Davison, *Reform in the Ottoman Empire*, especially pp. 146–151; Shaw and Shaw, *History of the Ottoman Empire*, Vol. 2, pp. 89–91.

[16] Davison, "Turkish Attitudes Concerning Muslim-Christian Equality," p. 252.

[17] For further information on the Reforms in Syria see: Isabel Burton, *The Inner Life of Syria, Palestine and the Holy Land* (London, 1868), p. 29; John Murray, *Handbook for Travellers in Syria and Palestine* (London, 1868), p. xxxvii; FO 195/994, Skene to Rumbold, 18 January 1872.

Naturally, local intellectuals chose to support Ottomanism. Outstanding amongst them was Butrus al-Bustānī. From the 1850s on, he became an adherent of Ottomanism as did other Christian-Arab intellectuals; he called for its recognition as a political principle. He believed that the 1856 decree was an important step towards integration of the Empire's communities, regarded this as the most suitable solution for Syria and a means for achieving his ultimate goal of Syrian patriotism.[18] Other intellectuals from the Beiruti middle stratum understood that integration of the population in the Empire would bring prosperity with it, thereby advancing the well-being of the inhabitants. Ottomanism strove to replace religious solidarity; at the same time, these intellectuals acted to weaken religious power through the patriotism they invoked.[19] The Porte, for its part, assented in silence to the intellectuals' activities by not objecting to their views; thus, perhaps it also gave this process some kind of legitimisation. In several cases, it was prominent Ottoman personages such as Fu'ād Pāshā or Midhat Pāshā who helped to reinforce these notions.

Ottoman Policy toward Syria 1860–1880:
The Establishment of the Vilâyet *of Syria*[20]

In 1865, Syria became one of the first regions to which the *Vilâyet* Law was applied. The new Ottoman administrative entity was created by the union of the provinces of Damascus and Sidon, without the province of Aleppo, which remained separate. The province extended from the area south of Aleppo in the north to the Sinai Peninsula in the south, without the autonomous *Mutaṣarrifiyya* of Mount Lebanon.[21] Hence, the *vilâyet* was composed of almost the entire geographical area known as "Greater Syria," which included

---

[18] Abu-Manneh, "The Christians between Ottomanism and Syrian Nationalism," pp. 288–298.

[19] *Al-Jinān*, Vol. 1, No. 2, 1870, p. 28; *Ḥadīqat al-Akhbār*, No. 218, 19 April 1862.

[20] This chapter will focus on the years 1865–1880. For details regarding the province in later years see: Najib E. Saliba, *Wilayet Suriya 1876–1909*, Ph.D. dissertation, University of Michigan, 1971, pp. 15–16.

[21] Butrus Abu-Manneh, "The Establishment and Dismantling of the Province of Syria 1865–1888," in J. P. Spagnolo (ed.) *Problems of the Modern Middle East in Historical Perspective* (Reading, 1992), p. 9; FO 195/787, Jackson to Bulwer, 27 October 1865; US/NA, Eldridge to Payson, 15 September 1879.

Ottoman Palestine, eastern Transjordan, present-day Syria and Lebanon, without Aleppo and Deir al-Azūr.[22] This *vilâyet* formalised and paved the way for the existence of a territory under Ottoman rule bearing the name "Syria" (for the borders of the *Vilâyet* of Syria see the map on page 97).[23]

Of interest in the establishment of the *Vilâyet* of Syria was that, in contrast to the usual custom of the Porte, this province or *paşalık* was not named after its capital. The Porte chose instead a pre-Islamic term, namely "Syria." This decision carries importance, since in the long run, this secular name would become the object of the Christian-Arab intellectuals' secular identity, who would see their *Vilâyet* of Syria as one territorial entity and as their own homeland. More than that, gradually and especially after the establishment of the Syrian province, these intellectuals began more intensively to identify their homeland as Syria and themselves as Syrians. What exactly drove the Ottomans to choose this Western and pre-Islamic name remains puzzling, especially when a Muslim term, *al-Shām* was already in use.

Starting from the seventh century, the Muslim population used the term *al-Shām*, which was perhaps taken from the word *Shimāl*—left, meaning north, for a person at al-Ḥijāz looking eastward. Other terms used were *Barr al-Shām*, meaning the land mass of *Shām*, and *Bilād al-Shām*, meaning the lands of *Shām*. Unfortunately, an exact answer to this question is difficult to find. Several explanations could

[22] With the Ottoman occupation in the sixteenth century, three provinces were established in the Syrian region: Aleppo, Damascus and Tripoli. In 1660 another province, Sidon, was added to the region, which now had four provinces. This was the situation until the beginning of the nineteenth century. Probably between 1809 and 1810, the province of Tripoli disappeared and became the *sancak* of Tripoli. The latter was subordinate to the province of Sidon and in times to Damascus. Again, the region came to have three provinces, Aleppo, Damascus and Sidon, and this remained so until the 1860s.

[23] The borders of the *Vilâyet* of Syria encompassed a population that approximately doubled in 35 years. Although estimates vary, according to McCarthy, who bases his figures on Ottoman sources in 1878, there were approximately 660,000 people in the whole *vilâyet* during this year; in 1890, 794,000 and in 1913, there were already 1,040,000 people. The American Consul put the same populations during the Hamidian rule at 604,170 in 1878 and 1,300,000 in 1913. See: Justin McCarthy, "The Population of Ottoman Syria in Iraq, 1878–1914," *Asian and African Studies*, Vol. 15 (1981), p. 13; FO 195/2277, Davey to O'Connor, Damascus, 16 January 1908; FO 195/1305, Consul Henderson, Memorandum on the Population of the *Vilayet* of Syria, 28 August 1880; Gharāyiba, *Sūriyya fī al-Qarn al-Tāsiʿ ʿAshar*, pp. 40, 43, 59, 66–69; ʿAbd al-ʿAzīz Muḥammad ʿAwaḍ, *al-Idāra al-ʿUthmāniyya fī Wilāyat Sūriyya, 1864–1914* (Cairo, 1969), pp. 66–81.

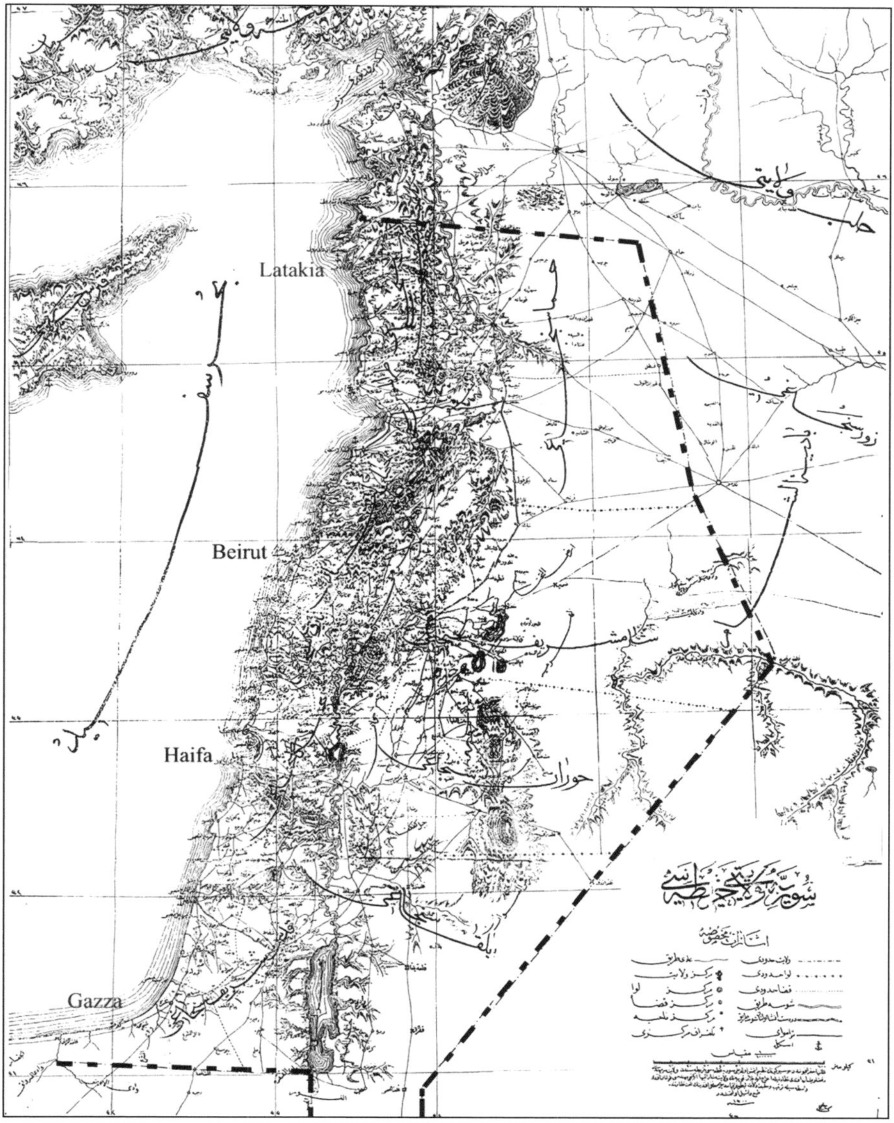

Map of *Vilâyet* of Syria
[*Salname-yi Vilâyet-i Suriye* 1300AH/1882]

clarify the matter and will show how, during this period, the term began to be used in the region itself.

In the West, the term Syria had already been in use from the Greek period and on until the nineteenth century and afterward, at least partly because the name appears in the New Testament as well as in Western travelogues.[24] During the second half of the nineteenth century, due to the penetration of the West, especially under the influence of missionaries[25] and consuls, Christian-Arab merchants and intellectuals and some Muslims began using the name "Syria" more extensively. Moreover, apparently from the 1830s, when the crisis between Muḥammad ʿAlī and the Porte took place, this term was used in diplomatic parlance among the Powers. Nevertheless, in the correspondence between Muḥammad ʿAlī and his son Ibrāhīm Pāshā, terms such as *al-Shām* and *Barr al-Shām* were still in use.[26] Thus, during all this time, the Muslim names for the region were used concurrently with the name "Syria."[27] Eventually, it received formal legitimisation by the central Ottoman government, in line with the reformist policies of the *Vilâyet* Law, when it gave the name to the enlarged province. Still, the answer as to why the Ottomans made in fact this atypical choice for the Syrian province requires further research.[28]

The establishment of the *Vilâyet* of Syria should not be perceived as a simple administrative measure. Apparently, it was the first step taken by the Empire to express a new attitude regarding the Syrian region. The concept of a "federalised Empire" or the decentralisa-

---

[24] "Syria" appears a number of times in the New Testament where it stands for the northern and central parts of "Greater Syria." Luke 2/2; Acts of the Apostles 15/23, 41, 18/18, 20/3, 21/3. Famous, too, is of course the dramatic account of Saul's conversion "on the road to Damascus," in Acts 9/1–9. See, for examples in Western travelogues: Constantin F. Volney, *Travels through Syria and Egypt in the Years 1783, 1784 and 1785*, 2 vols., translated from French by G. G. J. and J. Robinson (London, 1788); John L. Burckhardt, *Travels in Syria and the Holy Land*, 2 vols., ed. by Fuat Sezgin (London, 1995). Other books referred to cities in Syria or defined it as "the Levant"; Josias L. Porter, *Five Years in Damascus*, 2 vols. (London, 1855); Charles T. Newton, *Travels and Discoveries in the Levant*, 2 vols. (London, 1865).

[25] The American missionaries in Syria had probably introduced the extensive use of the name "Syria" into Arabic starting in 1825. Daniel Pipes, *Greater Syria—The History of an Ambition* (Oxford, 1990), p. 14.

[26] Asad Rustum, *al-Maḥfūẓāt al-Malakiyya al-Miṣriyya*, 4 vols. (Beirut, 1940–1943).

[27] The term "Syria" was also used by the Muslim population but mainly toward the end of the nineteenth century.

[28] For more details on this name and its development see Appendix II, pp. 245–251.

tion method that had, as its main goal, the unity of the Empire, should be also kept in mind. Ottoman statesmen such as Fu'ād Pāshā and Midhat Pāshā and probably Rāshid Pāshā wanted to create a federative or conceivably a confederative basis for the Empire.

Furthermore, passage of the *Vilâyet* Law followed not long after the civil war in Mount Lebanon and Damascus in 1860, which was the backdrop for its formulation.[29] As Davison himself wrote, "the revision of the statute of the Lebanon by the Porte and the Powers in the conference in 1864 influenced both the form and the time of issuance of the *Vilâyet* Law."[30] The events of 1860 were a milestone in the thinking of Christian-Arab intellectuals and served as a catalyst for building their identity as an integral part of their communal imagination in the years until the early 1880s.

These events also marked a milestone in Ottoman policy regarding Syria and constituted one of the important factors for establishing the province of Syria. After 1860, the Porte grew fearful that the political intervention by Western Powers in the Syrian region might become permanent rather than a passing episode. It is reasonable to assume that Fu'ād and ʿAlī thought this might create a situation in which the Christian population would attempt to bring the region under the patronage of the West, or that the Western Powers would try to take advantage of their regional influence to annex this area.

The Porte saw the developments of 1860 with the resultant French military intervention in Syria as a grave warning that the situation in Syria was liable to get out of hand if not dealt with properly. These Ottoman fears only increased after the Beirut Committee was established following the events of 1860, in order to restore tranquillity in the region and to reorganise the administration of Mount Lebanon.[31] In the framework of this committee, discussions were held between

[29] On the civil war of 1860 and the events leading up to it and its consequences see: Iskandar ibn Yaʿqub Abkariyus, *The Lebanon in Turmoil—Syria and the Powers in 1860*, trans. by Johann F. Scheltema (New Haven, 1920); Linda S. Schatkowski-Schilcher, "The July Riots in Damascus" in her *Families in Politics: Damascus Factions and Estates of the 18th and 19th Centuries* (Stuttgart, 1985), pp. 87–106; Leila T. Fawaz, *An Occasion for War*; Ussama Makdisi, *The Culture of Sectarianism—Community, History and Violence in Nineteenth-Century Ottoman Lebanon* (Berkeley and Los Angeles, 2000).

[30] Davison, *Reforms in the Ottoman Empire*, p. 143.

[31] For further details on the Beirut Committee see: Asad Rustum, *Lubnān fi ʿAhd al-Mutaṣarrifiyya* (Beirut, 1909), pp. 216–217; Engin D. Akarli, *The Long Peace—Ottoman Lebanon, 1861–1920* (London, 1993), pp. 6–33.

the Western Powers and the Porte regarding solutions for Syria. Suggestions ranged from the desire to create a semi-autonomous Syrian province, to the desire that Mount Lebanon be ruled separately from the rest of the Syrian lands. In fact, in 1860, Lord Dufferin, the British representative to the Beirut Committee, suggested a plan for the establishment of a single semi-independent Syrian *paşalık*, which would act in conjunction with the West.[32] He also recommended appointing Fu'ād, who was at that time the Ottoman Foreign Minister and the Ottoman representative on the Beirut Committee, as Governor-General of the province. The plan was never carried out, and consequently, in 1861, Mount Lebanon, without Beirut, became an autonomous *mutaṣarrifiyya* and as such was separated from the rest of the region of Syria. In the years to come, this *mutaṣarrifiyya* was the centre for a developing Lebanese identity. The rest of the Syrian region continued to be regarded by the Beiruti middle stratum as one territorial entity, the target of the construction of a Syrian identity.

Even though Fu'ād Pāshā managed to keep Mount Lebanon under Ottoman dominion and out of the hands of the French who had a growing interest in the area, he knew that the Porte must come up with a solution for the rest of the Syrian region as well. In the ensuing years until the establishment of the Syrian province, Fu'ād strove hard and succeeded in creating a Syrian entity that would be an Ottoman creation far removed from the solution proposed in the Beirut Committee by Lord Dufferin.[33] He was also, as we have seen, a supporter of Christian intellectuals such as Khalīl al-Khūrī, who was one of the first promulgators of the idea of Syrian patriotism. After the establishment of the *Vilâyet* of Syria, al-Khūrī's newspaper, *Ḥadīqat al-Akhbār*, became its semi-official organ. Consequently, it received a subsidy from the Ottoman government that lasted for five years.[34]

---

32 For further details on this plan, see: Zachs, "'Novice' or 'Heaven-born' Diplomat? Lord Dufferin's Plan for a 'Province of Syria': Beirut, 1860–61," *Middle Eastern Studies*, Vol. 36, No. 3 (2000), pp. 160–176. The plan itself appears in FO 78/1626; PRONI, D1071H/C5, Dufferin to Bulwer, 3 November, 1860.

33 Fruma Zachs, "'Novice' or 'Heaven-born' Diplomat?," pp. 170–173.

34 When Fu'ād served as the Ottoman representative on the Beirut Committee, al-Khūrī was appointed as his translator. From this time on Fu'ād became al-Khūrī's patron. Al-Khūrī even wrote a *dīwān* glorifying him. Khalīl al-Khūrī, *al-Nashā'id al-Fu'ādiyya* (Beirut, 1863). See also, Fruma Zachs, "Building a Cultural Identity: The Case of Khalil al-Khuri"; Agafangel E. Krymskii, *Istoria Novoi Arbskoi Literaturyi, XIX-Nachalo XX Beka* (History of New Arab Literature, XIX-Beginning of XX Century), (Moscow, 1971), p. 481. I would like to thank Ms. Olga Borymchuck for translating this text from Russian.

As the events brought about the establishment of the autonomous *mutaṣarrifiyya* of Mount Lebanon, the Porte feared that areas around the *mutaṣarrifiyya* would begin to demand similar autonomy for themselves. The populations in these regions were envious of the special status of the Mountain's *mutaṣarrifiyya* and of the unique rights granted to its inhabitants. For example, the taxes of residents of the *mutaṣarrifiyya* were fixed and they were exempt from compulsory military service. This situation differed from that of the neighbouring areas, whose populations were subject to heavy and increasing taxation and whose circumstances were less advantageous. The Porte, which was concerned by such demands, believed that the establishment of the *vilâyet* under a strong governor would curtail the wish of the neighbouring areas for autonomy and put the Mountain itself under better control. The new governor of the province of Syria would supervise the autonomy of Mount Lebanon in order to avert incidents that might upset the ruling order and would deal with local opposition. The Porte believed that it could reinforce its rule over the local government in Syria, by wholly controlling it from one powerful centre.[35]

There were additional but more marginal reasons that led Fuʾād Pāshā and ʿAlī Pāshā to establish the province. The *Tanẓīmat* reforms, especially the idea of equality between Muslims and non-Muslims, aroused Sunni Muslim opposition, which included the Ottoman elite in Damascus and Istanbul. The latter widely viewed the decree of 1856 as a violation of the *Sharīʿa*. This group upheld the ideals of the Islamic state in which the *Sharīʿa* was held supreme and was the fundamental law. These views contrasted with the new political concept and policy of Fuʾād Pāshā and ʿAlī Pāshā, which was influenced by the West; it upheld the idea of the supremacy of the state in the sense of an all-powerful and corporate body with the privilege of making laws.[36]

ʿAlī and Fuʾād were concerned that the growing opposition in Damascus would undermine the spirit of reforms. Bearing in mind the involvement of Fuʾād in the *Vilâyet* Law, we can assume that he was probably the one who hoped that by establishing a Syrian

[35] US/NA Johnson to Seward, 25 May 1865; FO 195/866, Rogers to Elliot, 29 December 1867; FO 195/994, Eldridge to Rumbold, 29 April 1872.

[36] For further details on this opposition see: Abu-Manneh, *Studies on Islam*, pp. 128–129; Davison, *Reforms in the Ottoman Empire*, pp. 57–58, 65–68, 101–103; Maʿoz, *Ottoman Reform in Syria and Palestine*, pp. 200–209; Butrus Abu-Manneh, "The Sultan and the Bureaucracy: The Anti-Tanzimat Concepts of Grand Vizier Mahmud Nadim Pasha," *International Journal of Middle East Studies*, Vol. 22 (1990), pp. 257–274.

province he could restrain the aspirations of this Islamic opposition by creating a more secular solution in the spirit of the *Tanẓīmāt*. Since he did not want this province to be conceived as a Western entity, Fuʾād chose Damascus as the capital and the administrative centre of the new *vilâyet* rather than Beirut, which was identified with Western influence.

Another reason for doing so was the Ottoman fear of Egypt which bordered the Syrian region and which frequently threatened the central government in Istanbul. According to several British reports, the Ottomans apparently suspected that there was a tendency among certain circles in the Syrian region (even after the establishment of the *Vilâyet* of Syria) to try to attach it to Egypt. The Ottomans hoped that the establishment of the *vilâyet* would prevent these kinds of aspirations.[37] They also believed that by encouraging local patriotism and supporting the rising Syrian identity, they would reduce this desire to be annexed to Egypt, since the local population would have an alternative solution.

The Ottoman policies and the establishment of the province of Syria seemed to be successful in the years that followed. In fact, the *Vilâyet* of Syria endured for more than a quarter of a century. During those years, considerable tranquillity prevailed in the region, and Syrian patriotism gradually developed. The reduction of the *Vilâyet* of Syria began in the summer of 1872, when the *sancaks* of Jerusalem, Nablus, and Acre were detached from the *vilâyet* in order to create the province of Jerusalem.[38] This province survived for just two months. Thereafter, Nablus and Acre were restored to Syria, while the *sancak* of Jerusalem was made a separate entity. A second stage occurred in December 1887, with the separation of five *sancaks* from Syria (Latakia, Tripoli, Beirut, Acre, and Nablus) and the establishment of the Beirut province in March 1888. In territorial terms, Syria remained a province on the edge of the desert, from Hama in the north to Maʿān in the south.[39]

---

[37] US/NA, Johnson to Seward, 18 December 1865; FO 424/27B, Burton to Elliot, 19 July 1871.

[38] FO 195/ 994, Eldridge to Elliot, 31 July 1872.

[39] Abu-Manneh, "The Establishment and Dismantling of the Province of Syria," pp. 23–26.

The Vilâyet *of Syria and Local Patriotism: Big* Waṭan, *Small* Waṭan

As Benedict Anderson wrote, "one has to look at the ways in which administrative organisations create meaning."[40] Referring to South America, he noted that administrative units there foreshadowed new states. Over a period of time, these units developed a firmer reality due to geographic, political and economic factors. Eventually, they would come to be conceived as fatherlands.[41]

Such was the case regarding the province of Syria. Its establishment formalised links, notions and aspirations that were already in the process of crystallisation among the Beiruti middle stratum. Their connection with the Syrian territory that now had defined and formal borders was strengthened; gradually, these ties provided the basis for the construction of the homeland/*waṭan* for its people. In other words, an incipient Syrian entity was not only emerging as a product of the economic and political imagination of the Beiruti stratum, but taking shape as an administrative reality. Under these circumstances, it was easier for the stratum to mould its identity. During the following years, additional factors inside the Syrian *vilâyet* helped to strengthen this notion, and other factors undermined it.

In general, during the period between the 1860s and the end of the 1880s, and even later, Christian intellectuals promoted their Syrian *waṭaniyya* as part of the political framework in the Ottoman Empire. Also, from the second half of the 1860s and the beginning of the 1870s, the idea of a "federalised Empire" constituted an important topic of discourse among the Beiruti middle stratum.

By "federalised Empire" the Christian intellectuals meant having the same parameters as the American federal system, which they wanted to apply to the Ottoman Empire. This vision of theirs evolved under the influence of the *Vilâyet* Law and that of the American missionaries, in whose schools most of these intellectuals had studied. Evidently, Syrian intellectuals noticed a degree of similarity between the *Vilâyet* Law and the American federal system. The essence of both concepts was paradoxically "to decentralise in order to centralise." Obviously, the American model did not correspond exactly to the structure of the Ottoman Empire. In their vision, the intellectuals

---

[40] Anderson, *Imagined Communities*, p. 53.
[41] *Ibid.*, pp. 47–53.

saw the Ottoman Empire as a decentralised, federal, multi-national state capable of accommodating rapid modernisation and secularisation.

The periodical *al-Jinān* reflected part of this discourse through the publication of several articles on the subject. In them, Buṭrus and Salīm al-Bustānī called upon the Syrian population to embrace the ideas of the American system, since it was the best solution for the Ottoman Empire in general and for Syria in particular. America, they wrote, is progressing because it constitutes "one fatherland (*waṭan*) composed of many fatherlands."[42] Each *waṭan* (or *vilâyet*, as they frequently wrote) was connected with the central government, but had its own uniqueness and looked after its own interests.[43] Influenced by this model they wrote, "the Empire is our *waṭan*, but our country (*bilād*) is Syria."[44] In their imagination, they visualised the Ottoman Empire as a big *waṭan* (or *al-waṭan al-ʿāmm*) divided into small *waṭans* (*al-waṭan al-khāṣṣ*), one of these being the Syrian *waṭan*. As they did not see any contradiction between Ottomanism and Syrianism, they believed that under this complex unity both identities could exist side by side. In this way, the Christians could build their own local and cultural identity, while their political loyalty would remain Ottomanism. Consequently, whenever a *vali* appeared who was true to the policy of the *Tanẓīmāt* reforms or the idea of the "federalised Empire" the intellectuals welcomed and supported him.

Muḥammad Rāshid Pāshā (1866–1871)[45]

Most of the research examining the *Vilâyet* of Syria emphasises the important government of the Syrian *vali*, Midhat Pāshā. Another *vali*, less known, Rāshid Pāshā, was no less important: it was his government of the *Vilâyet* of Syria that established a model which would be used in later years by Midhat Pāshā. The latter ruled the *vilâyet* for less than twenty months, while Rāshid headed it for more than five years. In fact, he ruled for one of the longest periods in the

---

[42] Salīm al-Bustānī, "al-Ghad," *al-Jinān*, Vol. 1, No. 22, 1870, p. 675.

[43] Sālīm al-Bustānī, "al-Ams," *al-Jinān*, Vol. 1, No. 21, 1870, pp. 641–648.

[44] Hourani, *Arabic Thought in the Liberal Age*, p. 274.

[45] The name "Rāshid" appears here as it is written in Arabic sources. In Turkish sources it is written as Mehmet "Raşit" or "Raşid." Also, in sketching Rāshid's image and policy I shall focus mainly on the material that Beiruti intellectuals wrote and published during and after his governorship in order to show how they perceived it as contributing to their Syrian identity.

Vilâyet of Syria, and it was a fruitful one for the development of Syrian patriotism and identity.

Muḥammad Rāshid Pāshā (1824–1876) was born in Cairo, although his family originated in Macedonia. In 1844 he was sent by Muḥammad ʿAlī to study in Paris where he stayed for five years, later joining his father, who had meanwhile moved to Istanbul. On Rāshid's arrival there he joined the staff of interpreters for the Porte, since he was fluent in Turkish, French, and Arabic. He excelled at his work, was promoted and began to climb the bureaucratic ladder, appointed to several positions in Istanbul and the provinces. In 1853, for example, he was appointed governor of Gallipoli, a position he held until 1857. During the Crimean War in 1856, Gallipoli became a base for the soldiers of the Western Powers, diplomats and others. Due to this, daily conflicts erupted between the foreigners and local population. Rāshid succeeded in balancing this complicated situation to the satisfaction of both sides, and became known and distinguished for resolving disputes. He was also admired by the local inhabitants for his just policy with both the Muslim and the Christian populations.

In 1863 he was appointed as *vali* of Izmir. He remained in this position for 20 months. Izmir during this time had developed into an important economic and multi-cultural centre in the Empire. Like Beirut, its population included foreigners and non-Muslims who profited from its economic prosperity.[46] At this stage, Rāshid's connections with the West and the Christian population were constantly improving.[47] From Izmir, in 1866, Rāshid was sent to serve as the Governor General of the *Vilâyet* of Syria, where his background was very useful in his new position and in the years to come during his governorship of the province.

Almost all available sources make a special point of noting that two of his outstanding characteristics were his kindness and receptivity to the appeals of the poor and oppressed. He was considered

[46] See: Edhem Eldem, Daniel Goffman and Bruce Masters (eds.), *The Ottoman City between East and West, Aleppo, Izmir, and Istanbul* (Cambridge, 1999), pp. 125–134.

[47] w.n, "Tarjamat al-Marḥūm Rāshid Pāshā," *al-Jinān*, Vol. 7, No. 14, 1876, pp. 473–475; Ibrahim Alāttin Gövse, "Raşit Paşa Mehmet," *Türk Meşhurları Ansiklopedisi*, p. 315; Eugene L. Rogan, *Frontiers of the State in the Late Ottoman Empire* (London, 1999), pp. 48–52; Max L. Gross, *Ottoman Rule in the Province of Damascus 1860–1909.* Ph.D. Dissertation, Georgetown University, 1979, vol. 1, pp. 116–167; *Ḥadīqat al-Akhbār*, No. 493, 14 January 1868; Buṭrus al-Bustānī (ed.), "Rāshid Pāshā," *Dāʾirat al-Maʿārif*, Vol. 8, pp. 480–482; As far as I know, no comprehensive biography of Rāshid Pāshā exists in the Ottoman language.

by the Muslims to be faithful to Muslim interests, while both Christians and Jews considered him just. He was also a liberal, a partisan of the Ottoman reform movement, and a modernist, understanding well the reformist doctrine of the equality of all subjects.[48] ʿAlī Pāshā, the Grand Vizier, was his patron, and he was considered a strong *vali* who could carry out ʿAlī Pāshā's policies in a problematical region such as Syria. In addition to this, his close familiarity with the West, his preference for the European style of dress and entertainment, and his knowledge of the Arabic language, made him an attractive figure to the Beiruti middle stratum.

Hence, on entering the province, Rāshid was warmly welcomed especially by this stratum, but also by the rest of the population, who believed that such a "liberal man" could contribute to the *Vilâyet* of Syria and that "now Syria stood to win a better future."[49] Yet the condition of the province still caused concern. The effects of the events of 1860 were still evident. The Muslim population had been punished in the aftermath of the civil war and forced to pay many taxes, a circumstance that weakened their economic condition. On the other hand, the Christian population was fearful of Muslim agitation and the intellectuals, both Muslim and Christian, acted to prevent an escalation of tension between the two sides that might lead to regretful results.[50]

From this stage onward, it seems that two forces drove Rāshid's policy. The most important of them was his determination to implement the *Tanzīmāt* reforms in the *Vilâyet* of Syria; the second was his Western education and his espousal of liberal ideas. This policy translated itself into the creation of a centralised and better integrated Syrian entity, which would be responsible for its affairs but remain subordinate to the Porte. In line with this policy, Rāshid Pāshā sought to satisfy the immediate needs of the *vilâyet*. He seems to have been an extraordinarily able man who could accomplish what he wanted without alienating his potential enemies.[51] From the moment of his arrival he tried to pacify the Muslims and at the same time to help in improving the condition of the Christians. In order to calm the

---

[48] Gross, *Ottoman Rule in the Province of Damascus*, Vol. 1, pp. 121–123; US/NA, M. Johnson (consular clerk) to A. Johnson (Consul General), 31 December 1869.

[49] *Ḥadīqat al-Akhbār*, No. 368, 13 March 1865; No. 420, 21 August 1866.

[50] FO 195/1027, Green to Elliot, 12 December 1873.

[51] Gross, *Ottoman Rule in the Province of Damascus*, Vol. 1, p. 121.

Christian population's fears of a repeat of the events of the 1860s, he himself took up residence in the Christian quarter of Damascus.[52]

His tolerant attitude led him to employ Christians in senior government posts in the province. For example, Khalīl al-Khūrī, publisher of the weekly *Ḥadīqat al-Akhbār*, was the official responsible for connections with foreigners, and Nawfal Ni'matallāh Nawfal (1812–1887) of Tripoli served as Chief Customs Officer of the province.[53] But Rāshid did even more. He was the first Syrian *vali* who provided a forum for the activities of Christian intellectuals. During his regime and with his encouragement, privately published newspapers and magazines started to appear, especially in Beirut but also in Damascus. As Gross noted, "the flowering of the so-called Arabic literary revival in Syria which continued for the rest of the century, dates from the period of Rāshid Pāshā's governorship." With his permission, newspapers such as *al-Janna* and *al-Jinān* were published as well as Khalīl al-Khūrī's journal *Ḥadīqat al-Akhbār*, the latter so patriotic that it became the semi-official newspaper of the *vilâyet*. Moreover, an official government newspaper of the *vilâyet*, entitled *Sūriyya*, began to be published, and the first annual *Salname* (yearbook) of the province came out.[54]

The Christian press under Rāshid Pāshā could express itself more freely and ideas regarding the Syrian identity were often voiced. The periodical *al-Jinān* and also *Ḥadīqat al-Akhbār* enjoyed considerable freedom of expression. They dealt with issues such as governance, the condition of the subjects, the need for internal unity, concern for the good of the province and a wide variety of subjects regarding Syrian patriotism. In their articles, they addressed the *umma al-Sūriyya* (The Syrian nation), or referred to the territory of the province as *waṭan Sūrī* (Syrian homeland). *Al-Jinān* also praised the Porte for giving the Arabs the opportunity to restore the Arabic language.

Although the journal declared its loyalty to the Empire, it criticised it on a number of matters and denounced acts of bribery and swindling. Prior to Rāshid Pāshā's incumbency, such boldness would have been unthinkable.[55] In fact, the years 1870–1871 turn out to

---

[52] FO 195/806, E. G. R. to Lyons, 19 March 1867.

[53] Abu-Manneh, "The Establishment and Dismantling of the Province of Syria," p. 17.

[54] Gross, *Ottoman Rule in the Province of Damascus*, Vol. 1, p. 123.

[55] *Ibid.*

be the best period for tracing the aspirations of Syrian patriotism via the writings of local intellectuals.

During the end of Rāshid Pāshā's rule, as noted earlier, most of the ideas of the Christian-Arab intellectuals regarding the vision of a "federalised Empire" appeared in the local newspapers. Accordingly, it is reasonable to assume that Rāshid allowed and supported written expression of this vision. Even though no direct evidence for it exists, Rāshid's policies in the province reinforce this thesis.[56] In the long run, by allowing for this kind of activity, Rāshid helped translate the *Tanẓīmāt* reforms into actual practice and daily reality. All this was to be changed when in 1871 Rāshid Pāshā left the *vilâyet*. Strictures were placed on freedom of the press and ideas of Syrian patriotism became less evident or more hidden.

Rāshid seems also to have had an abiding interest in education and the field of literature, making efforts to cultivate literacy and the diffusion of learning. Under his auspices, a number of new government primary schools were established in various cities such as Damascus, Beirut and Jerusalem.

The condition of the *Vilâyet* of Syria also improved. Rāshid wished to create a more relaxed atmosphere in the *vilâyet*, and saw to it that the residents did not feel that they were paying taxes or serving in the army without getting something in return. In this way, he hoped to attract them to his side. Taking pains to establish just rule and to suppress corruption, he strove to win the support of the Muslim notables, whose status was shaken after the events of 1860. Rāshid attended to the security of the *vilâyet*'s inhabitants and took serious steps towards settling the Bedouin.[57] In the economic sphere, he encouraged investment of private capital in land and ensured that the Land Law of 1858 was properly implemented.

Evidently, changes that Rāshid made in the administration of the *vilâyet* drew the inhabitants one step closer towards perceiving the province as one entity. Rāshid tried to construct a single system for the entire *vilâyet*. The *Vilâyet* Law, among other things, called for the establishment of an elected general council (*al-Majlis al-ʿUmūmī*) for each Ottoman *vilâyet*. Four deputies, two Muslims and two non-Muslims, were to be elected in each *mutaṣarrifiyya* as delegates to this

[56] For further details, see: Abu-Manneh, "The Christians between Ottomanism and Syrian Nationalism," pp. 297, 303 (footnote 92).

[57] US/NA, M. Johnson to Fish, 29 August 1870.

council, which was to meet once a year for a period not to exceed forty days.

In 1867, Rāshid Pāshā established a local *Majlis ʿUmūmī* which was planned to convene every year in Beirut.[58] This appears to be the first time that this aspect of the *Vilâyet* Law was implemented in this province, and no evidence has come to hand that a session of the general council was ever held again during the rest of the century.[59] This event, therefore, was unique, a fact that is quite surprising since this session of the council appears to have been a great success.[60]

Al-Majlis al-ʿUmūmī was given the task of electing its members from the council of every *sancak* in the *vilâyet*, and then of sending them to the centre of the *vilâyet* to meet and deliberate. It was chaired by the *vali* (meaning Rāshid Pāshā) and discussed public issues connected with the various parts of the *vilâyet* and its development. The council's resolutions were submitted to the *vali*, who had to inform the government in Istanbul of his conclusions.

The Christian Arabs well understood the significance of this event for Syria. Khalīl al-Khūrī wrote an article in his journal devoted entirely to this council, noting that Rāshid's purpose in creating it was to improve the situation of the *Vilâyet* of Syria and its population. He pointed out that emissaries had been sent to the various *sancak*s with the aim of informing them that they must send two Muslim and two non-Muslim delegates from the *sancak* council to Beirut,[61] illustrating the policy of Christian and Muslim equality adopted by Rāshid.

The council focused on four topics: road construction and maintenance; erection and maintenance of public buildings; police; and measures relating to agriculture and commerce. Another decision was taken as well—to establish a literary society, *al-Jamʿiyya al-Sūriyya al-ʿIlmiyya* (The Syrian Scientific Society), which turned out to be an important gathering for the middle stratum in advancing Syrian patriotism. Evidently, Rāshid took the discussions of the council seriously, and tried to implement them under his governorship.

---

58 FO 78/1978, Beirut, Rogers to Elliot, No. 77, 21 December 1867.

59 Gross, *Ottoman Rule in the Province of Damascus*, p. 135.

60 Gross expanded on this subject. See: Gross, *Ottoman Rule in the Province of Damascus*, Vol. 1, pp. 135–141.

61 *Ḥadīqat al-Akhbār*, No. 485, 19 November 1867.

Naturally, this policy increased the admiration of the Christian-Arab intellectuals for Rāshid. This admiration can be traced in the province's local newspapers. The intellectuals praised Rāshid for doing everything he could to advance the condition of the Syrian population in general and of themselves in particular. They wrote about his call to promote the development of learning without differentiating between religious groups and affiliations.[62] The provincial newspaper *Ḥadīqat al-Akhbār* wrote that he acted "for the homeland and the people," and that his governorship is proving to them that it was possible to live in brotherhood.[63] Salīm al-Bustānī emphasised the admiration of the inhabitants to Rāshid Pāshā in one of his articles on the *Vilâyet* of Syria.[64] Western officials also took note of his policies and praised them. Johnson, the American Consul General in Syria, described Rāshid as "one of the enlightened people and an honest man." He also noted that Rāshid was known in Istanbul as "a scholar of great learning."[65]

In 1871, following the death of his patron ʿAlī Pāshā, Rāshid lost his position in Syria.[66] When he left the *vilâyet*, the British Consul wrote that "No governor has departed Syria when the population there across all its strata regretted it, as occurred in his case."[67] The writing of the local population also reflects these sentiments. Indeed, Rāshid Pāshā's goals in working for equality and unity among the people, for pacifying the Muslim population, for administrative unification of the region, and for the betterment of the population and the *vilâyet*, created a sound foundation for the development of Syrian identity.

He left the treasury free of debts. As a result, government officials and army personnel became accustomed to being paid on time. Crime had gradually reduced in the province and for the first time

---

[62] See: Salīm al-Bustānī, "Wilāyat Sūriyya," *al-Jinān*, Vol. 1, No. 1, 1870, p. 1; Salīm al-Bustānī, "al-Difāʿ," *al-Jinān*, Vol. 1, No. 16, 1870, pp. 245–247, 537–539.

[63] *Ḥadīqat al-Akhbār*, No. 456, 30 April 1867.

[64] Sālim al-Bustānī, "Wilāyat Sūriyya," *al-Jinān*, Vol. 1, No. 1, 1870, p. 1; *al-Jinān*, Vol. 2, No. 7, 1871, pp. 245–247; No. 16, 1871, pp. 537–539.

[65] US/NA, M. Johnson to A. Johnson, 31 December 1869.

[66] FO 78/2259, Damascus, Burton to Elliot, No. 27, 19 July 1871; Jago to Elliot, No. 33, 28 September 1871. After Rāshid's governorship in Syria, he was unemployed for 10 months. Then he served consecutively as the governor of Herzegovina, Yenipazr and Bosnia in the Balkans until early 1873. He was then called to Istanbul and appointed as Minister of Public Works. Three years later he was appointed as Foreign Minister in the government that deposed Sultan Abdül Aziz. He was assassinated before the constitution came into existence.

[67] FO 195/976, Eldridge to Earl Granville, 5 October 1871.

in decades, the inhabitants of the province of Syria lived in an atmosphere of general peace and security. Christians and Jews especially regretted Rāshid's departure, as under his administration they had been treated equally.

In fact, when Rāshid left, the conditions of Ottoman rule in the Syrian province were as good as they would ever be during the rest of the century.[68] Jago, the American Consul in Damascus at that time, wrote that in contrast to him, "his successors (especially, between 1872 and 1877), some of whom were honest and capable but lacked power, left the country as they found it."[69]

Tanẓīmāt *Regressions*

The Vilâyet *of Syria between 1871–1878*

Between Rāshid's departure and Midhat's arrival, the Christian middle stratum continued to construct its identity as a Syrian one, but indirectly, and it kept a low profile. During this time the concept of big *waṭan*/small *waṭan* was pushed aside. A chain of events had led to this state of affairs.

At the beginning of the 1870s, Syrian *vali*s were appointed, whose policy hindered the existence of Syrian patriotism. Such were the policies of Ṣubḥī and Khālid (Hālit) Pāshā, who ruled the province in the early 1870s.

Ṣubḥī Pāshā, like Rāshid, had been raised in Egypt under Muḥammad ʿAlī and knew the Arabic language. During his governorship he reversed some of Rāshid's policies and demonstrated favouritism toward Muslims in making appointments. Unlike Rāshid Pāshā, he leaned heavily on the opinion of the *ʿulamā*ʾ and the traditional notables of the province.[70] As he wished to win the support of the Muslim population, he resolved to abolish the array of benefits granted by foreigners to local people; he also dismissed many Christians from administrative positions. Nevertheless, as a Muslim, he displayed none of the religious fanaticism that the Christian population or the Europeans so feared.[71]

---

[68] FO 78/2228, Beirut, Eldridge to Rumbold, No. 32, 29 April 1872.

[69] FO 195/1263, Jago to Malet, 14 April 1879.

[70] FO 78/2282, Beirut, Green to Granville, No. 33, 15 December 1873, Enclosure, Ottoman Conservatism in Syria, by Jago.

[71] Gross, *Ottoman Rule in the Province of Damascus*, Vol. 1, pp. 181–182; FO 78/2191,

Khālid Pāshā, who was not a man of the reform school, went even further. He announced that he was a pious Muslim, and during his rule the condition of the Christians grew worse. His advisors were shaykhs and *ʿulamāʾ*, whom he also appointed as chief officers of his government. He embarked on a policy in the *vilâyet* in accordance with the *Sharīʿa* or Islamic law, ignoring the legislation of the *Tanẓīmāt* as much as possible.[72] Under these circumstances, it was difficult for the Beiruti Christian middle stratum to continue developing its identity.

At this stage I would like to emphasise a few points regarding the Muslim movement of 1877, which began its activity a short time before Midhat's arrival. Concurrently, the war with Russia caused some deterioration in the situation within the Syrian province that found expression in both the Muslim and Christian populations.[73] Under such circumstances, some of the Muslims who were conscripted directed some of their rage towards the Christians, who could pay the *badal* to avoid conscription. The Muslims could also pay it but at a higher price.[74] Once again, the voices of those who had previously opposed the rights granted to the non-Muslims began to be heard. Some Christians were dismissed from government posts, and an attempt was made to reduce the influence of the consular representatives. Nevertheless, in most cases, Muslim-Christian relations remained cordial during the war, both in Beirut and in Damascus, and practically no evidence of religious tension was manifest. "The new class of Syrian notables"[75] as Gross called it, was responsible for this calm; both Christians and Muslims made an effort to ensure that nothing similar to the events of 1860 would occur again.

However, the general situation in the *vilâyet* was so grim that it created a general and widespread feeling of dissatisfaction with the Ottoman government among wide strata of the population of Syria. The greatest disaffection was among the Muslim clerics and within

---

Damascus, Jago to Elliot, No. 39, 6 December 1871; FO 78/2228, Damascus, Green to Rumbold, No. 4, 9 February 1872; FO 195/1027, Green to Elliot, 12 December 1873; FO 195/976, Jago to Elliot, 6 November 1871.

[72] FO 195/1027, Green to Granville, 17 September 1873.

[73] For some of the Muslim critiques of the Porte's policy in Syria, see: *Thamarāt al-Funūn*, No. 283, 31 May 1880; *Thamarāt al-Funūn*, No. 233, 16 June 1879.

[74] The Porte conscripted 115,000 soldiers from the Syrian province, including the Aleppo province. FO 195/1201, Jago to Earl Derby, State of Feelings in Damascus, 27 March 1878; FO 195/1153, Jago to Elliot, 21 January 1877.

[75] Gross, *Ottoman Rule in the Province of Damascus*, Vol. 1, p. 246.

the Muslim populace itself, whose masses were called upon to enlist in the war against Russia and to pay taxes. These feelings were not new, but the events of the past year had intensified them to the point that some of the population was beginning to resist the central government openly, and anti-Ottoman feelings began to be apparent.

As the research of Saliba and Steppat has shown,[76] there was indeed a movement in 1877 among some of the Muslim leading notables in Damascus, aimed at securing Syrian "independence." This was mainly due to the growing fear among these notables as to what might happen if a foreign Power would show ambitions for Syria. After a series of meetings in Damascus, it was agreed that the assembled notables would work for the establishment of an independent Syrian state, and the exiled Amīr, ʿAbd al-Qādir al-Jazāʾirī, was approached to serve as ruler of the new state. However, the participants decided that if Syria remained under Ottoman rule, they would aim at achieving autonomous status similar to that of Egypt or some Balkan countries. ʿAbd al-Qādir agreed in principle with the program, but requested that the decision be postponed until it was clear how the Ottoman Empire would emerge after the war. In case the Empire did collapse, they would seek an independent Syrian state.

Although this is not the place to analyse the activities of this Muslim movement, what is interesting is that some of the Muslim notables who participated in it in Damascus, such as Aḥmad al-Ṣulḥ, the leader of the movement, and Ḥusayn Bayhum, one of its members, belonged to families from the Beiruti middle stratum and had economic and cultural connections with Christians belonging to it as well.[77] For example, Buṭrus al-Bustānī and some members of the Bayhum family were close and were both active in the same cultural societies in Beirut. The latter also held a business partnership with the Bustrus family—leading Christian Beiruti merchants. Thus, when this movement brought forward ideas regarding a Syrian entity, certain Muslim personages had already been exposed to this kind of concept, since they had participated in cultural societies in Beirut that had called for similar ideas. Nevertheless, this time, they chose to do so in the framework of Muslim society.

---

[76] Saliba, *Wilayet Suriyya*, pp. 82–86; Fritz Steppat, "Eine Bewegung unter den Notabeln Syriens, 1877–1878," *Zeitschrift der Deutschen Morgenländischen Gesellschaft*, Sup. 1 (1968), pp. 631–649; see also, ʿĀdil al-Ṣulḥ, *Suṭūr min al-Risāla; Tārīkh Ḥaraka Istiqlāliyya Qāmat fī al-Mashriq al-ʿArabī Sanat 1877* (Beirut, 1966), pp. 92–94.

[77] Gross, *Ottoman Rule in the Province of Damascus*, Vol. 1, pp. 247–248.

More than that, members of the 'Abd al-Qādir circle were joined by a larger group of Damascus men of religion who became convinced of the necessity to modernise their country along European lines. From among this circle began to appear the first formulations of a rationalist reform of the traditional disciplines.[78]

Apparently, within this atmosphere, Christian-Arab intellectuals in the province hoped to find a common language with the Muslim population. At its core and in theory, Syrian identity was intended to apply also to the Muslim population, but in reality, since it was a secular identity, only a few Muslims, mainly from Beirut, took part in its development. At this time, the Christians might have understood that this was perhaps the best moment to raise notions of Syrian identity among Muslims and Christians, since they were experiencing similar difficulties. They sensed that the hour was ripe; the Muslims in the *vilâyet* despaired of Ottoman rule which now placed a heavy burden on them, drafting many into the army because of the Russian war. This, along with the heavy drought, caused an economic crisis. Christian intellectuals now hoped that together with the Muslims they could act to influence the Porte and achieve a better future for Syrian society.[79] Such was the atmosphere when Midhat arrived to govern the province.

Midhat Pāshā (1878–1880)

A great deal of research has been conducted on the government of Midhat Pāshā in Syria.[80] I will focus on several aspects of Midhat's policies that contributed to the development of Syrian patriotism. Even though Midhat was unsuccessful in implementing his goals in Syria, his governorship constituted the second important phase in which Syrian patriotism flourished among the Christian stratum, reaching yet another peak in its development.

---

[78] Weismann, *Taste of Modernity*, pp. 194–195.

[79] FO 195/1369, Dickson to Dufferin, 5 October 1881; FO 195/1369, Eldridge to Dufferin, 19 December 1881.

[80] Najib E. Saliba, "The Achievements of Midhat Pāshā as Governor of the Province of Syria, 1788–1880," *International Journal of Middle East Studies*, Vol. 9 (1978), pp. 307–323; Gross, *Ottoman Rule in the Province of Damascus*, Vol. 1, pp. 255–316; Shimon Shamir, "Midhat Pasha and the Anti-Turkish Agitation in Syria," *Middle Eastern Studies*, Vol. 10 (1974), pp. 115–141; Butrus Abu-Manneh, "The Genesis of Midhat Pasha's Governorship in Syria 1878–1880," in Thomas Philipp and Birgit Schaebler (eds.), *The Syrian Land—Process of Integration and Fragmentation in Bilad al-Sham from the 18th to the 20th Century* (Stuttgart, 1998), pp. 251–267.

In 1878, when Midhat was appointed governor of the *Vilâyet* of Syria, he had already established a reputation as a leading reformer who had been appointed to several important posts in the Empire. Midhat (1822–1884) was born in Istanbul. In his childhood he received religious schooling, but during the course of his lifetime he acquired a Western education. In 1862, on reaching the age of forty, he served as governor of the Danube province and in 1869 he was appointed governor of the Baghdad province. In these positions, he proved himself to be a skilled administrator. In 1872, he assumed the office of Grand Vizier under the Sultan Abdül Aziz. He is best known for being responsible for the promulgation of the Ottoman constitution in 1876. Later, the constitution was suspended and Midhat was exiled by the new Sultan, Abdül Hamid II, who feared his growing power.[81]

In 1878, Midhat was recalled from exile to govern Syria. This step gave the impression that Sultan Abdül Hamid II might soon reverse his policy and restore both Midhat and the constitution to imperial favour. Midhat was familiar with the region for over 30 years. In the past, he had served as the chief clerk of the Damascus province. In 1850, he was sent to the region again on a brief mission. The Syrian inhabitants looked forward joyfully to the arrival of this experienced reformer. As in the case of Rāshid, they believed that his appointment heralded a new era for Syria, one of good government, prosperity, and equality. The foreign consuls were likewise pleased with this appointment, and thought that it would effect an improvement in the administration of the country, and that his governorship would be beneficial for Syria.[82]

From the beginning, Midhat's policy was based on the same vision as that of Rāshid: the demand for decentralisation of the Empire. It is commonly known that in the 1870s Midhat Pāshā supported "a plan" for a "federalised Empire." His model was Germany, and the plan's essential aim was to bind the Rumanian principalities and Serbia to the Ottoman Empire in the same way as Bavaria and Württemberg were bound to the newly created German Empire.[83]

[81] For further details on Midhat, see: Midhat A. Haydar, *The Life of Midhat Pasha* (London, 1903); Davison, *Reforms in the Ottoman Empire*, pp. 136–171; Edwin Pears, *The Life of Abdul Hamid* (London, 1917), pp. 34–37; Shaw and Shaw, *History of the Ottoman Empire*, Vol. 2, pp. 66–69.

[82] FO 195/1263, Jago to Malet, Damascus, 14 April 1879; FO 195/1202, Jackson to Layard, 25 November 1878; FO 195/1202, Jackson to Layard, 8 December 1878.

[83] Davison, *Reforms in the Ottoman Empire*, pp. 290–291.

The idea of decentralisation was also repeated in article 108 of the constitution of 1876, of which Midhat had been the main architect.[84] His Syrian policies were based on this vision as well. Midhat drew up an elaborate programme of reforms, based on the powers granted to the governor according to the terms of the *Vilâyet* Law, of which he was also one of the architects. The programme stressed two principles: Ottomanism and decentralisation. Both were not acceptable by the Sultan. This was the main reason that Midhat Pāshā's plans (unlike those of Rāshid Pāshā who enjoyed the support of ʿAlī Pāshā) could not always be put into practice.

Midhat's programme reveals his vision regarding Syria. Since he was sensitive to the needs of the province, he attempted to introduce reforms that would answer these needs. The programme aimed at transforming the Syrian *vilâyet* into a strong entity (small *waṭan*) that could look after its own requirements but still remain subordinate to the Porte. Once again, the idea of big *waṭan*/small *waṭan* had returned.

Midhat requested a broad range of powers and tried to implement the policy of decentralisation in the province. For example, in economic aspects, he strove to safeguard local interests in Syria by the development of local projects and resources, believing that the *Vilâyet* of Syria could thus respond to the needs of the local economy. He attempted to retain some of the monies that were transferred to the Porte and use them within the *vilâyet*'s borders for the benefit of its population.[85] Another of his requests was to have command over the local army. The Sultan unsurprisingly refused, since this would lead to the weakening of Istanbul's direct authority over Syria.

In order to improve the situation of the *Vilâyet* of Syria and to build a strong and stable administrative system, Midhat concentrated on several areas of reform. He succeeded in implementing those for which he received support from Istanbul, although he was not prevented from acting upon others. He managed to improve public safety.[86] He also succeeded in raising the level of responsibility in public offices by engaging qualified people, and managed to improve communications inside the *vilâyet*. The telegraph system that had

---

[84] Abu-Manneh, "The Genesis of Midhat Pasha," p. 260.

[85] *Thamarāt al-Funūn*, No. 218, 3 March 1879.

[86] FO 195/1306, Jago to Layard, 31 May 1880; FO 195/1262, Jackson to Malet, 15 March 1879.

already been developed was extended, carriage roads were built and the number of postal facilities doubled.[87]

Midhat believed, as Rāshid had, in equality between Muslims and Christians. Hence, during his term of office, the Christian population enjoyed favourable treatment. He further encouraged the Arab population to participate in the administration and stressed that in Syria this had to be conducted "in keeping with the nature and customs of the inhabitants."[88] With regard to the Muslim population, he encouraged education. As most of the schools in Syria were funded by private sources, such as missionaries, Midhat prodded wealthy notables to contribute money to build and maintain schools that were aimed at serving local as well as Ottoman interests.[89]

He also called for the reform of the civil administration and even requested the restoration of the office of *mutaṣarrif* of the Damascus *sancak* so that the *vali* might attend to the affairs of the *vilâyet* as a whole and free himself from the need to administer those of the *sancak*. Yet, he did not receive the Sultan's approval in this respect.[90]

Eventually, due to Midhat's repeated requests for additional powers as well as the appearance of revolutionary placards in Beirut in June 1880, the Sultan, Abdül Hamid II ended Midhat's governorship. In 1880, Midhat was transferred from his position as *vali* of Syria and was made governor of Izmir. The British Consul wrote that one of the reasons for the termination of Midhat's tenure was his desire to give "self-government" to the people of the *vilâyet* when they were not yet ready for it."[91] However, this interpretation was wrong. Midhat was loyal to the Porte, and he was also loyal to his vision of a "federalised Empire." Still, he had clearly acted within the framework of the Empire and for its sake, and did not try to detach the *vilâyet* from it. His plans to establish a strong administration in the province were carried out in accordance with the principles

[87] For more details on the new roads, see: FO 78/2989, Tripoli, Blance to Eldridge, No. 5, 1 September 1879; FO 78/2989, Latakia, Vitali to Eldridge, 30 August 1879.

[88] FO 78/3130, Dickson, Beirut, 21 June 1880; US/NA, Eldridge to Payson, 15 October 1880.

[89] FO 78/2985, Damascus, Jago to Malet, No. 10, 2 March 1879.

[90] Muḥammad Kurd 'Ali, *Khiṭaṭ al-Shām*, Vol. 5, p. 189; Shimon Shamir, "The Modernization of Syria—Problems and Solutions in the Early Period of Abdul Hamid" in William R. Polk and Richard L. Chambers (eds.), *Beginnings of Modernization in the Middle East* (Chicago, 1966), pp. 351–381.

[91] FO 195/1306, Jago to Goschen, 16 August 1880.

of the *Tanẓīmāt* reforms and not as a means to create an independent Syria.

Midhat's policy was probably influenced by the success of Rāshid Pāshā, and he tried to follow in the latter's footsteps. Like Rāshid, he wished to obtain broad authority so as to implement necessary reforms as he saw them. Most of Midhat's projects were not put into practice but his period, as in the case of Rāshid, was important for its attempt to give the *Vilâyet* of Syria the form of a region or entity headed by a strong administrator who was able to manage its affairs efficiently. These ideas were obviously absorbed by the Beiruti middle stratum, since they corresponded to their own aspirations, and also, as we shall see shortly, by other sectors of the population.

At this juncture, a few points should be made regarding the *Vilâyet* of Syria until the period of Midhat Pāshā and beyond it. Relying on the spirit of the words of Anderson quoted earlier, it is evident that the establishment of the *Vilâyet* of Syria and its daily existence over time constituted milestones in the popular imagination and an important phase in the gradual construction of Syrian localism. This was true not only for the Christians but also in part within Muslim and Ottoman minds. *Vali*s such as Rāshid and Midhat contributed toward this development.

Also, over the years, the strong centralist government within the *vilâyet*, and its subordination to one centre (Damascus), strengthened the connection between the various areas of the province (which is an important stage in the formation of any local identity).[92] This situation contrasted to that of the past, when the Damascus and Sidon provinces had been placed under one overall ruler, but each of them had been administered separately and had its own capital.

In 1865, with the establishment of the *Vilâyet* of Syria, the two provinces were joined administratively for the first time (except for the union during Ibrāhīm Pāshā's reign). These boundaries of the *vilâyet* were identical with those that would later be called "Greater Syria" (without the *vilâyet* of Aleppo in the north, and after 1872, without the *sancak* of Jerusalem). Since the *vali* resided at the centre of the *vilâyet*, namely in Damascus, a single Syrian province was created, whose centre was this city. The name of the province was also an important innovation for the inhabitants of the area, who could

[92] FO 195/1202, Jago to Layard, 22 December 1878.

now identify with a particular name and with a defined region called "Syria," not merely with part of the region, as they had in the past.

Over the years, this administrative entity produced journals and founded societies to discuss its own economic, social and cultural issues.[93] Among the Beiruti middle stratum, this semantic and formal change from *Bilād al-Shām* to Syria, together with the establishment of the *vilâyet*, marked a turning point in their self-identity. Both innovations helped to further define a new affinity and territory and a new selective past. Of course, people retained their traditional identities and their self-images. What changed over the course of time was that a new parameter of the self-image was added to that of the traditional multiple identities, i.e. a Syrian identity. Finally, the impact of these ongoing changes under the *Tanẓīmāt* would bring out the appearance of "political local patriotism" embracing both Muslims and Christians, towards the end of Midhat's governorship.

Muslim-Christian Interrelationships: The Beiruti Secret Society—Arab Nationalism or Syrian Localism?

One of the topics which were examined in regard to the governorship of Midhat Pāshā was "The Beiruti Secret Society." Most research regarding this society focuses primarily on two issues: whether or not Midhat Pāshā was behind it, and whether or not the revolutionary placards, made by this society that appeared in Beirut, marked the beginning of the political movement of Arab nationalism.

The first issue, Midhat's loyalty to the Porte and the *Tanẓīmāt* reforms, has already been discussed in the previous section of this chapter. This section will offer a different interpretation of the second issue, concerning the contents of the placards and their meaning. The analysis will show that the activities of the Beiruti society did not mark the beginning of the Arab National Movement as George Antonius[94] stated, but actually constituted the end of a long, continuous

[93] After the establishment of the *Vilâyet* of Syria, in Muslim writings (in journals and societies) the region is usually termed "*Bilād al-Shām*," but gradually the terms "Syria" and "Syrians" appear more frequently.

[94] George Antonius, *The Arab Awakening: The Story of the Arab National Movement* (New York, 1965).

process that had started at the beginning of the nineteenth century and reached its zenith toward the end of Midhat's governorship—the construction of a Syrian patriotic identity.

Even though the importance of this society as a major movement was somewhat exaggerated (as far as we know it included twenty-two participants), this historical study allows us a glance into the aspirations and states of mind of some of the local intellectuals of the time. Some members of the society were Christians, e.g. Ibrāhīm al-Yāzijī, while others were Muslims. Most of the participants were also students of the Syrian Protestant College in Beirut that was established by American missionaries, such as Fāris Nimr, a society member who also gave his testimony to Antonius regarding this issue.

The members chose to distribute their ideas by posting anonymous placards written in Arabic in the streets, mainly in Beirut but also in Tripoli and Sidon. In summarising some of the placards' contents, Antonius wrote that they called for "violent denunciations of the evils of Turkish rule, and exhorted the Arab population to rise in rebellion and overthrow it."[95] Relying mainly on one of the placards, which was published on 31 December 1880,[96] Antonius concluded that the roots of the Arab National Movement dated back to the nineteenth century. Focusing mainly on the second and fourth points,[97] he believed that this placard marked a new conception, namely, that of a politically independent state resting on a truly national foundation.[98] He saw this programme as "the first recorded statement of an Arab political programme."[99]

However, a close examination of this placard, while taking into account the development of the Beiruti middle stratum, especially during the *Tanẓīmāt* reforms, can lead to a different conclusion—that it reveals an advanced phase of the development of Syrian patriotism, a process that had already begun at the start of the nineteenth century. Albert Hourani was the first to note that the only important conclusion about this society is that "it teaches us about

---

[95] *Ibid.*, p. 80.

[96] The placard can be found in the Public Record Office (PRO) in London. See: FO 195/1368, Dickson to Goschen, 1880.

[97] This placard in the PRO includes three, and not four points, as Antonius describes. In fact, Antonius divided the third point into two. Nevertheless, in analysing the placards I will follow Antonius and refer to it as having four points.

[98] Antonius, *The Arab Awakening*, p. 86.

[99] *Ibid.*, pp. 81, 85.

the political awakening of the Christians."[100] Moreover, beyond its ideological platform, the placard shows the more obvious desire of its authors to improve daily life and satisfy the needs of the local population.

Taking into consideration the fact that in most ideological platforms, the demands are written in the order of their importance, the subject of primary importance on the agenda of the society was the call for "*Istiqlāl nashtarik bihi*[101] *maʿa Ikhwatinā al-Lubnāniyyīn biḥaythu taḍummunā jamīʿanā al-ṣawāliḥ al-waṭaniyya.*" Antonius summarised it as "Granting independence to Syria in union with Lebanon."[102] Yet, the meaning of the word *istiqlāl* here should not be translated as independence but as autonomy.[103] Thus the translation should be that "Autonomy, which we [the Syrian people] will share [i.e. a similar status] with our Lebanese brethren so that the patriotic interests will join us together." The key words in this sentence are *nashtarik bihi*, meaning that the authors of the placard aspired to the same status as that of Mount Lebanon, which of course was not independent of the Porte but did have an autonomous administration.

The second point was translated by Antonius as "recognition of Arabic as an official language of the country,"[104] i.e. Syria. Indeed, from the second half of the nineteenth century there was an Arabic revival among the Beiruti middle stratum. As this stratum strove to revive the knowledge of Arabic and Arab culture as the heritage of their new identity, it was natural for them to ask the Porte to recognise Arabic as the formal language of the country. However, at this time the Porte was actively imposing use of the Turkish language on local administrators. As a result, a gap occurred between the local population who spoke Arabic and the bureaucrats of local institutions

---

[100] Hourani, *Arabic Thought in the Liberal Age*, p. 274.

[101] Emphasis was added by me.

[102] Antonius, *The Arab Awakening*, p. 84.

[103] In the nineteenth century the word "*istiqlāl*" meant "autonomy" and not "independence," as this term is translated today. For example, in the *Salname* of Jerusalem, the Porte used the word "*istiqlāl*" when it was obvious that this *sancak* had a special status under the Porte. Only in the twentieth century did the term "*istiqlāl*," with the additional term "*tāmm*" (complete), come to mean independence. Butrus Abu-Manneh, "The Rise of The *Sanjaq* of Jerusalem in the Late 19th Century," in Gabriel Ben-Dor (ed.), *The Palestinians and the Middle East Conflict* (Tel-Aviv, 1979), p. 30, footnote 23; Abdul Latif Tibawi, *A Modern History of Syria including Lebanon and Palestine* (London, 1969), p. 165.

[104] Antonius, *The Arab Awakening*, p. 84.

who spoke Turkish.[105] The first two points of the placard can therefore be summarised as a call for Syrian autonomy with Arab culture at its core.

The third and fourth points reflected the distress caused by Abdül Hamid II's regime at that time. The third point called for abolishing censorship and for lifting the restrictions on freedom of speech and information that was so widely enforced under Abdül Hamid II. The fourth point was *"An tanḥaṣir ʿasākirunā fī khidmat al-waṭan wa-tatakhallaṣ min ʿubūdiyyat ruʾūs al-Atrāk."* This was translated by Antonius as "Employment of locally-recruited units for local military service only."[106] Yet this demand, as Tibawi also suggested,[107] was that "the service of our soldiers shall be confined to the homeland [in times of peace] and they be saved from servitude to the Turkish officers."

In fact, Muslim men from the region of Syria were sent (as in other parts of the Empire) under obligatory conscription both in times of peace and war to serve outside their region. The demands of the placard came after the war with Russia, when conscription in the Syrian region was at its highest; taxes had been raised and the cultivation of lands was adversely affected. The Christian and Muslim populations suffered great economic hardship: the resources of the region were exhausted and people of the *vilâyet* were reduced to starvation.[108] In consequence, the writers of this placard demanded that in times of peace the soldiers serve within Syria and only in times of war should they serve wherever necessary.

Finally, the placard refers specifically to the people of Syria or to the people of the homeland (*Yā abnāʾ Sūriyā/Yā abnāʾ al-waṭan*) and not to the Arab people. It demanded autonomy for the Syrian region without calling for autonomy of the other Arab provinces. The request to make the Arabic language the official language of the country came for cultural and practical purposes rather than for political or national reasons. Hence, what may be concluded from these points

[105] It seems that the problem had been known in the region for a long time. For example, after the events of 1860 it was already discussed with regard to Mount Lebanon. FO 78/1626, Dufferin to Bulwer, 3 November 1860.

[106] Antonius, *The Arab Awakening*, p. 84.

[107] Tibawi, *A Modern History of Syria*, p. 166.

[108] FO 195/113, Eldridge to Elliot, 11 December 1876; FO 195/1113, Dickson to Elliot, 5 August 1876; FO 195/1113, Jago to Elliot, 21 November 1876; FO 195/1201, Jago to Derby, 27 March 1878; FO 195/1202, Jago to Derby, 27 March 1878.

is that the placard reveals the needs of the population, as well as their desire to have a Syrian autonomous entity similar to that enjoyed by Mount Lebanon. This supposition supports the analysis of the historian Zeine Zeine that Arab nationalism as a political ideology did not develop until the beginning of the twentieth century and that it evolved in response to the rise of Turkish nationalism.[109]

Antonius' interpretation, as is known, was motivated by political and ideological considerations. He attempted to show that the desire for an Arab nationalist awakening had already existed in the nineteenth century. He received encouragement for his germ of an idea after his visit to London in 1934, when he sensed that demand would be great for a book on the subject, and that the sooner such a book was published the better.[110]

Thus, even though Midhat was unsuccessful in realising his vision regarding a Syrian entity, his period constitutes the peak of the process in which local patriotism was created among sections of the local population. His policy and vision probably helped to reinforce such thoughts among the local intellectuals and even to transform them into a political platform.

As noted above, this was a difficult time for the Syrian population, both Muslim and Christian. More importantly, as reflected by membership in the societies, the ideas about Syrian autonomy were shared not only by the Christian middle stratum but by many Muslims from this stratum. As Abu-Manneh observed, "This collaboration in political agitation between Christians and Muslims was a new and a striking phenomenon in the nineteenth century."[111]

From 1875 onward, a growing number of cultural activities were organised by Muslim notables for the sake of the Syrian population and the Syrian province and Muslim-Christian cultural relationships flourished. In 1875, when the Muslim newspaper *Thamarāt al-Funūn* was established, Christians from families such as Thābit and Bīṭār worked on its staff side by side with educated Muslims. ʿAbd al-Qādir al-Qabbānī, who established the newspaper, studied in al-Bustānī's school, *al-Madrasa al-Waṭaniyya* (the Patriotic/National School),

[109] Zeine N. Zeine, *The Emergence of Arab Nationalism, With a Background Study of Arab-Turkish Relations in the Near East* (New York, 1973), pp. 47–46, 60.
[110] SAC (St. Antony's College), Oxford, Antonius Papers, Antonius to Rogers (6 April 1934).
[111] Abu-Manneh, "The Genesis of Midhat Pasha," p. 266.

one of the aims of which was the promotion of Syrian patriotism. Other Muslim notables, such as Yūsuf al-Asīr, who held the position of *qāḍī* in Syria, or Ibrāhīm al-Aḥdab, who belonged to one of the prominent Muslim families in Beirut, were in close relationships with Christians from the Beiruti middle stratum. This circle of notables established the Muslim society *al-Maqāṣid al-Khayriyya*,[112] which tried to promote education among the Muslim population and in fact *Thamarāt al-Funūn* was one of their projects. Some members of this circle directed criticism against the Porte, as can be seen in newspaper publications especially during the years 1878–1881. They called for the improvement of the situation in the *Vilâyet* of Syria under Ottoman rule.

Another explanation can be given for the background surrounding some of the ideas of the Beiruti society. The movement itself and its view of Syria as an entity were among the changes occurring in the thinking of Muslim notables in Beirut and Damascus. When the Beiruti society was established, the call for Syrian patriotism had already been voiced. At this point, it seemed as though the interests of the Muslims and Christians of the middle stratum had coincided. In general, they both wanted a strong Syrian entity. Both sides decried the injustice and corruption of their rulers and wished to assert their Arabism, as well as to acquire equal rights for both Arabs and Turks. Yet this tendency did not last for very long. Towards the end of the nineteenth century, their courses diverged and in the years that followed, each community utilised different methods to reach their common goal. For the Christians, Midhat's rule was not only a peak of their patriotic aspirations but also the beginning of their eclipse. In the periodical *al-Jinān*, we can see how these aspirations still occasionally surfaced throughout the 1880s. The Christians continued to search for a secular Syrian identity, but gradually, especially after the Hamidian regime with its anti-*Tanzīmāt* tendencies, some of them, mainly those who emigrated from Syria, aspired and acted in behalf of a secular Arab nationalism. In the meantime, the Muslims tried to find their solution within the Islamic framework. After their disappointment with Hamidian rule, they would focus on a Muslim Arab identity.

---

[112] For further information on this society see: Linda Schatkowski-Schilcher, *The Islamic Maqased of Beirut—A Case Study of Modernisation in Lebanon*. M.A. thesis, American University of Beirut, 1969.

As mentioned, behind the Beiruti Secret Society stood students from the SPC which was established by American missionaries. These missionaries provided another catalyst in advancing the idea of a Syrian identity, which reflected their own vision and interest during the nineteenth century. Tracing the vision of some of these missionaries in the Levant and its contribution to the identity of the Beiruti middle stratum will shed additional light on the influence of the encounter with the West and the construction of local identity.

CHAPTER FOUR

REVISITING THE AMERICAN PRESBYTERIAN MISSIONARIES IN NINETEENTH CENTURY SYRIA[1]

As part of the cultural encounter with the West, among the most important influences on the Christian Arabs in the Syrian region were the American missionaries. Their activities during the nineteenth century in this region should be grasped not as primarily those of agents of a hegemonic Western culture, or as has been called in some of the studies as "cultural imperialism,"[2] but as constituting an actual process of inter-cultural communication or cultural interaction. This development accelerated the process of local transformation of the identity of the Christian-Arab intellectuals, or as Dunch[3] saw them, as one of the elements in a globalising modernity, that has altered Western societies as well as non-Western ones in the nineteenth and twentieth centuries. . . ."[4] Some of these missionaries had their own non-governmental reasons for acquiring and disseminating knowledge. A number of these reasons were almost certainly largely recreational, having little to do with their professional pursuits and duties as missionaries.[5]

From the mid-nineteenth century, certain American Presbyterian missionaries living and working in Beirut and other parts of the

[1] This chapter is based mainly on an article that I published in *Die Welt des Islams*. See: Fruma Zachs, "Toward A Proto-Nationalist Concept of Syria? Revisiting the American Presbyterian Missionaries in Nineteenth-Century Levant," *Die Welt des Islams*, Vol. 41, (2001), pp. 145–173.

[2] "Cultural Imperialism" as Dunch explains, "reduces complex interactions to a dichotomy between actor and acted upon, leaving too little place for the agency of the latter." For more details on "Cultural Imperialism and its Problems," see: Ryan Dunch, "Beyond Cultural Imperialism: Cultural Theory, Christian Missions, and Global Modernity," *History and Theory*, Vol. 41 (2002), pp. 302–307: See also, Eleanor H. Tejirian and Reeva S. Simon (eds.), *Altruism and Imperialism: Western Religious and Cultural Missions to the Middle East* (New York, 2002).

[3] Dunch, "Beyond Cultural Imperialism," pp. 301–325.

[4] *Ibid.*, p. 301; see also: Jean and John Comaroff, *Of Revelation and Revolution: Christianity, Colonialism, and Consciousness in South Africa* (Chicago, 1991).

[5] See: Oddie Geoffrey, *Missionaries, Rebellion and Proto-Nationalism—James Long of Bengal 1814–1887* (London, 1999), p. 185. See also, Eleanor A. Doumato, "Extra Legible Illustration of Christian Faces: Medicine, Medical Ethics and Missionaries in the Arabian Gulf," *Islam and Christian-Muslim Relations*, Vol. 13 (2002), pp. 388–389.

region significantly helped define and promote a concept of "Syria." Given their preoccupation with "Syria," another parameter which contributed to the emergence of a Syrian identity among local Christian-Arab intellectuals, it comes as somewhat of a surprise that this aspect of the American missionaries' activities has so far received little or no attention.

Some scholars have claimed that the Arab Awakening, or *Nahḍa*, received some of its impetus from the educational activities the American Presbyterian missionaries engaged in. A few have gone so far as to relate the impact that the missionaries made through education to the emergence of Arabism and then, later, to Arab nationalism.[6]

At the other end of the spectrum we find, for example, ʿAbdūl Latif Tibawi. Though Tibawi acknowledges their achievements in the fields of education and religion, he wrote that the alleged contribution of the American missionaries to the *Nahḍa* was "a fanciful picture."[7]

My point of departure will be Tibawi's criticism. I will show that the main contribution of the missionaries was not to the *Nahḍa* or to Arab nationalism but rather to the idea of Syria or the Syrian identity.[8] Thus, the chapter will trace how some American Presbyterian missionaries who went to the region in the early nineteenth century with the prime objective of spreading the Gospel, ended up helping to shape and promote a concept of "Syria". Local Christian-Arab intellectuals then used this concept as the spindle, so to speak, around which they could further coil the thread of their Syrian *waṭaniyya*.

How the missionaries arrived at this concept of "Syria" and the content they gave it will be analysed from two interrelated perspectives:

---

[6] Rao H. Lindsay, *Nineteenth-Century American Schools in the Levant: A Study of Purposes*, (Ann Arbor, 1965); Adnan Abu-Ghazaleh, *American Missions in Syria: A Study of American Missionary Contribution to Arab Nationalism in Nineteenth-Century Syria* (Vermont, 1990). See also, Anīs al-Naṣūlī, *Asbāb al-Nahḍa al-ʿArabiyya fī al-Qarn al-Tāsiʿ ʿAshar* (Beirut, 1985), pp. 57–58, 85–92, 184–195; Faith M. Hanna, *An American Mission: The Role of the American University of Beirut* (New York, 1979); Cf. Bassam Tibi, *Arab Nationalism: A Critical Inquiry* (London, 1981), pp. 73–79; Antonius, *The Arab Awakening*, pp. 35–43, 79–100.

[7] ʿAbdūl Latif Tibawi, "Some Misconceptions about the *Nahḍa*," *Middle East Forum*, Vol. 47 (1971), esp. p. 17.

[8] Other studies have emphasised the connection between missionaries and the rise of national consequence and identity. See for example: Ryan Dunch, *Fuzhou Protestant and the Making of a Modern China, 1857–1927* (New Haven, 2001). See also the introduction by Eleanor A. Doumato who discussed, among other things, missions and identity formation in the Middle East in a volume of *Islam and Christian Muslim Relations*, Vol. 13, No. 4 (2002), pp. 373–376; Oddie, *Missionaries, Rebellion and Proto-Nationalism.*

the development of their own views and ideas as can be culled from their private and public literary products; and the educational activities through which they made their presence felt in the region. These activities include, most notably, the College they established in 1866 in Beirut, as well as the cultural societies they helped to found.[9]

The analysis is primarily based on the manuscripts and books the missionaries produced and on the voluminous correspondence they left behind, now kept at the Houghton Library, Harvard,[10] and of course on the writings and publishings of their local followers, many of whom were graduates of the SPC and some of whom were prominent Arab literati.

Imagining "Syria"

When the American missionaries arrived in the region of *Bilād al-Shām*, they named it as was generally known in the West, that is, as "Syria." This region, besides the Lebanon, included Palestine, the "Holy Land."[11] Their arrival was described by Tibawi, stating that "Unlike Spanish, Dutch or English missionaries in other parts of the world, who often followed in the footsteps of soldiers, the American missionaries were preceded only by merchants."[12]

---

[9] On the attitude of the Porte toward the American missionaries see: Selim Deringil, *The Well-Protected Domains: Ideology and the Legitimization of Power in the Ottoman Empire 1876–1909* (London, 1998), pp. 112–134.

[10] The Houghton Library (HL) at Harvard University houses the main archive of the American Board of Commissioners for Foreign Missions (ABCFM) which was established in 1810 in Boston and supervised all American missionary activities. On the Syrian Mission between 1823 and 1902 the archive contains the following: Formal documents, including Annual Reports (of the various stations, schools and the Syrian Protestant College), formal policies, deployment of the mission; correspondence between the missionaries, including personal views on the interaction between the Syrian mission and the local population and personal papers; correspondence between the missionaries and local literati.

[11] As shown, e.g. by popular travelogues, such as Volney, *Travels through Syria and Egypt*; Burckhardt, *Travels in Syria and the Holy Land*; Frederick A. Neale, *Eight Years in Syria, Palestine and Asia Minor from 1842–1850*, 2 vols. (London, 1851); Josias L. Porter, *Five Years in Damascus*, 2 vols. (London, 1855); idem, *The Giant Cities of Bashan and Syria's Holy Places* (London, 1867); Newton, *Travels and Discoveries in the Levant*; Murray, *Handbook for Travels in Syria and Palestine*; Drake and Isabel Burton, *Unexplored Syria*, 2 vols. (London, 1872); Karl Baedeker, *Palestine and Syria: A Handbook for Travelers* (Leipzig, 1876).

[12] Tibawi, *American Interests in Syria*, p. 4; the "only" is of course less innocent than here implied.

The first American Protestant missionaries arrived in Beirut in 1823. They were sent by and came under the supervision of the American Board of Commissioners for Foreign Missions (ABCFM, the "Board", the home authority of missionaries in Syria) located in Boston, Massachusetts, and their main mission was to evangelise the region.[13] They introduced a printing press to Beirut in 1834 and by 1850 had managed to establish a number of schools in the region.[14] Their crowning event was undoubtedly the founding of the SPC in 1866, the first college in the region with Western features, which would later become the American University of Beirut (AUB). For the Americans, education was of course a way of getting closer to the local population and of leading the younger generation to "true Christianity," but it was also a principle of fundamental importance. The Americans were drawn from the smaller towns and farms of New England, led narrow, parochial lives, and were imbued with the spirits of puritan saintliness and patriotism.

The Americans chose "Syria" for their missionary activities because of the religious importance this part of the world had for them. They wanted to prepare for the Second Coming by trying to convert the region's population, a process they knew would take a major commitment over a long period of time. Syria had been the cradle of Christianity and incorporated the Holy City of Jerusalem and other important Christian sites. Their Protestant belief held that the population, now largely Muslim, should be prepared for the second coming of Christ at the turn of the millennium when, at Armageddon, the region would become the battleground for the forces of light and darkness.[15] They also thought of Syria as a bridge between Asia and Africa, a melting pot of cultures and civilisations and thus an eminently suitable locality for their missionary activities.[16]

---

[13] Frederick Bliss, *The Religions of Modern Syria and Palestine* (New York, 1912), pp. l, 314; Rufus Anderson, *Memorial Volume of the Fifty Years of the A.B.C.F.M.* (Boston, 1862), p. 242.

[14] Gharāyiba, *Sūriyya fī al-Qarn al-Tāsiʿ ʿAshar*, pp. 173–174; Frederick Bliss (ed.), *The Reminiscences of Daniel Bliss* (New York, 1920), pp. 102, 120; John M. Munro, *A Mutual Concern: The Story of the American University of Beirut* (New York, 1977), pp. 6–11; Antonius, *The Arab Awakening*, pp. 41–45; *The Missionary Herald*, Vol. 34, December 1838, p. 473.

[15] HL, series ABC: 16.8.1, Vol. 4, Bliss to Anderson, 27 August 1858; Samir Khalaf, "Leavening the Levant: New England Puritanism as a Cultural Transplant," *Journal of Mediterranean Studies*, Vol. 7 (1998), pp. 270–272.

[16] Bliss, *The Religions of Modern Syria and Palestine*, p. 314; Lindsay, *Nineteenth Century American Schools*, p. 69; Tibawi, *American Interests*, p. 11.

The missionaries were fully aware of the strategic importance of the region in providing access to millions of "unsaved" souls. Of equal importance was the fact that the Near East was neither part of the British Empire nor under its sphere of influence. Also, the missionaries wanted to save the local population from the corruptness of the "nominal Christians", i.e. Catholics. Moreover, what is striking in the first annual reports of the ABCFM is the almost total absence of an overall strategy or program, or a preference for any particular geographic area.

They arrived with a fair knowledge of the ancient history of the region, most of it drawn from the travel literature that the West was familiar with at that time, from references appearing in the New Testament,[17] and from the education that they had received during their training period. This may explain why it was natural for them to refer to the region as "Syria." For the same reason, they had a clear idea in their minds concerning the area's territorial borders. As one of them, Eli Smith, wrote in 1833:

> [Syria is the] general name for the country that lies along the whole breadth of the eastern end of the Mediterranean sea, extending inland to the deserts of Arabia, and having the territories of Egypt on the south, and the river Euphrates with the mountains of Cilicia on the north. . . . The southern part of it is Palestine, the ancient land of promise. On the north of it, beyond the Euphrates, is Mesopotamia. . . .[18]

If it was the religious significance of the area that had motivated the American missionaries to come and work in Syria, it did not take long for many of them to develop a growing sense of affinity with the land and its population. For a number of them, this meant that their interests soon extended beyond the goals set by the Board in Boston. Before long, their diaries abounded with remarks that reveal their obvious love for the country and the sympathy they felt towards the local people—Christians mainly—with whom they were in daily contact; gradually we find them speaking of Syria as their adopted homeland.

---

[17] "Syria" appears a number of times in the New Testament where it stands for the northern and central parts of "Greater Syria": Luke 2/2; Acts of the Apostles 15/23, 41, 18/18, 20/3, 21/3, 9/1–9. See also, Walter K. Kelly, *Syria and the Holy Land* (London, 1884), pp. 2–5.

[18] Eli Smith, *Missionary Sermons and Addresses* (Boston, 1833), p. 147.

They report on the extensive amount of travelling they do throughout the country and reveal a good deal of interest in its archaeological past, collecting fossils, coins and other items including the flora and fauna of Syria, which are then displayed in museums established by the College.[19] Their interest in contemporary Syria comes to the fore in much of their writings, be they diaries, correspondence or books. In 1896, one of the missionaries, Dr. George E. Post, published a book on the *Flora of Syria, Palestine and the Sinai Region*.[20] Others wrote about the region's population and their customs and manners.[21]

A closer look at the writings the American Presbyterian missionaries produced in various forms will help reveal what their concept of "Syria" consisted of, i.e. how through their "missionary" imaginings, they went about shaping the grammar of their "Syria." After that, the chapter will take up one important aspect of their educational activities, i.e. the cultural societies they founded, in order to trace how they went about concretising and disseminating it.

As the "Orient", the Middle East was of course "almost a European invention," far less so an American one. Still, "Even the legendary American missionaries to the Near East during the nineteenth and twentieth centuries took their role as set not so much by God as by *their* God, *their* culture, and *their* destiny."[22] In other words, propelled

---

[19] For example, see: HL, series ABC: 16.8.1, Vol. 7, Jessup to Anderson, 27 January 1865; 16.8.2.5, Vol. 2, Annual reports of the SPC, June 1869, 18 July 1873, 1877, 17 July 1884, 1886; Henry H. Jessup, *Fifty-Three Years in Syria*, Vol. 1 (New York, 1910), pp. 26–27, 43, 123–125, 128–135, 281; Vol. 2, pp. 596–597; William M. Thomson, *The Land and the Book* (London, 1888), pp. 19–178 (especially on Phoenician history); Bliss (ed.), *The Reminiscences of Daniel Bliss*, pp. 116–117, 137; Howard S. Bliss, *The Modern Missionary* (Beirut, 1920), pp. 8, 20. This "missionary" archaeology has, of course, little to do with Anderson's "museumising imagination," which is "profoundly political"; see: Anderson, *Imagined Communities*, p. 178. But the underlying mechanism is perhaps not so very different. As we will see, the American missionaries' "peculiar imagining of history" helped shape the "grammar" of their "Syria" and "Syrians," no less a concretisation of possibilities than the colonial state's "Burma" and "Burmese," "Indonesia" and "Indonesians" (p. 185).

[20] Post contributed the 300 items he had gathered during his travels to the flora collection of the SPC. Jessup contributed plant fossils from his private collection, which included all the types that could be found in Syria at the time. HL, series ABC: 16.8.2.5, Vol. 2, Annual Reports of the SPC, June 1869 and 17 July 1886; Forty-Third Annual Report of the College in 1908–9, p. 43.

[21] For example, Jessup, *Fifty-Three Years in Syria*, Vol. 1, pp. 123–128; HL, Bliss Papers, Wayland to Bliss, 22 March 1864.

[22] Said, *Orientalism*, pp. 1, 294–295; as an instance of this Said refers to Jessup's *Fifty-Three Years in Syria*.

as they were by the ideologies of the modern, Christian West, the American Presbyterians in their perception of the "other" inevitably often appear blinkered by the prejudices of their religion and culture. At the same time, they differed from their European counterparts, whose missionary efforts were almost inextricably interwoven with Europe's expansionist drive into the eastern Mediterranean, in that before long they developed an obvious sense of belonging to the region, even if that would in many cases be *their* "Syria."[23]

What is immediately striking—though not surprising—is how utterly disappointed the American missionaries were by the "reality" they found in the region and how incongruent it seemed next to the magnificence that had characterised its past history. The "present" was immediately evident to them upon arrival: it was one of neglect and inadequacy. The state of the educational system, of the economy and of the means of general transportation left much to be desired. The existing school systems, Muslim as well as Christian, were still highly traditional, which meant almost no formal education for girls, and that non-religious books were a luxury.[24]

To turn things around meant reviving Syria's glorious past, a task the missionaries saw as lying on the shoulders of the present generation of Syria's Christians. It is in this context that we come across descriptions in their writings of a "New Syria," of the way they envisioned the country's future. References to a historic past crop up immediately, that is, to a "Syria" they knew from their New Testament and to the "Phoenicians," the sea-faring inhabitants of the coastal region during the first millennium BCE, whose trade routes and colonies extended as far as Carthage in Northern Africa or perhaps even further. In creating this kind of continuity with the past, the missionaries may well have been inspired by the foreshortening immediacy that New Testament texts tend to impart when read in the original Greek.[25]

---

[23] On Europe's "peaceful crusade," see: Schölch, *Palestine in Transformation*, pp. 47–75.

[24] The Muslim secular public education began to develop primarily as of the 1870s. For further details, see: Donald J. Cioeta, "Islamic Benevolent Societies and Public Education in Ottoman Syria 1875–1882," *The Islamic Quarterly*, Vol. 25 (1981), pp. 40–55.

[25] One wonders, for example, what they felt when reading such passages as Acts 21/1–3 (here in The New English Bible translation): "When we had parted from them and set sail, we made a straight run and came to Cos; next day to Rhodes, and thence to Patara. There we found a ship bound for Phoenicia [eis Phoiniken],

Their archaeological interests, of course, served the same imagining purpose. For Henry Jessup, William Thomson and Daniel Bliss, who frequently mention it, the period of the Phoenicians formed a pinnacle in the economic and cultural history of the region.[26] More importantly, it allowed them to shape their grammar of "Syria" and "Syrians" as exclusive of Islam: investing their concept of "Syria" with pre-Islamic features signalled their belief that Islam equalled tradition and "thus" stagnation. "New Syria" meant progress, and Gospel and education were to combine to help it advance: divine enlightenment would be the country's guidance into the future and a highly developed educational system was to prepare "Syrian youth" for all aspects of modern life.[27]

This vision of a "New Syria" comes to the fore especially in the writings of those missionaries who later formed part of the SPC staff. For Henry Jessup, who spent more than half a century in the region, the "Syrian race" had reached the moment in which "it should awake." "There will yet be," he continued, "a new Phoenicia, a new Syria, better cultivated, better governed, with a wider diffusion of Christian truth." In 1902, he wrote that the students of the SPC would learn to "act together harmoniously in the future as citizens of a free country, to respect each other and to be the leaders in reform and progress."[28]

---

so we went aboard and sailed in her. We came in sight of Cyprus, and leaving it to port, we continued our voyage to Syria [eis Syrian], and put in at Tyre, for there the ship was to unload her cargo."

[26] Thomson, *The Land and the Book*, pp. 19–178; Bliss (ed.), *The Reminiscences of Daniel Bliss*, p. 116; Jessup, *Fifty-Three Years in Syria*, Vol. 1, p. 26. Henry Jessup arrived in Syria in 1856 and stayed for 53 years. In the beginning he was active in Tripoli and later on in Beirut. William Thomson had come to the region as early as 1833 and was a medical doctor; in 1836 he founded a girls' boarding school in Beirut; Gregory M. Wortabet, *Syria and the Syrians*, Vol. 1 (London, 1856), p. 59; Bliss (ed.), *The Reminiscences of Daniel Bliss*, p. 105. Daniel Bliss (1823–1916) received his education at the Kingsville Academy. In 1848 he entered Amherst College and after that studied in Andover Seminary. He arrived in Beirut in 1856. For two years he studied Arabic and carried out duties at the ʿAbeih station. In 1858 he was sent to *Sūq al-Gharb*, in western Lebanon, as principal of the boarding school for girls that had just then been transferred from Beirut. During the years of 1866–1902 he served as president of the SPC. See: Bayard Dodge, *The American University of Beirut* (Beirut, 1958), pp. 9–10.

[27] HL, series ABC: 16.8.1, Vol. 6, Jessup, Annual Report of the Beirut Station, 1866; R.W. Smith, "The American University of Beirut," *Middle Eastern Affairs*, Vol. 7 (1956), pp. 292–334; Stephen B. L. Penrose, *That They May Have Life: The Story of the American University, 1866–1941* (Beirut, 1970), p. 16.

[28] Jessup, *Fifty-Three Years in Syria*, Vol. 1, p. 27; one chapter is actually called "New Syria," Vol. 2, pp. 596–597, 788.

Daniel Bliss, who served for more than three decades as the SPC's first president (1866–1902), expressed a strong sense of optimism regarding Syria's future in *The Missionary Herald*, the Mission's official newspaper. His son, Frederick Bliss, later portrayed his father as a person whose mind was ever on the future, a man with "visions and dreams." Writing three years before it was actually established, Bliss clearly saw the College as one of the tools that was to help them create this "new society."[29]

Eager to translate their vision into practice, the American missionaries proved indefatigable in their effort to create a local audience through their educational programs, transmitting their ideas to their local students via daily lectures, studies in their schools and the College, the sermons they preached during church services and other forms of contact. Their main goal always remained religious, but they realised they ought to serve simultaneously as a medium to improve the state of the country and better the lot of its inhabitants.[30] This they did through education.

Throughout the years, the missionaries accelerated the establishment of elementary schools. In 1846, there had been 528 pupils in the American schools. In 1858, the number doubled and was 1,065, while four years later 1,925 pupils already studied in their schools. On the eve of the First World War, the American missionaries operated 675 schools with a total of 34,317 pupils.[31] As William Eddy stated, the Mission's aims were to educate as wide a population as possible, "reviving the spirit of literature among themselves, nourishing a sympathy for each other and creating a love for their own country and language and race."[32] In 1866, when they inaugurated the SPC, its doors were "opened to all religions." One of its principles was equal education for all and anyone could join the college, no matter what religious community he or she belonged to.[33] As the missionaries set out sowing the seeds they believed they would be

[29] *The Missionary Herald*, Vol. 56, Bliss, 17 February 1860; Bliss (ed.), *The Reminiscences of Daniel Bliss*, pp. 137–138; HL, series ABC: 16.8.1, Vol. 6, Bliss to Treat, 18 November 1863.

[30] Henry H. Jessup, "Syria," *Foreign Missionary*, 37 (1878), p. 201.

[31] HL, series ABC: 16.8.1, Vol. 7, Jessup to Anderson, 7 February 1866; Roderic H. Davison, *Essays in Ottoman and Turkish History 1774–1923, The Impact of the West* (Austin, 1990), pp. 167–168; Lindsay, *Nineteenth Century American Schools*, p. 101.

[32] HL, series ABC: 16.8.1, Vol. 4, part 2, Eddy to Baton, 5 June 1856.

[33] Bliss (ed.), *The Reminiscences of Daniel Bliss*, p. 198.

reaping in years to come, a dilemma they faced at first but quickly solved was in which language to teach. Soon Arabic won out over English, because they realised that without Arabic they would be unable to reach the locals. Also, the notion that without English, graduates might be less prone to leave the country also played a part.[34]

It remains a bit of a puzzle how the missionaries thought they could hope to attract the majority Muslim population to their concept of "Syria."[35] It is true that following the civil war in 1860 they tried to seek out a common denominator in which the various religious communities could find themselves—the events formed Syria's "darkest hour," a clear signal that from now on sectarian strife ought to be prevented at all costs.[36] But their response proved to be a renewed emphasis on a shared history and culture in the more remote past, their concept of "Syria" again serving as the lode star toward that brighter future.[37]

Thus, we find that for their concept of "Syria" the American Presbyterian missionaries valorised elements that remained firmly within traditional conceptions of identity, though they attached these to a clear territorial referent. That is, when they spoke of love for one's country, they meant love for "Syria", when they referred to history and culture, they meant "Syrian" history and culture, but "country" for them at this stage was *balad*, not *waṭan*, "patria." It was not patriotism they were after but the creation of a community of Christian Syrians, i.e. Arabs who could lead their society into the reality of the modern, Westernised world. Moreover, as there was no doubt in their minds that the "progress" the West had been able to achieve was directly related to its being Christian, their foremost goal remained Christianising Syria.

---

[34] HL, series ABC: 16.8.1, Vol. 7, Jessup to Anderson, 7 February 1866.

[35] Admittedly, they counted some Muslims among their pupils (e.g., 12 percent of the student body of the SPC were Muslim), while several Muslims, among them Yūsuf al-Asīr and Ibrāhīm al-Aḥdab, participated in the activities organised by the missionaries or attended meetings of their cultural societies; cf. Jessup, *Fifty-Three Years in Syria*, Vol. 2, pp. 787–789.

[36] HL, series ABC: 16.8.1, Vol. 7, Jessup to Anderson, 29 August 1860.

[37] Jonas King (1792–1869) was the first American missionary in the region to use the term "Syria" in his book, which was written in Arabic: *Wadāʿ Yunas Kīn ilā Aḥbābihi Fī Filasṭīn wa Sūriyya* (Beirut, 1825). Pipes maintains that the term "Syria" came into use in Arabic and Turkish through the Protestant missionaries. He especially mentions Jonas King that already in 1825 used this term in his book. In his opinion, afterwards, i.e. from the middle of the nineteenth century, the term was in more frequent use with the American missionaries. Pipes, *Greater Syria*, p. 14.

The shift to Syrian patriotism came later and was made by local Christian literati who were or had been closely involved with the activities of the American missionaries. Nevertheless, the shift to this Syrian patriotism occurred in two stages. First, we find local literati such as As'ad Khayyāṭ and Gregory Wortabet referring to a Syria that still carried an obvious Christian emphasis. Later, as we shall see in the last chapter, other Christian literati, though also strongly influenced by these missionaries' ideas, began talking of a non-sectarian Arab Syria.

Khayyāṭ was born in Beirut in 1811 as a Greek Orthodox. He was in contact with the missionaries while still a teenager and studied English and Arabic grammar in their school. In 1847, after touring the country and making several trips to Europe, he published *A Voice from Lebanon*, in which he gives an impressionistic account of the country's social and economic situation. Khayyāṭ writes that he had given up the "honourable" office of dragoman at the British consulate general in Syria in order to promote the welfare of Syria through education and every other means that seemed practicable and proper. In his invention of the past, he follows the missionaries and takes the Phoenicians to be his ancestors.[38] Furthermore, the book is the first to reflect the Western idea of territorial loyalty.

The same tendency is evident in Gregory Wortabet's writing. Wortabet was the first local Armenian to convert to Protestantism. Like Khayyāṭ, he developed a close relationship with the American missionaries but as early as the 1820s. In his *Syria and the Syrians*, which was published in 1856, the Phoenician past of the region is again extolled and its magnificence contrasted to the present. Wortabet speaks of "the natural talent of the Syrian mind" and hopes that the inhabitants of Syria may again become what they once were.[39]

In the case of Khayyāṭ, Wortabet and others, we find them increasingly speaking of their territorial identity as "Syrians." Khayyāṭ, for example, saw himself as "the greatest Syrian traveller in mod-

---

[38] Khayyāṭ, *A Voice from Lebanon*, pp. 142–143, 161, 316, 365. See also, Isaac Bird, *Bible Works in Bible Land* (Philadelphia, 1872), p. 218. For further details on Khayyāṭ, see: Kamal S. Salibi, "The Two Worlds of As'ad Y. Kayat," in Benjamin Barude and Bernard Lewis (eds.), *Christians and Jews in the Ottoman Empire*, Vol. 1 (New York, 1982), pp. 135–155.

[39] Wortabet, *Syria and the Syrians*, especially Vol. 1, pp. 33, 267. On Wortabet's life, see: Tibawi, *American Interests*, pp. 38, 51; Gharāyiba, *Sūriyya fī al-Qarn al-Tāsi' 'Ashar*, p. 196.

ern times."[40] Other obvious examples are the titles that Wortabet chose for his books, *Syria and the Syrians* and *Researches in the Religions of Syria and Palestine.*[41] Again, the semiotic meaning of the shift from "*Bilād al-Shām*" with its Muslim connotation, to "Syria," a term predating Islam, is very important. It encapsulates an affinity to a defined territory, along with a selective past, culture and thus identity.

A short but illuminating study by Haim Gerber about the "territorial concept" of "Palestine" in the seventeenth century can be extrapolated to a discussion of *Bilād al-Shām*, i.e. that one can speak of a territorial awareness of *al-Diyār al-Shāmiyya* much before the appearance of nationalism.[42] One implication for our purposes here would be that inhabitants of the Ottoman provinces of Aleppo, Sidon and Damascus shared a territorial identity one may call *Shāmiyya.* The other is that when the socio-political changes in the fabric of Ottoman society which occurred during the nineteenth century led local Christians—increasingly set apart from their fellow Muslims—to seek out a new socio-cultural identity for themselves, "Syrian" was a natural candidate. In this sense, the missionaries' concept of "Syria" appears as a cultural-semiotic construct, successful almost by default.

With this in mind, I want to turn next to one other important aspect of the interaction between missionaries and locals, to try and pinpoint the shift among the latter toward a Syrian identity; that shift made use of Arab culture as a means to this end.

Al-Jamʿiyya al-Sūriyya li-Iktisāb al-ʿUlūm wal-Funūn *(1847–1852)*

One way in which the missionaries were *active* was the establishment of cultural societies. Here, conversations and lectures on general

[40] Khayyāṭ, *A Voice from Lebanon*, p. 142.

[41] Gregory Wortabet, *Researches in the Religions of Syria and Palestine* (London, 1860). "Syria" also appears in poems Wortabet wrote, e.g. "When Syria's now degraded sons rise / and learn her daughter's rights and worth to prize / When Freedom's banner wide shall be unfurled / Proclaiming loud to an astonished world / On Syria's plains, and Lebanon's green heights / Lo! Freedom reigns—God and sacred rights" (idem), *Syria and the Syrians*, Vol. 1, p. 267).

[42] Cf. Haim Gerber, "'Palestine' and Other Territorial Concepts in the 17th Century," *International Journal of Middle East Studies*, Vol. 30 (1998), pp. 563–572. Much as Dawn wrote about the late nineteenth century, Gerber has little doubt that "the human mind . . . [can] accommodate multi-faceted phenomena such as a double identity." (p. 563).

subjects enabled them to reach the adult population they could not reach through their schools. In 1847 the American missionaries, in collaboration with local Christian Arabs, established a cultural society in Beirut which they called *al-Jamʿiyya al-Sūriyya li-Iktisāb al-ʿUlūm wal-Funūn* (The Syrian Society for the Acquisition of Sciences).[43] This was the first such society established in the region[44] that carried the term "Syria" in its title. One important activity of the Society was collecting books and manuscripts, mainly in Arabic but of course also in English, intended to help its members broaden their knowledge but to avoid "controversy between the different faiths [which] has no place in this Society."[45]

The Society was active for about five years; its meetings were conducted in Arabic. Two years after its establishment, it had about fifty members, all of whom were Christian. Among the missionaries the following were especially active: Henry De Forest (head of the girls' boarding school in Beirut), William Thomson (first chairman of the Society), Cornelius Van Dyck (head of the ʿAbeih seminary), Eli Smith (chairman of the Society) and Simeon Calhoun.[46] Most

[43] There are conflicting accounts as to who the actual founders were. Choueiri names three missionaries: William Thomson, Cornelius Van Dyck and Eli Smith, while according to Antonius and Abu-Ghazāleh, the honour should go to local literati, al-Bustānī and Yāzijī; see: Yussef M. Choueiri, *Arab History and the Nation State—A Study of Modern Arab Historiography, 1820–1920* (London, 1989), p. 50, note 3; Antonius, *The Arab Awakening*, pp. 51–52; Abu-Ghazaleh, *American Missions in Syria*, p. 65.

[44] There is some controversy regarding the primacy of this kind of society. Tibawi claimed that in 1846 a society by the name of *Majmaʿ al-Tahdhīb* was established; Tibawi, "Some Misconceptions About the Nahda," p. 17; see also, al-Bustanī, *al-Jamʿiyya al-Sūriyya lil-ʿUlūm wal-Funūn*, pp. 5–6. Antonius, on the other hand, wrote that the society was the first of its kind, not only in the region of Syria but in the entire Arab world; Antonius, *The Arab Awakening*, p. 52; see also, Jān Dāya, "Bākūrat al-Jamʿiyyāt al-Thaqāfiyya fī Sūriyya wal-ʿĀlam al-ʿArabī," *Fikr*, Vols. 20–21 (1984), pp. 173–181.

[45] Buṭrus al-Bustānī, *Aʿmāl al-Jamʿiyya al-Sūriyya* (Beirut, 1852), p. v (as the first pages in this book are not numbered, I indicate them here with Roman numerals).

[46] De Forest had arrived in Syria in May 1842 and managed the girls' boarding school in Beirut until 1854; Tibawi, *American Interests*, p. 103; Jessup, *Fifty-Three Years in Syria*, Vol. 1, pp. 95–97. Van Dyck came to Syria in 1840. He was the American Mission's medical doctor; see Douglas and Belle D. Rough and Alfred H. Howell (eds.), *Daniel Bliss—Letters from a New Campus* (Beirut, 1994), pp. 267–270. Calhoun had arrived in Syria in 1844 and in 1846 he replaced Van Dyck as the head of the ʿAbieh Seminary; Jessup, *Fifty-Three Years in Syria*, Vol. 1, pp. 95, 97–98; Ghada Y. Khoury, *The Founding Fathers of the American University in Beirut—Biographies* (Beirut, 1992). pp. 105–125.

local members have several features in common. A number of them studied or worked in the American mission, while others were sons of merchants from the new middle stratum families. Most of them were part of the intelligentsia that emerged in Beirut in the course of the nineteenth century, and included such figures as Khalīl Mishāqa, Nakhla Mudawwar, John (Yohanna) Wortabet, Nāṣīf al-Yāzijī and Buṭrus al-Bustānī.[47]

In 1852, the Society's final year of activities, Buṭrus al-Bustānī selected eighteen of the many lectures that had been given at the society's meetings and published them as a book, called *Aʿmāl al-Jamʿiyya al-Sūriyya.* The collection contains all the elements that make up the missionaries' concept of "Syria," i.e. the country itself as a territorial unit, its history and culture, and of course the predominance of Arabic. Some of these elements would also later constitute the parameters of the local intellectuals' Syrian patriotism. The book is important for the glimpse it gives us into the nature and activities of the Society, of course, but also for the connection between Eli Smith and Buṭrus al-Bustānī which it reflects. The former played an important role among the American missionaries in the formation of their concept of "Syria" through his many writings, lectures and activities. Buṭrus al-Bustānī had already become one of the leading figures among the literati of Beirut, and one of the first to talk of a Syrian *waṭaniyya.* The two were close friends. As a young man, al-Bustānī had found shelter in Smith's household when in the 1840s, following his conversion to Protestantism, he had to escape the wrath of the Maronite patriarch. Smith and Buṭrus al-Bustānī worked closely together on the translation of the Bible into Arabic, and Smith was best man at al-Bustānī's wedding.[48]

Born in 1801, Eli Smith had graduated from Yale and in 1821 received his diploma in theology from Andover Seminary in Boston. In 1826, the Board decided to send him to the region of Syria and he arrived in Beirut on February 1827. His first position was with the missionary press but in 1828, when military conflict loomed following the rebellion in Greece, he and other missionaries left temporarily

[47] Ṭarrāzī, *Tārīkh al-Ṣiḥāfa*, Vol. 4, p. 112.

[48] Cf. Jessup, *Fifty-Three Years in Syria*, Vol. 2, p. 484; HL, Smith Papers, ABC: 60, box 2, Smith to Anderson, 3 August 1843; Abdul Latif Tibawi, "The American Missionaries in Beirut and Buṭrus al-Bustani," St. Antony's Papers, *Middle Eastern Affairs*, No. 16 (1963), p. 161.

for Malta. There he was put in charge of improving the American press, in existence there since 1822, which he did by, among other things, adding Arabic to the Italian, Greek and Armenian print the press was capable of producing.

He was also the first American missionary to show a clear interest in Arabic as a missionary tool, as he was very well aware that optimal contact with the local population could be achieved only via its own native language.[49] Not only was Smith himself fully conversant in colloquial Arabic, his writings reveals a fluent command of *fuṣḥā* (literary Arabic). In 1830 he ordered an Arabic letterset from Germany and when the press moved from Malta to Beirut in 1834, it was able to start printing in Arabic.[50] During the same year, Smith and his wife founded the first school for girls in Syria, in Beirut. Smith remained interested in Arabic typography and made a special trip to the USA in 1838 in order to learn more about certain technical details. Starting in 1840 he devoted several years to the study of other Semitic languages.

In 1847 he was assigned to head one of the Mission's important projects—the translation of the Bible to Arabic. His devotion to this project was so complete that one of his fellow missionaries at one point demurred and thought he ought to put more emphasis on his religious activities, to which Smith responded that he was acting in this issue upon his own judgment and that he believed the Board would tolerate some straying.[51] In 1851 he founded the first Arabic newspaper in Beirut and named it *Majmūʿat Fawāʾid*[52] (Useful Lessons). His knowledge and love of Arabic no doubt help explain why he developed such close ties with local literati, such as Buṭrus al-Bustānī and Nāṣīf al-Yāzijī, with whose assistance he was able to publish books on other than religious topics.[53] Salīm Nawfal, a local Christian intellectual, asked Smith in 1851 to help him set up a Syrian Arabic newspaper dealing with trade, politics and culture.[54]

---

[49] Tibawi, *American Interests*, pp. 49–50; Munro, *A Mutual Concern*, pp. 5, 95.

[50] Joseph L. Grabill, *Protestant Diplomacy and the Near East: Missionary Influence on American Policy, 1810–1927* (Minneapolis, 1971), p. 21.

[51] HL, Smith Papers, ABC: 60, box 2, Smith to Hallock, 17 April 1840; Smith to Anderson, 17 June 1851.

[52] Ṭarrāzī, *Tārīkh al-Ṣiḥāfa*, Vol. 2, p. 31; Ami Ayalon, *The Press in the Arab Middle East—A History* (New York, 1995), p. 34.

[53] SAC, Tibawi Papers, box 2, file 3, Yaziji to Smith, 16 August 1845.

[54] HL, Smith Papers, ABC: 50, box 1, Nawfal to Smith, 1 August 1851; for some reason nothing came of the project.

At the same time, Smith devoted many hours to the study of "Syria." He had a keen interest in its geography and pioneered transferring the Arabic names of local places onto English-made maps. His private library included three travelogues about Syria and several books that described its past and present, both significant themes in his thinking and very much evident in the lecture he gave to the members of the Society in 1852.[55] This lecture in fact opens Buṭrus al-Bustānī's collection. Curiously, Smith does not use the term "Syria" but instead speaks of *bilādukum* ("your country") and immediately connects it with the Arab race and culture which he highlights as the "link" between the ancient and the modern world.[56] That is, that it was thanks to Arab civilisation that the achievements of the ancient Greeks and Romans were safeguarded for the West, where they became the foundation of the "modern world":

> It is evident that our numbers are small, our work limited and our resources poor, but this does not mean we have to stop hoping or let our will slacken, since the country you were born in and the race to which you belong and the tongue in which you speak . . . come to your help and lend you a hand [*Iʾanna nafs al-bilād allatī wulidtum fīhā wal-jins alladhī tanāsaltum minhu wal-lisān alladhī tatakallamūna bihi narāhā qad wāfat ilā najdatikum wal-akhdh biyadikum*]. As to your country, its long history [*fatārīkhuhā al-mustaṭīl*] tells us what happened in it and is being studied with a great deal of enthusiasm by all those who love religion and find pleasure in [studying] the events. [This history] is carved in its stones and walls and buried in its mountains and hills. Regarding your Arab race, its culture served as a link [*fa-ādābuhu wasīla tarbuṭ*] between the ancient world, graced with the Greek and Roman sciences, and the modern world, graced with the science and culture of the European people. In addition, you possess books that have come to us from this past that shed light on the wonderful and significant events that make up the era.[57]

Together with his clear notion of Syria as a territorial unity, the way in which he discusses "country," "race," "language," "history" and

---

[55] On Smith's library, see for example, Edward W. Hooker, *Memoir of Mrs. Sarah Lanman Smith* (Boston, 1840), pp. 183, 327; Patton, *The Modern Syrians*, p. 68.

[56] In general, we find that when members of the society talked about the Ottoman Empire they used the word "*dawla*", while for Syria they used "*bilād*"; cf. Al-Bustānī, *Aʿmāl al-Jamʿiyya al-Sūriyya*, pp. 2, 9, 41–43.

[57] *Ibid.*, pp. x–ix. Smith's idea of Syria as a territorial unit appears as early as 1833 in a lecture he delivered during a stay in Boston; Smith, *Missionary Sermons and Addresses*, p. 147.

"culture" clearly meant to tell his listeners that they ought to revive these elements—in the past these had helped them to get out of "difficult situations;" if they wished to "improve the present state" of their country they ought to revive its "glorious past." For Smith, as for other missionaries, no clear contradiction existed between being "Syrian" and having an Arab cultural identity. In their eyes, the latter carried no religious implication, and was pre-Islamic. By endowing the Arab culture with a secular connotation, being Arab would not prevent a person from accepting the Gospel. Moreover, the apparent ambiguity between a Phoenician past and an Arab culture was also not contradictory in the eyes of the missionaries, or for their local listeners. They saw the concepts as complementary—two sides of a whole or two cultural identities that do not contradict each other but rather two discourses that contest the power to shape "New Syria."[58]

Smith's lecture was delivered in 1852 but, as noted above, he had already developed some of his notions before that. Furthermore, local Christian intellectuals, such as Mīkhā'īl Mishāqa, Buṭrus al-Bustānī, Wortabet and the young Khalīl al-Khūrī, were in close contact with Smith and other missionaries during these same years, and no doubt were also exposed to and influenced by their ideas.

Towards the end of his lecture Smith hinted at how important bridging the gaps between the different religious communities was, in his opinion. The Society had a rule which forbade members to oppose views expressed by the faiths (*madhāhib*) of the many religious communities that inhabited the country (*abnā' hādhā al-balad*). Anybody interested in the sciences could participate in the meetings of the Society, whatever their denomination. This message applied to the limited context of the Society, but the principle later received a broader interpretation in the writings of the local literati, where the "Society" was replaced by the inhabitants of the entire region, united in their concern about the country's future.[59]

Of the other seventeen lectures Buṭrus al-Bustānī chose to include, another three had been given by the missionaries; thus, the lion's share of the book was devoted to the local Christians.[60] As we find

---

[58] On a similar duality in the case of Egypt see: Gabriel Piterberg, "The Tropes of Stagnation and Awakening in Nationalist Historical Consciousness—The Egyptian Case" in James Jankowski and Israel Gershoni (eds.), *Rethinking Nationalism in the Arab Middle East* (New York, 1997), pp. 48–50.

[59] Al-Bustānī, *Aʿmāl al-Jamʿiyya al-Sūriyya*, p. xiii.

[60] Bustānī writes that the Society ran a total of 53 gatherings. Perhaps some

the motives Smith had outlined in his opening lecture—country, history, language and culture—re-occurring throughout those of all the others, Buṭrus al-Bustānī's collection is clear testimony not just of how great a share the Society had in disseminating the missionaries' concept of "Syria", but also of how deeply interwoven that concept was with the importance of modern (Western) science.

For example, Van Dyck called his contribution "On the Pleasures of Knowledge and its Benefits," in which he stressed the importance of knowledge and of broadening one's education.[61] Others dealt with modern science. Buṭrus al-Bustānī himself, for example, talked about matters of astronomy and Salīm Nawfal discussed "The Origins of Natural Laws."[62] Many of the lectures, of course, centred on Syria, and focused not only on history, geography, culture and language, but primarily on education. One of Buṭrus al-Bustānī's lectures was on "The City of Beirut," in which he highlighted the city's ancient Phoenician glory.[63] William Thomson lectured "About the Sabti River" that flowed north of Mount Lebanon, while Nawfal talked "About the Flora."[64] Others addressed the country's future and the state of its education. Buṭrus al-Bustānī, significantly, in his "About Women's Education," wrote that promoting female education would benefit not only women but also the country as a whole.[65]

In "The Extent and Causes of the Development of Education in Syria" John Wortabet reviewed the positive cultural and educational developments Syria had seen throughout the first half of the nineteenth century, which for him had much to do with Syria's extended trade with Europe and the introduction of the new sciences.[66] He pointed to the important contribution the new schools were making; to the increase in the number of women receiving a better education; and to the distribution of books on culture and science. All this, he felt, entitled him to proclaim a bright future for Syria:

---

meetings included more than one lecture. Bustānī's choice reflected the topics he himself was interested in. See al-Bustānī, *Aʿmāl al-Jamʿiyya al-Sūriyya*, p. xiv; al-Bustānī, *al-Jamʿiyya al-Sūriyya lil-ʿUlūm wal Funūn*, p. 13.

[61] Al-Bustānī, *Aʿmūl al-Jamʿiyya al-Sūriyya*, pp. 2–10.

[62] *Ibid.*, pp. 91–99 and pp. 10–13, respectively.

[63] *Ibid.*, pp. 61–64.

[64] *Ibid.*, pp. 64–69 and pp. 79–91, respectively.

[65] *Ibid.*, pp. 27–40.

[66] *Ibid.*, pp. 10–13. Wortabet probably delivered several lectures on Syria at the Society's meetings, which he later translated into English and published in his *Syria and the Syrians*; HL, Smith Papers, ABC: 60, box 5, Wortabet to Smith, 15 January 1852.

> We have slept enough, if the dawn rises now, let us rise and awake with it. We have missed much and have much to accomplish before we achieve our goal and I wish I had a trumpet to startle this country [*bilād*], to awake its dwellers . . ."[67]

Other lectures, especially those dealing with the region's history and economics, invariably go back to pre-Islamic times. Mīkhā'īl Mudawwar's lecture "On the Origin and Development of Trade" traces the economic history of the Syrian region from the pre-Islamic period until the present. Mīkhā'īl Mudawwar, as do other local Christians, follows the missionaries in giving a great deal of attention to the Phoenician period, for example, surveying their main trading centres: Tyre, Sidon and Tadmor. According to him, the success of these cities lay in their highly developed cultures and their economic significance as bridges between the West and Syria's hinterland, suggesting that reviving Syria's glory was dependent on enhancing its cultural features and expanding trade through its ports.[68]

Directly connected with this is the recurring call in Buṭrus al-Bustānī's collection for the revival of the Arabic language and Arab culture. For Van Dyck, it was clear that as the local Arab population was no longer able to fully appreciate the richness of their own language, they had lost access to the splendour of the poetry and literature that was their heritage. He pointed to the example of the Abbasid Caliphs and suggested to his contemporaries that they start incorporating foreign (especially Greek) loan words into Arabic so as to facilitate the study of the new sciences.[69] To reinforce the link with the achievements of the past, Buṭrus al-Bustānī includes Nāṣīf al-Yāzijī's contribution "About the Arab Sciences," in which the author recalls the great heights Arab science had reached in the *al-Jāhiliyya* period (the pre-Islamic period).[70] With much the same aim in mind, Buṭrus al-Bustānī himself wrote about al-Ḥarīrī, the fourth-century Persian literati and a poet famous for his Arabic *maqamāt*.[71]

The trend we find running throughout Buṭrus al-Bustānī's collection is recognisably one of restructuring images of the past for a contemporary purpose. And it is Mudawwar's lecture, perhaps more

---

[67] Bustānī, *Aʿmāl al-Jamʿiyya al-Sūriyya*, p. 13.
[68] *Ibid.*, pp. 43–50.
[69] *Ibid.*, pp. 9–10.
[70] *Ibid.*, pp. 41–43.
[71] *Ibid.*, pp. 77–79; *Ḥadīqat al-Akhbār*, No. 103, 30 May 1861.

than any other, that may be seen as representative of the new kind of awareness that the process of "modernisation" had sparked, of the "new perceptions of the traditional heritage and attempts at adaptation to new conditions" it brought about.[72] Read in this way, Buṭrus al-Bustānī's collection reaffirms that American missionaries and local Christian Arabs met, fortuitously, in the interstices thrown up by the very same process—as agents of modernisation. The encounter enabled the missionaries to "concretise" their imagined "Syria" and "Syrians," while it was crucial for the local Christians, as part of the newly emerging middle stratum, in grounding their search for a new socio-cultural identity in the missionaries' concept of "Syria."

What emerges most clearly from Buṭrus al-Bustānī's collection is that as early as 1852 a group of local Christians had begun to conceive of "Syria" as a single geographically unified region with its own socio-cultural characteristics and a shared history and economy. Religion is not mentioned anywhere, neither Christianity nor Islam. Given that talks and discussions were held in Arabic, this underscores the fact that in cultural and linguistic terms the Society's members conceived of "Syria," not as Muslim or Christian, but as Arab, possibly the earliest instance of the pull of secularism which was to play such an overriding part in the way Christian-Arab nationalism was to develop.

Khuṭba fī Ādāb al-ʿArab: *A Case Study*[73]

As noted, Buṭrus al-Bustānī and Eli Smith had become close friends over the years and obviously discussed their philosophies together, developing a fair amount of cross-fertilisation of ideas between them. Thus we find that when al-Bustānī gave his own famous lecture, *Khuṭba fī Ādāb al-ʿArab* (A Lecture on the Culture of the Arabs) in 1859, seven years after Eli Smith's speech in *al-Jamʿiyya al-Sūriyya*, it contained several clear echoes of Smith's earlier effort.[74] In the intervening seven years, interest in Arab culture and literature had increased

---

[72] Sharabi, *Arab Intellectuals and the West*, p. ix.

[73] I am referring mainly to the last part of the lecture entitled "On the Current Culture of the Arabs."

[74] Al-Bustānī, *al-Jamʿiyya al-Sūriyya lil-ʿUlūm wal Funūn*, pp. 101–117; Abu-Manneh, "The Christians between Ottomanism and Syrian Nationalism," p. 291.

gradually. For example, Iskandar Agha Abkāryūs' book, *Rawḍat al-Ādāb fī Ṭabaqāt Shuʿarāʾ al-Arab*, was published in Marseilles in 1852. The book includes biographies and information about the lives of Arab writers from the Classical Period. It was reprinted in Beirut in 1858, indicating that a demand existed during this period for this type of literature. Therefore, it can be said that Buṭrus al-Bustānī's interest in Arab culture was part and parcel of an existing atmosphere. At the same time, his lecture represented a significant push towards involvement in Arabic language and culture.

The lecture was divided into three parts. In its third part, titled "On the Current Culture of the Arabs", Buṭrus al-Bustānī called for the revival of Arabic language and culture. The importance of this lecture, which was also conceived as marking the beginning of the *Nahḍa*, is evident on two levels. The first is that it deals with the cultural shades of modern Syria. Secondly, it was one of the first lectures that joined Arabic language and culture to the Syrian idea. Although Buṭrus al-Bustānī does not make use of the term "Syria" in his lecture, he does link the country with Arabic language and culture. Nevertheless, in this lecture there is as yet no clear call for Syrian patriotism. That development became evident in Buṭrus al-Bustānī's writing only after 1860.

A comparison of the two lectures, those of Smith and Bustānī, makes it possible to evaluate not only what the principal concepts that the American missionaries imparted to the local Christian-Arab intellectuals were and what the degree of their influence on the latter was, but also how the intellectuals re-interpreted the ideas of the missionaries according to their own views. Smith's influence on al-Bustānī is evident from the very start of the lecture, where the latter returns to Smith's first idea, holding that to reach the best results in science people had to work in coordination and cooperation. Accordingly, Buṭrus al-Bustānī, like Smith, stressed that to obtain good results in scientific research, minds have to be united. However, al-Bustānī advanced this idea a step further than had Smith. Smith spoke of the assembly of individual people to achieve knowledge; Buṭrus al-Bustānī added the need for the fusion of tribes and peoples—a hidden call for unity.

The major theme of al-Bustānī's lecture was his call for the resurrection of Arabic language and culture, while admonishing Arabs for their dismal cultural and linguistic state. This subject was also a foremost issue for Smith. In contrast to the latter, al-Bustānī developed it in the third part of his lecture, detailed it more extensively, and added a review of the state of knowledge among the Arabs from the *Jāhiliyya* to the nineteenth century. He emotionally called on the Arabs to emerge from their present depressed condition and revitalise their illustrious past.[75]

Buṭrus al-Bustānī sought to instil in his listeners pride in their ancestors' culture, in order to awaken them to achievements as great as those of the past. He therefore explained the scientific contribution of the Arabs and praised their earlier attainments. He stressed that the search for knowledge was an Arab quality. Al-Bustānī raised this point after he tried to explain to his audience why the Arabs had achieved so much in the past. He claimed that when science and culture were in danger of being lost because of wars, disputes and civil conflicts in the Western world, they found refuge in the schools of the Arabs, in which the Arabs protected and safeguarded the mediating link in the chain of science joining the ancient sciences with the modern ones. When Buṭrus al-Bustānī presented Arab culture as a link connecting the early sciences to the modern, he was in fact repeating the principal idea that Smith had espoused in 1852.[76]

In his lecture, al-Bustānī expanded on the ways in which the Arabs could realise the revival of their culture. He viewed the generation of the nineteenth century as a generation striding on the right path and for which the door of hope was opening on the opportunity to achieve the objects he preached. He exhorted the local population to encourage education since it would bring about the revitalisation of the culture.

The high point of the speech came towards its end. Buṭrus al-Bustānī turned to his countrymen with an emotional call to arise and resurrect their culture:

> People of the land (*waṭan*), descendants of those honourable men, progeny of the tribes (*maʿāshir*) of Syrians and Greeks, riding on the crest of the nineteenth generation, a generation of knowledge and light, a generation of inventions and discovery, a generation of culture and knowledge, a generation of skills and sciences, Arise! Awake! Hark! And begin to act with vigour.[77]

Although Smith's influence on al-Bustānī is evident in the lecture, it may be discerned that the latter sharpened Smith's ideas by developing

[75] Al-Bustānī, *al-Jamʿiyya al-Sūriyya lil—ʿUlūm wal Funūn*, pp. 113–117.
[76] *Ibid.*, p. 115.
[77] *Ibid.*, p. 117.

the concept of revival of the Arab culture. Smith and al-Bustānī indeed drew on the grandeur of the past, but it was Buṭrus al-Bustānī who stressed the significance of the Arab cultural revival and its direct contribution to the good of the homeland. Thus, he talked of this revival in the Syrian setting as early as 1859. In contrast to Smith, who spoke before a small audience of members of the Society, Buṭrus al-Bustānī addressed the entire community, whom he called, the sons of the homeland (*abnāʾ al-waṭan*).

Beyond this, it is evident that al-Bustānī was influenced by a number of Smith's ideas and charged them with wider meaning. For example, Smith had claimed that the will to bridge the gaps between the various sects would contribute to society and its goals. Buṭrus al-Bustānī took this idea as his starting point and transferred it to the framework of the *waṭan*. For him, unity of minds, tribes, and peoples would help in the development of science and knowledge, a circumstance that would bring peace and quiet to Syria.

Apparently, the influence on Buṭrus al-Bustānī by the American missionaries in general, and the inspiration he received from Smith's words and friendship in particular, laid the foundation for some of the ideas that subsequently (after 1860) became the basis for the development of his pattern of thinking regarding Syrian patriotism. During this period he did not yet speak in patriotic-secular terms, such as *ḥubb al-waṭan* (love of the homeland). These themes characterised his writing only later. At this stage, his doctrine focused mainly on preaching the Arab-cultural resurrection of the land. Evidence of this is the fact that the ideas he set out in his lecture concentrate on the cultural sphere.

The Nahḍa *and the American Missionaries*

Where does this leave the American Presbyterian missionaries vis-à-vis the *Nahḍa*? Attempting to answer this, my point of departure will be Tibawi's rejection of claims that the missionaries were instrumental in the rediscovery of the Arabic literature. Instead, he emphasised that this heritage was never lost, adding that anyone who claimed to have "rediscovered" it can never specifically point out any Arabic classics they had edited or printed.[78]

---

[78] Abdul Latif Tibawi, *A Modern History of Syria Including Lebanon and Palestine*

At least one other historical element that is important here has generally been overlooked. Already from about the beginning of the nineteenth century, i.e. before the arrival of the American missionaries, a literary circle of Arab writers and poets had existed that produced many books and collections of poetry some of which are well-known and read until today. As was shown in the first chapter, this was the circle maintained in the court of Amīr Bashīr II.

Then also, and much better known, there is the fact that as far back as the early nineteenth century, presses were printing in Arabic both in Egypt and the Lebanon.[79] In fact, most of the books the missionaries published would be printed on these presses. In 1822, quite a number of books in both Arabic and Turkish were printed in Būlāq (Cairo).[80]

Later, during the period of the Egyptian occupation, local Christians and Muslims from various places in Syria, such as Aleppo, Damascus, Tripoli and Jaffa, began ordering volumes in Arabic on a wide variety of topics (medicine, science, theology, literature, history, geography, etc.) from Egypt.[81] We find that, whereas the missionaries were mainly interested in bringing out religious and textbook literature, the local literati were very much involved in publishing books that dealt with cultural topics and classical Arabic.[82] Significant, too, in this context are the activities of ʿAyn Waraqa, the Maronite college. Buṭrus al-Bustānī and Fāris al-Shidyāq were only two of the several well-known literati who received their Arabic education there.[83] Consequently, because of his command of the language, al-Bustānī became the Arabic tutor of a number of American missionaries while

(London, 1969), p. 145; idem, "The American Missionaries in Beirut and Butrus al-Bustani," pp. 141, 151. Most of the books the missionaries published in Arabic on secular topics were textbooks on the basic subjects they taught in their schools, e.g. Smith's Arithmetic, Bustānī's Arithmetic, Van Dyck's Geography and Algebra, in addition to Arabic Alphabet, Elements of Arabic Grammar, Arabic Grammatical Structures, etc. On religious topics I counted 33 titles; cf. HL, series ABC: 16.8.1, Vol. 1, "Printing Done at the Mission during 1810–1860;" Vol. 6, "Annual Report of the Beirut Station, February 1862;" Vol. 8, pt. 1, "Records of the ʿAbeih Seminary 1848–1878"; see also Rufus Anderson, *The Missionary Herald*, Vol. 34, December 1838, p. 473.

[79] Tibawi, *American Interests*, pp. 68–71.

[80] For further details see: Abū al-Futūḥ Raḍwān, *Tārīkh Maṭbaʿat Būlāq wa Lamḥa fī Tārīkh al-Ṭibāʾa fī Buldān al-Sharq al-Awsaṭ* (Cairo, 1953), pp. 256–257.

[81] Tibawi, *American Interests*, pp. 68–69.

[82] *Centennial of the American Press, 1822–1922* (Beirut, 1923), pp. 3, 12, 38–39.

[83] Hourani, *Arabic Thought in the Liberal Age*, p. 99.

also working for the Mission in his capacity as Arabic teacher.[84] As we saw, in 1850 he assisted Smith in his project of translating the Bible into Arabic.

Thus, the most we can say is, again, that the American Presbyterian missionaries encouraged a process of local dynamics already underway, but did not initiate it. The impetus which they may have given to the existing process of Arabic revival was not considered by them a goal in and of itself, but as a means towards construction of a Syrian concept or idea. The increased use of Arabic created a by-product—the increased interest in it among local intelligentsia. During the final years of the nineteenth century, the language which served these missionaries as an educational and cultural instrument, also came to serve as an important element of the Arab Nationalist Movement, among which numbered several of the missionaries' students and local Muslims as well.

From Evangelical Activities to Secular Enterprise: The Syrian Protestant College

By the 1850s and independently from the declared policy of the Boston-based home organisation, which remained centred on evangelising, some of the Americans had begun to identify with the region and its population to such an extent that they spoke of "Syria" as their adopted country. Before long a clear "concept of Syria" emerged in their writings; they then set out to give these concepts tangible form through educational and cultural activities.

The civil strife of 1860 provided a sense of added urgency, and the concept of Syria became the cornerstone of the SPC that the missionaries founded in 1866. I would like to emphasise some hitherto ignored points regarding the college. On other issues of the college much research was already conducted.[85]

With the passing years, the SPC grew more and more detached from the Mission, while some of the missionaries who taught there

[84] Rustum, *Bashīr Bayna al-Sulṭān wal-ʿAzīz*, p. 274.

[85] For example, see: Dodge, *The American University of Beirut*; E. Kedouri, "The American University of Beirut," *Middle Eastern Studies*, Vol. 3 (1966), pp. 74–90; Munro, *A Mutual Concern: The Story of the American University of Beirut*; Smith, "The American University of Beirut," pp. 292–334.

put less and less emphasis on its religious character, focusing instead on cultural, scientific and secular aspects.[86] From the beginning, one of the purposes of the College was to meet the educational needs of the Syrian youth and thus to bridge the gap between the various Syrian communities. The College was to include all conditions and classes of men without regard to colour, nationality, race or religion. For Daniel Bliss (1823–1916), the first president of the College, who served in this role for 36 years, these principles were the essence of his policy. The missionaries working in the College believed that such an establishment would, in the American style, combine Christian ideals with modern outlooks and provide an advanced Western education.[87] Jessup for example, wrote that, "A right and solid system of education such as we propose to give will do more for Syria than all the diplomacy of any five powers on the face of the earth."[88]

Also, the missionaries believed that, by making available good college education locally, the more ambitious local people, including potential leaders, would remain in Syria, rather than go abroad for their higher education. The missionaries held that those who left found it very difficult to fit into local society and did not contribute to its successes.[89] Simultaneously, the demand for higher education among the local population was growing. With the economic development of Beirut, the population needed new professions and diverse education. They believed that the American missionaries were the ones to fulfil this demand for higher education. The local community was sympathetic towards these missionaries, among other reasons due to the fact that America had not participated in the Beiruti Committee after the events of 1860. Moreover, they were already known for the good education that they provided in their primary schools.[90]

---

[86] SAC, Tibawi Papers, box 3, file 1, Anderson to the Syrian Mission, 21 March 1862; Ussama Makdisi, "Reclaiming the Land of the Bible: Missionaries, Secularism and Evangelical Modernity," *The American Historical Review*, Vol. 102 (1997), pp. 707–713.

[87] Penrose, *That They May Have Life*, p. 4.

[88] HL, Bliss Papers, Jessup to Bliss, 6 January 1866.

[89] HL, Annual Report of the ABCFM, 1863, p. 84; 1864, p. 90; HL, series ABC: 16.8.2.5, Vol. 2, Thirty-Sixth Annual Report of the SPC, 9 July 1902; ABCFM, series ABC: 16.8.1, Vol. 8, part 1, Annual Meeting, Bliss, 17 January 1862.

[90] *The Missionary Herald*, Vol. 59, December 1863, p. 366.

The American missionaries in the College were aware of this atmosphere and tried, by means of the SPC, to take advantage of the new circumstances after the events of 1860, and help establish a modern Syrian society wherein its people would work together in harmony for the good of their Syrian country. Of course, these activities were also conducted in order to preserve the successes that they had achieved in the Syrian region until that time.

During these years, they tried to create a sense of Syrian citizenship with a vision common to all its sects, which would provide Syrian youth with experience and training in this direction, so that as adults in the coming years, they would function as Syrians. The missionaries believed that the College would be "an institution which shall furnish to native youth an education such as the country demands, in their own tongue, in their own land and at the lowest cost."[91] They preached for a "good" Syrian society and government and tried to expose their students to various professions in all aspects of life that were needed by society.

The students were engaged in activities that would enlarge their knowledge regarding the history of the Syrian region. The missionaries used to conduct trips during some of the classes, involving their students in collecting artefacts from Syria for display in the museums they established.[92]

Finally, it is important to emphasise that until 1881, the language used for teaching in the college was Arabic. Also, the college's name was "The Syrian Protestant College" emphatically proclaiming that this educational establishment was to be a symbol to the entire population of the modern Syrian society.

In the beginning of the twentieth century, when Howard Bliss, son of Daniel Bliss, served as president of the College (between the years 1902–1920), it became active not only in cultural and educational activities but also in political issues regarding the Syrian region.[93] In contrast to the past, when the college had emphasised its apolitical nature, it and its president now began to take part in the political activities regarding the future of the region after the First World War. In 1918, the American government attempted to inquire into the desires of the local inhabitants regarding their future. In that

[91] HL, Bliss Papers, Correspondence Regarding the SPC, n.d.
[92] HL, ABC: 16.8.2.5, Vol. 2, Annual Report of the SPC, 1873; 1877; 1884; 1886.
[93] Bliss, *The Modern Missionary*, pp. 5–6.

year, Howard Bliss wrote to Woodrow Wilson, the American President, that he believed that any report prepared by anyone with an education would show that the Syrians aspire to a free country or at least to a country that would temporarily be placed under the mandate of a Great Power or the League of Nations. Later he explained that it is desirable that the Americans would be the ones to come and investigate the region.[94]

The encouragement of Syrian patriotism in the College over the years stood out in 1919 in the King-Crane report. This report, which Howard Bliss participated in creating, remarks upon "the spirit revealed in American educational institutions in Syria, especially the college in Beirut, with its well known and constant encouragement of Syrian national sentiment . . ."[95]

In conclusion, from the second half of the nineteenth century on, a number of local, educated Christians became active on behalf of Syrian patriotism. One of the characteristics they had in common was that they all were or had been in touch with the missionaries or had received all or part of their education in missionary schools or in the College. In their publications and activities one also recognises many of the features of *al-Jamʿiyya al-Sūriyya*, the society that had brought missionaries and local intellectuals together between the years of 1847–1852.

In other words, when in the 1860s and 70s local literati took up and further developed the American missionaries' concept of Syria, they turned it into the linchpin for the construct of the Syrian *waṭaniyya* that they were already developing. In this sense, one can say that Syrian patriotism had some of its roots in the presence of the American missionaries and the challenges thrown up by discrete local dynamics.

The most illuminating example of this process is Buṭrus al-Bustānī. His relationship with the missionaries illustrates the changing relationships between the Christian intellectuals and the missionaries as well as the changing attitudes among the American missionaries toward Syria over the years. As early as the 1840s, Buṭrus al-Bustānī, then in his twenties, was in touch with the missionaries, in particular with Eli Smith, with whom he was to form a close friendship. But,

---

[94] Harry N. Howard, *The King-Crane Commission* (Beirut, 1963), p. 26.
[95] *Ibid.*, p. 353.

as the years went by, he realised that, however strong they might feel about the future of modern Syria, the missionaries would never be prompted to transcend the main purpose for which they had come to the region, the spreading of the Gospel and the creation of a Christian Syria. In 1856, following the death of Smith, Buṭrus al-Bustānī distanced himself from the Mission.

Then, in 1864, Bustānī established *al-Madrasa al-Waṭaniyya*, a school based on patriotic and secular principals and open to all, regardless of religious or sectarian origin. When two years later the SPC was established, Buṭrus al-Bustānī renewed his relationship with the missionaries who taught there, and his institution was chosen as a preparatory school for the College.

Later, as he contemplated the events of 1860, he understood only too well that for his society to regain its balance and have its different communities live together in peace, Syrian patriotism had to be encouraged. In other words, al-Bustānī took the missionaries' concept of Syria one crucial step further and helped transform it into what he saw as the only valid goal—a Syrian *waṭaniyya*.

Hence, the relationships between the American missionaries and the Christian-Arab intellectuals was not a dichotomy between actor and acted upon but rather a complex matrix of interactions, cross cultural exchanges wherein both sides were active. The encounter between these missionaries and the Christian-Arab intellectuals should be treated dialectically, emphasising the dynamic role not only of the missionaries but also of that of the local Christian Arabs.[96] The missionaries were another catalyst contributing to the process of building this Syrian identity. Yet, the final touch was to be that of the local Christian-Arab intellectuals. The methods they used to process and transform these concepts will be elaborated in the next chapter.

96 For more details on this attitude, see: Jean Comaroff and John Comaroff, *Of Revelation and Revolution*, pp. 6–11.

CHAPTER FIVE

NARRATING AN IDENTITY: NEW GENRES, NEW IDENTITY (1858–1881)

New topics or concepts, in our case identity, are expressed in new styles of writing, which include new subjects, or create new genres in their wake. Thus, changes in content may lead to changes in style, or vice versa.[1] The emergence of the concept of *waṭan* (homeland) as opposed to *umma* or *milla* (mainly the Muslim community) was a pivotal factor in the changing world view that led to the genesis of new forms of discourse.[2] In order to introduce a new identity, it was necessary to find new ways of writing that would express this new way of thinking, to discover the tools and methods to portray and narrate the saga of the Syrian nation, and to turn it into reality by embedding it into a broader semantic field of "civilisation" and "progress."

Syrian identity was expressed in three new genres that were first formed by the Beiruti middle stratum and that had hardly existed before in the Arab provinces: the press, a "new historiography" and historical novels. The evolution of these modern genres attests to a new kind of self-awareness or self-identification. Syria as a unified political entity would not exist for several decades, but it had already begun to take conceptual shape in the cultural productions of this rising Beiruti middle stratum.

From the second half of the nineteenth century, especially after the events of 1860 and until the middle of the 1880s, a more creative and active side of the Beiruti middle stratum can be seen. During these years these Christian-Arab intellectuals took another step toward building their identity and managed to mould it into its final shape. Emphasis will be laid in this chapter on the creative

---

[1] Alastair Fowler, "Transformation of Genre," in David Duff (ed.) *Modern Genre Theory* (London, 2000), pp. 232–233; Alastair Fowler, *Kinds of Literature: An Introduction to the Theory of Genres and Modes* (Oxford, 1982), pp. 170–183.

[2] Sabry Hafez, *The Genesis of Arabic Narrative Discourse: A Study in the Sociology of Modern Arabic Literature* (London, 1993), p. 97.

potential of cultural interaction, i.e. the result of adopting Western traits of culture as inherently original rather than accentuating the actual act of imitation.

For example, local intellectuals transformed the Western experience and influence into their own society, translating them into their existing cultural matrices and codes, where they took on different meanings or were employed in different ways. These intellectuals played an active role in resisting, selecting, and re-shaping the cultural products by which they were influenced. They added new components, enlarged or re-interpreted others that already existed, or gave them different interpretations by means of new genres that were influenced by the West. The members of this group served as a kind of "blender" which selectively absorbed new concepts and ideas in order to translate them to their own cultural environment and then reinvented them in their own imagination, giving these adopted genres their own authentic mark.[3]

Concentrating on the way in which the intellectuals constructed their identity shows that they combined different influences, sometimes opposed to one another, but combining together to create this Syrian identity; it contained influences from the Islamic East and from the West, from the local and the foreign, translated into the Syrian and Arab heritage. This eclectic, multi-cultural hybridian identity was Syrian in its new tenor, Ottoman in its political aspects, and Arab in its traditional heritage and cultural tone.

In many cases, and in all three literary genres, the intellectuals adapted genuine "old" traditions to new situations and at the same time built "new" traditions to meet new needs. The game between the self and the "other", the self with the "other", or the traditional with the modern, created the balance or the dichotomy of their identity. In this way the Christian Arabs invented their identity, but at the same time re-constructed it.

---

[3] As Chaterjee puts it, "If nationalisms in the rest of the world have to choose their imagined community from certain 'modular' forms already made available to them by Europe and the Americas, what do they have left to imagine?" Partha Chatterjee, *The Nation and its Fragments: Colonial and Postcolonial Histories* (Princeton, 1993), p. 5.

Characteristics and Goals of the Syrian Press

From 1858, with the publication of the first privately owned newspaper in Beirut, *Ḥadīqat al-Akhbār*, and as part of the *Nahḍa*, a domestic Arabic press developed in Beirut, especially among Christian-Arab intellectuals. The medium of the press had hardly existed here previously. Some newspapers were published before 1858 in the Ottoman Empire, but none of them represented the intellectual challenge that the Beiruti press did. For example, the government's newspaper *al-Waqāʾiʿ al-Miṣriyya* (Egyptian Events), founded by Muḥammad ʿAlī in 1828, and written in Egypt in the Arabic and Ottoman languages, was official in nature and of little interest to the public.[4] Later, from 1860, Ottoman newspapers began to appear. These publications were initiated from above, i.e. by the central government.

In contrast to these newspapers, the Beiruti press developed from within local society by the Christian-Arab intellectual elite, and in many cases as the private initiative of the Beiruti middle stratum, merchants and intellectuals working side by side.[5] This new medium quickly came to serve the needs of these intellectuals. The development of newspapers in Beirut was principally due to European influence and to the *Tanẓīmāt* reforms. In many cases, the Beiruti press was reminiscent of its European counterpart, and it developed many similar characteristics.

Four prominent newspapers, already mentioned, were published in Beirut: *Ḥadīqat al-Akhbār* (1858–1868),[6] *al-Jinān* (1870–1886), *Nafīr Sūriyya* (1860–1861) and the only newspaper published by Muslims at that time *Thamarāt al-Funūn* (1875–1908). The three newspapers edited by Christians were filled with secular issues in many fields of

[4] Another example of a newspaper that published before 1858 is *Mirʾāt al-Aḥwāl* (Mirror of Events). It was privately published by Rizqallāh Ḥassūn in Istanbul and appeared for only a single year—1855.

[5] *Ḥadīqat al-Akhbār*, No. 1, January 1858; No. 5, February 1858.

[6] Some claim that *Ḥadīqat al-Akhbār* continued to be published only until 1911, while others say it ran as far as 1913. In any case, only the first ten years (1858–1868) are available in the Bodleian Library (Oxford). I could not locate later issues, neither in the UK nor in the US. As far as I know, copies of the newspapers which were published in the 1880s are extant in the Jafet Library of the American University of Beirut. For more information on this newspaper, see: Ṭarrāzī, *Tārīkh al-Ṣiḥāfa*, Vol. 1, pp. 55–56; Krymskii, *Istoria Novoi*, p. 481.

daily and intellectual life. Several newspapers managed to keep publishing for years, sometimes for decades, and heralded the beginning of the press in the Arab provinces. This process continued, especially from the mid-1870s, mainly in Egypt. Yet it should be borne in mind that the cultural roots of this process originated in the region of Syria, and only later emerged in Egypt, in many cases by the same Beiruti middle stratum that had fled to Egypt to avoid the censorship of Hamidian rule, or by their following generation. In Beirut, the press became the centre of the cultural and the socio-economic life of the Beiruti stratum, and eventually of other places in the *Vilâyet* of Syria.

It was only natural that Syria would be exposed to this development due to the infrastructure already established in the region. The multiplication of printing houses and schools provided it with the instruments to train accomplished and well-educated people, capable of publishing this press.[7] The activities of the missionaries and their educational network provided secular and religious studies for girls as well as boys, in contrast to traditional education, which was religious in nature and intended for boys. This created, relative to other areas of the Arab provinces, a growing audience that included literate women and men.

The population in the region found considerable interest in the press though it is difficult to know how many people actually bought and read newspapers, since such information is almost unobtainable.[8] It is also difficult to assess what kind of audience read these newspapers or what impact it had on them. Yet, the growing number of newspapers in Beirut indicated their success. By the end of the nineteenth century, 25 newspapers were published in the city.[9] Also, the fact that they were published for long periods of time obviously meant that people actually bought them.

The only figures available for subscribers of newspapers in Beirut are for *Ḥadīqat al-Akhbār*. This newspaper published almost 3,000

[7] For more details on the development of the Syrian press during this time, see: Shams al-Dīn al-Rifāʿī, *Tārīkh al Ṣiḥāfa al-Sūrriya*, Vol. 1 (Cairo, 1969), pp. 27–28; Jūjīf Ilyās, *Taṭawwur al Ṣiḥāfa al-Sūriyya fī Miʾat ʿĀm 1860–1965* (Beirut, 1982–1983), pp. 9–17; Ayalon, *The Press in the Arab Middle East*, pp. 28–39.

[8] This problem was already discussed in research on Palestine at the end of the nineteenth century and the beginning of the twentieth century. Rashid Khalidi, *Palestinian Identity*, pp. 53–55; See also, Ami Ayalon, "Modern Texts and Their Readers in Late Ottoman Palestine," *Middle Eastern Studies*, Vol. 38 (2002), pp. 20–21.

[9] Ayalon, *The Press in the Arab Middle East*, p. 36.

issues; it had acquired 400 regular subscribers within three months of its first appearance. This was a relatively high number, given that most newspapers were sold via retail vendors.[10]

Other figures can be deduced from recent research by Ayalon on the channels through which Palestinians found access to the new cultural fruits that had ripened in neighbouring provinces or cities such as Beirut toward the end of the nineteenth century. The research presents preliminary conclusions or rough estimates on the number of people in Palestine who probably read *al-Jinān*. This periodical was published twice a month by Buṭrus al-Bustānī and was very well known among the population of *Bilād al-Shām*, Iraq, and Egypt; it even reached readers in European capitals such as London, Paris, and Berlin.[11] Every issue included between 32 and 36 pages, sometimes containing drawings. It was the first pan-Arab publication, i.e. it reached most parts of the Arab world. As Ayalon could not find a list of subscribers of *al-Jinān*, he focused on another record that was published in this newspaper—those who were interested in buying *Dāʿirat al-Maʿārif*, the first Arabic encyclopedia which was published between the years 1876 and 1900. Ayalon managed to find 1,022 names of subscribers listed in *al-Jinān* who were interested in buying this encyclopedia. Eventually, many of them changed their minds once the time to pay for it had arrived.

Nevertheless, it is interesting to see that such a large number of people wanted to buy it in the first place. This could give us an idea regarding cultural life during this time. More interesting for our case is the fact that most of them, around two thirds, lived in Lebanon and in Egypt. There were 154 names from towns in the Syrian provinces; most were Christians. Of course, through these figures we can assume that the people who were interested in buying the encyclopedia also had access to *al-Jinān* itself or were exposed to the newspaper.[12] This will also help to provide a rough estimate of the number of readers of *al-Jinān*, and eventually the number of people that apparently were exposed to ideas of Syrian identity.

We already know that *al-Jamʿiyya al-Sūriyya li-Iktisāb al-ʿUlūm wal-Funūn* alone had more than two hundred members. If we add this

---

[10] Krymskii, *Istoria Novoi*, p. 487; Ayalon, *The Press in the Arab Middle East*, pp. 31–32, 37.

[11] Ashraf A. Eissa, "Majallat al-Jinan: Arabic Narrative Discourse in the Making," *Quaderni di Studi Arabi*, Vol. 18 (2000), p. 42.

[12] Ayalon, "Modern Texts and Their Readers," pp. 22–26.

number to the participants in other cultural societies, the figures increase proportionately, although the fact that some individuals participated in more than one society should be taken into account. In addition, people of other strata who had the ability to read and write but were not considered intellectuals nor belonged to these societies were interested in such publications.

Some of the newspapers, and thus their ideas, were read out loud in coffee shops for people who could not afford them or were illiterate, and some were passed from hand to hand. These were also bought all over the *Vilâyet* of Syria. Marketing agents circulated them in cities and areas such as Mount Lebanon, Haifa, Acre, Jerusalem, Deir al-Qamar, and also in regions outside the *Vilâyet* of Syria such as Iraq and Egypt. For example, another newspaper of the Bustānī family, *al-Janna*, published from the end of the 1870s, had 40 agents distributing and promoting it in 40 different places.[13] Of course, the fact that so many newspaper agents were active does not provide precise information as to the extent that this network reflected demand for the printed products in these places. However, it is an indication that the press, and thus the ideas it promulgated, were distributed in many places throughout the *Vilâyet* of Syria.

Thus, a general figure of newspaper readers can be estimated. Ayalon's research regarding the Palestine region (which was part of the *Vilâyet* of Syria) toward the end of the nineteenth century and the beginning of the twentieth century concluded that in 1914 there were probably several hundred journal readers in a population of around 605,000.[14] Ayalon emphasises that this percentage was meagre compared with parallel activities in Lebanon and Egypt. The figures for Beirut and for other big cities in the *vilâyet* can be assumed to be higher than Ayalon provides for Palestine. Taking into account the *Nahḍa* activities, the local and foreign factors, the growing number of missionary schools, and Christian readers who had the ability to read and the money to buy these newspapers, the potential number of readers in Beirut and in a handful of smaller towns in

[13] The first page of several issues of the *al-Janna* newspaper includes a list of the names of the agents and their respective locations of marketing. In several cases the agents came from the Beiruti middle stratum and included merchants and educated figures, such as Asʿad Daḥdāḥ the agent of Ghazīr, Niqūlā Bustrus the agent in Egypt, Nuʿmān Maʿlūf the agent in Zahle and so on. See, for example, *al-Janna*, 25 July 1879.

[14] Ayalon, "Modern Texts and Their Readers," pp. 23, 32.

Mount Lebanon was possibly close to a thousand readers, or perhaps higher; but probably far less than that of the rest of the Syrian province, in cities such as Damascus and Aleppo (probably half as many). The likelihood is that each newspaper was read—or heard—by more than one person. These figures should be presented in comparison with the estimate of the Beiruti population, which in the 1870s (when the newspaper started publishing) was between 50,000 and 70,000 people.[15]

Hence, the circle of readers among the general population in the whole region of Syria was not a large one, but neither was it a marginal number. In proportion to the Christian population it was large, and thus had an influential effect in Beirut and probably in other cities of the *vilâyet* as well.

Journalism gradually became part of the cultural change taking place, accelerating the cultural transition and playing a significant role both in the self-identity of the new reading public, i.e. the Muslim and Christian intelligentsia, and in the new narrative discourse. It also became a vital medium of public communication.[16]

In 1870, Ḥusayn Bayhum, a contemporary Muslim notable and merchant from Beirut, wrote a poem on the Syrian press, highlighting the intellectuals' views about the press as an instrument to disseminate their concepts. The poem had added importance because the names of the leading journals of his day were inserted into its lines.[17]

Other reasons for the importance of the press are set out in *Ḥadīqat al-Akhbār*. Khalīl al-Khūrī wrote that the press was important because "this is how we feel in our local existence, and this is how we prepare that which accords us a seat among the developed nations." Khalīl al-Khūrī regarded his paper as "a star set on the forehead of our land (*balad*)," namely that the press elevated and "modernised" the country in which it appeared.[18]

The press was also perceived as bringing pride to local Syrian society. An anonymous article submitted to the editorial board of *Ḥadīqat al-Akhbār* noted that among the Europeans and "the enemies

---

[15] For further information see: Kais, Firro, "Silk and Socio-Economic Changes in Lebanon, 1860–1919," in Eli Kedouri and Sylvia G. Haim (eds.), *Essays on the Economic History of the Middle East* (London, 1988), p. 39; Fawaz, *Merchants and Migrants*, p. 128.

[16] Hafez, *The Genesis of Arabic Narrative Discourse*, pp. 71–72.

[17] Jiḥā Mīshāl, *Salīm al-Bustānī* (London, 1989), p. 50.

[18] *Ḥadīqat al-Akhbār*, No. 98, 17 November 1859.

of the Arab nation," the claim was widespread that the Arabs were incapable of publishing papers because they were not fond of reading and did not grasp what they read. The unnamed writer saw in this claim an expression of contempt and disdain for the Arab nation. In his view, the very existence of Khalīl al-Khūrī's paper proved precisely the opposite. The writer argued that the Arab nation proved that it was not without the ability to derive benefit from the press and that the Arabs were well aware of the value of such creativity and its purpose, which was the common good and the propagation of science.[19]

Buṭrus al-Bustānī also maintained a clear-cut perception of the importance of publishing papers. The entry "newspaper" (*Jarīda*) that he wrote for the encyclopedia *Dā'irat al-Ma'ārif*[20] indicates the importance of this matter in his eyes. The journals, al-Bustānī argued, had to be effective and nothing should be included in them that was incorrect, nor should they publish topics that served personal goals or incited to civil war and revolution. They should be free, and fulfil the critical and investigative responsibilities of the Fourth Estate, thereby improving the condition of the nation.

In general, most articles discussed the needs of *tamaddun* (civilisation) and argued that "a person who is without culture has no attributes and no importance."[21] The intellectuals believed that the solution to the conditions of society lay mainly in internal reform, i.e. arising from within society.

The papers published numerous articles on subjects such as literature, poetry, agriculture, medicine, plants, animals, chemistry, and so on in order to enlighten the Syrian society.[22] The education they recommended was for all strata, including women, who were gradually perceived as an important part of the population who should also be recruited for building the Syrian nation.[23]

After 1860, it is possible to observe in the Beiruti press components of the Syrian idea at an advanced stage, whereby the presentation had become more crystallised and clear, and was set forth openly before the entire population. The intellectuals believed that

---

[19] *Ibid.*, No. 31, 7 August 1858.
[20] Buṭrus al-Bustānī, "Jarīda," *Dā'irat al-Ma'ārif*, Vol. 6, p. 477.
[21] *Thamarāt al-Funūn*, No. 5, 18 May 1875; No. 9, 15 June 1875.
[22] *Al-Jinān*, Vol. 1, No. 1, 1870, pp. 10, 21.
[23] *Thamarāt al-Funūn*, No. 32, 2 November 1875.

through newspapers they could create in the individual a sense of belonging to his Syrian homeland. They also felt that their ideas would be distributed to a larger reading public and their aspirations would not remain within the closed framework of theoretical ideas solely among the educated elite.

In the past, information had been transmitted mainly orally, usually in the framework of religion. For example, most formal information in the Muslim community was transmitted in the Friday's *khuṭba*. In the Christian community, such information was promulgated through the chapel. In this way, the divisions between the religions were maintained, and information was sectionalised between the different communities of the region. The publication of newspapers, or as Anderson called it, "print capitalism,"[24] distributed uniform information, in many cases of a secular nature, to people from different communities, making it available to intellectuals of various religions or communities. Indeed, until the 1880s and even after that, newspapers served as a tool of translating the intellectuals' Syrian concept into reality.

Components of Identity in the Beiruti Press: How to Create Syrian Waṭaniyya

Tolerance, Brotherhood, and an Appeal to Abandon Sectarian Strife

After 1860, the intellectuals understood that the population of the region was unable to act in harmony, which prevented it from developing into "an advanced society." They saw that discord outweighed amity in their heterogeneous society, and called for unity, understanding, and tolerance, the basic components necessary to bring people together as one. They likewise stressed that the exposure to education and knowledge would improve the situation of the country and would facilitate the fulfilment of these desires.

Khalīl al-Khūrī, who had grasped the problem as early as 1858, before the events of 1860, preached tolerance. He called on "the Syrian nation", both Muslims and Christians, to avoid divisions that were eroding Syrian society. Even before the establishment of the

[24] Anderson, *Imagined Communities*, pp. 39–46.

Vilâyet of Syria, he was the first to address the population in the region as *al-jumhūr al-Sūrī* (the Syrian public), or *al-umma al-Sūriyya* (the Syrian nation) and used terms in his newspaper such as "Syrian pride" (*al-fakhr al-Sūrī*) and so on.[25]

The intellectuals reiterated that as long as the local population lacked cooperation among itself, it was harming the homeland in which it lived.[26] They urged the population to keep away from trouble and concentrate on farming its land so that it might be able to pick the fruits of success for itself and for the homeland.[27] Brotherhood and civic love (*maḥabba ahliyya*) would also help them.[28] They were warned against division, communal hatred, and sectarian zeal, which were considered the reasons for the destruction of the homeland.[29]

This is why the press also attempted to convince the population that war was the most terrible thing under the sun, and that civil war among children of the same soil was the vilest of all.[30] The intellectuals expressed the hope that henceforth the inhabitants of the homeland would not identify themselves by their religious origins but by national brotherhood and the region in which they lived.

For example, Salīm al-Bustānī stated in an article entitled "Why We Are Backward" that Syria's backwardness arose from disunity, religion, and ignorance. He pointed out that knowledge, unity, brotherhood, and sacrifice of personal interests for the sake of general interests were the remedy for the ills of society.[31]

The intellectuals promised that the good state of the homeland would bring personal fulfilment stemming from civic amity, patriotic affinity (*ulfa waṭaniyya*), concern for the benefit of all, and unification, without undermining personal desires.[32]

The call for unity was made not only in journals owned and edited by Christians but was echoed as well in one journal edited by Muslims, though more circumspectly. The Muslim newspaper *Thamarāt al-Funūn* noted in an article headlined "Unity" that people who argued that unity was brought about by means of religion, were misguided,

---

25 *Ḥadīqat al-Akhbār*, No. 29, 24 July 1858; No. 31, 7 August 1858.
26 *Nafīr Sūriyya*, 9 September 1860.
27 *Ḥadīqat al-Akhbār*, No. 125, 24 May 1860.
28 *Ibid.*, No. 165, 13 June 1861.
29 *Nafīr Sūriyya*, 14 January 1861.
30 *Ibid.*, 1 November 1860.
31 *Al-Jinān*, Vol. 1, No. 6, 1870, pp. 162–164.
32 *Ḥadīqat al-Akhbār*, No. 173, 8 August 1861.

and that instead this approach was the foundation of hatred. Such people, the paper believed, misused the laws of religion. The article stressed that people who did not possess much knowledge about religion claimed that the existence of a variety of religions ran counter to the possibility of unity. The writer argued that these people were mistaken because religion had its own way of bringing about unity, namely through a common faith in one God and in the need to perform good deeds.[33]

The newspaper was suffused with religious metaphors, and its writing was filled with Islamic connotations. At the same time, it did not make use of these factors for provocation against the faithful of other religions. Between the lines, indeed, one discerns a certain tendency of the Muslim intellectual in Beirut, and perhaps in other coastal cities too, to soften rigid opinions on matters of religion, and to consider religion as a factor that might unify and not merely single out. Moreover, in several cases the newspaper called for tolerance and brotherhood, albeit indirectly. The element of "religious fanaticism" was notable for its absence in this paper, while a common concern was the attempt to appeal to the rational, not the emotional side of the readership.

Two more methods were put forward to achieve unity. The first was through education and knowledge. Salīm Nawfal, in an article published in *Ḥadīqat al-Akhbār* in 1861, appealed for granting free education to all citizens of the country. He called for the establishment of a university in one of the cities of *al-Shām*, to benefit every student, regardless of religion. To create this school, he proposed placing a special tax on the "people of Syria" (*ahl sūriyya*). His wish was that this school would be "a station for the hopes of the people and all sons of the Arabs who would study there, with their different religions, in concord, harmony, and goodwill, would strengthen the bond with the land in an era of cooperation under the light of the sciences and the arts."[34]

The second method for achieving unity was patriotism—love of the homeland, the *waṭan*, which had to be shared by all. The love and unity that the Christian Arabs preached was "love as members of one family, whose father is the *waṭan*, whose mother is the land,

[33] *Thamarāt al-Funūn*, No. 3, 4 May 1875.
[34] *Ḥadīqat al-Akhbār*, No. 183, 17 October 1861.

and whose one Creator is God."[35] As Sheehi put it, "love of the nation is the central discursive element in the social and psychological process by which the self becomes a national subject."[36] The journals declared that all members of the homeland were equal. They called for a situation in which the Turk, the Arab, the Druze, the Jew, the Mutawali, the Maronite, the Orthodox, the Protestant, the Armenian, the Assyrian, and the Copt would all be brothers in the *waṭan*. They would have a single goal, namely the good of the land as a whole, not the good of a particular community.[37]

Ḥubb al-Waṭan[38] min al-Īmān *(Love of the Homeland is [an Article] of Faith)*

Syrian identity in the nineteenth century was not essentially a national territorial outlook in the Western sense. The motif of love of the *waṭan* was an abstract concept, and perhaps more difficult for readers to grasp. This could be one of the reasons that the press wrote many articles on this theme. In introducing the subject, the intellectuals started with a definition of the borders of their beloved *waṭan*, "Greater Syria." They wrote, "Syria is between the River Euphrates in the east and the Mediterranean Sea to the west, between the Arabian Peninsula to the south and Anatolia to the north."[39]

They then tried to explain the meaning of "patriotism." One of the first local intellectuals to absorb the full significance of patriotism as it was known in the West was again Khalīl al-Khūrī. He emphasised to *abnā' al-waṭan* (sons of the homeland) that a person had to sacrifice himself for the sake of the homeland, and to love its residents regardless of their religion.

Other intellectuals also explained the bilateral relationship between the *waṭan* and its inhabitants. They wrote that the population has

---

[35] *Nafīr Sūriyya*, 19 November 1860.

[36] Stephen P. Sheehi, "Inscribing the Arab Self: Buṭrus al-Bustani and Paradigms of Subjective Reform," *British Journal of Middle Eastern Studies*, Vol. 27 (2000), p. 14.

[37] *Al-Jinān*, Vol. 1, No. 14, 1870, pp. 435–436.

[38] The term "*waṭan*," as it is used in the newspapers, held several meanings. The first was the patriotic meaning, which referred to the Syrian homeland and was in use mainly by Christian Arabs. In contrast, the Muslims did not always use it in its patriotic connotation, but merely as a general term to describe a region that constitutes part of (and occasionally the whole territory of) the Ottoman Empire. Only towards the end of the nineteenth century did the Muslims also use it in its patriotic sense.

[39] *Ḥadīqat al-Akhbār*, No. 408, 29 May 1866.

rights within the *waṭan*, which had in turn responsibilities towards them. The homeland had to ensure the safety of its people, protect their rights, and grant them freedom of rights, religion, and culture. Members of the *waṭan* in return had to love it. If they departed from this purpose, because of sectarian zeal, "they sacrifice the good of their land to the good of their personal interests, and they do not deserve to belong to the *waṭan* but are its enemies."[40]

Khalīl al-Khūrī endeavoured to define the meaning of love of the homeland, especially as love of the people in the homeland for each other. He called attention to this interpretation as a solution for the main problem of society, i.e. its fragmentation. Already in 1858 he told his readers that in addition to the religious and moral demands for the welfare and the good of the people, for development and ascent up the ladder of human perfection, there was the love of the homeland.[41] This love was not merely for its landscapes, but primarily a love for the people, who lived in it, be they Muslims or Christians, and it had to be felt by all inhabitants of the land equally.[42]

Love of the homeland was also conceived as a requirement of faith (*ḥubb al-waṭan min al-īmān*). It was expressed, the intellectuals argued, as one of the homeland's rights (*al-ḥuqūq al-waṭaniyya*) and as serving the material and cultural resurrection of the nation. Its first appearance was probably in 1860 in the newspaper *Nafīr Sūriyya* in which Buṭrus al-Bustānī clarifies that one of the obligations of the people towards their homeland is to love it, as stated in the *ḥadīth*.[43] As of 1870, it was the motto of the periodical *al-Jinān* and appeared on the first page of every issue. It seems that both al-Bustānī's (father and son) used this motto, appearing, in their own words, in the *ḥadīth*, and gave it a secular interpretation according to their needs, hoping that this phrase would appeal to the Muslim population.[44]

---

[40] *Nafīr Sūriyya*, 25 October 1860; Zachs, "Building a Cultural Identity: The Case of Khalīl al-Khūrī."

[41] *Ḥadīqat al-Akhbār*, No. 31, 7 August 1858; No. 50, 18 December 1858; No. 114, 29 December 1859.

[42] *Ibid.*, No. 31, 7 August 1858; No. 50, 18 December 1858; No. 114, 29 December 1859.

[43] *Nafīr Sūriyya*, 25 October 1860.

[44] After searching the canonical *ḥadīth* I could not find this phrase. Moreover, I could not find it in the non-canonical *ḥadīth* either. Other historians who quoted this sentence did not offer the exact reference in the *ḥadīth*; nevertheless, the Egyptian Rifāʿa Rāfiʿ al-Ṭahṭāwī, who served as Shaykh al-Azhar, referred to this phrase in

A good example illustrating the zeal of the intellectuals for the idea of patriotism is the newspaper *Nafīr Sūriyya*, which began publication after the civil war in the summer of 1860. Every issue of the paper opened with the address *Abnā' al-waṭan* (sons of the homeland) and signed off with *muḥibb al-waṭan* (the one who loves the homeland), who was of course Buṭrus al-Bustānī.

Finally, the Muslim newspaper *Thamarāt al-Funūn* likewise spoke lovingly of the homeland, by grasping this love as opposite to the term *taʿaṣṣub* (fanaticism, extremism). It stated that *taʿaṣṣub* constituted a barrier for justice and entailed many obstacles. To clarify this point, the newspaper pointed to the example of Alexander the Great, who wished to conquer Persia and asked his adviser how he might do so. The adviser suggested that he should divide the tribes and place a ruler over each group; thus it would be easier to overcome the Persians because they would be engrossed in their own squabbles.[45] This principle of divide and rule was presented to impress upon the readers the importance of solidarity and cooperation.

Creation of a Common Identity

Even though the intellectuals were striving to create their Syrian identity as an all encompassing one, it is important to recognise that their self-image was a combination of four circles of overlapping identities: the Eastern (*Sharq*), the Ottoman, the Arab and the new circle they were promoting, the Syrian. This was evident as early as 1859 when they wrote that their past was "adorned by the crown of Syrian glory, set upon the pillars of Arab heroism and dwelling in eastern bravery."[46] The Eastern and the Ottoman circles were their global identities, while the Arab and Syrian circles served as their local ones, what Dawn called "smaller *waṭan*" or as referred to earlier as big *waṭan*/small *waṭan*.[47]

1869, saying that it belongs to the *ḥadīth*, without being specific as to where it actually appears. He also claimed that ʿUmar Ibn al-Khaṭṭāb said that God ordered the lands (*bilād*) to love the *waṭan*. Al-Ṭahṭāwī attributed similar terms, such as *ḥubb al-waṭan*, to the Prophet Muḥammad. See: Rifāʿa Rāfiʿ al-Ṭahṭāwī, *Manāhij al-Albāb al-Miṣriyya fī Mabāhij al-Ādāb al-ʿAṣriyya* (Cairo, 1889), pp. 7–10. This subject should be researched further.

[45] *Thamarāt al-Funūn*, No. 54, 27 April 1876.

[46] *Ḥadīqat al-Akhbār*, No. 104, December 1859.

[47] Ernest C. Dawn, "The Origins of Arab Nationalism," in Rashid Khalidi et al. (eds.), *The Origins of Arab Nationalism* (New York and Oxford, 1991), pp. 7–8.

The intellectuals, who were aware of these circles, believed that when a population has a sense of belonging to a defined region, a common identity would likely develop within it. This could be achieved through the instillation of collective memory, awareness and pride among readers for their homeland, language, and culture, and through the attempt to portray the historical and economic past of the region as shared by all. This attitude was emphasised by sentences such as "O sons of the homeland, you drink of the same water and you breathe the same air, and the language in which you speak, and the soil in which you are buried, and our interests and customs are one."[48]

In order to achieve this common identity, the intellectuals instilled pride in the local population by writing that the "Syrian race" (*al-jins al-sūrī*) constituted the supreme level of the population in terms of their intelligence and astuteness. It enjoyed high commercial and cultural abilities, and was equipped with the tools to develop *ādāb* (culture, literature) and the ability to rise up the ladder of civilisation. Also, the Syrian land was conceived as the best in terms of its air, water, and fertility. They published many articles devoted to Syria, including those depicting its past greatness and its present, stressing that the present could improve.[49]

The press tackled questions of identity such as: Who are we? Where are we going? Why is our present situation so amiss, compared with our eminence in the past? It made use of the comparison between past and present to create the wish to improve whatever possible for the future. For example, in an article entitled "Who are we?" Salīm al-Bustānī pointed out that the residents did not have to ask where they had been but rather where they are now.[50]

Pre-Islamic Heritage: Arabic Language and Culture

The Christian-Arab intellectuals emphasised the Arab heritage, its language and its culture, i.e. Arabism and its connection to Syrianism, not in the political sense of the word but in its cultural one. Their

---

48 *Nafīr Sūriyya*, 9 September 1860.

49 *Ibid.*, No. 9, 14 January 1861; No. 4, 25 October 1860; *Thamarāt al-Funūn*, No. 22, 30 October 1875.

50 For example, see: Salīm al-Bustānī, "Man Naḥnū?," *al-Jinān*, Vol. 1, No. 6, 1870, pp. 161–162; Salīm al-Bustānī, "Limādhā Naḥnu fī Ta'akhkhur," *al-Jinān*, Vol. 1, No. 6, 1870, pp. 162–164.

main focus was Arabism as the means of uniting Christians and Muslims in a common culture and language. These intellectuals did not see any contradiction between being "Syrian" and having an Arab cultural identity, since in their view Arabism and Syrianism complemented each other.

For the Christian intellectuals, the idea of Arabism was separate from the Islamic-religious context. This religious perception had prevailed in the first centuries following the rise of Islam and connected Arabic language and culture solely with Islam and with Muslims. By contrast, the new approach of these intellectuals referred to the cultural role of the Arabic language principally before the rise of Islam, and thus was adoptable by both Christians and Muslims. In several cases the intellectuals saw Bedouin life in the pre-Islamic period as an important period in the Syrian past and as a symbol of Arabism. In this way, Arabic was not presented mainly as the language of the Koran, but as the heritage of all Syrians. Hence, an Arabism of a secular character was created.

The intellectuals sought thereby to have the term "Arabic-speakers" cover all those whose culture was Arab. They did not want the term to be interpreted as an ethnic definition but to assume a purely linguistic-cultural shading. They tried to revive Arabic as the medium for teaching in general and for teaching science in particular. The language was extolled not for its religious context but for its glorious past in the domain of culture and science in the pre-Islamic period.

Furthermore, the intellectuals, like the American missionaries; believed that Arabic was the language that should serve as the connecting link between the old disciplines of the past and the new ones of the present. Being speakers of the language and inhabitants of the place, the Christian intellectuals saw themselves (and hoped that the Muslims would likewise perceive them) as Arabs. This stage in the crystallisation of the Syrian idea opened the way for Christians to construct a supra-communal concept based on territory, Arabic language and culture, which they could share with the Muslims amongst whom they lived.

In later years, towards the end of the nineteenth century, local intellectuals encouraged what they called *taʿmīm al-lugha*, i.e., the process of spreading the Arabic language among the population.[51]

---

[51] For more details, see: Salīm al-Bustānī, "al-Muʿallim Buṭrus al-Bustānī Faqīd al-Waṭan," *al-Jinān*, Vol. 14, No. 11, 1883, pp. 321–323.

This was also part of the *Nahḍa* movement; as an element in this process, newspapers and books written in Arabic were published. They truly believed that through this process they would become proud Arabs and not imperfect Europeans.[52]

The concept of the "Arab nation" (*al-umma al-ʿarabiyya*) in its modern sense apparently made its first appearance in print in 1858 in the newspaper *Ḥadīqat al-Akhbār* and only later in other Christian intellectual's writings.[53] Moreover, for the first time in local journalism, Khalīl al-Khūrī's writing contained a modern, secular, linguistic perception of Arab culture and language as part of a cultural Syrian identity.[54] Hence, the call for *Nahḍa* was not only a goal in itself but was mainly a means for creating a common and secular denomination for the Syrian population.

In contrast to the missionaries, the main aim of the intellectuals in calling for *Nahḍa* was not to create a Christian Syria, but rather to create a secular one. This concept became more obvious among the Beiruti middle stratum after 1860, and explains why most researchers until now have regarded the development of the Syrian patriotism as occurring only after the traumatic events in 1860 and not earlier.[55]

Arab culture was the core of Syrian identity, and its roots shown to be deeply embedded in pre-Islamic times. Nevertheless, Islam was not totally pushed aside but was reinterpreted as an important phase in the development of Arab culture. In this regard, Islam was conceived as the religious movement that took this glorious heritage (especially its language) and raised it to a higher level.

Arab culture was grasped as one that encompassed and amalgamated the influences of other cultures. Trying to define their self-identity, the intellectuals declared that the peoples of the Near East had many languages and influences, and this attested to the wealth of their cultural heritage. Some of Syria's population was indeed made of the descendants of the Arabs who ruled in the East and the West, and were famed for their conquests, their commerce, and their agriculture. Yet another portion of the population was Assyrian,

---

[52] See, for example what Bustānī wrote regarding the Arabic language. *Nafīr Sūriyya*, 22 December 1861.

[53] *Ḥadīqat al-Akhbār*, No. 22, 5 June 1858.

[54] *Ibid.*

[55] For example, see: Hourani, *Arabic Thought in the Liberal Age*, pp. 99–102.

who gained fame for their love of science and knowledge; while others were Greeks, renowned for their philosophical wisdom.[56] The rest, of course, were a mixture of all these great peoples. The intellectuals emphasised that the Syrian population was unique in that it was descendant of those who gave the world religions, taught it crafts, and bequeathed it the principles of civilisation.[57]

The perception of the intellectuals was that Syrian-Arab culture was eclectic, containing many layers. This is what eventually created its dynamics and made it flexible enough to suit intellectual needs. Naturally, the Muslim population could not accept such an attitude, since they saw their culture as having begun only with the rise of Islam. The pre-Islamic period was not conceived as important, and in fact this period was termed *al-Jāhiliyya*—literally also meaning state of "ignorance".[58]

Among the tools used to advance ideas regarding Arab culture were cultural societies. For example, at the beginning of 1860, local Christians and Muslims, mainly from Beirut, founded *al-ʿUmda al-Adabiyya li-Ishhār al-Kutub al-ʿArabiyya* (the Literary Society for the Publication of Arabic Books). The main goal of this society was to make Arabic literature accessible to the wider public, and to do so by printing literary and historical works in Arabic and selling them at reasonable prices in the Arab cities.[59]

An important principle adopted by the Society was the propagation of knowledge without taking a stand against one religion or another.[60] The Society's members believed that its work would not only contribute to the redemption of the Arabic language and culture, but would also bring benefit to the country (i.e. Syria) in that it would preserve and develop its culture. Khalīl al-Khūrī reinforced this point, stating that people who studied their own language were restoring their honour.[61] In contrast to *al-Jamʿiyya al-Sūriyya li-Iktisāb*

---

[56] Salīm al-Bustānī, "Man Naḥnu?." *al-Jinān*, Vol. 1, No. 6, 1870, p. 160.

[57] *Ibid.; Nafīr Sūriyya*, 14 January 1861.

[58] On the term "*Jāhiliyya*", see: Ignaz Goldziher, *Muslim Studies*, Vol. 1, trans. by C. R. Barber and S. M. Stern (London, 1967), pp. 201–208.

[59] For more details on this society, see: *Ḥadīqat al-Akhbār*, No. 112, 23 February 1860.

[60] US/NA, w.n., 13 April 1859.

[61] *Ḥadīqat al-Akhbār*, No. 22, 5 June 1858.

al-ʿUlūm wal-Funūn, in this literary society Christians and Muslims worked together without the support of the American missionaries.[62]

Already in March 1860, the Society announced the publication of two books in Arabic. The first was a book of poetry, the *Dīwān* of al-Mutanabbī (915–965) annotated by Buṭrus al-Bustānī. This choice was apparently not accidental. The poetry of al-Mutanabbī symbolised Arab pride at a time when the Arabs had lost effective political power in the territories of the Caliph. Another reason for this choice was the fact that his poetry expressed passion and courage, in addition to being replete with references to parables from Arab life in olden times. Likewise, it contained themes setting forth the differences between Arab and non-Arab.[63] The *Dīwān* merited another printing a few years later, a fact attesting to the demand for literature of this kind. The second work published was the *Dīwān* of ʿUmar Ibn al-Fāriḍ, a Ṣūfī poet nicknamed "the Sultan of Lovers," who wrote mainly Ṣūfī love poems in Arabic.[64]

An Application of Identity

Traditional Versus Modern: The Rise of Syrian Historiography

The transformation in Christian-Arab self-definition, from the traditional concept of *Bilād al-Shām* to the territorial concept of Syria, also introduced a new genre into Syrian historiography. The genre of traditional historiography that focused on cities in *Bilād al-Shām*, shifted to the genre of modern historiography which focused on the history of Syria as a country.

---

[62] Participating in the society were figures such as the Muslims: Ibrāhīm al-Aḥdab; Ḥusayn Bayhum; Saʿd Ḥamāda; Khālid al-Naṣr; and the Christians: Yūḥannā Abkāryūs; Mīkhāʾīl ʿAbrut; Buṭrus al-Bustānī; Salīm Bustrus; Jurjus al-Jāhl; Khalīl al-Khūrī; Shakrallāh al-Khūrī; Mīkhāʾīl Mudawwar; Niqūlā Naqqāsh; Nawfal Afandī Nawfal; Ayyūb Thābit; and Nāṣīf al-Yāzijī. For details on these people see: Antonius, *The Arab Awakening*, p. 53; Alan R. Taylor, *The American Protestant Mission and the Awakening of Modern Syria 1820–1870*, unpublished Ph.D. dissertation, Georgetown University, 1957, p. 144; *Ḥadīqat al-Akhbār*, No. 14, 32 August 1858.

[63] *Ibid.*, No. 113, 1 March 1860; No. 114, 8 March 1860.

[64] *Ibid.*, Several plays were also written in order to glorify Arabic culture. For example, Mārūn al-Naqqāsh's play concerns the Caliph Hārūn al-Rashīd.

Traditional Genre

The traditional genre in the region of Syria comprised an integral part of traditional Muslim historiography. The latter first appeared in the seventh century, developing until the nineteenth century and beyond. Its writers were principally Muslims, but also included several Christians. From the point of view of content, this genre focused mainly on three topics: large cities such as Aleppo, Damascus and so forth; smaller cities such as Zahle, Tripoli and Homs; and biographies of *ʿulamāʾ* and *aʿyān* from these cities, including descriptions of their customs. Such biographies allow us to study distinguished families and their dynasties, their education and fields of interest.[65]

These writers defined the region in which they lived as *Bilād al-Shām*. They did not conceive it as one entity, but rather referred to a regional concept lacking a country-encompassing identity. The definition of identity by these writers was narrow, based on the city or the region to which they belonged and focused mainly on the Muslim community and its elite.

A number of books belonging to the traditional genre serve as examples of this approach. In the seventh century Ibn al-ʿAdīm wrote the book *Zubdat Ḥalab min Tārīkh Ḥalab* (The Best of the History of Aleppo). In 1874, Khalīl Sarkīs wrote a book entitled *Tārīkh Ūrshalīm* (History of Jerusalem). At the end of the Mamluk period, Ṣāliḥ Buḥtur wrote *Tārīkh Bayrūt wa Akhbār al-Umarāʾ al-Buḥturiyyīn min Banī al-Gharb* (The History of Beirut and the Story of the Buḥturiyyīn Princes from the People of al-Gharb), which was printed in 1898, and so forth.[66]

---

[65] Franz Rosenthal, *A History of Muslim Historiography* (Leiden, 1968), pp. 16–17, 87–93, 100–110.

[66] See for further details and for additional examples, Kamāl al-Dīn Ibn al-ʿAdīm, *Zubdat al-Ḥalab min Tārīkh Ḥalab*, 3 vols. (Damascus, 1991). The book was first published in the seventh century. Also, Lūwīs Shīkhū, *Bayrūt-Tārīkhuhā wa-Āthāruhā* (Beirut, 1925); Mīkhāʾīl Mūsā Alūf, *Tārīkh Baʿlabak* (Beirut, 1908); ʿĀrif al-Zayn, *Tārīkh Ṣaydā* (Sidon, 1913); Khalīl Sarkīs, *Tārīkh Ūrshalīm—Ayy al-Quds al-Sharīf* (Beirut, 1874); Nuʿmān al-Qasāṭilī, *al-Rawḍa al-Ghannāʾ fī Dimashq al-Fayḥāʾ*, 2nd ed. (Beirut, 1982). The book was first published in 1879; ʿAbd al-Razzāq al-Bīṭār, *Ḥilyat al-Bashar fī Tārīkh al-Qarn al-Thālith ʿAshar*, 3 vols. (Damascus, 1961–1963); Ṣāliḥ Buḥtur, *Tārīkh Bayrūt wa Akhbār al-Umarāʾ al-Buḥturiyyīn min Banī al-Gharb*, ed. Lūwīs Shīkhū, 2nd ed. (Beirut, 1927). The first publication of this book was in 1898; Kāmil al-Ghazzī, *Kitāb Nahr al-Dhahab fī Tārīkh Ḥalab*, 2nd ed., 3 vols., eds. Shawqī Shaʿth and Maḥmūd Fākhūrī (Aleppo, 1991). The first edition was published in 1926.

The writing style of this traditional Muslim genre was that of a chronicle. Hayden White defined this type of writing, in contrast to historical writing, which will be discussed in reference to the modern genre. Chronicle writing, he explained, provides mainly a list of unconnected chronological facts rather than a meaningful narrative that strives to connect different events. He also emphasised that it "lacks closure, that summing up of the 'meaning' of the chain of events with which it deals that we normally expect from the well-made story. The chronicle typically promises closure but does not provide it."[67]

Books that were written according to the traditional genre included details on leading figures and events as seen through the eyes of the author. In most cases the author was an eyewitness to the events described, but tried not to take sides in presenting the story, nor share his views with his readers. He neither analysed nor criticised events, and did not give his readers information regarding the economic nor social life of the community. Finally, these authors did not include a narrative nor a summary nor a conclusion, but only a description of the events themselves.

In between Genres

Before discussing modern historiography, it is important to point out that the transformation to this genre was gradual, proceeding through a transitional period containing characteristics from both genres. Transformations in style progressed slowly, but changes in content moved considerably faster. One can find books that in style still belong to the traditional genre, yet the contents of which had begun to change according to the evolving identities of their authors. These books are still written as chronicles. Very detailed, at the same time they show the first signs of change toward the modern genre. This tendency was evident first among Christian writers who came from the literary circle in the court of Amīr Bashīr II.

Geographically, they focused on Mount Lebanon, i.e. on a relatively narrow region, as was the common practice in the traditional genre. However, careful scrutiny of their writing reveals that they began to grasp the region of Syria as a whole, within which Mount

---

[67] Hayden V. White, *The Content of the Form: Narrative Discourse and Historical Representation* (Baltimore, 1987), p. 16; see also, Lionel Gossman, *Between History and Literature* (Cambridge, Mass., 1990), pp. 118–120.

Lebanon is seen as an integral region.[68] They persisted in using the term *Bilād al-Shām* to describe the region, but alongside of it we can discern the term "Syria."

This change in concept and in the terminology can also be found among Muslim writers, mainly toward the end of the nineteenth century. They wrote in the traditional style but, in addition to terms such as *Bilād al-Shām,* they began to use the name "Syria" and, to some extent, several other parameters of the Syrian self-concept characterising the modern genre, which will be elaborated upon shortly. Their description of a particular city was accompanied by the acknowledgement that the city was a part of a wider entity—Syria. The seven-volume book written by Muḥammad Rāghib al-Ṭabbākh entitled *Aʿlām al-Nubalāʾ bi-Tārīkh Ḥalab al-Shahbāʾ*[69] (The Most Prominent Notables in the History of Aleppo) is a good example of this. Nevertheless, it is important to note that the book was written in the early twentieth century, a few decades after the establishment of the *Vilâyet* of Syria in 1865, a time in which it was perhaps already obvious to refer to the region as Syria.

As evident by the title of the book, it was part of the traditional genre and as such its main topic was the city of Aleppo and the biographies of its important *ʿulamāʾ*. On the other hand, already in the beginning of the book, Aleppo is described as belonging to the Syrian entity. Ṭabbākh describes the borders of Syria and the inhabitants of ancient Syria.[70] Thus, the concept of Syria as an entire region was gradually assimilated, perhaps partly due to administrative changes taking place under the Ottoman Empire, although the shift among Muslim writers occurred at a slower pace.

The Modern Genre: Syria as a Country

From the second half of the nineteenth century, Christian intellectuals, especially Greek Orthodox, mainly from coastal towns such as Beirut and Tripoli, began to publish books in Arabic with titles that included the term "Syria." This transformation was not only semiotic but marked a new concept that was the source of a new identity. The main subject of these books was Syria as one entity, as a country.

---

[68] For further details, see: Zachs, "Mīkhāʾīl Mishāqa," pp. 79–81.

[69] Muḥammad Rāghib al-Ṭabbākh, *Aʿlām al-Nubalāʾ bi-Tārīkh Ḥalab al-Shahbāʾ*, 2nd ed., 7 vols. (Damascus, 1988).

[70] *Ibid.*, Vol. 1, pp. 29, 77–79.

This modern genre developed in parallel with traditional historiography but did not replace it, even later on, towards the end of the nineteenth and into the twentieth century. Most of the books in this genre were written after 1860, following the civil war in Mount Lebanon and Damascus.[71] Five books published between 1860 and the beginning of the twentieth century can be seen as belonging to it. Each book represents a different level of Syrian identity and the development of this modern genre and its parameters. In each book, the historical narrative of Syria includes a growing number of details and is constructed according to the needs of the evolving identity of their writers.

Not surprisingly, the first book in a series of volumes that wished to stimulate interest in Syria is that of the Greek Orthodox Khalīl al-Khūrī titled *Kharābāt Sūriyya* (Ruins of Syria). Al-Khūrī's family moved from Mount Lebanon to Beirut in 1841. As mentioned earlier, at an earlier age he devoted his time to poetry, mainly active in the press and in the cultural endeavours in Beirut. He held a number of governmental positions in the Ottoman Empire.[72] His rather small book was published in Beirut in 1860, but it was first delivered as a lecture at the cultural society *al-ʿUmda al-Adabiyya li-Ishhār al-Kutub al-ʿArabiyya* in 1859.[73]

It was the first book written in Arabic by a local Syrian with a title that included the name "Syria." The style of the book is akin to diaries of Western travellers in the region, and can serve as a kind of geographic-archaeological lexicon for those interested in the Syrian region. The "Syrian" sites of Greater Syria are arranged according to the importance of their cities and these cities' histories in pre-Islamic times are presented. In this way, Khalīl al-Khūrī tried to shape the collective memory of the local population. Al-Khūrī, as did other authors, made it clear that he wrote this book in order to highlight the contemporary condition and suffering of Syria, in

---

[71] Gregory Wortabet's book, which was written in English, and can be seen as part of this genre, was published already in 1856. See: Gregory M. Wortabet, *Syria and the Syrians*, 2 vols. (London, 1856). This is probably the first local book on Syria.

[72] Yūsuf Sarkīs, *Muʿjam al-Maṭbūʿāt al-ʿArabiyya wal-Muʿarraba*, Vol. 1, pp. 845–846; Jurjī Zaydān, *Tarājim Mashāhīr al-Sharq*, Vol. 2, pp. 121–125; Lūwīs Shīkhū, "Tārīkh Fann al-Ṭibāʿa fī al-Mashriq," *al-Mashriq*, Vol. 3, 1900, pp. 998–999.

[73] Parts of the book were later published in Khūrī's newspaper. *Ḥadīqat al-Akhbār*, No. 116, 22 March 1861; No. 136, 20 June 1861.

contrast to its glorious history and past economic state, to encourage the people to restore it according to its magnificent heritage.[74] This motif was to re-emerge in the writing of the intellectuals—lamentations for a lost past coupled with aspirations for a better future.

The second book, which was partly discussed in the first chapter in connection with Amīr Bashīr's court, was that of Mīkhā'īl Mishāqa, *al-Jawāb 'alā Iqtirāḥ al-Aḥbāb*. It was written in Beirut in 1873 but published only in 1955.[75] Even though the book was published so many years after it was written, it does indicate the mind-set and thoughts of Mishāqa when writing it.

The book's historical review covers almost a century. It begins some time before the rise of Aḥmad Pāshā al-Jazzār. Mīkhā'īl Mishāqa focuses on al-Jazzār's ties with Amīr Bashīr II, who was the object of his admiration. He goes on to describe the various feuds between the pāshās of the area and the civil war in the 1840s in Mount Lebanon; he ends with a detailed description of the civil strife of 1860. These events are presented through Mishāqa's eyes, who took part in most of them and personally knew the people he described.

The book introduces the history of the *Vilâyet* of Syria and Mount Lebanon as one continuous entity. This tendency is especially revealed in the way Mīkhā'īl Mishāqa uses the term "Syria." For instance, Amīr Bashīr is described as the ruler of Mount Lebanon with all Syrian clans (*'Ashā'ir*) seeing themselves as his children.[76]

Mishāqa not only holds a territorial concept of Syria, he also perceives its people as one. He commonly uses such terms as *rijāl Sūriyya* (men of Syria), *sukkān Sūriyya* (inhabitants of Syria) or *ahālī al-mudun fī Sūrriya* (people of the cities of Syria).[77] Interestingly, Mīkhā'īl Mishāqa enlarges on the minority groups of the region, in accordance with his aspiration to present all parameters of Syrian society. The book also describes and analyses the economic and social background of the region.

---

[74] Khalīl al-Khūrī, *Kharābāt Sūriyya* (Beirut, 1860), pp. 2–7.

[75] Mīkhā'īl Mishāqa, *Muntakhabāt min al-Jawāb 'alā Iqtirāḥ al-Aḥbāb*, eds. A. Rustum and Ṣ. Abū-Shaqrā (Beirut, 1955). Earlier in 1868, another book with the name "Syria" in its title appeared. Yet it was not a history book but a quodlibet of Arabic literature. See: Anṭūn Būlād, *Rāshid Sūriyya* (Beirut, 1868).

[76] Mishāqa, *al-Jawāb*, p. 47.

[77] *Ibid.*, pp. 295, 304, 315.

Finally, even though Khalīl al-Khūrī's book includes a historical survey of the region, it is chiefly a separate history of each Syrian city. As in the case of the traditional genre, it does not treat Syria as one territorial entity as did Mīkhā'īl Mishāqa. Hence, Mishāqa could be viewed as the first historian of modern Syria.[78]

The third book, *al-ʿUqūd al-Durriyya fī al-Mamlaka al-Sūriyya* (Selected Events [Pearl Necklace] in the History of the Syrian Region) was published in Beirut in 1874. Its author was the Greek Orthodox Ilyās Maṭar (1857–1910). His family immigrated to Beirut from the Mountain after the events of 1860. The book was published with the encouragement of Faris Nimr, his chemistry teacher in the SPC and his spiritual patron.[79] In the introduction, Maṭar claims that he sees his writing as fulfilling a moral obligation and a patriotic need. He further explains that the motivation driving him to write this book is the fact that every *mamlaka* (in the sense of region) has its historical literature, yet only the history of Syria is not available.[80] Indeed, the contents of the book reveal the author's love for his homeland, which he sees as the place of "the birth of civilisation."[81]

In general, the book consists of two parts. The first is a general introduction to the region and its features, and the second surveys Syria's important cities in terms of history and geography. In contrast to the books of Mīkhā'īl Mishāqa and Khalīl al-Khūrī, Ilyās Maṭar evidently attempted to produce a more accurate territorial definition of Syria. He often describes Syria as a chain (range) of mountains. As had al-Khūrī, he begins his book in the pre-Islamic period but without mentioning the Phoenicians. Also, and in contrast with the first two, this book typifies and classifies the people of the region according to their qualities and nature, and even provides numerical estimations of population sizes for each group. He describes the region's climate and its animals, and the economic aspects (e.g. crops, resources, etc.). He also discusses the source of the name "Syria," a subject that is crucial in the quest for identity.[82]

---

[78] For more details, see: Zachs, "Mīkhā'īl Mishāqa."

[79] Ilyās Maṭar, *al-ʿUqūd al-Durriyya fī al-Mamlaka al-Sūriyya* (Beirut, 1874). For further details on Maṭar, see: Choueiri, *Arab History and the Nation State*, p. 53; Yussef M. Choueiri, "Two Histories of Syria and the Demise of Syrian Patriotism," *Middle Eastern Studies*, Vol. 23 (1987), p. 498.

[80] Maṭar, *al-ʿUqūd al-Duriyya*, pp. 2–3.

[81] *Ibid.*, p. 21.

[82] *Ibid.*, pp. 5–6, 21–26.

In Ilyās Maṭar's book, Syria is perceived as a geographical unit populated by a particular people. True, Maṭar includes many characteristics central to the depiction of a nation, but he does not convey any clear-cut political message. In fact, what he omits in patriotic tone is compensated for by the space he devotes to the portrayal of a defined territorial unit, to which he imparts the characteristics of a nation.

The fourth book is that of the Greek Orthodox Jurjī Yannī (b. 1854), entitled *Tārīkh Sūriyā* (History of Syria), which was published in 1881.[83] The Yannī family was active in the literary movement in Tripoli but also dealt in commerce. Jurjī studied in 1868 at the school of the American missionaries in ʿAbeih and later in Buṭrus al-Bustānī's school (*al-Madrasa al-Waṭaniyya*). He himself established a school, similar to that of al-Bustānī, in Tripoli. In 1882 he became the acting Belgian Consul in Tripoli.[84]

Yannī's thick volume was an extensive compilation on Syria, including more than 600 pages on its history from the pre-Islamic period, especially the Phoenician period, to which over fifty pages were devoted. As Buheiry wrote, Yannī saw Syria "as a coherent and meaningful historical unit in the sense that it was the location of some of the oldest urban conglomerations and interactions in history."[85] Before writing this book, Yannī conducted extensive research, obtaining most of his sources from the library of the SPC, relying on classical Islamic works such as those of Yāqūt al-Ḥamawī, Ibn Baṭūṭa and Ibn Khaldūn, but also on Western sources such as Herodotus, Strabo and so on. Similar to the other writers, he defined the Syrian territory, its people, its flora, and so on.

The last book is that of Yūsuf al-Dibs (1833–1907), a Maronite Archbishop of Beirut, which was also entitled *Tārīkh Sūriyya*. Al-Dibs was born in northern Lebanon. From a young age he studied Arabic and, in addition, learned Syriac which was for many centuries the language of liturgy of the Maronite church. In 1847 he joined the college of ʿAyn Waraqa where he stayed for three years in which

[83] Jurjī Yannī, *Tārīkh Sūriyā* (Beirut, 1881).

[84] For further details on the family, see: SAC, Tibawi's Papers, box 3, file 1, Yanni to Smith, 6 November 1848; Nawfal, *Tarājim ʿUlamāʾ*, pp. 110, 219–220; Ṭarrāzī, *Tārīkh al-Ṣiḥāfa*, Vol. 2, pp. 45–47, 57.

[85] Marwan Buheiry, "Lebanese Christian Intellectuals and the Ottoman State: Azuri, Nujaym, Yanni and Bustani," in Abdeljelil Temimi (ed.), *Les Provinces Arabes à l'Époque Ottomane* (Zaghouan, 1987), p. 83.

he continued to study not only Arabic and Syriac but in addition French, Italian and Latin along other theological and secular topics. In 1860, the Patriarch Būlus Masʿad, himself a graduate of ʿAyn Waraqa, appointed him as secretary to the Patriarchate, a post he fulfilled for the next 12 years. In 1872 the seat of the diocese of Beirut became vacant and al-Dibs was appointed as the Maronite Bishop of the city.

Al-Dibs' book is the most comprehensive book written on Syria in the nineteenth century. It includes eight volumes published between the years 1893 and 1905.[86] The book traces Syrian history from Creation up until the nineteenth century. Yūsuf al-Dibs refers to the territory of Mount Lebanon, in his first volume, as part of the Syrian entity. He defined the territory of Syria and enlarged on its characteristics in the very first pages of the book. In general, he conceived this entity as a homeland of defined and clear borders.

Through these books, the main characteristics of the modern genre are gradually revealed. Differing from the chronicle style of the traditional genre, most of the above-mentioned books are closer to being historical narratives, or what Hayden White calls "proper history," that is, one that includes historical narrative and continuity regarding the order of events as well as a complete analysis. White wrote that it was not enough that an historical account dealt in real, rather than merely imaginary, events. The events must not only be registered within the chronological framework of their original occurrence but narrated as well, which means that the events will be revealed as possessing a structure and an order of meaning, and not a mere sequence.[87] In fact, the writers of these books did construct a vast historical narrative, which they analysed and interpreted. In other words, they introduced historical events, enlarging on the backgrounds, circumstances and significance of these events according to their own understanding and interests.

From the point of view of content, the main topic of this genre was Syria as a country. Thus, the modern genre created a new historiography, the main purpose of which was to document the history, culture and geography of the region of Greater Syria. In addition

[86] Yūsuf al-Dibs, *Tārīkn Sūriyya*, 8 vols. (Beirut, 1893–1905). For more details on al-Dibs, see: Zaydān, *Tarājim Mashāhīr al-Sharq*, Vol. 2, pp. 226–229; Yūsuf Dāghir, *Maṣādir al-Dirāsa al-Adabiyya*, Vol. 2 (Sidon, 1950), pp. 357–358.

[87] White, *The Content of the Form*, pp. 4–5.

and in contrast to the traditional genre, these books did not refer only to the Muslim community, but also enlarged on the history of the minorities.

In their historical overview of the region the authors not only downplayed the Islamic era, they practically omitted the Umayyad Caliphate in which Damascus played a notable role, thus neglecting a crucial chapter in the history of the region. They resumed with an account of the Crusades and went on to describe their own times.

Another characteristic of the modern genre was the origin and educational background of its authors. Most of them, as already mentioned, were Greek Orthodox from Beirut and Tripoli and had some kind of contact with the American missionaries. The majority of them received their education in the missionaries' schools. For example, Khalīl al-Khūrī was close to the American missionaries and served as a teacher in their school in ʿAbeih.[88] Due to his close relationship with the missionaries, Mīkhāʾīl Mishāqa converted from Catholicism to Protestantism and between the years 1859–1870 served as the acting American Consul in Damascus. In fact, when reading the personal correspondence between the missionary Eli Smith and other local intellectuals in the region, one can see that Smith's correspondence with Mīkhāʾīl Mishāqa was greater in volume than that of any other local intellectual, including Buṭrus al-Bustānī.[89] Ilyās Maṭar studied chemistry at the SPC and Jurjī Yannī studied at the American missionary school in ʿAbeih.

The missionaries' ideas were transmitted through the cultural societies they established with the locals or through the missionary schools, as well as through the library of the College. Yet, it is important to note that in parallel to the influence of the American missionaries, these ideas also developed among local intellectuals through mutual interactions at their meetings.

Nevertheless, the question that still intrigues is why most of these writers of Syrian history, as well as of the newspapers, came from the Greek Orthodox community. Examining the structure of the Greek Orthodox Patriarchy can partially explain this, and will also show that the notion of Syria had been evolving within Christian-Arab society and was due to local factors, not only to external influence.

---

[88] HL, series ABC: 16.8.1, Vol. 8, part 1, Records of the Abeih Seminary, 1848–1878.

[89] HL, Smith Papers, ABC; box 1, Mishaqa to Smith, 13 March 1842.

The seat of the Patriarch of the Greek Orthodox community was in Damascus, and the Patriarch headed the church in the regions known today as Syria and Lebanon. The Patriarchy maintained good relations with the Porte. This, coupled with the fact that the Greek Orthodox community was spread throughout the region, may have led its members to see the region as a whole and to feel internally affiliated with it[90] and yet at the same time conceive it as an integral part of the Empire. Finally, the communal jurisdiction of the Patriarch extending to present-day Syria and Lebanon might have served as a basis for developing a notion of one large geographical entity, the feeling of belonging to it and the desire to see it advance.

An opposite case was that of the Maronites, who were greatly influenced by the Catholic missionaries and by the French and hence were treated by the Ottomans with some suspicion. Furthermore, toward the end of the nineteenth century and the beginning of the twentieth century, their external affiliation increased when they became subject to the control of the papacy in Rome. Last but not least, the Maronites, based mainly in the Mountain, had accordingly a more localised view of the region, eventually contributing to the emergence of the Lebanese identity.

The rise of the modern historiography allowed local intellectuals (as well as other sectors of the population) to be exposed to Arabic works on Syrian history. In this way, they did not have to make do only with Western works, such as travel books, as some of them had done in the past. The modern genre was more accessible to wider portions of the local population and exposed them to this new concept or identity, in their own language. Through these books, the local intellectuals could transmit their own vision as a reality to the inhabitants of Syria.

"Historical Novels"[91] *as Building Identity: The Role of Heritage, Myth and Women in the* Waṭan

The formation of a new reading public as well as the shaping of its new experience or identity are also necessary preludes to the emergence

[90] The Greek Orthodox in Israel/Palestine and the region of Jordan of today belonged to the Patriarchy of Jerusalem.

[91] The term "novel" (*riwāya*) that was used by the intellectuals for writing their historical texts/stories or popular prose carried a problematic definition in the nineteenth century. During this time, the term was generally used for various types of

of a new literary discourse capable of codifying this experience.[92] The role of literature in serving patriotic needs and the connection between history and literature is not new. In recent years, various critical schools have reaffirmed the view that literary text does not exist separately from the world that creates it.[93] Thus, literature can also be perceived as an agent of history and as an historical or social document that reflects the needs of the society for which it was written. Through it, one can learn about the world in which the writer lived or the fictional world that he was inspired to create. In this regard, the development of the historical novel or the narrative fiction among the Christian Arabs could indicate how the idea of patriotism was introduced to the people through literature and what kind of audience it addressed.

The historical novel had already been developed in the West during the eighteenth century by the bourgeoisie (middle stratum) and had a central role in shaping attitudes toward class, gender and nation, assuming a crucial role in the constitution of the nation as an "imagined community."[94] As we shall see, similar developments and dependencies appeared in the Arab society. Since my main aim is to stress the creative aspect of Christian-Arab intellectuals, I will show that even though the novel was a literary genre influenced by the West, local intellectuals managed to mould and change it in accordance with their own new identity.

The emergence of the Arabic novel dates back to the beginning of the twentieth century.[95] Yet, until 1950s, poetry remained the leading literary genre. During this time the novel was perceived by

---

fiction writing, for example, for short stories and novellas. I chose to use the term "historical novel" (even though it is not similar to the Western term) since these novels can be seen as initial examples of this genre.

[92] Hafez, *The Genesis of Arabic Narrative Discourse*, pp. 102–103.

[93] Edward W. Said, *The World, the Text, and the Critic* (Cambridge, Mass., 1983), p. 5.

[94] Deidre Lynch and William B. Warner (eds.), *Cultural Institutions of the Novel* (London, 1996), introduction, pp. 4–5; Todd C. Kontje, *Women, the Novel and the German Nation 1771–1871—Domestic Fiction in the Fatherland* (Cambridge, 1998), pp. 1–17.

[95] For example, in the Middle East the development of the concept of "*waṭaniyya*", alongside the novel, is known in Egypt especially at the beginning of the twentieth century. See: Muḥsin Jāsim al-Mūsawī, *al-Riwāya al-ʿArabiyya al-Nashʾa wal-Taḥawwul*, Vol. 2 (Beirut, 1988), p. 294. For the association between the novel and national identity, see: Martin Strohmeier, *Crucial Images in the Presentation of the Kurdish National Identity: Heroes and Patriots, Traitors and Foes* (Leiden, 2003), pp. 151–195. For more details on the Arabic novel, see: Roger Allen, *The Arabic Novel: An Historical and Critical Introduction* (New York, 1982).

intellectuals as a lower or non-canonical genre compared to that of poetry. Only in the second half of the twentieth century was poetry pushed into the margins of the literary canon, and prose, especially the novel, became the leading form of literature.[96]

Nevertheless, the first examples of this kind of literary genre had already appeared in the 1870s in the writings of Salīm al-Bustānī who helped his father, Buṭrus al-Bustānī, in editing the periodical *al-Jinān*.[97] Salīm was raised in an intellectual house. He studied in the English school in ʿAbeih, learning French with Khaṭṭār al-Daḥdāḥ and Arabic with Nāṣīf al-Yāzijī. In 1862, he replaced his father as a dragoman in the American consulate in Beirut, a position he held until 1871. Later, he was elected to the Beirut municipal council.

Al-Jinān was the first Arab magazine to devote considerable attention to narrative fiction and Salīm al-Bustānī himself was one of the pioneers of this genre. Hafez terms this phase in the development of Arabic narrative discourse "the embryonic" stage. He linked it to the growth and development of a new Arabic reading public in Egypt and the Levant, and to the change in their artistic sensibilities resulting from the social and historical mutations that occurred during the second half of the nineteenth century.[98]

In general, historical novels by Salīm al-Bustānī did not receive much attention in research; their contents have barely been analysed, and in fact they have only been mentioned on a few occasions. Brief references to these novels can be found mainly in the writings of Muḥammad Yūsuf Najm, who defined them as "historical tales," and treated them with some contempt. Other researchers simply quoted him on this subject later.[99] The lack of interest was mainly

---

[96] Reuven Snir, *Modern Arabic Literature: A Functional Dynamic Model* (Toronto, 2001), pp. 68–69.

[97] It is important to emphasise that the Ottoman novel developed in the 1860s. Apparently, these novels were similar in topic to those of Salīm. They dealt with the place of women in society and with Westernisation. See: Şerif Mardin, "Super Westernization in Urban Life in the Ottoman Empire in the Last Quarter of the Nineteenth Century," in Peter Benedict, Erol Tümertekin and Fatma Mansur (eds.), *Turkey—Geographic and Social Perspectives* (Leiden, 1974), p. 403.

[98] Hafez, *The Genesis of Arabic Narrative Discourse*, pp. 105–111.

[99] Muḥammad Yūsuf Najm, *al-Qiṣṣa fī al-Adab al-ʿArabī al-Ḥadīth*, 3rd ed. (Beirut, 1966), pp. 41–77; ʿAbd al-Raḥmān Birmū, *al-Riwāya al-Tārīkhiyya fī al-Adab al-Sūrī al-Muʿāṣir 1870–1938* (Damascus, 1996), pp. 41–45, 153–175; al-Ṣādiq Qassūma, *al-Riwāya Muqawwimātuhā wa Nashʾatuhā fī al-Adab al-ʿArabī al-Ḥadīth* (Tunis, 2000), pp. 75–88; ʿAbd al-Raḥmān Yāghī, *Fī al-Juhūd al-Riwāʾiyya Mā Bayna Salīm Bustānī*

due to the fact that these novels were considered as deficient in artistic merit, since the style of writing used deviated from the strict rules of the later modern novel as it developed mainly in the beginning of the twentieth century. The plots were unsophisticated and the images were seen as plain.

However, the artistic level of the novels was of less interest to Salīm al-Bustānī, and thus they appeared under the title *fukāhāt*—amusements. Salīm's main goal was to create a style of writing that would stimulate the imagination of his readers, educate them and kindle their awareness of their society and homeland, rather than adhere to artistic restrictions. In this way, he believed that he could transmit the ideas of patriotism to the younger generation more effectively. In this respect they were "didactic novels" (*riwāya taʿlīmiyya*) as ʿAbd al-Muḥsin Ṭāhā Badir defined them.[100]

Indeed, other researchers claimed that these novels proved to be popular and influential, since they set the pattern for narrative writing for years to come, particularly among the writers of the Levant. It was also claimed that they contributed to the emergence, development and shaping of the modern Arabic novel.[101]

If we examine these novels as historical and social documents and focus on their contents and messages rather than on their artistic aspects, we find much more in them. Their contents reveal the connection between the emergence of this genre and the development of Syrian patriotism and the way it was spread among men and women of the region.

The Case of al-Jinān—*First Experience*

Al-Jinān symbolised the apex of the construction of Syrian identity as seen by the local intellectuals until the time of Abdül Hamid II, who brought its publication to an end. From the very beginning, its

---

wa-Najīb Maḥfūz, 2nd ed. (Beirut, 1981), pp. 23–34; Ibrāhīm al-Saʿāfīn, *Taṭawwur al-Riwāya al-ʿArabiyya al-Ḥadītha fī Bilād al-Shām 1870–1967* (Baghdad, 1980), pp. 13–126.

[100] ʿAbd al-Muḥsin Badir, *Taṭawwur al-Riwāya al-ʿArabiyya al-Ḥadītha fī Miṣr* (Cairo, 1963), pp. 51–66.

[101] Hafez, *The Genesis of Arabic Narrative Discourse*, p. 111; Eissa, "Majallat al-Jinān," pp. 45–48; Moosa Matti, *The Origins of Modern Arabic Fiction* (Boulder, 1997), pp. 157–183. See also the recent book of Stephen P. Sheehi, *Foundations of Modern Arab Identity* (Gainesville, Florida, 2004). Sheehi discusses the work of Arab Renaissance pioneers. He argues that these intellectuals planted the roots of modernity in Arab society through their experiments in language and literature.

motto was *ḥubb al-waṭan min al-īmān*, which appeared in every issue under the title of the journal.

In contrast to other newspapers in the region of Syria and in the Arab provinces until that time, *al-Jinān* gave special attention and devoted large and regular sections to literary issues. It included genres such as the *uqṣūṣa* (short story) and also the *mulḥa* (anecdote, funny story), which appeared in the last pages of every issue. Another genre included the historical novels that were used to promote ideas of Syrian patriotism. In this respect, *al-Jinān* was probably the first Arabic journal to publish this new literary genre. Some of the novels were more than one hundred pages long and were published serially for more than a year so that people would continue to buy the newspaper. These novels were examples of authentic Arabic literature, mass-produced; they disseminated the ideas of local identity in an enjoyable and popular way.

Until that time, novels had simply been translated from other languages into Arabic, especially from the French. The novels in *al-Jinān* were authentic and original works written in Arabic. In publishing them, the journal focused its attention not only on the intellectual elite within local society but also on other sections in it that could read and write, but felt more comfortable with a style that was not highly sophisticated.

Salīm al-Bustānī probably aspired to write in this new genre in order to disseminate the ideas of patriotism more intensively to those not yet exposed to them. This was one of the reasons why it was important for him to publish them in a language that the *ʿāmma* (the common people) could read but that the intellectuals would not reject."[102] He was aware that the novels would be read out in coffee shops and other gathering places to people who could not read them. Perhaps this was also the reason that in some of the novels he illustrated his messages by interspersing pictures throughout the novel. In this way, people without the ability to read could still be exposed to the ideas contained in the novels. Thus, he was one of the first to use what I define as "visualising identity."

Also, it was important for Salīm al-Bustānī to insert sentences in *lugha wusṭā* (middle language) defined relatively to his period, adapting

[102] Fīlīb Dī Ṭarrāzī, *Tārīkh al-Ṣiḥāfa*, Vol. 2, p. 47.

through this a new style of writing so as to make Arabic more accessible to his readers or listeners. The language in the text combined *fuṣḥā* (literary language), in which the novel was primarily written, with occasional sentences in the *wusṭā* language. Thus, he chose a non-canonical style sometimes free from the manacles of *maqāma*, instead combining influences and motifs from Arab classical writing (*Adab*) and modern Western writing, especially French, by which he was influenced. The texts of these novels can be defined as semi-historical, fictional or popular.

Salīm al-Bustānī knew that in the nineteenth century, the Romantic Movement had spread throughout Europe and that the Arabs were influenced by it, and also that there was a great public demand for this kind of literature, even though it was disregarded by some intellectuals.[103] He tried to convince those well versed in European literature that although these amusing (*tankītīyya*) novels seem to deal with issues that are of no concern to them, if they were to look carefully, they would realise that the situations described in them existed perhaps in every family. Salīm believed that such novels are the best tools for reforming the attitudes and behaviour of men and women in Syrian society.[104]

In fact, women were a specific target audience for whom the novels were written, in order to introduce them to ideas concerning Syrian patriotism. As early as 1870, *al-Jinān* carried Salīm's call for the emancipation of Arab women from the repressive traditional ideas concerning their role and position in society. Some of his articles deal with issues concerning the status of women in society.[105] The newspaper also provided the first platform for Arab women to participate in the Arabic press. They contributed articles to the periodical, and from time to time addressed their fellow female readers. In 1870, Idlīd al-Bustānī wrote a short story entitled *Hinrī wa-Imīlyā*, published in *al-Jinān*. At the end of it she called on her female readers to read the journal, underscoring her view that they were privileged to have the newspaper publish something for them as well.[106] Maryāna Marrāsh of Aleppo, as another example, published, as early

[103] Salīm al-Bustānī, "Budūr," *al-Jinān*, Vol. 3, No. 12, 1872, pp. 430–431; Salīm al-Bustānī, "al-Huyām fī Futūḥ al-Shām," *al-Jinān*, Vol. 5, No. 1, 1874, p. 29.

[104] Salīm al-Bustānī, "Asmā," *al-Jinān*, Vol. 4, No. 23, 1873, pp. 826–827.

[105] Salīm al-Bustānī, "al-Inṣāf," *al-Jinān*, Vol. 1, No. 12, 1870, pp. 369–371.

[106] Idlīd Bustānī, "Hinrī wa-Imīlyā," *al-Jinān*, Vol. 1, No. 12 and 13, 1870, pp. 366–367, 406–407.

as April 1871, a series of articles on issues concerning the status of women.[107]

Thus, *al-Jinān* became one of the first publications to approach women as a potential audience. At the end of Salīm al-Bustānī's story *Asmā*, he wrote that "What concerns men [in this story] is no less than what concerns women." He continued, "If we were not sure that these novels were read by a lot of (*kathīrāt*) women we would not put into them many issues that concerned them [the women]."[108] Of course, the meaning of the term "a lot" does not help us estimate how many women actually read these novels, although we do know that by the 1870s a growing number of women in the region could read. For example, between 1834 and 1860 more than thirty-three schools were founded by the American missionaries in the region of Syria, attended by approximately 1,000 pupils, of whom nearly one fifth were girls.[109] The number was even higher if we take into consideration the girls who studied in other missionary schools such as the Roman Catholic or Anglican ones, and yet there were still more male than female readers.[110]

Hence, it is reasonable to assume that the novels were not written only for women, since women were not the majority of the readers. Apparently, Salīm al-Bustānī mainly intended to expose women to the ideas of Syrian patriotism, but did not neglect his male audience, whom he believed still needed to understand the importance of women in the homeland and to the nation. In any case, the demands for this genre were relatively high; al-Bustānī himself admits in one of his novels that he could not meet the craving of the people for this kind of writing and claims that he does not even have time to edit them before publishing.[111] Finally, in contrast to his father, who chiefly addressed the male educated elite, Salīm al-Bustānī tried to transmit his views about patriotism to a larger audience—both men and women. This aspect of his contribution to the

---

[107] Eissa, "Majallat al-Jinān," p. 43.

[108] Al-Bustānī, "Asmā," p. 826.

[109] In 1846–1847, 150 girls studied in the American missionaries' schools. In 1857, 277 girls studied in them. From 1860 the number of girls studying in these schools increased. Iskandar Barūdī, "Ta'līm al-Mar'a 'Indanā," *al-Kuliyya*, June 1912, pp. 233–234; Abdul Latif Tibawi, "The Genesis and Early History of the Syrian Protestant College," in Fuad Sarruf and Suha Tamim (eds.), *American University of Beirut, Festival Book (Festschrift)* (Beirut, 1967), pp. 264–267.

[110] Hafez, *The Genesis of Arabic Narrative Discourse*, p. 53.

[111] Al-Bustānī, "Asmā," p. 827.

dissemination of the idea of a Syrian identity should be emphasised.

In the analysis below I will concentrate on three historical novels written by Salīm al-Bustānī. They are the only ones that were written for serialisation in the periodical. Other Christian-Arab intellectuals, such as Nuʿmān al-Qasāṭilī, tried to promote the same ideas through novels or short stories. These authors criticised local society and it's Westernisation, trying to draw the lines for a better Syrian society through their writing. Standing out, Salīm al-Bustānī encapsulates most of the parameters of Syrian identity as reflected through literature, representing the general outlook of many members of the Beiruti middle stratum in this regard.

Selective Heritage and Myths

> . . . identities are about questions of using the resources of history, language and culture in the process of becoming rather than being: not "who we are" or "where we came from", so much as what we might become, how we have been represented and how that bears on how we might represent ourselves. Identities are therefore constituted within, not outside representation. They relate to the invention of tradition as much as to tradition itself, which they oblige us to read not as an endless reiteration but as "the changing same": not the so-called return to roots but a coming-to-terms with our routes.
>
> Stuart Hall[112]

This statement on cultural identity in general is revealed in the historical novels pertaining to Syrian identity. The main goal of the novels was to revive the glorious past of the Syrian people and the region in the collective memory of their readers. The novels used the success of the past in order to instil pride in the hearts of the Syrian inhabitants, contrasting Syria's history with the degraded contemporary situation. As Hobsbawn wrote "The past gives a more glorious background to a present that doesn't have much to celebrate."[113]

Hence, the importance of the historical novels is that they allowed the birth of an "invented tradition." They had the ability to connect people to the past, thus helping them to become familiar with their magnificent heritage and the roots of their new identity, one which would often be introduced as their primordial one. Writing

---

[112] Stuart Hall and Paul Du Gay (eds.), *Questions of Cultural Identity* (London, 1996), p. 4.

[113] Eric Hobsbawm, *On History* (London, 1997), p. 6.

the story of the past influences both the present and the future. As Salīm al-Bustānī wrote, "The past brings the person to the present and to the future, the future is the child of the past and the present." He also wrote that "History is the knowledge of the past and the watchful eye for the results of present events."[114]

The past was utilised to fulfil present social needs. Through these novels, myths and a new heritage were constructed according to a selective historical account of the region. Every novel represents a highlight in this new history and heritage of Syria. This was the manner chosen by the intelligentsia to rediscover and reinterpret a popular living past for the collective memory. The cultivation of these shared memories was essential for the survival and destiny of such a collective identity, in order to share meaning and ideals, to guide actions and determine the direction of changes and the evolving identity. Analysing the novels will illustrate, as Sethi stated, "what lies behind the writing of 'true' and 'authentic' histories of the nation."[115]

Building the New Self: Zenobia Queen of Palmyra (Tadmor)

The first novel, published in 1871, deals with Zenobia (d. 274 CE), the warrior Arab queen of Tadmor.[116] As we shall see, her myth was selected since it incorporates almost all the aspects that the new self was requested to fulfil. In Arab culture her name is Zaynab or Zabbā'. In Aramaic her name was Bat Zabbai, which according to one interpretation has two meanings, the daughter of Zabbai or the "daughter of a merchant,"[117] perhaps from the Arabic word *zabūn*, meaning "buyer" or "purchaser." Zenobia's father was possibly a member of the proud, cultured Arab merchant elite who inhabited this prosperous city.

In the third century, Tadmor itself was a half-religious, half-commercial centre, situated at a vital confluence of caravan routes in the Syrian Desert. These caravan routes "linked the city to the seaboard cities of Phoenicia, to Emesa, [present-day Homs], to Damascus and to Egypt itself."[118] Tadmor linked these places with

---

[114] Al-Bustānī, "Zanūbyā," Vol. 1, No. 1, 1870, p. 26.

[115] Rumina Sethi, *Myth of the Nation: National Identity and Literary Representation* (New York, 1999), p. 1.

[116] Al-Bustānī, "Zanūbyā," Vol. 1, No. 1–24, 1870.

[117] Antonia Fraser, *The Warrior Queens: Boadicea's Chariot* (London, 1988), p. 108.

[118] *Ibid.*, p. 111.

Seleucia and more distant eastern regions. The city was also halfway between the two mighty and contending empires or cultures of that period: Persia vs. Rome, the East vs. the West or European vs. Asian cultures.

In fact, what the myth of the Phoenicians symbolised for the Syrians in connection with the sea, the myth of Tadmor represented for the land.[119] Both are pre-Islamic and emphasise a cultural and economic highlight in the Syrian past similar to the role of Beirut at present. Also, the tie between land and sea, i.e. the Phoenicians' maritime dominance, and Tadmor's control of land/desert routes, reflected the essence of daily life in which the Beiruti middle stratum acted as commercial mediators between land and sea. As in the case of Beirut, Tadmor was a convergence of cultures and races and an important economic centre linking East and West. It is obvious why the Beiruti middle stratum was attracted and fascinated by both accounts. As with the Phoenician idea, the myth of Zenobia was probably obtained from Western travel books and the American missionaries.[120]

Zenobia ruled Tadmor, an autonomous principality subject to Rome, from 267 to 272, following the death of the previous ruler, her husband Odainathus. At first, Zenobia continued to recognise the ascendancy of Rome, although she soon tried to extend her rule over the whole of Syria. Her aspiration was that Tadmor would rule the East.

After the death of Emperor Claudius, she grew bolder, aggrandising territory, minting her own coinage, and declaring herself formally independent of Rome. When the new Emperor Aurelian cast himself in the role of "restorer of the Orient," Zenobia resolved in 271 to rebel against Roman dominance and its emperor, and to expand her authority over large portions of Syria.

Her armies stood against the Roman legions and repelled them. Her realm extended as far as Egypt and the heart of Asia Minor. Finally, in 272, she was deposed by the Roman Emperor, and was led to Rome in golden shackles. Aurelian had evidently saved her to be the crowing glory of his triumphal procession. Zenobia, the

---

[119] William Wright, *An Account of Palmyra and Zenobia with Travels and Adventures in Bashan and the Desert* (London, 1895), p. 138.

[120] For example, in 1920 we find exhibits on Phoenicia and Palmyra in the SPC's museum. Leonard Woolley, "The Archeological Museum of the SPC," *al-Kuliyya*, Vol. 7, 1920, pp. 23–25.

proud queen of Palmyra and the Empress of the East, made her last historic appearance.[121]

Fascinated by her story, Salīm al-Bustānī wrote his novel and added or even enhanced various aspects of her image, changing it according to his evolving sense of identity and its needs. He conducted a preparatory study of her history before writing his own one.[122] Salīm's novel presents her as both Arab and Syrian. Zenobia's army is described as an Arab and Syrian army. Tadmor itself is described as part of the Arab Syrian heritage. The novel focuses on her conquest of Egypt, her government in Syria, her war against Rome and her relationship with her daughter and with the people of Tadmor. As in Western versions, it enlarges on her strength and victory over Rome, but in contrast to them it mainly emphasises her leadership, her love and loyalty towards her people and homeland.

Undoubtedly, it is a patriotic novel that attempts to explain to its readers that the *waṭan* should be the most important entity for them, as it was for this magnificent queen. The story of this novel, as in the case of the two other historical novels examined here, has two levels. On one level, the true historical story of Zenobia is presented; the other is a fictional love story between her daughter, Jūlyā, and a distinguished Roman prince, from the ruling dynasty, by the name of Bīzū. The latter came to Tadmor as a result of differences with the Roman Emperor. Zenobia disliked his association with her daughter, fearful that some day he might rule Rome, and would demand her surrender. Nonetheless, during the course of the novel she changes her attitude towards him.

Throughout the novel Jūlyā is torn between her love and duty to her *waṭan*. Eventually she chooses duty over love, and willingly sacrifices her own happiness for the sake of her nation. At one point, Zenobia even considered marrying Jūlyā to the Persian King so as to gain him as Tadmor's ally in its war against Rome. The message is clear: *ḥubb al-waṭan* (love of the homeland, i.e. spiritual love) is more important than *ḥubb al-jasad* (love of the body, i.e. physical love).

A third female character in the fictional story is Fūstā, the daughter of one of Zenobia's advisers, who admires Zenobia's love for the

---

[121] For more details on Zenobia's story, see: Nabia Abbott, "Pre-Islamic Arab Queens," *The American Journal of Semitic Languages and Literatures*, Vol. 58 (1941), pp. 12–16; Wright, *An Account of Palmyra and Zenobia*, pp. 109–115.

[122] Al-Bustānī, "Zanūbyā," No. 1, pp. 26–28.

homeland. She differs from the figure of Jūlyā, as she unquestioningly and totally believes that love of thy country is above love for a man. Fūstā goes hunting with Zenobia, and follows her in battle as well.

The people of Tadmor are also a substantial element of the story, whose love for the Syrian country and Syrian queen is paramount. Through the Tadmorians, the novel presents another principal message, that the present inhabitants of Syria should put aside their religious differences and be united in their love for their homeland, as the Tadmorians did.[123]

Other patriotic messages are interwoven in the story, such as that the success of the homeland depends on the education of the new generation; differences among the population would weaken the homeland; and that the homeland should defend the people and their right to independence.[124]

The main figure, of course, remains that of Zenobia. She is the ultimate patriotic woman, because she unhesitatingly puts the interests of her country before her own. She is willing to sacrifice herself and her daughter's happiness for the sake of the homeland. She is presented as a wise, just ruler, who introduced reforms for advancing her people. Always looking towards the future, she understands that her power derives from them. Her character is employed in order to show the unity of the Syrian nation and its magnificent past. She is described as the queen of the desert, a Bedouin queen. The military help she receives from the Arab tribes is also highlighted, implying her ties with Arabism.

Zenobia's desire for independence is admired, yet her lust for power is criticised. Her own daughter tries to convince her not to initiate a battle while Tadmor is enjoying a period of prosperity, and the culture of the Arabs has overcome that of the Romans.[125] Perhaps Salīm al-Bustānī was trying to deliver a message by indicating that the Syrian population in his time should not hold such aspirations against the Ottoman Empire.

The high points of the novel are the battles led by Zenobia. The first battle, described with much patriotic enthusiasm, was fought against the Egyptians. The loyalty of the army and its love for

---

[123] *Ibid.*, No. 2, pp. 61–62, 99.
[124] *Ibid.*, No. 13, p. 465.
[125] *Ibid.*, No. 1, pp. 30–31 and No. 3, p. 102.

Zenobia's just rule are accentuated. Before the battle, Zenobia delivers a speech in order to encourage her soldiers. She calls, "Lead your country on the wings of victory.... Whoever dies for the *waṭan* will die a precious death, while the coward will fall into the pit meant for despicable people.... Your law is the law of your homeland."[126] The second high point of the novel depicts the battle against Rome. In this scene Salīm emphasises again that Tadmor included different people from diverse communities but that they overcame their differences and were willing to fight together against Rome.[127]

In the end, Zenobia and her army were defeated, but only after a heroic battle. With regard to her personal life, the novel has a happy ending. Zenobia marries a distinguished Roman figure; her daughter marries Bīzū. It is important to note that there are two historic versions of Zenobia's end. The first is the version that Salīm al-Bustānī used, and is the happier and perhaps more generally accepted one by historians. The second version provides her with a tragic end. It describes how, after her ruin, Zenobia refused all food, languished and died.[128] Why Salīm al-Bustānī chose the happier ending is not clear. After all, he could have represented Zenobia as the tragic heroine who sacrifices her life for the homeland. Perhaps he sensed that his readers would prefer a happy end for this queen who had done so much for the sake of the Syrian nation. Also, the fact that Zenobia was defeated was not important, since according to this version she was not defeated in spirit. Thus, another lesson could be learned from her story: the result is not important, the process is what counts.[129]

The myth of Zenobia was chosen since it brought together, in a single powerful vision, elements of historical fact and legendary elaboration to create an overriding commitment and bond for the Syrian community. Zenobia resembles what Smith terms a "myth of the heroic age"—the golden age of Syrian heritage.[130] Her story is convincing proof of ethnic ancestry and common history. As in the case

---

[126] *Ibid.*, No. 5, p. 172.
[127] *Ibid.*, No. 12 and 13, pp. 423–457.
[128] Wright, *An Account of Palmyra and Zenobia*, p. 168.
[129] In nineteenth-century Ottoman theatre, tragic endings often symbolised a threat to the existing government; happy endings were considered as entertaining, and did not raise any suspicions.
[130] Smith, *Myths and Memories of the Nation*, pp. 65–67.

of other myths, her image serves to legitimise the needs of the intellectuals who supported the construction of this identity.[131]

Salīm al-Bustānī was not exceptional in nurturing this myth. Zenobia became a main figure and a leading Syrian myth among other Christian-Arab intellectuals as well. In modern Syrian historiography she also receives attention. Ilyās Maṭar, for one, was fascinated by Zenobia's tragic tale, seeing her as a heroic figure, the goddess of war, the queen who carved her name forever in the annals of nations. Maṭar presumably wished to revive this period because Syria was then strong, autonomous, and under Arab rule.[132] Jurjī Yannī introduced her as the symbol of the Syrian will for self-government,[133] and al-Dibs presented her as the educated woman she was, fluent in several languages.[134]

In general, Christian Arabs considered her period as a highlight in the region's history. By setting forth the history of Zenobia, they aimed to underline the fact that even in the pre-Islamic era, there had been a domestic and autonomous Arab ruler in Syria. Her myth can still be found in Syria today. Some of today's political elite use her as a symbol to encourage Syrian nationalism. Her image decorates the one hundred Syrian lira note, dramatic plays and books are written about her, and Tadmor is still considered to be one of the important archaeological and tourist sites of Syria.[135]

Towards the end of the nineteenth century, as well as during the twentieth century, her myth was used in several other Arab countries such as Egypt and Iraq in the framework of Arab nationalism. In Egypt, for example, her image was very prominent in the writing of women at the beginning of the twentieth century. She became an exemplary figure for her political acumen and as one who brought glory to her community and to all women.[136] Nevertheless, it is important to note that the Christian Arabs were probably the first to use her image as part of their new secular identity.

---

[131] *Ibid.*, pp. 57, 61.
[132] Maṭar, *al-ʿUqūd al-Duriyya*, pp. 59–61.
[133] Yannī, *Tārīkh Sūriyā*, pp. 476–485.
[134] Al-Dibs, *Tārīkh Sūriyya*, Vol. 1, p. 23.
[135] For example, see the novel by Nawwāf Ḥardān, *Ẕanūbyā al-Aẕīma; Qaḍiyya wa-Sayf wa-Kitāb* (Beirut, 1995); Moustafa Tlass, *Zenobia: The Queen of Palmyra* (Damascus, 2000).
[136] Marilyn Booth, *May Her Likes Be Multiplied: Biography and Gender Politics in Egypt* (Berkeley, 2001), p. 94.

The novel of *Zanūbyā* was written during the governorship of Rāshid Pāshā, and this was one of the reasons that allowed Salīm al-Bustānī to highlight the pre-Islamic period in order to create the new self and vividly describe Syrian patriotism. The other two novels were written during a more problematical period in the *Vilâyet* of Syria, when a less liberal attitude prevailed. Syrian patriotism was less accentuated and the main focus of intellectual discourse was on a new interpretation of the heritage of the "other"—i.e. the Muslim heritage.

Building the New Self with the "Other": Al-Andalus *and the Conquest of* Bilād al-Shām

Salīm's next two novels in *al-Jinān* are entitled, *Budūr*, published in 1872,[137] and *al-Huyām fī Futūḥ al-Shām* (Love during the Conquest of *al-Shām*), published in 1874.[138] They represented the two other high points in this constructed Syrian heritage, but this time were connected to the cultural heritage of Islam. Even the name Budūr is taken from the local literary heritage, namely the stories of *Arabian Nights*. Budūr is the name of the heroine, a princess, in the tale of *Qamar al-Zamān* (literally, the Moon of Times but in meaning—The Ever Most Beautiful).[139]

In his novels, Salīm al-Bustānī uses parameters taken from the heritage of the "other" and gives them new interpretations in the framework of the new self, in order to show that Christians and Muslims could share the same identity. Because Islamic culture was also the heritage of the local Christian Arabs, they naturally utilised it as part of their own identity and truly saw their heritage in this way. In these novels Islam is perceived as the cultural heritage of the Muslims and the Christians, rather than as the religion of Syria and the Syrians. As we shall see in the analysis of these two novels, the Islamic past was transformed and its Arab nature emphasised.

Even though the novel *Budūr* takes place in Andalusia in the eighth century, evidently Salīm al-Bustānī tried to paint it with the

---

[137] Al-Bustānī, "Budūr," No. 1–24, 1872.

[138] Al-Bustānī, "al-Huyām fī Futūḥ al-Shām," No. 1–24, 1874. The story was published again in the beginning of the twentieth century under a different title: "*Mar'at al-Gharb*," in the newspaper *New-York*, which was published by Syrian immigrants. Birmū, *al-Riwāya al-Tārīkhiyya*, p. 43.

[139] *The Arabian Nights: Book of the Thousand Nights and One Night*, Vol. 2, ed. by J.C. Mardrus and trans. by E.P. Mathers (London and New York, 1994), pp. 1–69.

characteristics of Andalusia in a later period, i.e. that of its golden age. Apparently, this shift was intended to connect the imagination of his readers with this period, which was also one of the golden ages of the Arab Empire with flourishing science and culture, erudition and education. For Salīm's purposes, this era was ideal: it was primarily known for the close communal cooperation between the three religions, Islam, Christianity and Judaism, when members of all three lived and created together in cultural and economic prosperity.[140] The Arab dynasty that ruled Andalusia, in the period in which the novel takes place, was the Umayyads (661–750). They came to power with the help of Bedouin and Arab tribes and are perceived as Arab rulers, in contrast with the ʿAbbasid dynasty whose emphasis was notably on Islam and the Muslims. The policies of the former aspired to transform Islamic theocracy into an Arab Caliphate under Arab rule. Moreover, the centre of the Umayyad dynasty was Damascus, which was also the centre of the *Vilâyet* of Syria. Obviously, this period perfectly fitted the needs of Salīm al-Bustānī for constructing a new Syrian heritage.

The hero and the heroine of the novel are Muslim Arabs and not pre-Islamic figures. Again, the novel includes two levels, the known historical narrative and the fictional love story. The historical account takes place in the middle of the eighth century at the time when the ʿAbbasids emerged as the new Muslim dynasty. The novel starts with a description of the massacre of the former dynasty of the Umayyads by the ʿAbbasids. The only one who survived this massacre was the Umayyad prince ʿAbd al-Raḥmān, the grandson of the Caliph Hishām, who is known in Muslim historiography by the name "The One who Enters" (*al-Dākhil*). The prince managed to escape to Spain through North Africa in the year 750, and in 756, with the help of Arab tribes in the south of the Iberian Peninsula, he became the prince of Andalusia and ruled it until 788.

Salīm al-Bustānī adds a central fictional figure to the story, Budūr, an Umayyad princess, who is in love with ʿAbd al-Raḥmān, her cousin. The novel introduces Budūr as the person who urges ʿAbd al-Raḥmān to escape from the new rising dynasty and is thus credited with saving the future Arab leader of Andalusia.[141]

---

[140] About the same time, the symbol of the Golden Age of Andalusia also developed in Europe.

[141] Al-Bustānī, "Budūr," No. 1, pp. 33–34.

The plot traces the many adventures of Budūr and ʿAbd al-Raḥmān. First it describes ʿAbd al-Raḥmān's escape from the ʿAbbasids, and his flight to Egypt. Later, when war between the Spanish and Arabs begins, a group of distinguished "Syrian Arab" men from Damascus decide to establish a strong Arab government, and they suggest that ʿAbd al-Raḥmān head it.[142] So, he leaves Egypt for Andalusia.

In the meantime, and throughout most of the novel, Budūr tries to find her love. She escapes from the ʿAbbasid Caliph and on her journey she disguises herself as various men, one of them an Arab soldier.[143] She travels by ship, but pirates kidnap her. The pirate chief wants to marry her, but she manages to escape with the help of her Spanish teacher, who falls in love with her as well. At the end of the story, ʿAbd al-Raḥmān and Budūr find each other, marry and together rule Andalusia.

Throughout the novel, the spirit of the Arab Umayyads is presented, thus focusing on the fact that in Arab heritage, figures from Damascus or the region of Syria were central. Even though the story does not take place in Syria, there is Syrian involvement. The hero and the heroine and the group that sends ʿAbd al-Raḥmān to Andalusia are Syrians from Damascus; and thus Syria is at the centre of the magnificent Arab Empire and the bond between Arabism and Syrianism is constructed.

In the last novel, *al-Huyām fī Futūḥ al-Shām*, another high point in Muslim heritage is revealed, that of the Muslim conquest of *Bilād al-Shām* from the Byzantines in the seventh century (634–638). Yet again, the novel presents it as an Arab conquest. In contrast to the other novels, the didactic side of the story is accentuated at the expense of the plot. In the text, Salīm al-Bustānī interweaves several short heroic stories about Muslim heroes and heroines that are known in Muslim historiography.[144] For example, he mentions Khawla bint al-Azwar (d. 635), a poet who used her poetry to inflame the soldiers in this battle for *al-Shām*.[145]

---

142 *Ibid.*, No. 14, p. 499.

143 *Ibid.*, No. 4, pp. 141–142; No. 8, pp. 354–355; No. 10, p. 646; No. 24, p. 861. The motif of women disguised as men already existed in Arabian Nights stories and can be found in Western novels of the eighteenth and nineteenth centuries as well.

144 Salīm also uses classic Muslim sources such as: al-Wāqidī, Ibn al-Athīr and Ṭabarī.

145 For example, see: al-Bustānī, "*al-Huyām fī Futūḥ al-Shām*," No. 16, p. 575;

In doing so, he indicates, perhaps with his women readers in mind, the important role of women in the Arab-Syrian past. Salīm al-Bustānī himself notes that the main goal of this novel was to describe the transformation of the ancient Syrians under Byzantine rule into an Arab nation: how, from many nations, the local inhabitants were moulded under Arab culture, language and customs, and became part of the Arab Empire.[146] In other words, the novel emphasises the establishment of an Arab entity in Syria, i.e. the beginning of the Arabisation of the Syrian region for both its Muslim and Christian populations, over the Islamisation of *Bilād al-Shām*, as described in Muslim historiography.

The novel begins with a poem written by the poet al-Mutanabbī, whose writing is infused with pride of Arab culture.[147] The fictional story includes two parallel love stories, on both sides of the battling parties. The first one follows the tale of two Muslim lovers, Salmā and Sālim. Salmā is the daughter of a distinguished man from Yemen and Sālim is the son of a Yemenite Amīr. Sālim participates in the battle of *al-Shām* and Salmā, in disguise, helps him in the battlefield by taking care of the wounded and encouraging the soldiers. Later, she is arrested and sent to prison in Aleppo. At the end of the story she is released and returns to her beloved Sālim.

The second love story is between Jūlyān, a Byzantine commander and Ūghustā, the daughter of one of the Byzantine ministers. Ūghusta's character is similar to that of Salmā. She is educated and defends her loved one and her homeland, by accompanying Jūlyān to the battle where she manages to save his life. After that, she also tries to spy on the Muslim camp and is arrested, but her beloved saves her. In the end, Ūghustā is reunited with her treasured Jūlyān.

The Role of Women in the Waṭan

> *"Inna allatī Tahuzzu al-Sarīr bi-Yasārihā Tahuzzu al-Arḍ bi-Yamīnihā"* (She who rocks the cradle in her left hand, shakes the earth with her right.)
>
> Salīm al-Bustānī[148]

No. 19, p. 681; No. 23, p. 823. It should be emphasised that Khawla bint al-Azwar was most involved in the Islamic conquest of *al-Shām*.

[146] Al-Bustānī, "Asmā," No. 23, p. 827.

[147] Al-Bustānī, "*al-Huyām fī Futūh al-Shām*," No. 1, p. 29; No. 3, p. 105.

[148] Salīm al-Bustānī, *al-Muqtaṭaf*, Vol. 7, 1882, p. 709.

The three historical novels reveal new role models in the evolution of the Syrian identity, i.e. Syrian patriotic women and their place in society. An analysis of this literature utilising modern gender theory is outside the scope of this book, yet perhaps some of the resource material will be the subject of such future study.

That Salīm al-Bustānī chose women heroines as patriotic symbols and myths is not accidental, since the discourse of the proto-national and national context clearly called for a change in the status of women in society.[149] This topic occupied Salīm's thoughts as early as 1870, when he called for the emancipation of Arab women from their repressive traditional roles. In another instance he argued that women, entrusted with bringing up children, could shape the whole society by their actions and attitudes. A society of free men cannot be hoped for when they are brought up by women who are shackled by prejudice.[150] In this regard he was probably influenced not only by his father, who was among the first to talk about this issue,[151] but also by his educated mother, Raḥīl (1823–1894) who was trained by her own father in the literary arts. She also completed the course of studies in the first females' school run by the American missionaries in the 1840s, and could read both Arabic and English literature.[152] Her role in his life probably set an example, at least in part, for the image of women that he portrayed.

Salīm al-Bustānī's writing reveals how male writers defined Syrian patriotism through the image of the women both for the audience of men and women. The novels introduced female readers to historical or fictional models in order to show them how they should act as patriotic women in the framework of the homeland and in

---

[149] For example, see: Deniz Kandiyoti, "Slave Girls, Temptresses, and Comrades: Images of Women in the Turkish Novel," *Feminist Issues*, Vol. 8 (1988), pp. 33–50; Afsaneh Najamabadi, "The Erotic Vatan [Homeland] as Beloved and Mother: To Love, To Possess, and To Protect," *Comparative Studies in Society and History*, Vol. 39 (1997), pp. 442–467; Beth Baron, "Nationalist Iconography—Egypt as a Woman," in James Jankowski and Israel Gershoni (eds.), *Rethinking Nationalism in the Arab Middle East* (New York, 1997), pp. 105–124.

[150] Salīm al-Bustānī, "al-Inṣāf," *al-Jinān*, Vol. 12, 1884, pp. 369–371; Salīm al-Bustānī, "Inna allatī Tahuzzu al-Sarīr bi-Yasārihā Tahuzzu al-Arḍ bi-Yamīnihā", *al-Muqtaṭaf*, Vol. 7, 1882, pp. 709–712 and Vol. 8, 1883, pp. 7–11.

[151] Already in 1849 Buṭrus al- Bustānī gave a lecture on the issue of educating women. See: Buṭrus al-Bustānī, "Khiṭāb fī Taʿlīm al-Nisāʾ," in al-Bustānī, *al-Jamʿiyya al-Sūriyya lil- ʿUlūm wal-Funūn*, pp. 50–53.

[152] Booth, *May Her Likes Be Multiplied*, pp. 135–136; Iskandar Barūdī, "The Education of Women Among Us," *al-Kuliyya*, Vol. 3, June 1912, pp. 233–240.

the new modern society. The active role of women in the homeland was portrayed in two ways: as mother of the homeland/nation or in other words modern motherhood, and that of a woman, assisting her man to build the homeland, defend or fight for it. She is the patriotic woman behind or alongside the patriotic man.

The image of the mother of the Syrian nation is presented in the case of Zenobia. In this respect it is important to note that the figure of the woman as a mother often symbolises in many cultures the spirit of collectivity, i.e. the collective nature of culture.[153]

The second image, of the patriotic woman who fights alongside her love for the sake of the Arab culture and empire, is presented in the next two novels, *Budūr* and *al-Huyām fī Futūḥ al-Shām*. The heroines, Budūr and Salmā, help their men and are willing to do their utmost in order to save and support the patriotic hero. Salīm al-Bustānī enlarges on this issue in an article he wrote in *al-Muqtaṭaf* which was published in two parts, in the years 1882–1883.[154] In it, he explains that one of the important roles of women in the homeland is on the battlefield where they take care of the wounded and encourage their children to fulfil their patriotic obligations.[155] Sometimes, as in the case of Zenobia, the woman herself becomes the patriotic warrior who defends her homeland.

However, this message is delivered in all three novels along with a dichotomous one, also stressing the duties of the woman in her domestic role in the family and private sphere. Göçek called this "The concept of ambivalence in representation,"[156] similar to the difference between the idealised and the actual figures of women. This was also due to the possibility that while Salīm al-Bustānī strove to encourage increased involvement in public life by a group of the educated and middle class women, perhaps he wanted to send a different message to an increasingly large number of other women. These women were expected to contribute to the process of *tamaddun* and to the homeland, not only by becoming warrior women but

---

[153] Nira Yuval-Davis, *Gender and Nation* (London, 1997), p. 45.

[154] Al-Bustānī, "Inna allatī Tahuzzu al-Sarīr," Vol. 7, pp. 709–712 and Vol. 8, 1883, pp. 7–11.

[155] *Ibid.*, Vol. 8, 1883, p. 10.

[156] Fatma Müge Göçek, "From the Empire to Nation, Images of Women and War in Ottoman Political Cartoons, 1908–1923," in Billie Melman (ed.) *Borderlines, Gender and Identities in War and Peace, 1870–1930* (London, 1998), pp. 70–71.

also by preserving their traditional role, taking care of their families and their homes (see figures 5.1–5.3 as compared with figure 5.4).[157]

The ambivalent attitude was blatant in a lecture that Salīm al-Bustānī delivered in 1882 to the graduates of the school for girls which was established by the American missionary De Forest. The title of his lecture was "She Who Rocks the Cradle in Her Left Hand, Shakes the Earth with Her Right." The first part of this title symbolises the domestic role of women, while the second part symbolises their contribution to the public sphere. He illustrates his lecture with names of women who managed to perform heroic actions for the sake of the homeland. Salīm al-Bustānī provides the examples of Esther and Deborah from the Bible as well as Zenobia, Jean d'Arc and Elizabeth I, Queen of England. Yet, in parallel he stresses that a "good (*ṣāliḥa*) woman" is one who mainly fulfils her domestic role, as this is the road that will allow her to "shake the earth."

Earlier, in 1872, in order to encourage among his readers the image of a woman active for the sake of her homeland, he chose to "visualise identity,"[158] that is, portrayed the image of the patriotic women (and the patriotic man as well) through a collection of illustrations which were included in a single novel—*Budūr*.

These images were created by two illustrators who probably received their training in Europe—Luṭufallāh Arqash and Mīkhā'īl Faraḥ.[159] Their illustrations portray a material representation of public consciousness. Through them, Salīm al-Bustānī tried to construct patriotic images in the imagination of his readers.

[157] Yeşim Arat, "The Project of Modernity and Women in Turkey," in Sibel Bozdogan and Reşat Kasaba (eds.), *Rethinking Modernity and National Identity in Turkey* (Seattle, 1997), pp. 99–100.

[158] This process also appeared in Egypt towards the end of the nineteenth century. See: Baron, "Nationalist Iconography, Egypt as a Woman," pp. 105–106.

[159] I could not find any biographical information on these illustrators.

The Patriotic Woman

Fig. 5.1. Budūr riding on horseback, citing "As God eased my path of rescue, thus he shall assist my path of rejoining, and he will be my aid." ["Budūr," *al-Jinān*, Vol. 3, 1872, p. 137.]

Fig. 5.2. Budūr escaping on a horse. ["Budūr," *al-Jinān*, Vol. 3, 1872, p. 677.]

Fig. 5.3. Budūr crying out "Woe to war!" ["Budūr," *al-Jinān*, Vol. 3, 1872, p. 712.]

Fig. 5.4. Budūr weaving. ["Budūr," *al-Jinān*, Vol. 3, 1872, p. 281.]

The Patriotic Man

Fig. 5.5. Amīr ʿAbd al-Raḥmān. ["Budūr," *al-Jinān*, Vol. 3, 1872, p. 497.]

In figure 5.1, Budūr has escaped from the ʿAbbasid Caliph, who wants to marry her against her will. She is riding a white horse, is dressed in black, with a veil on her face, and is said to be disguised as a man. The illustration transmits mobility and power. Her image seems very active, and she appears strong and confident in God's help. In her hand, raised aloft, she holds a spear. It is possible that Luṭufallāh Arqash was influenced by images of Jean d'Arc contemporaneously produced in Europe, particularly in France. However, Budūr's image is indigenous (as indicated by her clothes). In other words, Budūr appears local but the setting appears to be influenced by contemporary European painting.

In figures 5.2 and 5.3 Budūr is again riding a horse, yet this time disguised as a Spanish man (it is difficult to determine whether she is portraying a warrior or a noble man). In these images her face is unveiled.[160] According to the story, she is running from the pirate chief, who kidnapped her while she tried to find her beloved ʿAbd al-Raḥmān.

In figure 5.5, we can see the image of ʿAbd al-Raḥmān as a patriotic warrior and perhaps the saviour of the nation. Of course, differences exist between his illustration and that of Budūr. His shiny spear is much larger and his horse is on the attack.

These illustrations found in *al-Jinān* also contain other messages, yet this is not the place to offer a full analysis of them.[161] Noteworthy to our understanding of the construction of the Syrian patriotism is the fact that women were portrayed in the Syrian region in this manner as early as 1872, thus exposing readers to such ideas.

Illustrations aside, the novels themselves also offered other messages for the Syrian woman. For example, in each novel they were called to dedicate themselves to preserve their local Arab culture. Hence, in many cases all three heroines had the qualities of outstanding Bedouin women in pre-Islamic times. In portraying the role of the woman in the *waṭan* simultaneously as a warrior and as an educated individual, Salīm al-Bustānī introduced his audience to heroic women from both pre-Islamic and Islamic historiography.

[160] In some research, the debates on un-veiling coincided with the rise of nationalism.

[161] I am already conducting additional research on this issue. In this chapter I presented some of my conclusions regarding the illustrations and the way in which they represent the role of the women in the homeland. Still, there is work to be done in analysing illustrations in the novel, such as the manner in which local intellectuals perceived women's modernisation and Westernisation.

Apparently, the three heroines had the qualities of Tamāḍur bint ʿAmr, known as "al-Khansāʾ" (575–645 CE), the Arab poet and warrior who converted to Islam, or perhaps that of the poet and warrior Khawla Bint al-Azwar, whom Salīm al-Bustānī mentioned in the novel *al-Huyām fī Futūḥ al-Shām*.[162] Salīm chose these figures of Arab women in order to remind the women of his time that what European women were now doing, had already been done by Arab women in the past. Thus, for a woman to become patriotic, or in other words "modern," meant that she had to return to her heritage and preserve it by adapting it to the new and modern changes taking place.

Women were also called upon to preserve and defend the local economy and to help in developing the industry and agriculture of the homeland. Zenobia, for example, was described as dressing in local attire in order to serve as an example, eventually encouraging local industry and bringing about prosperity.[163] As local economic support was an important factor among the Beiruti middle stratum it was also a clear message in the novel. In order to reduce the tendency of local women to buy Western clothes, such behaviour was presented as an unpatriotic act. In fact, several of Salīm's non-historic novels and short stories deal in the over imitating of Western fashion, accentuating his view that ones' appearance is not an indication of his/her *tamaddun*.

In general, Salīm emphasised the importance of education for women. All three heroines were portrayed as educated ones (see figure 5.6), in order to better raise the future patriotic generation and thus to advance their society and homeland.

In contrast to the patriotic women, her non-patriotic counterpart was described as one who is interested in a comfortable life. She lacks education, and instead of preserving her own culture, she prefers to embrace everything from the West. She neglects her commitment towards her family and does not care about her homeland.

In essence, the image of the "new educated woman" (*al-marʾa al-jadīda al-ʿāqīla*) and her significant contribution to the homeland is largely identified with Qāsim Amīn's landmark book, *Liberation of Woman* (*Taḥrīr al-Marʾa*), which was published in Egypt in 1898.

---

162 Al-Bustānī, "*al-Huyām fī Futūḥ al-Shām*," No. 16, pp. 574–575.

163 Al-Bustānī, "Zanūbyā," No. 23, pp. 823–825; al-Bustānī, "Budūr," No. 8, p. 281.

Fig. 5.6. Budūr writing.
["Budūr," *al-Jinān*, Vol. 3, 1872, p. 318.]

Previous research has found that well before Amīn, this critical modern social issue had already been raised and debated by several Middle Eastern Muslim and Christian writers. In fact, attention to the role of women in society or the homeland had already increased after the first quarter of the nineteenth century.[164] Indeed, the Syrian case shows that as part of the emergence of the Arab Syrian historical novel, the issue of women's roles appeared among Christian-Arab intellectuals nearly thirty years prior to Amīn. Of course, this may partially be due to the West's influence on Christian Arabs at the time. Somewhat similar to the contemporary situation in the West, Syrian women were recruited in the effort to build the nation and the homeland and to educate the new generation to patriotism.

The actual impact of these ideas on female readers, ideas written by men but concerning Syrian women, is difficult to measure. While Christian-Arab intellectuals were dealing with the definition of their own Syrian identity and discussing the place of women in society, women themselves were beginning to reconsider their own place in it. Later, towards the end of the nineteenth century and the beginning of the twentieth century, after massive immigration of Syrians to Egypt, many of them, who were in fact sisters or daughters of

[164] Byron D. Cannon, "Nineteenth Century Arabic Writing on Women and Society: The Interim Role of the Masonic Press in Cairo" (*al-Laṭā'if*, 1885–1895), *International Journal of Middle Eastern Studies*, Vol. 17 (1985), pp. 463–471.

these Christian-Arab intellectuals' families from Beirut, such as Warda al-Yāzijī (1838–1924) and Hind Nawfal (1859–1920), became prominent figures in the Egyptian press.[165] These women, who were most probably among the young readers of the Beiruti newspapers, now had the ability to write and even publish journals of their own, in Arabic. In analysing their writing, one can trace several ideas that belonged to the Beiruti stratum. Later, some of these women took elements of these concepts another step forward, enlisting them in the feminist discourse. They added new ideas and thoughts and thus moulded their own views regarding these issues, finally taking practical steps in the struggle for their own freedom.

These Syrian women living in Egypt did not construct their identity as a Syrian one, but mainly tried to shape it in the direction of an Arab identity. They tended to stress shared identities while largely ignoring separatist histories and divergent religions. Of significance is that one of their interests was in writing biographies of non-Egyptian Arab women from pre-Islamic times to the present.[166] Andalusia was another topic of choice. They stated that Andalusia's golden period included many female poets and authors whose intelligence and talents were hardly below those of men.[167]

Another characteristic was their attention to the lives of al-Khansāʾ or Zenobia.[168] Warda al-Yāzijī wrote an article in the newspaper *al-Ḍiyāʾ* on *al-Marʾa al-Sharqiyya* (The Eastern Woman). Some of her ideas are similar to those emanating from the middle stratum to which she belonged. She blamed local women for trying to be similar to the Western ones, and by so doing neglecting their heritage and roots.[169] Through the newspaper, she called upon her female readers to aim for the qualities of women in the period of the *Jāhiliyya*. She claimed that female poets of that era were loyal to their language and culture and in this way achieved an important place in society.

* * *

[165] For more details on the Syrian women and the foundation of the press in Egypt, see: Beth Baron, *The Women's Awakening in Egypt: Culture, Society and the Press* (Chelsea, Michigan, 1994), pp. 13–27.

[166] Booth, *May Her Likes be Multiplied*, pp. 52–53.

[167] *Ibid.*, p. 96.

[168] *Ibid.*, p. xv.

[169] Warda al-Yāzijī, "al-Marʿa al-Sharqiyya," *al-Ḍiyāʾ*, Vol. 12, 1906, pp. 357–360, 392–396; Vol. 12, 1906, pp. 453–456.

In summary, we can say that the topics chosen for the three novels were not accidental and were intended for both women and men. They aspired to create a new heritage for the region of Syria by selectively adopting portions of its glorious past, starting in the third century and continuing to the seventh and eighth centuries. The point of departure was the pre-Islamic period. The story of Zenobia was intended to detach Arabism from Islam by creating a secular, pre-Islamic didactic history. Central to the depiction of this pre-Islamic period was the rise of an Arab Empire and culture and its development as part of the Syrian past. In other words, the heritage was based on pre-Islamic times, with the Arabic language and Arab culture at its centre.

Salīm al-Bustānī himself emphasised this historical view in one of his stories. He explained that his main goal in writing the novels was to describe the emergence and development of the Arab Empire and culture, both before and after the emergence of Islam. The rise of Islam was interpreted merely as another high point of this magnificent Arab Empire, which had already emerged before the rise of Islam. In this way the Muslim culture of the "other" was not pushed aside nor perceived as the most important culture. Rather, the Muslim culture was viewed as part of the continuum of a more ancient culture, the Arab one.

Throughout the novels, Salīm al-Bustānī tried to portray and emphasise the expansion of this empire stretching from the Middle East and North Africa to Southern Europe and West Asia. He saw the apex of its development in the occupation of Spain when the gates were opened for a new period, in which the Arab nation became the centre of science and culture for the world. During this time the West was undergoing a period of darkness and was enlightened by the achievements of the Arab Empire.[170]

The novels also highlight periods in which, in his eyes, Arab culture transcended Western culture. This was in order to indicate to the readers that in the past the former had been more advanced than that of the West, and that this could be achieved once again in the present. The magnificent past was remoulded in the seventh

[170] Al-Bustānī, "Asmā", No. 23, p. 827. This tendency to build up the magnificent past of the Arabs can be seen in the stories of Nuʿmān al-Qasāṭilī, "Murshid wa-Fitna," *al-Jinān*, Vol. 11, No. 5–24, 1880, and Vol. 12, No. 1, 1881, pp. 159–767.

and eighth centuries after the rise of Islam when it reached its zenith, yet it was interpreted as a continuation of the pre-Islamic Arab past.

Through building this new concept of the past, pre-Islamic and Islamic Syrian myths were constructed for the first time. Yet, in order to build this Syrian identity as a secular and multi-cultural one, the pre-Islamic era and phases within the Islamic period underwent a process of Arabisation and Syrianisation. The use of Islamic and Arab culture accentuated the similarity rather than the dissimilarity within the Syrian heterogeneous society. In later years, towards the end of the nineteenth century and during the twentieth century, other Christian intellectuals made use of some of these historic motifs and myths, but this time as part of the ideology of Arabism. They also added new myths. Examples can be found in the work of Jurjī Zaydān (1861–1914), who studied in the SPC. Zaydān is well known for his historical novels and yet it is obvious that Salīm al-Bustānī wrote about the same topics and periods, and was perhaps the first to enlarge on these symbols of Syrian Arab culture, at least a decade earlier. Yet, we can trace in Zaydān's writing, new motifs such as that of the legendary Ṣalāḥ al-Dīn, who was not mentioned in Salīm's writing.

Salīm's novels encouraged patriotism, and in each one of them the hero gives up everything for the sake of his/her *waṭan*.[171] Bedouins played central roles in the novels, since they were considered to be "true Arabs." However, this created an unresolved contradiction since patriotism is a territorial loyalty, while in Bedouin life territorial borders do not exist; the Bedouin is free to move from one land to another. This contradiction probably resulted from combining factors of local heritage and Western ideologies.

The importance of unity is emphasised several times in the texts of each novel.[172] In *Budūr*, the civil war during the period of Arab rule in Spain is explained by the fact that the "Arabs stopped taking care of each other" and this made them weak.[173] In *al-Huyām fī Futūḥ al-Shām* the main message is that the conquest of *Bilād al-Shām* was not due to the new religion, i.e. Islam, but because the Arabs

[171] For example, see: al-Bustānī, "*al-Huyām fī Futūḥ al-Shām*," No. 1, p. 31; No. 3, p. 101.

[172] Al-Bustānī, "Budūr," No. 1, pp. 393–395; No. 12, pp. 425–430.

[173] *Ibid.*, No. 13, p. 467.

were unified at the time that their enemy was divided. The novels attempt to indicate that unification is the basis for the success of Arab culture in the past, and that the Syrians in the present should strive to achieve it again.

To conclude, new genres, or new uses of genres existing in the West, were utilised to formulate a new local identity and new concepts of proto-nationalism in Greater Syria; and to educate the public about these ideas. By developing territorial ideas of a homeland that encompassed all religious minorities equally, and a more influential role for women, the Christian middle stratum developed its own identity as an integral part of community. They made use of journalism, historiography and historical novels to process and define their concepts of self identity and homeland.

EPILOGUE

When in 1876 Sultan Abdül Hamid II came to power, some aspects of his policy stood in contrast to that of the *Tanẓīmāt.* Under his rule, Islam received more emphasis, mainly in order to strengthen his status as a Muslim Caliph. In parallel, censorship increased, and for the Christian Arab intellectuals, especially from the 1880s on, it became more difficult, albeit not impossible, to formulate and disseminate ideas regarding their Syrian identity.

In this atmosphere, many Syrian intellectuals emigrated from the *Vilâyet* of Syria to places such as Egypt, North America, or Brazil. Some, such as those in America, continued to promote Syrian identity. The Christian Arab intellectuals who stayed in the *Vilâyet* of Syria, as the newspaper *al-Jinān* reveals, continued to encourage this identity, but not quite as intensively as under former *vali*s such as Rāshid Pāshā or Midhat Pāshā. For example, in 1880 Adīb ʿAbduh Afandī Kaḥīl wrote an article in *al-Jinān* entitled *al-Waṭan wa-Maḥabbatuhu* (The Homeland and the Love for It). In the article, he made use of terms such as *taʿaṣṣub waṭanī* (in the sense of patriotic devotion), *muwāṭin Sūrī* (Syrian citizen), and so forth. This patriotic article describes the Syrian homeland as the best in the world and the Syrians as the most intelligent people in existence.[1] Another example is that of Salīm al-Khūrī Sarkīs, one of the editors of the Beiruti newspaper *Lisān al-Ḥāl* (Voice of the Present), who in 1882 wrote an article entitled *Ḥubb al-Waṭan.* The piece encapsulates the components of the Syrian identity as it developed before the period of Abdül Hamid II.[2]

One possible explanation for the continued appearance of these ideas under Abdül Hamid II is that he did not oppose them, since his main interest was to undermine the growing demands of the Arabs for an Arab Caliph as the spiritual head of the Muslim World. These demands were made during the end of the nineteenth and early twentieth century. For example, in the late 1890s ʿAbd al-Raḥmān

---

[1] For example, see: Adīb ʿAbduh Afandī Kaḥīl, "al-Waṭan wa-Maḥabbatuhu," *al-Jinān*, Vol. 11, No. 3, 1880, pp. 81–85; Salīm al-Bustānī, "Tārīkh al-ʿIlm al-Qadīm," *al-Jinān*, Vol. 13, No. 1, 1882, pp. 11–15.

[2] Salīm al-Khūrī Sarkīs, "Ḥubb al-Waṭan," *al-Jinān*, Vol. 13, No. 8, 1882, p. 240.

al-Kawākibī proposed a detailed plan for a spiritual Caliphate. Al-Kawākibī believed that the Ottoman Empire could not affect the regeneration of Islam and that such a rebirth could only be achieved by the Arabs, who would supply an Arab Caliph acting as the world-wide Muslim spiritual head.

Abdül Hamid II's main fear may have been that if the idea of an Arab Caliph materialised, it could endanger his position as an Ottoman Caliph in the Muslim world. As Buzpınar wrote ". . . his mind was always occupied with opposition to his caliphate."[3] Perhaps this was one of his reasons for refraining from opposing some of the ideas that developed during the period of the *Tanẓīmāt* reforms, such as the territorial concept of Syria. In this way, he could undermine current ideas of an Arab Caliphate or the growth of Arab separatism in the region south of Anatolia. In other words, the idea of Syrian localism under the Ottoman Empire would displace the notion of Arab separatism.

Some clarification is important here. Apparently, Abdül Hamid II did undermine the development of Syrian patriotism as a political concept, but did not oppose, at least in his early years of rule, the development of a local Syrian identity. This could explain why he preserved the entity and the title "*Vilâyet* of Syria" until the end of his reign. This argument regarding Abdül Hamid's attitude toward the Syrian identity should be studied further; such additional research could shed new light on the development of this identity towards the end of the nineteenth century. Perhaps a causative link may be shown between the growth of this identity and the Syrian nationalism that developed later on, during the beginning of the twentieth century.

Strikingly, only towards the end of the nineteenth century did a territorial concept of Syria become meaningful among the modern educated Muslim class and had penetrated into their parlance and discourse, which began to define the region as Syria, and as such, to adopt it as part of their own identity. Such was the case even though this population continued to use the traditional term of *Bilād al-Shām* to denote the region, as is evident in Muslim newspapers such as *Thamarāt al-Funūn*, which appeared from the mid 1870s. In

[3] Tufan Buzpınar, "The Question of the Caliphate under the Last Ottoman Sultans," in Itzchak Weismann and Fruma Zachs (eds.), *Ottoman Reform and Islamic Regeneration*, forthcoming (London, 2005).

1876, ʿAbd al-Qadir al-Qabbānī, *Thamarāt al-Funūn*'s editor, already used such terms as "*abnāʾ waṭaninā al-Sūrī*" (sons of our Syrian homeland) or "*bilādunā al-Sūriyya*" (our country Syria).[4]

This tendency continued around the turn of the century when other Muslim newspapers such as *al-Manār* (The Lighthouse, published in Cairo) and *al-Muqtabas* (Acquired Learning, published first in Damascus and later on in Cairo) used the name "Syria" more and more. *Al-Manār* actually defined the meaning of the term and in 1899 wrote that "Syria is the country (*bilād*) that lies between Asia Minor in the north and Egypt in the south,"[5] that is Greater Syria. In fact, Muḥammad Kurd ʿAlī, the publisher of *al-Muqtabas*, and Rashīd Riḍā, the publisher of *al-Manār* were prominent figures who influenced the younger Muslim generation. Their newspapers reveal that during Abdül Hamid II's period and prior to the First World War, the Muslim educated class used and defined the term Syria throughout the Syrian region and beyond. Over the years, the name probably became current among the Muslim population in general and those who read and wrote for these newspapers in particular.[6]

Even though "Syria" was already in use in Muslim newspapers and periodicals, it appeared in certain historiographical works written in interior cities such as Damascus and Aleppo only after the First World War. However, some of these books were probably being composed before the war. One example is Kāmil al-Ghazzī's *Kitāb Nahr al-Dhahab fī Tārīkh Ḥalab*, published in Aleppo in three volumes from 1923 to 1926. Al-Ghazzī defined Aleppo as part of "*al-Bilād al-Sūriyya*."[7] Thus, the territorial concept of Syria was developing and

---

[4] *Thamarāt al-Funūn*, No. 83, 16 November 1876; No. 84, 22 November 1876.

[5] *Al-Manār*, Vol. 2, 1899, pp. 278–281.

[6] See especially in *al-Muqtabas*: Yūsuf Jirjis Zakhm, "Safḥa Tārīkhiyya fī Sūriyya," *al-Muqtabas*, Vol. 1, 1906–1907, pp. 561–570; M. Khayrallāh, "al-Mas'ala al-Ijtimāʿiyya wal-Madrasiyya fī Sūriyya," *al-Muqtabas*, Vol. 2, 1907, p. 551; w.n., "Tahdhīb al-Shabība al-Sūriyya," *al-Muqtabas*, Vol. 3, 1908, pp. 599–600; Dūsū, "ʿArab Sūriyya qabla al-Islām," *al-Muqtabas*, Vol. 2, 1907, pp. 293–294 (this article was probably translated from French); w.n., "Ghābāt Sūriyya," *al-Muqtabas*, Vol. 6, 1911, pp. 24–35, this volume abounds with the word "Syria"; w.n., "al-Zirāʿa fī Sūriyya," Vol. 8, 1914, p. 555.

[7] Ghazzī, *Kitāb Nahr al-Dhahab*, pp. 28, 30. Other books that were written by Muslims and were published outside the region of Syria used this term. For example, Muḥammad ʿAlī Bāshā, *al-Riḥla al-Shāmiyya* (Beirut, 1981), pp. 5, 22, 48, 66, 68. Muḥammad ʿAlī Bāshā was a "prince" from the ruling family in Egypt. There were also Muslim Tunisian authors that had taken up this term in their writing of the early 1880s. For example, Muḥammad al-Sanūsī, *al-Riḥla al-Ḥijāziyya*, Vol. 2. ed. ʿAlī al-Shanūfī (Tunis, 1976), p. 320. Al-Sanūsī distinguished between *al-Shām*

becoming assimilated not only in port cities such as Beirut and Tripoli, as emphasised throughout this book, but could also be found in interior cities of the region. Plainly, this was also the result of the long administrative existence of the *Vilâyet* of Syria, and the Porte's acceptance of the name, among other things.

In the meantime, the notions of an Arab identity, which had begun to prevail in the region before 1908, were transformed to become the component of the evolving Arab National Movement,[8] which had begun to gain adherents, reaching its peak only after the Young Turks Revolution in 1908. On the eve of the First World War, when the split between the Arabs and the Turks in the Ottoman Empire became visible, the first Arab National Conference took place in Paris in 1913. The main aim of the conference was to bring the Arab question to the public's awareness and to express the Arab demand for full political rights and an effective share in the administration of the Empire. The representatives to the congress came from the Party of Decentralisation in Cairo (consisting mainly of Syrians living in Cairo) and from the Committee of Reform in Beirut, which accepted this initiative warmly and made an obvious impact on the congress. In fact, 23 of the 25 Muslim and Christian representatives were Syrian Arabs. The other two were from Iraq. Three of the participants came from the Beiruti middle stratum. They were from the Bayhum, Sursuq, and Thābit families.[9]

An examination of the conference's minutes shows that the components of the Syrian identity, as it developed in the latter part of the nineteenth century among the Christian Arab intellectuals in Beirut, were in effect the essence of the lectures delivered at this congress. The main topic of most of the lectures was the future of Syria. From the minutes, it is clear that the Muslim and Christian participants accepted the territorial concept of Syria and declared

(Damascus) and Sūriyya (region of Syria), yet he still felt the need to explain the meaning of the latter. Finally, Muḥammad Bayram did not use the term "Syria" but gave a positive account of the role and contribution of Beiruti and Muslim intellectuals and refered to the work of the American missionaries and of Buṭrus al-Bustānī. See: Muḥammad Bayram, *Tārīkh Ṣafwat al-Iʿtibār bi-Mustawdaʿ al-Amṣār wal-Aqṭār*, Vol. 5 (Cairo, 1885), pp. 38–42.

[8] For more on Arab Nationalism, see: Ernest C. Dawn, "The Origins of Arab Nationalism," in Rashid Khalidi et al. (eds.) *The Origins of Arab Nationalism* (New York, 1991).

[9] Muḥibb al-Dīn Khaṭīb (ed.), *al-Muʾtamar al-ʿArabī al-Awwal* (Cairo, 1913), pp. 14–16.

unequivocally that "Syria is for the Syrians."[10] In his talk, the Beiruti Muslim Aḥmad Ṭabbāra defined the sphere of the Syrian region, discussed its inhabitants and reviewed the pre-Islamic (for example, the Phoenician) and Arab history of the region.[11] Other representatives stressed the equality between the Christian and Muslim populations, by reiterating that "the Arab nation is both Muslim and non-Muslim."[12]

It is also clear that the Muslim and Christian representatives treated the other Arab territorial provincial divisions as defining Arab countries (*Bilād ʿArabiyya*).[13] The participants discussed Iraqi, Egyptian and Lebanese territorial entities but above all the territorial entity of Syria. In addition, they supported the secular interpretation of the Arab culture and heritage as attested by the lecture of the Beiruti ʿAbd al-Ghanī al-ʿArīsī, who was one of the conference's organisers and served as its secretary. Another lecture, that of Nadra Muṭrān, on "Preserving Patriotic Life in the Arab Ottoman Countries,"[14] concentrated mainly on the history of the Arabs.[15]

After six days, several resolutions were adopted by the conferees, among them was the request that Arabs take part in the central government and that the Porte recognise their political privileges. Finally, they demanded that the Arabic language be accepted in the Ottoman parliament.

Considering that the conference was defined as Arab, and accepting that it was a formative activity during the course of the early period of the National Arab Movement, we may conclude that this movement adopted some of its components from the Christian Arab intellectuals and their notions regarding a Syrian identity. Also, the Syrian Christian Arab intellectuals, despite their relatively small number, were the first to promote territorial concepts along with secular interpretations of Arab culture.[16] These ideas were to become an

---

[10] *Ibid.*, pp. 9, 54.

[11] *Ibid.*, pp. 83–94; See also the speech delivered by Nadra Muṭrān on the preservation of patriotic life in the Arab-Ottoman countries, pp. 54–74.

[12] Khaṭīb, *al-Muʾtamar al-ʿArabī al-Awwal*, p. 61 but also pp. 54–66, 83–94.

[13] *Ibid.*, especially pp. 14–15, 48.

[14] *Ibid.*, pp. 43, 54–64.

[15] *Ibid.*, pp. 58–59. The motif of the Ghassāniyyūn (defined in the lecture as Christian Arabs) is mentioned here as an example of Christians collaborating with Muslims, at the time when the latter invaded *al-Shām*.

[16] Egyptian intellectuals promoted territorial concepts during the nineteenth century, but this was done especially under the rule of Ismāʿīl Pāshā, by people such

important legacy in the political life of the Arab countries of the Middle East during the twentieth century. In other words, an examination of this middle stratum's activities and the notion it developed, reveals that it's most significant contribution lies in the processes it set in motion.

Finally, the Paris Conference reveals conceptual developments and differences in the thinking of some Christian Arab intellectuals. Many who supported the Syrian identity during the nineteenth century became part of the Arab National Movement, whose strength was mounting as the new century started. This movement developed in two phases. The Paris Conference ended the first phase of the development of Arab identity and marked the growing influence of the Arab National Movement. Two years later, the second phase in the development of the Arab National Movement began, this time in a different region—al-Ḥijāz; but again, the region of Syria was to stand at its heart.

as ʿAlī Mubarak or Rifāʿa Rāfiʿ al-Ṭahṭāwī. Thus, the Egyptian territorial concept only arose starting in the 1860s, namely when the Syrian identity was already in the process of evolving. Muḥammad ʿAlī is credited with the initiative of encouraging Egyptian identity. However, two points must be drawn in this regard. First, this was not a local development arising from Egyptian society (such as from its intellectuals, as was the case with Syria) but an initiative that came from the ruler. Secondly, Muḥammad ʿAlī encouraged such ideas mainly in order to advance his own interests and in order to safeguard his own status.

APPENDIX ONE

Biographies of Leading Families and Individuals from the Syrian Middle Stratum[1]

The Abkāryūs family

This was a Beiruti family of Armenian origin. **Iskandar** and **Yūḥannā** were the sons of **Yaʿqūb**. Iskandar was a poet, writer, and historian, while Yūḥannā was a merchant and became one of the wealthiest people in Beirut. He died in 1889. Yaʿqūb served as a consular representative in Sidon. Yūḥannā was a dragoman at the British consulate in Beirut.[2]

Ibrāhīm al-Aḥdab

Ibrāhīm (1826–1891) was a native of Tripoli, an intellectual with extensive knowledge of Arabic culture, literature, and poetry. He belonged to one of the leading Muslim families of nineteenth-century Beirut. In 1860, he served as a member (*nāʾib*) of the *Sharīʿa* court in Beirut. He also edited the journal *Thamarāt al-Funūn* and was a member of the educational council of the *Vilâyet* of Syria.[3]

Mīkhāʾīl ʿArmān

In 1838, **Mīkhāʾīl** studied at the English School operated by the American missionaries, and was among the first students at the boys'

---

[1] The appendix includes names taken from the member lists of three Syrian cultural societies which were active in Beirut, and engaged in promoting the Syrian identity: *al-Jamʿiyya al-Sūriyya li-Iktisāb al-ʿUlūm wal-Funūn* (1847–1852), *al-ʿUmda al-Adabiyya li-Ishhār al-Kutub al-ʿArabiyya* (1860) and *al-Jamʿiyya al-ʿIlmiyya al-Sūriyya* (1858–1860, 1868–1869). Information was gleaned from numerous sources, much of it incomplete, leading sometimes to contradiction, duplication, and gaps in family histories. The aim of these sources was not to provide extensive family histories but to demonstrate their economic and intellectual backgrounds and their ties with the American missionaries, when available.

[2] FO 195/1113, Eldridge to Elliot, 6 June 1876; Zaydān, *Tarājim Mashāhīr al-Sharq*, Vol. 4, pp. 320–321.

[3] Ṭarrāzī, *Tārīkh al-Ṣiḥāfa*, Vol. 2, pp. 101–104.

seminar at ʿAbeih. After completing his studies, he became a teacher at the college. In 1863 he and his wife established a girls' school.[4]

Yūsuf al-Asīr

Yūsuf al-Asīr (1815–1889) was of Muslim origin. He was born in Sidon, where his father was a merchant, but he was not interested in commerce and preferred to study. At the age of 17 he moved to Damascus, later settling in Egypt and studying at al-Azhar, where he specialised in Islamic theology and Arabic literature. Upon completion of his studies he served as a judge in Tripoli, became the *Muftī* of Acre, and was the attorney general for Mount Lebanon. Finally, he settled in Beirut.

He was the first Muslim to work with the American missionaries. In 1847 he assisted the American missionary Cornelius van Dyke in translating the Bible into Arabic. He also taught at al-Bustānī's National School and was a teacher of Arabic at the SPC. In addition, he worked in the Ministry of Education and was appointed by the government as teacher of Arabic at *Dār al-Muʿallimīn*. He was made *qāḍī* in Syria and was known as an authority on Muslim law, considered liberal in outlook. In the 1870s he edited the journals *Thamarāt al-Funūn* and *Lisān al-Ḥāl*.[5]

The ʿAytānī family

This was a Sunni Muslim family from Beirut. Originally, most of its members belonged to the lower class, and worked at fishing and farming. In time some of them became well-to-do merchants and property owners. Others chose liberal professions (for example, **Muḥammad Zakariyya** was a lawyer)[6] or were employed as officials, public functionaries, or tax collectors. Many members of the family belonged to the "*petit-bourgeoisie*" and owned small shops. The Bayhums were the patrons of the family.

[4] Tibawi, *American Interests in Syria*, pp. 83, 163.

[5] Zaydān, *Tarājim Mashāhīr al-Sharq*, Vol. 1, pp. 164–166. *Lisān al-Ḥāl* is also an expression meaning the state of current affairs.

[6] Johnson, *Class and Client in Beirut*, p. 92; Ḥallāq, *al-Tārīkh al-Ijtimāʿī*, p. 101.

Yūsuf Bākhūs

Yūsuf Bākhūs came from a respected Christian family from Mount Lebanon, of Assyrian origin, with close ties to the Thābit family. Yūsuf belonged to the Maronite branch of the family. Born in Kisrawān, he later taught Arabic at the Jesuit school at ʿAyn Ṭūra. He subsequently moved to Beirut and wrote chapters on philosophy for the book *Āthār al-Adhār* (Remnants of Time) together with his friends Salīm Shaḥāda and Salīm al-Khūrī. He continued teaching Arabic there, at the Maronite school of Bishop Yūsuf al-Dibs. In 1880 he published a journal called *al-Mustaqill* (The Independent) which was supported by the Italian consulate.[7]

The Bayhum family

This was a family of Muslim notables from Beirut that settled in the region of Syria as early as the Middle Ages. The Beirut-born **Ḥusayn** can be called the founder of the family, having changed his name from ʿAytānī to Bayhum, to distance himself from inferior branches of the family. As an importer and exporter, he became rich in the nineteenth century, although his main inclination was towards scholarship. In addition, he served in several senior positions in the Ottoman government. In 1876, he was elected to serve as the Beirut delegate in the first Ottoman Parliament. A year later, he became a member of the Beirut appeals council. In 1878, he and several others founded the cultural society *al-Maqāṣid al-Khayriyya.*

In general, the Bayhum family was one of the few Muslim families that succeeded in penetrating the export business in the Syrian region. Its members profited from the developing trade between Beirut and Europe during the nineteenth century. They dealt in agricultural products such as silk, wool, and cotton and they imported finished goods. Their commercial importance is attested to by the fact that the market in Beirut came to be known as *Sūq Bayhum.* In addition to their commercial activity the family owned much land.

Aḥmad Mukhtār (1878–1920) was one of the most successful merchants in import and export; his uncle, **ʿAmr**, dealt in clothes. The family had strong associations with Christian merchants. For

[7] Najīb Fāris Bākhūs, "Yūsuf Ḥabīb Bākhūs," *al-Mashriq*, Vol. 5, 1902, pp. 497–503; Dāghir, *Maṣādir al-Dirāsa*, Vol. 2, pp. 155–156.

example, ties existed between **Muḥammad** Bayhum, Ḥusayn ʿAytānī's grandson, and Yūsuf Sursuq, a member of a well-known Christian merchant family.

During the Ottoman period Bayhum family members served on several councils. Muḥammad and at least two of his cousins were members of the City Council and the administrative council of the *sancak* and the *vilâyet.* In 1875, **Waḥyī al-Dīn** was elected to the Beirut City Council. At the end of the Ottoman period family members were involved in the Arab National Movement, and during the Mandate period they were involved in the pan-Syrian opposition. Their political predominance in the Ottoman and the Mandatory periods rested mainly on their commercial strength, and was manifested in the second half of the nineteenth and until the first half of the twentieth century.[8]

The Bustānī family

The Bustānīs were a Christian family of Maronite roots, who began apparently as farmers. The family may have originated from Latakia. They owned property in northern Lebanon. At the beginning of the eighteenth century, some members of the family moved to Dalhamiyya (south of Tiberius). As time passed, most of the family members became teachers.

The American missionary Henry Jessup described **Buṭrus** al-Bustānī (1819–1883) in his book as "the most learned, most productive, and most successful man, and also the man with the most influence on modern Syria."[9]

At the age of ten, Buṭrus started attending the Maronite ʿAyn Waraqa school. For about ten years he studied various subjects there, as well as languages: Arabic, Syriac, and Latin. After completing his schooling, he taught at his *alma mater* until 1840. At that stage he decided to learn English as well, moving from Mount Lebanon to Beirut, where he was employed by the British as a translator. During that period he formed close relationships with the American mis-

---

[8] Fawaz, *Merchants and Migrants*, pp. 96–97; Johnson, *Class and Client in Beirut*, pp. 14, 60–67; *Thamarāt al-Funūn*, No. 93, 1 February 1877 and No. 32, 26 November 1875; Ḥasan Ḥallāq, *Awqāf al-Muslimīn fī Bayrūt fī al-ʿAhd al-ʿUthmānī-Sijillāt al-Maḥkama al-Sharʿiyya fī Bayrūt* (Beirut, 1988), pp. 135–136.

[9] Jessup, *Fifty-Three Years in Syria*, Vol. 2, p. 483.

sionaries. He was on particularly close terms with two of them, Eli Smith and Dr. Cornelius van Dyke. In time, these acquaintances turned into close friendships and spiritual cooperation and eventually Buṭrus converted to Protestantism.

In the 1840s, Buṭrus was employed as dragoman at the American consulate in Beirut, and in 1846 was hired by the missionary school in ʿAbeih to teach Arabic. The following year he was among the founders of the cultural society *al-Jamʿiyya al-Sūriyya li-Iktisāb al-ʿUlūm wal-Funūn*. In 1848 he was appointed as Smith's assistant in translating the Bible into Arabic. Throughout the 1840s and '50s, in addition to his other activities, he wrote and published a number of books and articles, and worked with the American missionaries at their printing house. In 1854, it was suggested that Buṭrus enter the ministry and he began negotiations with the missionaries. The aim was to make him the Americans' first local minister, but this did not take place. His good friend, the missionary Eli Smith, explained to him in one of his letters that he was not suited for the ministry, since he had developed a secular character and was not essentially a man of religion. Smith described him as an intelligent person, one astute in commerce, and a diligent manager of businesses.

Around 1857, namely from Smith's death, his relations with the mission began gradually to fray. In 1863, he established the National School, which was open to children of all sects and religions. Buṭrus became well known primarily as a leading intellectual. He published journals such as *Nafīr Sūriyya*, *al-Janna* and *al-Jinān*. He also wrote many books on grammar, mathematics, and other topics, contributing significantly to the revival of the Arabic language and literature. For example, Buṭrus al-Bustānī edited and published the first Arabic dictionary in the nineteenth century, *Muḥīṭ al-Muḥīṭ*, and the first Arabic encyclopedia, *Dāʾirat al-Maʿārif*. He is considered to be one of the first Syrian patriots to use the terms *waṭan* and *abnāʾ al-waṭan*.[10]

Raḥīl (1823–1894), Buṭrus' wife, had been trained by her own father in the literary arts and in household management. She also

---

[10] For example, see: John W. Jandora, "Butrus al-Bustani, Arab Consciousness and Arabic Revival," *Muslim World*, Vol. 74 (1984), pp. 77–84; HL, series ABC: 16.8.1, Vol. 7, H. Jessup to Anderson, 27 January 1865; *The Missionary Herald*, Vol. 57, No. 4, April 1864, Annual Report of the Beirut Station; Hourani, *Arabic Thought in the Liberal Age*, pp. 97–100; Abu-Manneh, "The Christians between Ottomanism and Syrian Nationalism."

studied in the 1840s in the first school for females operated by the American missionaries and was well versed in Arabic and English literature.[11]

Salīm (1846–1884) was Buṭrus's first-born son. In 1862 he replaced his father as dragoman at the American consulate in Beirut. The following year he was made deputy principal to his father at the National School, where he headed the departments of history, nature, and English. At the same time, he continued to work as dragoman at the consulate until 1871. In order to work on the journals that his father had established, he resigned as dragoman in that year. In addition he assisted his father in writing the encyclopedia *Dā'irat al-Ma'ārif*. In 1882, upon the death of his father, he became editor-in-chief of the encyclopedia which he continued to publish until his own death. Later he was elected as a member of the Beirut City Council. Salīm was considered the finest dragoman of Western languages in the East. He was also one of the first Christian Arabs who tried to write fiction. Starting in 1871, he wrote short stories and historical novels in the periodical *al-Jinān*.[12]

The Bustrus family

This was a family of merchants of Greek Orthodox origin that migrated from Cyprus to Beirut in the sixteenth century. During al-Jazzār's rule (1776–1804), the family fled the city. In the 1820s 'Abdallāh Pāshā returned several Christian families to Beirut, including that of the Bustrus'. He offered them a partnership in certain businesses. The Bustrus family returned to Beirut and settled in the Ashrāfiyya district. Over the years, they became one of the wealthiest and foremost families in the city. They owned olive groves and they acquired land in Beirut, in other parts of Syria and in Egypt. The family members exported and imported agricultural products, such as wheat, trading between the Levant and Europe, and were also agents of steamship companies headquartered in Liverpool.

Through their commercial activities they developed relations with Europeans and Ottomans. **Jūrj** was apparently the family head. His sons **Jūzīf** and **Mūsā** continued the family business, Mūsā's company representing a British firm in Syria.

---

[11] Booth, *May Her Likes Be Multiplied*, pp. 135–136.
[12] Jīḥā, *Salīm al-Bustānī*, pp. 26–27; Dāghir, *Maṣādir al-Dirāsa*, Vol. 2, pp. 186–188.

Salīm, Mūsā's son, was born in Beirut in 1839. He became very rich but was not content just with commerce and spent more of his energies in acquiring knowledge. In 1859 he travelled to Europe where he wrote a book entitled *al-Riḥla al-Islāmiyya* (The Islamic Journey) setting out his views of the way in which his country could progress. He called on the people of his region to try to understand why Europe had advanced, and stressed that unity would bring about progress. In 1860, due to his commercial and business interests, he moved to Alexandria. In 1866 he returned to Europe again, establishing a trading house in Liverpool, which he transferred to London in 1869. Apart from his commercial occupation he was a poet and author. His brother-in-law, **Jūrj**, was a dragoman at the French consulate in Beirut.[13]

Al-Danā family

This was a Muslim family. **ʿAbd al-Qādir** was born in Beirut. He engaged in politics, became chair of the Beirut City Council, worked as a journalist, and took part in cultural activities. In 1907 he headed a society named *Jamʿiyyat al-Maqāṣid*, after having worked with his brother **Muḥammad Rashīd** on the journal *Bayrūt*. This paper ceased publication in 1902 with the death of Muḥammad Rashīd and reappeared only after several months, under the management of the younger brother **Muḥyī al-Dīn**, who handed the paper over to ʿAbd al-Qādir in 1905.[14]

Salīm Dyāb

Salīm was born in 1848 in Tripoli and studied medicine at the SPC in Beirut. Afterwards, he returned to Tripoli where he practiced medicine; well-versed in Arabic, he also wrote poetry. He subsequently worked as a doctor in Alexandria and wrote for several Egyptian journals. His brother **Kāmil** was an author who also published many articles in the Egyptian press.[15]

[13] Zaydān, *Tarājim Mashāhīr al-Sharq*, Vol. 2, pp. 145–147; Fawaz, *Merchants and Migrants*, p. 94.
[14] Salām, *Mudhakkirāt Salīm*, p. 112.
[15] Nawfal, *Tarājim ʿUlamāʾ*, pp. 193–195.

Ilyās Ḥabālīn

Ilyās (1839–1889) was a Maronite, a native of Mount Lebanon. He received his elementary education at the college of the Lazarist monks at ʿAyn Ṭūra, and so became well acquainted with French language and literature. He also taught at well-known schools in Beirut. In 1866, he was appointed editor-in-chief of the official journal *Lubnān*. From 1871 to 1874 he taught French at the American College, and in 1875 he received a post at the French consulate in Beirut.

The Ḥaddād family

The Ḥaddāds were a Christian family from Tripoli. **Faraḥ** had two sons: **Mīkhāʾīl**, who was a doctor, and **Ilyās**, a well-known merchant who settled in Alexandria. **Asʿad** (1853–1920), Mīkhāʾīl's son, was born in Tripoli and went to elementary school there. In 1869 he went to Beirut where he studied medicine at the American College, receiving his diploma in 1872 and returning to Tripoli. In 1881 he traveled to England and there he broadened his knowledge of medicine. A year later he returned to the East, settled in Alexandria, and became the private physician of many renowned Alexandrian families. Asʿad knew Arabic, English, and French. **Jibrāʾīl**, Mīkhāʾīl's youngest son, was born in 1865. He attended the American missionaries' elementary school in Tripoli, going on to study at the SPC in Beirut from 1879 to 1883. Upon graduating, he went to Alexandria and took up a position in the Egyptian government. **Ṭānnūs** was a Greek Orthodox teacher who converted to Protestantism and became a Protestant minister. He was the first local teacher to work for the missionaries.[16] **Tiyudūra** (d. 1889) wrote several essays on the importance of respecting women's status and their influence on society.[17] The family had intermarried with the Ḥasībī family of Damascus.

The Kātsifilīs family

This was a Christian family originating in the Greek island of Corfu. Its members were physicians, lawyers, dragomans, and merchants.

[16] *Ibid.*, pp. 200–201.
[17] Booth, *May Her Likes be Multiplied*, p. 83.

Many of them had a profound knowledge of Arabic. They engaged in literature and culture alongside their other occupations, particularly at the consulates. The father of the family, **Giyūvānī**, arrived in Tripoli in the middle of the eighteenth century to serve as an advisor to the English Consul. After the latter's death he replaced him as consul and married **Barbāra**, daughter of **Mīkhā'īl Yannī**.

Giyūvānī had two sons, **George** (aka **Jirjis** or **Jūrj**) and **Krīstūf**, and two daughters. The eldest daughter married **Niqūlā Ibrāhīm Nawfal** and the younger married Nicholas Lūmbār, a French merchant resident in Tripoli. Other members of the family were **Iskandar**, **Tiyudūr**, **Idwār**, and **Qayṣar** (1846–1889).

Iskandar was born in Tripoli in 1837 and studied English, Arabic, and French there. He later officiated as Russian Consul and was also an agent of the Russian *al-Fābūrāt* company in Tripoli. **Jūl** was head of the lawyers' association in Egypt. **Aliksī** was also a lawyer by profession. **George**, Iskandar's son, was the Russian vice-Consul in Tripoli. **Krīstūf**, Tiyudūr's son, was the vice-Consul of Britain and of Holland in Tripoli. Later on, he moved to Egypt and became a merchant in Alexandria. Qayṣar, Giyūvānī's son, was appointed vice-Consul of Holland, and in 1874 married **Barbāra**, daughter of **Anṭūnyūs Yannī**.

Krīstūf (1803–1867) knew Arabic, Italian, and French. He was made Consul of Austria in Tripoli and later represented Spain as well. Afterwards, in partnership with his brother George, he established a large commercial house in Tripoli. Krīstūf's son **Tiyudūr** was vice-Consul of Spain, and after his father's death replaced him as Consul of Austria and Hungary, representing the Austrian Lloyd's company.[18]

The Khlāṭ family

This was a Christian family that moved to Tripoli from the town of Khlāṭ. Its members included writers and merchants. The most famous of them, **Yūsuf**, was a well-known merchant who was also employed by the Ottoman government. **Jirjis** was appointed Persian

---

[18] Nawfal, *Tarājim 'Ulamā'*, pp. 78–81, 149–152, 186–187; Mārūn 'Īsā al-Khūrī, *Malāmiḥ min al-Ḥarakāt al-Thaqāfiyya fī Ṭarāblus Khilāl al-Qarn al-Tasi' 'Ashar* (Tripoli, 1982), pp. 17, 41–42, 57.

vice-Consul in Tripoli. He was succeeded in this position by **Jibrāʾīl**. **Rāmiz** was a merchant.

Ibrāhīm, **Mūsā**'s son, was born in Tripoli in 1825. He learned Arabic and became the secretary of the Chamber of Commerce (*al-Majlis al-Tijārī*) in Tripoli. Later he became a permanent member of the council. Similarly, he served as the Chief Secretary of the Tripoli City Council (*Bāsh Kātib lil-Majlis al-Baladī*). His son **Anīs** was born in 1848. At an early age, Anīs travelled to Europe and then to Egypt, where he served as a clerk in the government. Later, in Egypt, he founded a journal called *Ḥaqīqat al-Akhbār* (Validity of News). He had two brothers: **ʿAzīz**, who moved to Alexandria and engaged in business, and **Amīn**, an intellectual who lived in Egypt.

The Tripoli branch of the family, headed by **Isḥāq**, was also prominent. His son **Niʿma** had a son named **Nasīm** who was born in 1833. Nasīm was in touch with the American missionaries and learned English and Italian. In his early years, he served as dragoman at the American consulate in Tripoli. He later went to Egypt and set up a large business house in Alexandria together with his cousin **Asʿad Mīkhāʾīl**. The business prospered and expanded, and he brought his brothers **Tiyudūr** and **Qayṣar** into the business. Later on he married the widow of Jirjis Naḥḥās and opened another branch of his business house. During this period he was appointed as a member of the Tripoli City Council and was the largest shareholder of the tramcar company that linked the parts of the city with the docks, and of another transport company named al-Shūsa, plying between Tripoli, Homs, and Hama. Together with his commercial activities he engaged in cultural work, and wrote for the journals *al-Muqtaṭaf* and *al-Manār*. He had five sons and four daughters. Among his sons were **Imīl**, a writer, **Almaʿī** a well-known merchant in Alexandria, and **Nasīm**, who established an Orthodox school in Tripoli that stood for tolerance among the religions and sects.[19]

Khalīl al-Khūrī

Khalīl al-Khūrī (1836–1907) was from a Greek Orthodox family from Shuwayfat in Mount Lebanon. Only after the departure of Ibrāhīm Pāshā from Syria did the family move to Beirut. Khalīl

[19] Nawfal, *Tarājim ʿUlamāʾ*, pp. 103–104, 131–134, 196–198.

acquired his education and studied Arabic language at Orthodox Christian schools (elementary and secondary). He acquired his knowledge of literary Arabic from renowned teachers, including Nāṣīf al-Yāzijī, later learning Turkish and French as well. He started his career working for a merchant firm, which he did until age 18, simultaneously writing poetry and prose. In time, he drew close to the American missionaries and served as a teacher in their school in ʿAbeih. In 1858, aged 21, he founded the first Arabic journal in the region, *Ḥadīqat al-Akhbār*. In the 1860s he continued with journalism and specialised in various functions in the Porte's administration having been appointed dragoman for Fuʾād Pāshā, the Ottoman foreign minister, in 1860. From this time on Fuʾād became Khalīl's patron. He appreciated Khalīl's talents and became interested in the way his newspaper depicted the interests of the Ottoman government. Consequently, the newspaper began to receive a subsidy and was now able to appear twice a week. After the establishment of the *mutaṣarrifiyya* of Mount Lebanon, *Ḥadīqat al-Akhbār* became its semi-official journal. In 1865, with the formation of the *Vilâyet* of Syria, he served as editor of the *vilâyet* press and his journal became its official publication. Subsequently he was appointed as inspector of non-Muslim schools in the *vilâyet*, and was put in charge of the libraries in Lebanon. In 1880 he was made the government official responsible for matters involving foreigners in Syria.

Khalīl al-Khūrī's literary activities were wide-ranging and he supported Arabic periodicals and newspapers in Syria such as the journal *al-Muqtaṭaf*.[20] He took part in various cultural societies in Beirut, among them *al-Jamʿiyya al-ʿIlmiyya al-Sūriyya* which operated between 1858 and 1860; and he actively supported other Arabic newspapers when they began to take their first steps. He thus became one of the leading figures of the *Nahḍa* and a prominent persona among the rising generation of young journalists in Beirut. Examples of those whom he influenced include **Yūsuf Shalfūn**, a trainee who later launched the publishing house *al-Maṭbaʿa al-ʿUmūmiyya*; and **Khalīl Sarkīs**, who became publisher of the newspaper *Lisān al-Ḥāl* after having taken his first steps in journalism under Khalīl's tutelage.

[20] Ṭarrāzī, *Tārīkh al-Ṣiḥāfa*, Vol. 1, pp. 55–56; Zaydān, *Tarājim Mashāhīr al-Sharq*, Vol. 2, pp. 115–121; Sarkīs, *Muʿjam al-Maṭbūʿāt al-ʿArabiyya*, Vol. 2, pp. 745–746; Zachs, "Building a Cultural Identity: The Case of Khalīl al-Khūrī."

The Mishāqa family

Members of the family became rich from the commerce brought by the region's growing ties with the West, lost most of their earlier gains as a result of the oppression of Aḥmad Pāshā al-Jazzār, the *vali* of Sidon during the last quarter of the eighteenth century, and then recovered their initial success—if not becoming more affluent—under the patronage of Amīr Bashīr II. Following the end of the Egyptian occupation and Bashīr's fall and exile to Malta, other members of the family added clerical and white-collar jobs to their repertoire.

The head of the family, **Yūsuf Batrākī**, a Greek Orthodox and an important merchant in his native land, moved from the island of Corfu to Tripoli to deal in the silk trade. The family name "Mishāqa" is in fact derived from the process of filtering fibres of silk, linen, hemp and cotton. For example, the word *Mushāqa* refers to the waste that remains after the process of filtering, *al-mishq* (verbal noun) means filtering, and *bil-mushāqa* (noun) refers to the tools that filter the silk. So, because the head of the family, Yūsuf, dealt with filtration of silk fibres, in time it came to replace his original family name and he was thus the first to be known as "Mishāqa," even though the family name was originally Batrākī. Later on, Yūsuf's son **Jirjis** moved to Sidon and then to Tyre in order to export tobacco to Egypt. During this period he also converted to Catholicism.

Jirjis thus settled in an area ruled by al-Jazzār. His son, **Ibrāhīm**, became a tax collector under al-Jazzār in the regions of Bilād Bishāra and al-Shaqīf, south of Mount Lebanon. He was known as a wealthy man with extensive contacts. In later years al-Jazzār began to oppress the family and seized much of their property. At this point, Ibrāhīm's son, also named **Jirjis**, escaped from al-Jazzār's territory to Deir al-Qamar and changed his profession to silversmith. When Amīr Bashīr learned of his arrival he made Jirjis his secretary, and responsible for the emirate's finances.

Deir al-Qamar was chosen by the family due to economic considerations. In that town the family members could conduct their business and make a living from service with the Amīrs and the sheikhs, working in tax collection, bureaucracy, or money-lending. In addition, at that time Deir al-Qamar was developing into a commercial hub linking Sidon, Mount Lebanon, Damascus, and the Syrian hinterland. The Mishāqa family took advantage of the town's development and engaged in commerce and crafts, formed economic ties with the foreigners who came to it, and traded with the interior of the country and the coastal region. Jirjis worked under the Amīr until the former's death in 1832. From this point the destiny of the family became interwoven with that of Amīr Bashīr II. Under him the family prospered and acquired more property.

Jirjis's son, **Mīkhā'īl** (1800–1888), was born in Rashmayyā, but grew up in Deir al-Qamar. He claimed not to have received any formal education, having acquired most of his knowledge as an autodidact. In 1817 his father sent him to Dimyāṭ in northern Egypt to go into commerce. Three years later he returned to the Mountain and, during the 1820s (and for a short time during the 1840s as well), was involved in silk weaving. In the 1830s, he followed in his father's footsteps by working at the court of Amīr Bashīr II, representing him at the courts of his allies and collecting his taxes from the Mountain. This was due to the fact that the Misāhqa family had a reputation of being close to Amīr Bashīr II, and other Amīrs would ask its members to mediate between them and Bashīr. At this time Mīkhā'īl' name was already well-established. In 1833, Sa'd al-Dīn, the Amīr of Hāṣbayyā, after acquiring the consent of Amīr Bashīr II, appointed Mīkhā'īl as his representative (*wakīl*) in Damascus in order to safeguard his interests with the newly installed Egyptian government in Syria. Mīkhā'īl's financial situation improved, as he now received some property from his new employer: lands in the region of the Hula valley and a little village near Qunayṭira.

He settled in Damascus and extended his connections beyond the Mountain. Not only was he in touch with the middle stratum and the ruling class of the Mountain; he also socialised with Damascus' Muslim *a'yān* and merchants and, of course, had ties with Western representatives. The big city stimulated his appetite for knowledge even further. He began studying medicine. Traveling to Egypt for this purpose, he qualified as a physician in 1845. On his return to Damascus, Mīkhā'īl was appointed chief physician of the city. Practicing medicine was not lucrative enough for him, so he returned to commerce. In the 1840s he forged business ties with the American consulate and American missionaries, strengthening and nurturing these ties from that time on.

In 1848 he converted from Catholicism to Protestantism, and in 1859 he was appointed American vice-Consul in Damascus. During the second half of the nineteenth century, he became renowned as one of the leading intellectuals in the region in such fields as medicine, mathematics, history, and even music. In addition, he completed a statistical report on mosques and other Muslim institutions in Damascus, which constitutes a unique contribution to the study of Muslim urban history. His cultural life was not confined to activities in Damascus alone; he was also drawn to the cultural richness provided by Beirut at that time. Despite all this, the 1860s were problematic for him. During the riots of 1860 he was assaulted and received an axe-blow to his temple and a blow to his right side. Eventually, both his family and his own life were spared when a Muslim friend offered him asylum in his own house.

Mīkhā'īl had two brothers, **Jibrā'īl**, who served as a judge in Zahle, and **Rufā'īl** (or **Rafā'īl**), who was a member of the court of the *mutaṣarrifiyya*. Other family members also enjoyed foreign nationality and consular protection. Mīkhā'īl's son, **Salīm**, served as dragoman in the British consulate in Damascus. A second son, **Ibrāhīm**, was a doctor who received his education at the SPC. Another son, **Nāṣīf**, served as a dragoman in the American consulate in Damascus in 1869, while their cousin, **Khalīl**, was chief dragoman at the American consulate-general in Beirut.[21]

The Misk family

Members of this family served as dragomen in the British consulate.

The Mudawwar family

This was a family of Greek Catholic origin that had arrived in Beirut in 1492. In the nineteenth century, they were landowners and entrepreneurs, and engaged in commerce. In the 1850s the family grew silk near Beirut. They apparently developed a method of growing cochineal grubs for producing carmine dye, and came to specialise in the process. Later, the family requested that the government grant them exclusive rights to grow these grubs in any part of Syria, for

---

[21] For more details, see: Zachs, "Mīkhā'īl Mishāqa," pp. 67–87; Fawaz, "Zahla and Dayr al-Qamar," p. 53; FO 195/274, Moore to Rose, 13 February 1847; FO 195/806, Roger to Stuart, 22 November 1864; FO 195/787, Eldridge, 23 December 1864; FO 195/274, Rose, 27 May 1847; FO 195/965, Burton to Barron, 5 January 1870; FO 195/1047, Green to Elliot, 10 November 1874; FO 195/187, Rose to Bankhead, 28 December, 1841; Mishāqa, *al-Jawāb*.

a period of ten years, arguing that in other countries such rights were given to developers of new inventions. The profits of the family stemmed mainly from commerce. Its members were known to be shrewd operators who prospered economically because of their aggressive quest for methods of turning a profit.

Several family members enjoyed the protection of the French consulate in Beirut, serving in it as dragomans and clerks. They were close to the French Consul, an indication of their high social standing. However, because they needed the support of the local government, they nurtured their connections with the Ottoman rulers as well, and saw to it that one of the family members was appointed to a position within the administration. For example, in 1875, **Nakhla** was chosen as a member of the Beirut City Council. The six brothers of the family were each responsible for a particular task. One took care of the land, two more ran the business, the fourth was in charge of the finances, and the remaining two attended to public relations and legal matters.

The Mudawwar brothers inherited a fortune, and multiplied it several times through their gift of exploiting their protected status. One of the prominent members of this family was **Mīkhā'īl**, born in Beirut in 1822. As a young man, until 1852, he engaged in commerce, later becoming the dragoman of the French consulate, a position he held until his death. He was knowledgeable in poetry and history; in 1858, when Khalīl al-Khūrī established his newspaper *Ḥadīqt al-Akhbār*, Mīkhā'īl supported it financially. He also was a member of the Beirut City Council.[22]

The Naḥḥās family

This was a family of Christian origin. The grandfather of the family was named **Sulaymān**. He had migrated from Ḥawrān to Homs, where he raised two sons, **Ibrāhīm** and **ʿAbbūd**. The latter moved to Tripoli after his father's death, and evidently the Naḥḥās family that resided in Tripoli in the nineteenth century were his descendants. One member of this family, **Mūsā**, served as a member of the administration and the municipality. **Qayṣar Bey** was a dragoman

[22] Fawaz, *Merchants and Migrants*, pp. 90–91; *Thamarāt al-Funūn*, No. 32, 26 November, 1875 and No. 112, 21 June 1877; Ṭarrāzī, *Tārīkh al-Ṣiḥāfa*, Vol. 2, p. 112.

in the administration. **Sāmī Afandī** was a member of the court of Tripoli, and **Niqūlā** was a well known poet at the time. Another member of the family, **Maryam Naḥḥās Nawfal** (1856–1888), was born in Beirut, but later moved to Egypt. She was educated in the Syrian English School and was knowledgeable in Arabic and English. In 1872 she married **Nasīm Nawfal**, and in 1879 she published a book on famous women's lives.[23]

The Nawfal family

This was a Christian family originating in Ḥawrān; they moved to Tripoli in the seventeenth century and when al-Jazzār came to power they moved to Beirut. A large number of the family members served as officials in the Ottoman government. This family produced 17 male figures, all involved in promoting the Arab cultural movement. **ʿAbdallāh** was director of Ibrāhīm Pāshā's office of the Accountant-General. His sons were **Nasīm** and **Anṭwān**.

Nasīm was born in Tripoli in 1847 and spent part of his life in Beirut, studying at al-Bustānī's National School. Later he moved to Alexandria and managed a shop belonging to a family of big merchants from his own city, the Bārūdīs. He also published many books. Anṭwān studied in Beirut, and then at al-Bustānī's National School. He wrote and worked for various newspapers in Alexandria.

Nawfal Niʿmatallāh Nawfal (1812–1887) was one of the people who lead the Arabic revival in Tripoli. In 1820 he accompanied his father **Niʿmatallāh** to Egypt, where he studied Arabic, Turkish, and French, returning to the Syrian region in 1828. There he served as the official in charge of finances for the Tripoli and Latakia districts. He remained at this post for seven years. Then in 1850 he was appointed dragoman at the treasury in Tripoli and the following year he moved to Beirut, apparently to take the position of secretary at the administrative council of the *Vilâyet* of Sidon. In 1852 he was appointed head of the customs office in Beirut. Later he

[23] HL, ABC: 50, box 1, S. Nawfal to Smith, 1 August 1851; Nawfal, *Tarājim ʿUlamāʾ*, pp. 68–69, 81–82, 93–94, 114–120, 190–193, 206, 209–210; *Ḥadīqat al-Akhbār*, No. 109, 2 February 1860 and No. 9, 6 April 1859; Zaydān, *Tarājim Mashāhīr al-Sharq*, Vol. 2, pp. 152–156; Ṭarrāzī, *Tārīkh al-Ṣiḥāfa*, Vol. 2, pp. 45, 171–175; al-Dibs, *Tārīkh Sūriyya*, Vol. 8, p. 604; Sarkīs, *Muʿjam al-Maṭbūʿāt al-ʿArabiyya*, Vol. 2, pp. 1874–1875; w.n., "Tarjamat al-Marḥūma Maryam Naḥḥās Nawfal," *al-Muqtaṭaf*, Vol. 12, 1882, pp. 502–503; Booth, *May Her Likes Be Multiplied*, pp. 2, 143.

became dragoman at the German and American consulates, and engaged in composition and writing for the 20 years remaining until his death. He wrote a book on Arab history and another book entitled *Zubdat al-Khā'if fī 'uṣūl al-Ma'ārif*. The last was published in Beirut in 1873 and was about the history of the Phoenicians, the Persians, the Chinese, the Egyptians, and the Greeks. Nawfal tried to describe how their ideas and culture had reached the Arabs. His book also describes the origins of history, language, poetry, and engagement in modern sciences.

Salīm (1828–1902), as a young man, was the agent for a Russian shipping company in Tripoli. He learned Arabic and French in 1840 at the 'Ayn Ṭūra school in Mount Lebanon. During that period he studied with Nāṣīf al-Yāzijī and became friendly with Buṭrus al-Bustānī, returning to Tripoli in 1843. Subsequently, he took a leave from work and went off to tour Europe. Later, in 1851, before the publication of the journal *Ḥadīqat al-Akhbār*, Salīm wrote to Eli Smith requesting his help in establishing an Arabic journal for the region. At that time the proposal remained only an idea. When he returned to Syria, he worked as assistant to Khalīl al-Khūrī in editing *Ḥadīqat al-Akhbār*. In 1861, the Russian government invited him to St. Petersburg to teach Arabic at the St. Petersburg College, in order to prepare young Russians for posts in the East. In 1872 he served as dragoman for the Russian Tsar. In 1879 he was appointed as adviser to the Russian government on the Ottoman Empire.

Ibrāhīm Nawfal al-Thānī's son **Mīkhā'īl** had a son named **'Abdallāh**, who was born in Tripoli in 1815. He held several different posts in the government of the *mutaṣarrifiyya* of Mount Lebanon. For many years he was director of the office of the Accountant-General (*Dīwān al-Muḥāsaba*) in Mount Lebanon. He had four sons and a daughter.

The eldest son, named **Nasīm**, established a journal called *Majallat al-Fatā*. The second son, **Anṭwān**, was editor of the journal *Jarīdat al-Fallāḥ al-Miṣrī al-Yawmiyya* (The Egyptian Peasant's Daily Paper). The third son, **Hānī**, was a writer, while the youngest son, **Tawfīq**, was a clerk.

Niqūlā Bey, the son of **Luṭfallāh Jirjis** (1818–1895) knew Arabic, Turkish, and French. When in 1860 a commission was appointed under Fu'ād Pāshā to discuss matters concerning Syria and Mount Lebanon, he acted as dragoman for the Russian delegate. Afterwards, he was appointed *Qā'imaqām* of al-Qūra district, and was a member of the administrative council of Mount Lebanon. Still later, he presided over the commercial court in Tripoli. In 1877 he was appointed as Tripoli's delegate to the *Majlis al-Mabʿūthīn al-ʿUthmānī*. In 1845 he married his niece **Tiyudūra**, daughter of **Ḥannā**, Ibrāhīm Nawfal's son, and they had four sons and four daughters. The eldest, named **Luṭfallāh**, held various positions in the Ottoman state. He was director of the port in Tripoli, *Qāʾimaqām* of al-Marqab district, and a member of the Tripoli City Council. He knew Arabic, Turkish, and French.

Luṭfallāh's son **Azīz** was a merchant in the United States. Another figure in the family was **Wahballāh**, father of **Qayṣar**; the latter was British vice-Consul in Tripoli. Another member of the family, **Naṣrallāh**, had a son named **Jibrāʾīl** whose own son **Wadīʿ** was born in Tripoli in 1854, studied at al-Bustānī's school, and knew Arabic and French. He was appointed secretary to his father who was Director of Customs.

The Qabbānī family

The Qabbānīs were a Muslim family. **Aḥmad Ḥusayn** was the father of **Saʿd al-Dīn**. The family had *awqāf* lands in the area of al-Ḥadādīn market in Beirut port and in al-Qatan market in the Christian area in the centre of the city. **ʿAbd al-Qādir** was one of the Muslim notables who established the first Muslim newspaper in Beirut, *Thamarāt al-Funūn*.[24]

The Ṣābūnjī family

This was a Greek Catholic family. **Lūwīs** was a priest, and maintained good ties with the American missionaries. He and Yūsuf Shalfūn founded the journal *al-Naḥla* (The Bee).[25]

The Shaḥāda family

Mīkhāʾīl was the acting Russian Consul in Beirut in the 1860s. His son **Salīm** (1847–1908) was born in Beirut and studied Arabic and French at the Orthodox school at *Sūq al-Gharb*. Then he studied at the American missionaries' school learning English and science and

[24] Ḥallāq, *Awqāf al-Muslimīn fī Bayrūt*, p. 123.
[25] Tibawi, *American Interests in Syria*, p. 214; SAC, ABC: 50, box 1, 1856.

taking a special interest in history and geography. Salīm translated books from French into Arabic for the journal *Ḥadīqat al-Akhbār* and was in charge of its French-language edition. He co-authored a book in Arabic with Salīm al-Khūrī on history and geography entitled *al-Āthār* (The Remnants). In 1866, he succeeded his father as translator at the Russian consulate. Together they founded *al-Jamʿiyya al-Khayriyya al-Urthūdhuksiyya* (The Orthodox Society of Charitable Intentions), a society in Beirut, which Salīm headed for about 17 years.[26]

Yūsuf Shalfūn

The Shalfūns were a long-standing Maronite family originating in Beirut. **Yūsuf** lived from 1839 to 1895. His grandfather had been governor of the Lebanese coast under the rule of the Amīr Bashīr II. Yūsuf was a journalist. He worked at Khalīl al-Khūrī's journal, where he was in charge of typesetting. In 1871, in partnership with Rizqallāh Afandī Khaḍrā', he established a publishing company, focusing on the printing of religious books and literary compositions, and he directed the general printing house (*al-Maṭbaʿa al-ʿUmūmiyya*). In 1874, he founded *Maṭbaʿat al-Kuliyya* and published the journal *al-Taqaddum* (Progress), which appeared for thirteen years. He also headed several other journals, such as *al-Najāḥ* (Success) in 1871.[27]

The Shidyāq Family

Aḥmad Fāris (1804–1877) was a Maronite, born in ʿAshqūt in Kisrawān. He studied at ʿAyn Waraqa. His brother, **Asʿad**, was the first local to convert to Protestantism. The Maronite Patriarch did not take this calmly and he was persecuted to death. Soon after his brother's death, Aḥmad escaped from the Patriarchy and found shelter with the American missionaries. They sent him to Egypt, where he lived from 1825 to 1834, later leaving for Malta, to continue working with the missionaries. For fourteen years, he worked for

---

[26] Zaydān, *Tarājim Mashāhīr al-Sharq*, Vol. 1, pp. 230–231; Sarkīs, *Muʿjam al-Maṭbūʿāt al-ʿArabiyya*, Vol. 1, p. 1103; May Davie, "Ville, Notables et Pouvoir: Les Orthodoxes de Beyrouth au XIXème Siecle," *Cahiers de la Mediterranee*, No. 45 (1992), p. 187.

[27] Sarkīs, *Muʿjam al-Maṭbūʿāt al-ʿArabiyya*, Vol. 1, p. 1140.

their printing operation in Malta. Throughout his life he converted to Protestantism and then to Islam. He translated, adapted and produced original Arabic literature and acquired a reputation as a talented writer. Apparently, in 1859 he traveled to Istanbul. There, from 1861 to 1883, he published an Arabic journal called *al-Jawāʾib* (Circulating News), which became the most popular journal of its time.[28]

The Ṣulḥ family

This was a Muslim family, defined by Johnson as a family of "Ottoman notables and Beiruti *zaʿīms*." Originating in Sidon, it acquired its status in the second half of the nineteenth century, with some family members active in the new middle stratum in Beirut. During the last decades of the century the leading branch of the family in the city included landowners, judges, and senior officials in the administration. Family members traveled extensively throughout the empire, and were thus able to forge marriage ties with leading families of Damascus, Aleppo, Egypt, and Turkey. They developed an interest in a wide range of topics, including Arabism.

The brothers **Aḥmad Pāshā** and **ʿAbd al-Raḥīm** were the first to establish their home in Beirut. ʿAbd al-Raḥīm owned some land, but his brother Aḥmad Pāshā owned much land near Sidon. The latter also served as Governor of the *sancaks* of Acre and Latakia. His firstborn son **Kamīl** became a judge in the Balkans. Eventually, he too settled in Beirut and married local women of upper-class families. His youngest son **Riḍā** (1860–1934) was *Mutaṣarrif* of Salonika. Early in the twentieth century he was elected to the Syrian National Congress, a body which proclaimed Amīr Fayṣal as king.[29]

The Sursuq family

This was a family of Orthodox Christian origin. In the seventeenth century its members served as tax collectors. As a result, they were able to acquire *mīrī* lands in return for their services for the Ottoman government. At the turn of the nineteenth century some members of the family moved to Beirut. By 1832 they had attained respectable

[28] Sarkīs, *Muʿjam al-Maṭbūʿāt al-ʿArabiyya*, Vol. 1, pp. 1104–1105.

[29] Ḥallāq, *Awqāf al-Muslimīn fī Bayrūt*, p. 155; Johnson, *Class and Client in Beirut*, pp. 57–58.

status, becoming the wealthiest Christian family in the Ashrāfiyya district during the nineteenth century. **Dīmitrī** was an independent merchant who became a dragoman for the American consulate. **Nīqūlas**, who headed the family business, held a Greek passport and enjoyed Greek protection until 1862. In the 1870s, **Mūsā**, Nīqūlas' brother, benefited from German protection.

Ilyās Jibrāʾīl was the Iranian acting-Consul from 1841 to 1875. **Asʿad Jibrāʾīl** was the advisor to the court of appeals in the *Vilâyet* of Beirut. **George Dīmitrī** served as dragoman at the German consulate. Some members of the family enjoyed the protection of the Russian consulate. The family also dealt in shipping, silk, and grain transport to London and Cyprus. Other members of the family were bankers, who invested in the Suez Canal, the Beirut-Damascus highway, and the Beirut harbour company. The family had wide social ties and was close to key Ottoman and European figures.

Imilī Sursuq went to Egypt to complete her schooling. Later she built a school for girls in Beirut and initiated other philanthropic projects.[30]

The Thābit family

This was a Greek Orthodox merchant family. Its members held ties with the American missionaries from the 1840s on. **Ayyūb**, the son of the family head **Salīm**, was a wealthy trader in Beirut and also served as dragoman at the American consulate. In 1853, he travelled to Boston and formed ties with a company called Dabney and Cunningham, wool importers in the city. When one of its proprietors, Mr. Cunningham, died in 1864, Ayyūb succeeded him and entered into partnership with William Dabney. In 1866 the company acquired American consular protection in Beirut. The business flourished and they conducted extensive trade between Syria and the United States. In addition, in 1859 Ayyūb became the owner of two thirds of the land of the Bwareshe area. Apparently, the inhabitants of this village washed and prepared the wool at Ayyūb's factory.

Yūsuf was appointed as a member of the Beirut City Council in 1875. Another family member also named **Ayyūb** (1875–1945) studied at the American College. In 1905, he travelled to the United

[30] Fawaz, *Merchants and Migrants*, pp. 91–93; Ḥallāq, *al-Tārīkh al-Ijtimāʿī*, p. 205.

States and studied medicine, returning to Mt. Lebanon in 1908. In 1913 he participated in the Arab conference in Paris and he became a member of the City Council in 1926.[31]

The Ṭrād family

A respected Christian family of long standing, with many branches. Most of the Ṭrāds were rich. They originated in Ḥawrān and had arrived in Beirut in 1643. The family included businessmen and financiers, writers, and officials in the Ottoman government. They had ties with the Russian consulate as well. For example, **Iskandar** and **Salīm** worked as dragomans at that consulate. Another family member, **Jirjis ibn Niqūlā**, was a member of the city's Chamber of Commerce. **Najīb** (1859–1911) was a philologist, writer, historian, and journalist, and knew several foreign languages. He had studied at the Orthodox school in Beirut. Subsequently, he left the school and went into business, but his ventures did not meet with great success, and he returned to his studies and to teach at a school in Homs. Later on, he was appointed secretary in the railway administration in Egypt, and then held a post in the war ministry. In 1882 he was appointed translator for the famous ʿUrābī trial in Egypt. In 1898 he published the journal *al-Raqīb* (The Observer).

Asʿad Ṭrād (1835–1891) was born in Beirut and studied at the American school at ʿAbeih under Nāṣīf al-Yāzijī. Upon his arrival in Egypt in 1872 and until his death, he engaged in commerce in Alexandria and in al-Manṣūra. In the 1870s he wrote an article entitled "Unity and Brotherhood" for the journal *al-Jinān*; it called on all the communities of the region to live in unity. **Farīda**, daughter of **Isḥāq**, was head of the *Zahrat al-Iḥsān* school. **Imīlya**, the daughter of **Fāris** was the head of the patriotic school in Shuwayfat. **Salmā** wrote in several newspapers on the privileges of women. In 1910 she established the newspaper *al-Ḥasnāʾ* (The Beautiful). The family was close to the Sursuq family. For example, **Idmā**, the daughter of **Jurjī**, was married to Ilyās Sursuq.[32] The family con-

---

[31] *Thamarāt al-Funūn*, No. 93, 26 November 1875; Salām, *Mudhakkirāt Salīm*, p. 136; US/NA, Hay to Brown, 20 November 1871; US/NA, Eldridge to Campbell, 24 October 1876; US/NA, Moore to Appleton, 14 January 1861; US/NA, Eldridge to Payson, 10 May 1881; HL, ABC: 50, box 1, Tabet to Smith, 15 August 1841.

[32] Sarkīs, *Muʿjam al-Maṭbūʿāt*, Vol. 1, pp. 1236–1238; Zaydān, *Tarājim Mashāhīr*

tinued to be prominent also in the twentieth century. For example, in 1910, **Najīb** was elected to the Administrative Council (*Majlis al-Idāra*) of Beirut.[33]

The Wortabet Family

A family of Armenian origin. **Gregory** (1798–1832), was the first Armenian in the region to convert to Protestantism. Throughout his life he was friendly with the American missionaries, with whom he studied the scriptures. He travelled with them to Malta and worked for a short time in their publishing house there.[34] **Yūḥannā**, his son, attended the first American school in Beirut, starting when it was founded in 1838, and continuing to study there for six years, where he learned English and Latin. He also took private lessons in medicine, languages, and theology from the missionaries Smith and De Forest. Later, he travelled to the United States where he received his diploma in medicine. When the Faculty of Medicine opened at the American College in Beirut in 1867 he was made a lecturer in physiology, anatomy, and philosophy. He also wrote books in these fields.

The Yāfī Family

This was a respected Muslim family with branches in Damascus, Aleppo, Homs, Tripoli, and Beirut. The shaykh **Muḥyī al-Dīn Afandī al-Bakrī** (1803–1886) was born in Damascus and was an *ʿālim*. In 1843 he moved to Beirut.[35]

The Yannī family

This was an Orthodox Christian family of Greek origin. The name of the family was originally Kātsifilīs. Some of its members were associated with the literary movement in Tripoli. Others were active

al-Sharq, Vol. 2, p. 278; Zaydān, *Tārīkh Ādāb al-Lugha al-ʿArabiyya*, Vol. 4, p. 219; Ṭarrāzī, *Tārīkh al-Ṣiḥāfa*, Vol. 2, pp. 179–187.

[33] May Davie, "Ville, Notables et Pouvoir: Les Orthodoxes de Beyrouth au XIXème Siecle," *Cahiers de la Mediterranee*, No. 45 (1992), p. 189.

[34] w.n., "al-Duktūr Yūḥannā Wartābit," *al-Muqtaṭaf*, Vol. 34, 1909, pp. 1–7; HL, ABC: 60, box 5, J. Wortabet to Smith, n.d.; HL, ABC: 60, box 2, Smith to Anderson, 17 June 1851; HL, ABC: 60, box 5, J. Wortabet to Smith, 15 January 1852.

[35] Ḥallāq, *Awqāf al-Muslimīn fī Bayrūt*, p. 135.

in commerce, and enjoyed good ties with the American consulate. Still other branches of the family left for Egypt and the United States. The founder of the Syrian branch of the family was a sea captain, **Mīkhā'īl** Yannī. He had sailed from the island of Mykonos in about 1770 to trade with settlements on the Syrian seaboard. His ship was wrecked near Tripoli and he lost all his possessions and merchandise. Later, he found shelter with the English Consul (Cary), who also found him occupation.

Mīkhā'īl had three sons: **Ḥannā**, **ʿAbdallāh**, and **Jirjis**. The last-named also had three sons, **Anṭūnyūs**, **Niqūlā**, and **Isḥāq**. Anṭūnyūs went into the silk trade; in 1848 serving as the American acting-Consul in Tripoli and in 1863 as the Belgian vice-Consul. Due to his ties with the American missionaries, he converted to Protestantism, the first such convert in Tripoli. He enjoyed a broad education and knew Italian, English, Greek, and Arabic, as well as being well-versed in literature, politics, poetry, and prose. He acquired some of his education when he worked for the American and Belgian Consuls. In Tripoli, his house was a cultural centre, visited by Americans, Syrians, and Greeks. He believed that all religions were equal, and therefore he made efforts to develop ties of friendship with upper class Muslims as well. He had two daughters, **Tiyudūra**, wife of **Tiyudūr Kātsifilīs**, the vice-Consul of Spain, Austria and Hungary, and **Barbāra** (wife of **Qayṣar Kātsifilīs**, vice-Consul of Holland). Anṭūnyūs had two sons, **Samū'īl** (1865–1919) and **Jurjī**.

Jurjī was born in 1854. In 1868 he studied Arabic, English, mathematics, history, and geography at the English school established by the American missionaries in ʿAbeih. Afterwards, he moved to Beirut and studied at al-Bustānī's National School. In 1876, he helped establish a literary society, headed by Iskandar Kātsifilīs, in which he served as secretary. In 1881 Jurjī established a school similar to Bustānī's. That year, at the age of 27, he published his book *Tārīkh Sūriyā*. In 1882, following the death of his father, he was appointed as the latter's successor as American vice-Consul in Tripoli, filling this position simultaneously with serving as the Belgian vice-Consul in Tripoli. He was one of the founders of the literary *salon* (*al-Muntadā al-Adabī*). From 1908 to 1928, he and his brother published the journal *al-Mabāḥith* (Researches), using it as the medium to publish his articles on the history of Lebanon, Syria, Palestine, Iraq and Turkey. He was active in a wide range of cultural endeavors, particularly as a member of several societies: *al-Majmaʿ al-ʿIlmī al-Sharqī* (The Eastern Scientific Society) in Beirut, *Jamʿiyyāt al-Mashriqiyyāt* (The Eastern Societies) in Leiden, Holland, *al-Majmaʿ al-ʿIlmī al-ʿArabī* (The Arabic Scientific Society) in Damascus, and *al-Jamʿiyya al-Āsyawiyya al-ʿIlmiyya* (The Asian Scientific Society) in Paris.

Samū'īl, Anṭūnyūs' other son, studied at the American school in Tripoli and at Yūḥanna Mārūn's school in Batrūn. He subsequently transferred to the American College in Beirut.

Isḥāq (1827–1863) knew Arabic, French, and Italian. In his earlier years he dealt in business for a short time, and in 1855 was appointed Belgian acting-Consul in Tripoli. In 1856, he married **Idlāyid (Idlīd)**, daughter of Krīstūf Kātsifilīs, the vice-Consul of Austria and Spain.[36]

The Yāzijī family

Al-Yāzijī was a Greek Catholic family from Homs. The name apparently originates from the Turkish word *yazıji*, meaning clerk or scribe. **Nāṣīf** (1800–1871) was born in Mount Lebanon. From his twenties to his forties he served as secretary to Amīr Bashīr II. During this period he became famous for his knowledge of Arabic, and he published books of poetry. After the fall of Bashīr and the end of Egyptian rule in Syria, he moved from Mount Lebanon to Beirut and got in touch with the American missionaries. He held *salon*s in his home for intellectuals and writers.

Towards the end of the 1840s he assisted the Americans in printing books in Arabic and was employed as a proofreader for their press and as a teacher at the boys' seminar. From 1848 on, he assisted Smith in translating the Old and New Testaments into Arabic. In the 1870s he taught Arabic at the SPC. In addition to being considered one of the most important nineteenth-century poet in Arabic, Nāṣīf wrote many books in this language on grammar, logic, and rhetoric. **Ibrāhīm** (1847–1906), Nāṣīf's son, studied at an American missionaries' school. In addition to contributing to the rebirth of the Arabic language, he worked in journalism, editing the journal *al-Miṣbāḥ*

[36] SAC, Tibawi Papers, box 3, file 1, Yenni to Smith, 6 November 1848; Nawfal, *Tarājim ʿUlamāʾ*, pp. 110, 219–220; Ṭarrāzī, *Tārīkn al-Ṣiḥāfa*, Vol. 2, pp. 45–47, 56.

(The Illuminator) in 1873, and then the periodical *al-Ṭabīb* (The Doctor) in 1884. In 1894 he left Syria for Egypt, where he founded the periodical *al-Bayān* (The Declaration).[37] **Warda** (1838–1924), Nāṣīf's daughter, was a poet and wrote articles in the Egyptian press.

[37] SAC, Tibawi Papers, box 2, file 3, Yazagi to Smith, 16 August 1845; w.n., "al-Shaykh Ibrāhīm al-Yāzijī al-Lūbnānī," *al-Muqtaṭaf*, Vol. 33, 1908, pp. 993–994 and Vol. 34, 1909, pp. 12–14; Zaydān, *Tarājim Mashāhīr al-Sharq*, Vol. 4, pp. 240–241.

APPENDIX TWO

The Various Meanings and Definitions of the Name "Syria"

The Name "Syria" in Ancient Times

The use of the name "Syria" goes back to ancient times. In the Ugaritic literature it appears as "Sryn," and in old Hebrew as "Siryon," a name that stands for Anti-Lebanon (the mountains east of the Biqāʿ valley). To other peoples, the name referred to a larger area. The northern district of the Euphrates region was known to the Babylonians as "Su-ri."[1] The Bible does not mention "Surya;"[2] during that period the region was called "Aram." The name "Aram" apparently originates from a person of the same name, the fifth son of Shem, son of Noah. The addition of "Aram" to "Syria" was common in Biblical times; indeed "Aram" was added to many geographical names. For example, in Hebrew, "Aram-Naharayim" refers to the region between the rivers, or "Aram-Damesek" applies to the kingdom of Damascus.[3]

Yūsuf al-Dibs, the Maronite bishop of Beirut who set forth the history of Syria in eight volumes, is the source for three interpretations detailed in this appendix. He maintains that the Greeks were the first to use the term "Syria," at the end of the fifth century BCE.[4] The Greek poet Homer (ninth century BCE) called the inhabitants of Syria "Aramaeans." Al-Dibs notes that Herodotus (fifth century BCE) is known to be the first to call this land "Syria," and after him most Greeks and Romans did likewise.[5] In fact, the Greeks in the Hellenistic period used the term "Coele-Syria" to denote the territory stretching from the Mediterranean in the west to the river

---

[1] Philip K. Hitti, *History of Syria* (London, 1951), p. 51.
[2] Transliteration of words in Hebrew follows the phonetics of modern Hebrew.
[3] Al-Dibs, *Tārīkh Sūriyya*, Vol. 1, p. 11.
[4] Lamia R. Shehadeh, "The Name of Syria in Ancient and Modern Usage," *al Qantara*, Vol. 15 (1994), p. 286.
[5] Al-Dibs, *Tārīkh Sūriyya*, Vol. 1, p. 1.

Euphrates in the east. This was used to distinguish it from that part of Syria lying in Mesopotamia.[6]

In ancient times, Syria's borders were not clearly defined. At first, the Greeks considered it to be the area from the Euxine (the Black Sea) to Egypt, but sometimes confused it with the kingdom of Assyria. The name was applied to Aram and the Aramaeans, but also referred to the Persian *Eberhari* (across the river) and to Coele-Syria. Yet Syria was always clearly distinguished from Phoenicia and Judaea.[7] Confusion arose from the fact that in different times the Jews, Persians, and Greeks used the name differently, and also indicated different borders for the general area. For example, the first-century BCE historian Strabo defines the area of Syria almost as today's Lebanon—Mt. Lebanon, Anti-Lebanon, and the valley between them. But he was aware that other divisions of the region existed.[8]

According to al-Dibs, the origin of the name has other interpretations as well. He notes the following: The Syrian region is called so in connection with Ṣūr (Tyre), the famous Phoenician maritime city of Syria. The ancient Greeks knew the Tyrians because they frequently came to their cities to trade. Thus, the Greeks called the merchants they met "Sūriyyūn" and their country "Sūriyya." The replacement in "Ṣūr" of 'Ṣ', pronounced in Arabic as the letter *ṣād*, by 'S', pronounced in Arabic as the letter *sīn*, in "Sūriyya" stemmed from the Greeks' difficulty in pronouncing the letter *ṣād*.[9]

A second explanation offered by al-Dibs is that the Greeks called this country "Syria" in reference to "Ashur" (Hebrew) or "Assyria" (English, land of the Assyrians), as the country was occupied by the Assyrians before its conquest by the Greeks. Naturally, the Greeks would connect the region with this people. This explanation, too, involves a change in the pronunciation of the word. The Greeks dropped the first syllable, '*a*', in their pronunciation of the word, and replaced the '*sh*' by '*s*'. Hence, "Ashur" became "Sur."[10]

---

[6] Pipes, *Greater Syria*, p. 13; Paton states that the region of the Biqāʿ is Coele-Syria, and extends from Lebanon to Anti-Lebanon. See: Paton, *The Modern Syrians*, p. 11.

[7] Shehadeh, "The Name of Syria," p. 287.

[8] *Ibid.*, p. 288.

[9] Al-Dibs, *Tārīkh Sūriyya*, Vol. 1, p. 11. Le Strange supports this interpretation and states that the name "Syria" was given by the Greeks to the land surrounding Ṣūr (Tyre). See: Guy Le Strange, *Palestine under the Moslems* (Beirut, 1965), p. 14.

[10] Hitti, by contrast, believes that there was no connection between "Syria" and "Assyria". Hitti, *History of Syria*, p. 57.

Interestingly, "Ashur" is also related to Shem, son of Noah. It is the name of his second son.

Al-Dibs clarifies that archaeologists and historians of his time are divided in their views on these interpretations, and he presents yet another opinion as to the source of the name. He attributes its first use to the Egyptian period (in his opinion predating the Assyrian and the Greek eras. Today, the Assyrian empire is known to have had more than one phase, the first initiated by Shamshi-Adad in the nineteenth century BCE, declining in the wake of the Babylonians' rise (Hammurabi) and re-emerging in the so-called Neo-Assyrian period, re-creating their empire (Tiglat-Pileser) at the turn of the first millennium BCE). He notes that Egyptian archaeologists mention a people called "Asur," as one of the nations in league with the Hittites, that dwelt in the north of present-day Syria. This people fought against Ramses II, King of Egypt (ruled c. 1279–1213 BCE, third ruler of the nineteenth Dynasty),[11] namely many centuries before the Assyrians took control of the territory of Syria. Al-Dibs also indicates the existence of a certain Father dī Kārā, who tried to buttress this explanation with the claim that the name is of Greek origin, based on a stone tablet found in Egypt. On it, the name "Syria" appears in three languages: in hieroglyphics—"*Ruthānū*," in Greek—"Syria," and in the language of the Egyptian people—"*Asār*." Al-Dibs, however, states that for him the most ancient interpretation is closest to the truth.[12] Hence, in his opinion, the name "Syria" is older than the time of the Greek scholars.

After the Greek age the name continued to be in use. The Romans used it to designate that part of the their empire lying between Asia Minor in the north and Egypt in the south, retaining the name and applying it to the Roman province (for example, province of "Syria" in 14 CE; provinces of "Syria Coele" and "Syria Phoenicia" in 211 CE) extending at times from the River Euphrates to Egypt.[13] It remained in use in Byzantine times as well, referring to the same area as in the Roman period. This was the nature of things until the Muslim conquest in the seventh century.

---

[11] Al-Dibs, *Tārīkh Sūriyya*, Vol. 1, p. 11.
[12] *Ibid.*, p. 13.
[13] Hitti, *History of Syria*, p. 59.

After the Muslim Conquest

In the first century after the Muslim conquest, the name "Syria" was used also by the Muslims. For example, the geographer Yāqūt al-Ḥamawī, who set out the knowledge he had acquired in a geographical encyclopedia called *Muʿjam al-Buldān*, devotes a whole entry to the term "Syria." He writes that it is "a place in *al-Shām*."[14] He describes the battle of the Yarmuk (636 CE), in which the Muslims defeated the Byzantines and conquered Syria. He mentions the name "Syria" when describing the Byzantine Emperor Heraclius (ruled 610–641), who said to his men "O men of Rome. If the Arabs shall rise upon Syria, they will not be satisfied until they possess most of your cities and take your children."[15] Al-Ḥamawī describes the Muslim victory over the Byzantines, and the event of Heraclius ascending a Syrian hill before returning to Constantinople, and calling out "Farewell, Syria."[16] Aḥmad Ibn Yaḥyā al-Balādhurī, who lived in the eighth century, in his book *Futūḥ al-Buldān*, mentions the name "Syria," and he too gives an account of the Yarmuk battle and Heraclius' departure.[17]

Together with this term, the Muslims applied other names to describe the area (which Westerners continued to refer to as Syria). Starting from the seventh century, the Muslim population used the term *al-Shām*, which was perhaps taken from the word *Shimāl*—left, meaning north, for a person at al-Ḥijāz looking eastward. Other terms used were *Barr al-Shām*, meaning the land mass of *Shām*, and *Bilād al-Shām*, meaning the lands of *Shām*. This, in contrast with *al-Yaman* (present-day Yemen), the land to the right of al-Ḥijāz.[18] *Al-Shām* refered to a large expanse of territory, but not a defined or clearly bound land. According to al-Muqaddasī (a geographer, b. 946), another term in use was "*Shāmāt*", meaning "moles." This was derived from the patches of colour in Syria's fields that were likened to moles on a beautiful face.[19] Both writers used the term "*al-Shām*,"

---

[14] Yāqūt al-Ḥamawī, *Muʿjam al-Buldān*, Vol. 5 (Beirut, 1954), p. 171.
[15] *Ibid.*
[16] *Ibid.*
[17] Aḥmad Ibn Yaḥyā al-Balādhurī, *Futūḥ al-Buldān* (Cairo, 1901), pp. 6, 143.
[18] Hitti, *History of Syria*, p. 58; for more details see: Baedeker, *Palestine and Syria*, p. lvii.
[19] Le Strange, *Palestine under the Moslems*, p. 14.

as in fact it was in everyday use by the inhabitants of the region until the end of the Ottoman period. During the Mamluk period we can also find the term "Syria" in use. For example, in the book written by Ibn Faḍlallāh al-ʿUmarī (1301–1349), one of the chapters is actually entitled "*Fī Dhikr al-Mamlaka al-Sūriyya*."[20]

The Ottoman Period until the Nineteenth Century

At first, the Ottomans continued to apply the names "*al-Shām*" and "*Barr al-Shām*," as under the Arab Muslims. They also began to use the name *Arabistān* for this region, mainly in military context.[21] During the period of the *Tanẓīmāt* reforms, a *mushīr* was appointed over the Fifth Army in the area and he was called "Commander of the army of *Arabistān*." This commander was responsible for maintenance of order and security in this region. Apparently, the term "*Arabistān*" originated from the Arab population that inhabited the region. In parallel, the names "Syria" and *al- Shām* stayed in the awareness of both Muslims and Ottomans.

The Nineteenth Century and Revival of the Term "Syria"

At the beginning of the nineteenth century, the Ottomans did not customarily use the term "Syria," but it was preserved by its use in European languages, particularly in the literature of European travellers. Two examples are the books of the French traveller Constantin Volney and the German John Burckhardt.[22] When in 1820 the American missionaries arrived in the region, they used the term, as they encountered it previously in the New Testament. In general, the Europeans regarded what are now Jordan, Palestine, Israel and Lebanon as integral parts of Syria.

The application of the name "Syria" gradually infiltrated the Ottoman government due to its use by Europeans, probably during the international crisis over the conquest of Syria by Ibrāhīm Pāshā. At that time, the name referred to the entire geographical area that

---

[20] Ibn Faḍlallāh al-ʿUmarī, *al-Taʿrīf bil-Muṣṭalaḥ al-Sharīf* (Beirut, 1988), p. 224.

[21] Abu-Manneh, "The Formation and Dissolution of the Province of Syria," p. 10.

[22] Volney, *Travels in Syria and Egypt*; Burckhardt, *Travels in Syria and the Holy Land*; Murray, *Handbook for Travellers in Syria*, p. xxxvii.

he conquered. Yet, in their correspondence, Muḥammad ʿAlī and his son Ibrāhīm Pāshā both remained loyal to the terms that had been common following the Muslim conquest, i.e. *al-Shām* and *Barr al-Shām*.[23]

The first time that the Porte made official and administrative use of the name "Syria" was when the *Vilâyet* of Syria was created in 1865. In doing so, the Porte departed from its custom of naming the provinces after their capital city, instead using the name "Syria" for the new province.[24] From the second half of the nineteenth century until close to its end, the local intelligentsia also began to use this name. It took root first among the local educated Christian population,[25] and later by local Muslims. This apparently arose from the educational activities of the missionaries (mainly American Protestants) who arrived from the United States and Europe, and who continued to call the area "Syria" as was customary in the West.

The literary and cultural activities of the local Christians in the second half of the nineteenth century also promoted the revival of the term. These included publication of books and journals bearing the name "Syria" in their titles, compilation of dictionaries referring to the term, and the establishment of cultural societies including it in their designation. In 1859, Khalīl al-Khūrī published his book *Kharābāt Sūriyya*. This was the first book to have the name "Syria" in its title. A year later, the journal published by Buṭrus al-Bustānī, *Nafīr Sūriyya*, appeared. Then in 1866 Rāshid Pāshā, *vali* of the *Vilâyet* of Syria founded an Arab-Turkish paper in Damascus called *Syria*.[26] More books with the name "Syria" in their titles continued to appear: one by Maṭar (1874), *Tārīkh al-ʿUqūd al-Duriyya fī al-Mamlaka al-Sūriyya*, and one by Yannī (1881), *Tārīkh Sūriyā*. These books describe the borders of Greater Syria. The local intellectuals began to connect the term "Syria" with the traditional *al-Shām*, applying the pre-Islamic name "Syria" to the area hitherto known as *al-Shām*. The boundary demarcation became more precisely detailed in geographic accounts, and interest began to be paid not only to Syria as a geographic region but also to its history, archaeology, flora, and the population

[23] Rustum, *al-Maḥfūẓāt al-Malakiyya al-Miṣriyya*.
[24] Abu-Manneh, "The Formation and Dissolution of the Province of Syria," p. 10.
[25] Hourani, *Arabic Thought in the Liberal Age*, p. 276.
[26] Choueiri, *Arab History*, p. 26.

itself. Thus, as a result of local activity on one hand, and formal acceptance of the Ottoman establishment on the other, the name began to take root as part of a perception and as a source of self identification for the people living in this region.

BIBLIOGRAPHY

Primary Sources

Governmental Documents

Public Record Office (PRO)—London

a. FO 195—Consular correspondence and reports from the British consulate general of Beirut and from the consulates of Damascus and Aleppo to the British Embassy in Istanbul;
b. FO 226—Files of the Beirut consulate general; FO 78—Diplomatic and consular correspondence of the British Embassy in Constantinople to the Foreign Office, from 1820;
c. FO 424—Printed diplomatic and consular correspondence of the British Embassy in Constantinople to the Foreign Office, from 1820.

Public Record Office of Northern Ireland (PRONI)—Belfast

a. D1071H/C, Printed letters of British Consuls in Syria, 1858–1860;
b. Lord Dufferin and Ava papers: D1071/H/C, MD&A, mic. 22; MD&A, mic. 320—letters.

National Archives (NA)—Washington DC

Series T367—Dispatches from United States' Consuls in Beirut, Lebanon, 1836–1906.

Salname

Salname-yi Vilâyet-i Suriye of the years 1288AH/1871; 1300AH/1882, Haifa.

Non-Governmental Documents

Archives of the American Board of Commissioners for Foreign Missions (ABCFM)—Houghton Library (HL), Harvard University, Boston

1. *Miscellaneous papers relating to the Syrian Mission*:
   a. series ABC: 16.8.1—Reel 538, Vol. 1—journals, reports and letters, 1836–1844; Reel 542, Vol. 4—documents, reports and letters, 1847–1859; Reel 543, Vol. 4—documents, reports and letters, 1847–1859; Reel 544, Vol. 5—letters, 1846–1859; Reel 545, Vol. 6—documents, reports and letters, 1860–1871; Reel 546, Vol. 7—letters, 1860–1871; Reel 547, Vol. 7—letters, 1860–1871; Reel 548, Vol. 8—supplementary papers, documents, records and minutes, 1823–1870
   b. series ABC: 16.8.2.5: Reel 551, Vol. 2—annual reports of the SPC, 1866–1902
   c. Individual biographies, boxes 1–34; ABCFM, Manuscript histories of missions, box 32, no. 2, a brief chronicle of the Syrian Mission, 1818–1909
2. Eli Smith papers: ABC: 50 (3 boxes in English), ABC: 60 (5 boxes in Arabic)
3. Daniel Bliss papers: New series no. 1, 1861–1863
4. *The Missionary Herald* (Official Newspaper of the ABCFM)—1825–1865

Private Papers, St. Antony's College (SAC), Oxford
a. Antonius papers
b. Tibawi papers

Periodicals and Newspapers
Al-Ḍiyāʾ (Cairo)
Hadīqāt al-Akhbār (Beirut)
Al-Hilāl (Cairo)
Al-Janna (Beirut)
Al-Jinān (Beirut)
Al-Kuliyya (Beirut)
Al-Manār (Cairo)
Al-Mashriq (Beirut)
Al-Muqtabas (Cairo and Damascus)
Al-Muqtaṭaf (Beirut and Cairo)
Nafīr Sūriyya (Beirut)
Thamarāt al-Funūn (Beirut)

Other Primary Sources

Arabic

Alūf, Mīkhāʾīl Mūsā. *Tārīkh Baʿlabak.* Beirut, 1908.
Al-ʿAwra, Ibrāhīm. *Tārīkh Wilāyat Sulaymān Bāshā al-ʿĀdil 1804–1819.* Sidon, 1936.
Al-ʿAynṭūrīnī, Anṭūniyūs Abū Khaṭṭār. *Mukhtaṣar Tārīkh Jabal Lubnān.* Ed. Ilyās Qaṭṭār, Beirut, 1983.
Al-Balādhurī, Aḥmad Ibn Yaḥyā. *Futūḥ al-Buldān.* Cairo, 1901.
Bayram, Muḥammad, *Tārīkh Ṣafwat al-Iʿtibār bi-Mustawdaʿ al-Amṣār wal-Aqṭār,* 5 vols., Cairo, 1885.
Bāz, Rustum. *Mudhakkirāt Rustum Bāz.* Ed. Fuʾād Afrām al-Bustānī, Beirut, 1955.
Buḥtur, Ṣāliḥ. *Tārīkh Bayrūt wa Akhbār al-Umarāʾ al-Buḥturiyyīn min Banī al-Gharb.* Ed. Lūwīs Shīkhū, 2nd ed., Beirut, 1927.
Būlād, Anṭūn. *Rāshid Sūriyya.* Beirut, 1868.
Al-Bustānī, Buṭrus. *Aʿmāl al-Jamʿiyya al-Sūriyya.* Beirut, 1852.
——. *Al-Jamʿiyya al-Sūriyya lil-ʿUlūm wal-Funūn 1847–1852.* Ed. Yūsuf Quzmā Khūrī, Beirut, 1990.
——. *Khiṭāb fī al-Hayʾa al-Ijtimāʿiyya wal-Muqābala bayna al-ʿAwāʾid al-ʿArābiyya wal-Ifranjiyya.* Beirut, 1869.
Al-Dibs, Yūsuf. *Al-Jāmiʿ al-Mufaṣṣal fī Tārīkh al-Mawārina al-Muʾaṣṣal.* Beirut, 1987.
——. *Tārīkh Sūriyya.* 8 vols., Beirut, 1893–1905.
Al-Ḥamawī, Yāqūt. *Muʿjam al-Buldān.* 5 vols., Beirut, 1954.
Al-Ḥatūnī, Manṣūr. *Nabdha Tārīkhīyya fī al-Muqāṭaʿa al-Kisrawāniyya.* Beirut, 1887.
Ibn al-ʿAdīm, Kamāl al-Dīn. *Zubdat al-Ḥalab min Tārīkh Ḥalab.* 3 vols., Damascus, 1951.
Al-Khaṭīb, Muḥibb al-Dīn (ed.). *Al-Muʾtamar al-ʿArabī al-Awwal.* Cairo, 1913.
Al-Khūrī, Khalīl. *Al-ʿAṣr al-Jadīd.* Beirut, 1863.
——. *Kharābāt Sūriyya.* Beirut, 1860.
Al-Maʿlūf, ʿĪsā Iskandar. *Dawānī al-Quṭūf fī Tārīkh Banī Maʿlūf.* Beirut, 1907–1908.
——. *Tārīkh Zaḥla.* Beirut, 1984.
Maṭar, Ilyās. *Al-ʿUqūd al-Durriyya fī al-Mamlaka al-Sūriyya.* Beirut, 1874.
Mishāqa, Mīkhāʾīl. *Al-Jawāb ʿalā Iqtirāḥ al-Aḥbāb.* Beirut, 1874.
——. *Kitāb Mashhad al-ʿAyān bi Ḥawādith Sūriyā wa Lubnān.* Ed. Kh. ʿAbdu and A. H. Shakhāshīrī, Cairo, 1908.
——. *Muntakhabāt min al-Jawāb ʿalā Iqtirāḥ al-Aḥbāb.* Ed. A. Rustum and Ṣ. Abū-Shaqrā, Beirut, 1955.

Muḥammad ʿAlī Bāshā. *Al-Riḥla al-Shāmiyya*. Beirut, 1981.
Al-Munayyir, Ḥanāniyya. *Al-Durr al-Marṣūf fī Tārīkh al-Shūf*. Beirut, 1984.
Al-Qasāṭilī, Nuʿmān. *Al-Rawḍa al-Ghannāʾ fī Dimashq al-Fayḥāʾ*. 2nd ed., Beirut, 1982.
Al-Sanūsī, Muḥammad. *Al-Riḥla al-Ḥijāziyya*, 3 vols., ed. ʿAlī al-Shannūfī. Tunis, 1976.
Sarkīs, Khalīl. *Tārīkh Ūrshalīm—Ayy al-Quds al-Sharīf*. Beirut, 1874.
Al-Shidyāq, Ṭannūs. *Akhbār al-Aʿyān fī Jabal Lubnān*. 2 vols, ed. Buṭrus al-Bustānī. Beirut, 1954.
Al-Shihāb, Aḥmad Ḥaydar. *Lubnān fī ʿAhd al-Umarāʾ al-Shihābiyyīn*. 3 vols., eds. Asad Rustum and Afrām al-Bustānī, Beirut, 1933.
——. *Tārīkh Aḥmad Bāshā al-Jazzār*. Beirut, 1955.
Al-Ṣulḥ, ʿĀdil. *Suṭūr min al-Risāla: Tārīkh Ḥaraka Istiqlāliyya Qāmat fī al-Mashriq al-ʿArabī Sanat 1877*. Beirut, 1966.
Al-Ṭahṭāwī, Rifāʿa Rāfiʿ. *Manāhij al-Albāb al-Miṣriyya fī Mabāhij al-Ādāb al-ʿAṣriyya*. Cairo, 1869.
Al-Turk, Niqūlā. *Dīwān al-Muʿallim Niqūlā al-Turk*. 2 vols., ed. Fuʾād Afrām al-Bustānī, Beirut, 1970.
Al-ʿUmarī, Ibn Faḍlallāh. *Al-Taʿrīf bil-Muṣṭalaḥ al-Sharīf*. Beirut, 1988.
Yannī, Jurjī. *Tārīkh Sūriyā*. Beirut, 1881.
Al-Zayn, ʿĀrif. *Tārīkh Ṣaydā*. Sidon, 1913.
Anonymous. *Ḥasr al-Lithām ʿan Nakabāt al-Shām*. Cairo, 1895.

Books in European Languages

Anderson, Rufus. *Memorial Volume of the Fifty Years of the A.B.C.F.M.* Boston, 1862.
Baedeker, Karl. *Palestine and Syria: A Handbook for Travelers*. Leipzig, 1876.
Bird, Isaac. *Bible Works in Bible Land*. Philadelphia, 1872.
Bliss, Frederick. *The Religions of Modern Syria and Palestine*. New York, 1912.
—— (ed.). *The Reminiscences of Daniel Bliss*. New York, 1920.
Bliss, Howard S. *The Modern Missionary*. Beirut, 1920.
Bowring, John. *Report on the Commercial Statistics of Syria*. London, 1840.
Browne, William G. *Travels in Africa, Egypt and Syria from the Year 1792 to 1798*. London, 1806.
Burckhardt, John L. *Travels in Syria and the Holy Land*. 2 vols., ed. and trans. by Fuat Sezgin, London, 1995.
Burton Drake and Isabel. *Unexplored Syria*. 2 vols., London, 1872.
Burton, Isabel. *The Inner Life of Syria, Palestine, and the Holy Land*. 2 vols., London, 1875.
Churchill, Charles H. *The Druzes and the Maronites under Turkish Rule from 1840 to 1860*. 2nd impression, New York, 1973.
——. *Mount Lebanon: A Ten Years' Residence, 1842–1852*. London, 1853.
Egerton, Francis. *A Tour in the Holy Land in May and June 1840*. London, 1841.
Farley, Lewis J. *The Massacres in Syria*. London, 1861.
Guys, Henri. *Beyrout et le Liban*. Paris, 1850.
Hill, S. S. *Travels in Egypt and Syria*. London, 1866.
Hooker, Edward W. *Memoir of Mrs. Sarah Lanman Smith*. Boston, 1840.
Jessup, Henry H. *Fifty-Three Years in Syria*. 2 vols., New York, 1910.
Kelly, Walter K. *Syria and the Holy Land*. London, 1884.
Khayyat, Asʿad Y. *A Voice from Lebanon*. London, 1847.
Mardrus, J. C. (ed.). *The Arabian Nights: Book of the Thousand Nights and One Night*. 4 vols., trans. by E. P. Mathers, London and New York, 1994.
Mishaqa, Mikhayil. *Murder, Mayhem, Pillage, and Plunder—The History of Lebanon in the 18th and 19th Centuries*. trans. by Wheeler M. Thackston Jr., Albany, 1988.
Murray, John. *Handbook for Travelers in Syria and Palestine*. London, 1868.

Neale, Frederick A. *Eight Years in Syria, Palestine and Asia Minor from 1842–1850.* 2 vols., London, 1851.
Newton, Charles T. *Travels and Discoveries in the Levant*, 2 vols., London, 1865.
Oliphant, Laurence. *The Land of Gilead, with Excursions in the Lebanon.* London, 1880.
Osborn, Henry S. *The Holy Land, Past and Present.* London, 1868.
Paton, Andrew A. *The Modern Syrians.* London, 1844.
Porter, Josias L. *Five Years in Damascus.* 2 vols. London, 1855.
Rattray, Harriet. *Country Life in Syria.* London, 1876.
Rough, Douglas and Belle D. and Alfred H. Howell (eds.). *Daniel Bliss—Letters from a New Campus.* Beirut, 1994.
Salih, Nabil (ed.). *The Qadi and the Fortune Teller.* London, 1996.
Smith, Eli. *Missionary Sermons and Addresses.* Boston, 1833.
Thomson, William M. *The Land and the Book.* London, 1888.
Urquhart, David. *The Lebanon: A History and Diary.* 2 vols., London, 1860.
Volney, Constantin F. *Travels through Syria and Egypt in the Years 1783, 1784 and 1785.* 2 vols. trans. by G. G. J. and J. Robinson, London, 1788.
Wortabet, Gregory M. *Researches in the Religions of Syria and Palestine.* London, 1860.
——. *Syria and the Syrians.* 2 vols., London, 1856.
Anonymous. *Centennial of the American Press, 1822–1922.* Beirut, 1923.

Secondary Sources

Arabic

Abū ʿIzz al-Dīn. Sulaymān, *Ibrāhīm Bāshā fī Sūriyā.* Beirut, 1929.
Abū Khāṭir, Hīnrī. *Jumhūriyyat Zaḥla-Awwal Jumhūriyya fī al-Sharq.* Beirut, 1978.
Abū Ṣāliḥ, ʿAbbās. *Al-Tārīkh al-Siyāsī lil-Imāra al-Shihābiyya fī Jabal Lubnān 1697–1842.* Beirut, 1984.
ʿAwaḍ, ʿAbd al-ʿAzīz Muḥammad. *Al-Idāra al-ʿUthmāniyya fī Wilāyat Sūriyya, 1864–1914.* Cairo, 1969.
Badir, ʿAbd Al-Muḥsin. *Taṭawwur al-Riwāya al-ʿArabiyya al-Ḥadītha fī Miṣr 1870–1938.* Cairo, 1963.
Bawārdī, Basīliyūs. *Bayna al-Ṣaḥrāʾ wal-Baḥr: Baḥth fī Taʾthīr al-Qawmiyyatayn al-Lubnāniyya—al-Fīnīqiyya wal-Sūriyya ʿalā al-Adab al-ʿArabī al-Muʿāṣir*, unpublished M.A. Thesis, University of Haifa, 1998.
——. "Adab al-Qawmiyya al-Lubnāniyya al-Fīnīqiyya: al-Taṣwīnī Awwal Riwāya bil-Lugha al-Lubnāniyya Kanamūdhaj Nassī," *al-Karmil Abḥāth fī al-Lugha wal-Adab*, Vols. 20–21 (2001–2000), pp. 7–79.
Birmū, ʿAbd al-Raḥmān. *Al-Riwāya al-Tārīkhiyya fī al-Ādāb al-Sūrī al-Muʿāṣir.* Damascus, 1996.
Al-Bīṭār, ʿAbd al-Razzāq. *Ḥilyat al-Bashar fī Tārīkh al-Qarn al-Thālith ʿAshar.* 3 vols., Damascus, 1961–1963.
Al-Bustānī, Shukrī. *Dayr al-Qamar fī Ākhir al-Qarn al-Tāsiʿ ʿAshar—Muḥāwala Tārīkhiyya Ijtimāʿiyya wa Iqtiṣādiyya.* Beirut, 1969.
Dāghir, Yūsuf. *Al-Aṣūl al-ʿArabiyya lil-Dirasāt al-Lubnāniyya.* Beirut, 1982.
——. *Maṣādir al-Dirāsa al-Adabiyya.* 2 vols., Sidon, 1950.
Dāya, Jān. "Bākūrat al-Jamʿiyyāt al-Thaqāfiyya fī Sūriyya wal-ʿĀlam al-ʿArabī," *Fikr*, Vols. 20–21 (1984), pp. 173–181.
Gharāyiba, ʿAbd al-Karīm. *Sūriyya fī al-Qarn al-Tāsiʿ ʿAshar, 1840–1876.* Cairo, 1961.
Al-Ghazzī, Kāmil. *Kitāb Nahr al-Dhahab fī Tārīkh Ḥalab.* 2nd ed., 3 vols., eds. Shawqī Shaʿth and Maḥmūd Fākhūrī. Aleppo, 1991.
Ḥallāq, Ḥasan. *Al-Tārīkh al-Ijtimāʿī wal-Iqtiṣādī wal-Siyāsī fī Bayrūt wal-Wilāyāt al-ʿUthmāniyya fī al-Qarn al-Tāsiʿ ʿAshar.* Beirut, 1987.

——. *Awqāf al-Muslimīn fī Bayrūt fī al-ʿAhd al-ʿUthmānī-Sijillāt al-Maḥkama al- Sharʿiyya fī Bayrūt*. Beirut, 1988.
Ḥardān, Nawwāf. *Ẓanūbyā al-ʿAẓīma—Qaḍiyya wa-Sayf wa-Kitāb*. Beirut, 1995.
Ilyās, Jūjīf. *Taṭawwur al-Ṣiḥāfa al-Sūriyya fī Miʾat ʿĀm 1860–1965*. Beirut, 1982–1983.
Jiḥā, Mīshāl. *Ibrāhīm al-Yāziji*. London, 1992.
——. *Salīm al-Bustānī*. London, 1989.
Khūrī, Mārūn ʿĪsā. *Malāmiḥ min al-Ḥarakāt al-Thaqāfiyya fī Ṭarāblus khilāl al-Qarn al-Tāsiʿ ʿAshar*. Tripoli, 1982.
Kurd ʿAlī, Muḥammad. *Khiṭaṭ al-Shām*. 6 vols., 2nd ed., Beirut, 1969–1972.
Al-Mūsawī, Muḥsin. *Al-Riwāya al-ʿArabiyya—al-Nashʾa wal-Taḥawwul*. 2nd ed. Beirut, 1988.
Najm, Muḥammad. *Al-Qiṣṣa fī al-Adab al-ʿArabī al-Ḥadīth*. 3rd ed., Beirut, 1966.
Al-Naṣūlī, Anīs. *Asbāb al-Nahḍa al-ʿArabiyya fī al-Qarn al-Tāsiʿ ʿAshar*. Beirut, 1985.
Nawfal, ʿAbdallāh Ḥabīb. *Tarājim ʿUlamāʾ Ṭarāblus wa-Udabāʾihā*. 2nd ed., Tripoli, 1984.
Qassūma, al-Ṣādiq. *Al-Riwāya Muqawwimātuhā wa-Nashʾatuhā fī al-Adab al-ʿArabī al-Ḥadīth*. Tunis, 2000.
Raḍwān, Abū al-Futūḥ. *Tārīkh Maṭbaʿat Būlāq wa Lamḥa fī Tārīkh al-Ṭibāʾa fī Buldān al-Sharq al-Awsaṭ*. Cairo, 1953.
Al-Rifāʿī, Shams al-Dīn. *Tārīkh al-Ṣiḥāfa al-Sūrriya*. 2 vols., Cairo, 1969.
Rustum, Asad. *Bashīr Bayna al-Sulṭān wal-ʿAzīz. 1804–1841*, Beirut, 1956–1957.
——. *Lubnān fī ʿAhd al-Mutaṣarrifiyya*. Beirut, 1909.
——. *Al-Maḥfūẓāt al-Malakiyya al-Miṣriyya*. 4 vols., Beirut, 1940–1943.
—— (ed.). *Al-Uṣūl al-ʿArabiyya li-Tārīkh Sūriyya fī ʿAhd Muḥammad ʿAlī Bāshā*. 2nd ed., Beirut, 1987–1988.
Al-Saʿāfīn, Ibrāhīm. *Taṭawwur al-Riwāya al-ʿArabiyya al-Ḥadītha fī Bilād al-Shām* 1870–1967. Baghdad, 1980.
Ṣāfir, Buṭrus. *Al-Amīr Bashīr al-Shihābī*. Beirut, 1950.
Salām, Salīm. *Mudhakkirāt Salīm ʿAlī Salām*. Ed. Ḥasan Ḥallāq, Beirut, 1982.
Sarkīs, Yūsuf. *Muʿjam al-Maṭbūʿāt al-ʿArabiyya wal-Muʿarraba*. 2 vols., Cairo, 1928–1929.
Shīkhū, Lūwīs. *Bayrūt—Tārīkhuhā wa-Āthāruhā*. Beirut, 1925.
——. *Tārīkh al-Ādāb al-ʿArabiyya 1800–1925*. Beirut, 1991.
Smīlīyānskāyā, Īrīnā. *Al-Bunā al-Iqtiṣādiyya wal-Ijtimāʿiyya fī al-Mashriq al-ʿArabī ʿalā Mashārif al-ʿAsr al-Ḥadīth*. Trans. from Russian, Beirut, 1989.
Al-Ṭabbākh, Muḥammad. *Aʿlām al-Nubalāʾ bi-Tārīkh Ḥalab al-Shahbāʾ*. 2nd ed., 7 vols., Damascus, 1988.
Ṭarrāzī, Fīlīb dī. *Tārīkh al-Ṣiḥāfa al-ʿArabiyya*. 4 vols., Beirut, 1913–1924.
Yāghī, ʿAbd al-Raḥmān. *Fī al-Juhūd al-Riwāʾiyya Mā Bayna Salīm al-Bustānī wa-Najīb Maḥfūẓ*. 2nd ed., Beirut, 1981.
Zaydān, Jurjī. *Tarājim Mashāhīr al-Sharq fī al-Qarn al-Tāsiʿ ʿAshar*. 2 vols., 3rd ed, Cairo, 1922.
——. *Tārīkh Ādāb al-Lugha al-ʿArabiyya*. 4 vols., Cairo, 1957.
Ziyāda, Niqūlā. *Abʿād al-Tārīkh al-Lubnānī al-Ḥadīth*. Cairo, 1972.

Western Languages

Abbott, Nabia. "Pre-Islamic Arab Queens," *The American Journal of Semitic Languages and Literatures*, Vol. 58 (1941), pp. 1–22.
Abkariyus, Iskandar ibn Ya'qub. *The Lebanon in Turmoil—Syria and the Powers in 1860*. trans. by Johann F. Scheltema. New Haven, 1920.
Abu-Ghazaleh, Adnan. *American Missions in Syria: A Study of American Missionary Contribution to Arab Nationalism in 19th Century Syria*. Vermont, 1990.
Abu-Manneh, Butrus. "The Christians Between Ottomanism and Syrian Nationalism: The Ideas of Buṭrus al-Bustani," *International Journal of Middle East Studies*, Vol. 11 (1980), pp. 287–304.
——. "The Establishment and Dismantling of the Province of Syria 1865–1888,"

in J. P. Spagnolo (ed.), *Problems of the Modern Middle East in Historical Perspective*, Reading, 1992, pp. 7–26.

——. "The Genesis of Midhat Pasha's Governorship in Syria 1878–1880," in Thomas Philipp and Birgit Schaebler (eds.), *The Syrian Land—Process of Integration and Fragmentation in Bilad al-Sham from the 18th to the 20th Century*, Stuttgart, 1998, pp. 251–267.

——. "The Rise of The *Sanjaq* of Jerusalem in the Late 19th Century," in Gabriel Ben-Dor (ed.), *The Palestinians and the Middle East Conflict*, Tel-Aviv, 1979, pp. 21–32.

——. "The Sultan and the Bureaucracy: The Anti-Tanzimat Concepts of Grand Vizier Mahmud Nadim Pasha," *International Journal of Middle East Studies*, Vol. 22 (1990), pp. 257–274.

——. *Studies on Islam and the Ottoman Empire in the 19th Century 1826–1876*. Istanbul, 2001.

Akarli, Engin D. *The Long Peace—Ottoman Lebanon. 1861–1920*. London, 1993.

Allen, Roger. *The Arabic Novel: An Historical and Critical Introduction*. New York, 1982.

Anderson, Benedict. *Imagined Communities*. 2nd ed., London, 1991.

Antonius, George. *The Arab Awakening: The Story of the Arab National Movement*. New York, 1965.

Arat, Yeşim. "The Project of Modernity and Women in Turkey," in Sibel Bozdogan and Reşat Kasaba (eds.), *Rethinking Modernity and National Identity in Turkey*. Seattle, 1997, pp. 95–112.

Ayalon, Ami. "Modern Texts and Their Readers in Late Ottoman Palestine," *Middle Eastern Studies*, Vol. 38 (2002), pp. 17–40.

——. *The Press in the Arab Middle East—A History*. New York, 1995.

Baron, Beth. "Nationalist Iconography—Egypt as a Women," in James Jankowski and Israel Gershoni (eds.). *Rethinking Nationalism in the Arab Middle East*. New York, 1997, pp. 105–124.

——. *The Women's Awakening in Egypt, Culture, Society and the Press*. Chelsea, Michigan, 1994.

Ben-Arieh, Yehoshua. "The Population of the Large Towns in Palestine during the First Eighty Years of the Nineteenth Century, According to Western Sources," in Moshe Maʿoz (ed.), *Studies on Palestine during the Ottoman Period*. Jerusalem, 1975, pp. 49–69.

Bill, James. "Class Analysis and the Dialectics of Modernization in the Middle East," *International Journal of Middle East Studies*, Vol. 3 (1972), pp. 417–434.

Bodenstein, Ralph. "Housing the Foreign—A European's Exotic Home in Late Nineteenth-Century Beirut," in Jens Hanssen, Thomas Philipp and Stefan Weber (eds.), *The Empire in the City—Arab Provincial Capitals in the Late Ottoman Empire*. Beirut, 2002, pp. 105–127.

Bonne, Alfred. *The Economic Development of the Middle East*. New York, 1945.

Booth, Marilyn. *May Her Likes Be Multiplied: Biography and Gender Politics in Egypt*. Berkeley, 2001.

Buheiry, Marwan. *Beirut's Role in the Political Economy of the French Mandate, 1919–1939*. Papers on Lebanon, Centre for Lebanese Studies, Oxford, 1986.

——. "Lebanese Christian Intellectuals and the Ottoman State: Azuri, Mujaym, Yanni and Bustani," in Abdeljelil Temimi (ed.), *Les Provinces Arabes á l'Epoque Ottoman*. Zaghouan, 1987, pp. 77–85.

Burke, Edmund. "Rural Collective Action and the Emergence of Modern Lebanon—A Comparative Historical Perspective," in Nadim Shehadi and Dana Haffar Milles (eds.), *Lebanon: A History of Conflict and Consensus*. London, 1988, pp. 49–63.

Buzpınar, Tufan. "The Question of the Caliphate under the Last Ottoman Sultans," in Itzchak Weismann and Fruma Zachs (eds.). *Ottoman Reform and Islamic Regeneration*. forthcoming, London, 2005.

Cannon, Byron D. "Nineteenth-Century Arabic Writing on Women and Society: The Interim Role of the Masonic Press in Cairo (*al-Laṭā'if*, 1885–1895)," *International Journal of Middle East Studies*, Vol. 17 (1985), pp. 463–471.
Chatterjee, Partha. *The Nation and its Fragments: Colonial and Postcolonial Histories*. Princeton, 1993.
Chevallier, Dominique. *La Société du Mont Liban: A l'Epoque de la Révolution Industrielle en Europe*. Paris, 1971.
Choueiri, Yussef M. *Arab History and the Nation-State—A Study of Modern Arab Historiography, 1820–1920*. London, 1989.
——. "Two Histories of Syria and the Demise of Syrian Patriotism," *Middle Eastern Studies*, Vol. 23 (1987), pp. 496–511.
Churchill, Charles H. *Mount Lebanon: A Ten Years Residence, 1842–1852*. London, 1853.
Cioeta, Donald J. "Islamic Benevolent Societies and Public Education in Ottoman Syria 1875–1882," *The Islamic Quarterly*, Vol. 25 (1981), pp. 40–55.
Cohen, Amnon. *Palestine in the 18th Century*. Jerusalem, 1973.
Comaroff, Jean and John. *Of Revelation and Revolution: Christianity, Colonialism, and Consciousness in South Africa*. Chicago, 1991.
Davie, May. "Les Familles Grecques Orthodoxes de la Ville de Beyrouth—à Travers les Cahiers du Badal 'Askariyyat (1876–1895)," *Annales d'Histoire et d'Archéologie*, Vol. 5 (1986), pp. 1–43.
——. "Pouvoir Rural, Pouvoir Urbain: l'Èchec de l'Ètat au Liban," *Cahiers de la Mediterranee*, No. 46/47 (1993), pp. 255–271.
——. "Ville, Notables et Pouvoir: Les Orthodoxes de Beyrouth au XIXème Siecle," *Cahiers de la Mediterranee*, No. 45 (1992), pp. 184–200.
Davison, Roderic H. *Essays in Ottoman and Turkish History 1774–1923: The Impact of the West*. Austin, 1990.
——. *Reform in the Ottoman Empire 1856–1876*. Princeton, 1963.
——. "Turkish Attitudes Concerning Christian Muslim Equality in the Nineteenth Century," *American Historical Review*, Vol. 59, No. 4 (1954), pp. 844–864.
Dawn, Ernest C. "The Origins of Arab Nationalism," in Rashid Khalidi et al. (eds.) *The Origins of Arab Nationalism*. New York, 1991.
Deringil, Selim. *The Well-Protected Domains: Ideology and the Legitimating of Power in the Ottoman Empire 1876–1909*. London, 1998.
Dodge, Bayard. *The American University of Beirut*. Beirut, 1958.
Doumani, Beshara. *Rediscovering Palestine: Merchants and Peasants in Jabal Nablus, 1700–1900*. Berkeley, 1995.
Doumato, Eleanor A. "'Extra Legible Illustration' of Christian Faith: Medicine, Medical Ethics and Missionaries in the Arabian Gulf," *Islam and Christian-Muslim Relations*, Vol. 13 (2002), pp. 388–389.
Dunch, Ryan. "Beyond Cultural Imperialism: Cultural Theory, Christian Missions, and Global Modernity," *History and Theory*, Vol. 41 (2002), pp. 301–325.
——. *Fuzhou Protestant and the Making of a Modern China*, 1857–1927. New Haven, 2001.
Eissa, Ashraf A. "Majallat al-Jinān: Arabic Narrative Discourse in the Making," *Quaderni di Studi Arabi*, Vol. 18 (2000), pp. 41–49.
Eldem, Edhem and Daniel Goffman and Bruce Masters (eds.). *The Ottoman City between East and West, Aleppo, Izmir, and Istanbul*. Cambridge, 1999.
Enkiri, Gabriel. *Aux Origines du Liban Contemporain: Le Regene de Bechir II*. Beirut, 1973.
Exertzoglou, Harris. "The Development of a Greek Ottoman Bourgeoisie: Investment Patterns in the Ottoman Empire, 1850–1914," in Dimitri Gondicas and Charles Issawi (eds.), *Ottoman Greeks in the Age of Nationalism: Politics Economy and Society in the 19th Century*. Princeton, 1999, pp. 89–107.
Fawaz, Leila T. *An Occasion For War: Civil Conflict in Lebanon and Damascus in 1860*. London, 1994.

——. "The Changing Balance of Forces between Beirut and Damascus in the Nineteenth and Twentieth Centuries," *Revue de Monde Musulman et de la Mediterranee* (1990), pp. 208–214.
——. *Merchants and Migrants in Nineteenth Century Beirut.* London, 1983.
——. "Zahleh and Dayr al-Qamar—Two Market Towns of Mount Lebanon During the Civil War of 1860," in Nadim Shehadi and Dana H. Milles (eds.), *Lebanon: A History of Conflict and Consensus.* London, 1988, pp. 49–63.
Firro, Kais. *Inventing Lebanon: Nationalism and the State under the Mandate.* London, 2002.
——. "Silk and Agrarian Changes in Lebanon, 1864–1914," *International Journal of Middle East Studies,* Vol. 22 (1990), pp. 151–169.
——. "Silk and Socio-Economic Changes in Lebanon, 1860–1919," in Eli Kedourie and Sylvia G. Haim (eds.), *Essays on the Economic History of the Middle East.* London, 1988.
Fowler, Alastair, *Kinds of Literature: An Introduction to the Theory of Genres and Modes.* Oxford, 1982.
——. "Transformation of Genre," in David Duff (ed.) *Modern Genre Theory.* London, 2000, pp. 232–249.
Fraser, Antonia. *The Warrior Queens: Boadicea's Chariot.* London, 1988.
Gellner, Ernest. *Nations and Nationalism.* Ithaca, 1983.
Gelvin, James L. *Divided Loyalties—Nationalism and Mass Politics in Syria at the Close of Empire.* Los Angeles, 1998.
Gerber, Haim. "'Palestine' and Other Territorial Concepts in the 17th Century," *International Journal of Middle East Studies,* Vol. 30 (1998), pp. 563–572.
——. *The Social Origins of the Modern Middle East.* Boulder, 1987.
Göçek, Fatma M. *Rise of the Bourgeoisie, Demise of Empire—Ottoman Westernization and Social Change.* New York, 1996.
Goldziher, Ignaz. *Muslim Studies.* 2 vols., trans. by C. R. Barber and S. M. Stern. London, 1967.
Gossman, Lionel. *Between History and Literature.* Cambridge, Mass., 1990.
Grabill, Joseph L. *Protestant Diplomacy and the Near East: Missionary Influence on American Policy, 1810–1927.* Minneapolis, 1971.
Groiss, Arnon. *Religious Particularism and National Integration: Changing Perceptions of the Political Self-Identity among the Greek-Orthodox Christians,* Ph.D. dissertation, Princeton University, 1986.
Gross, Max L. *Ottoman Rule in the Province of Damascus 1860–1909,* Ph.D. dissertation, Georgetown University, 2 vols., 1979.
Haddad, Mahmoud. "The City, the Coast, the Mountain, and the Hinterland: Beirut's Commercial and Political Rivalries in the 19th and Early 20th Centuries," in Thomas Philipp and Birgit Scheabler (eds.), *The Syrian Land: Processes, Integration and Fragmentation.* Stuttgart, 1998, pp. 129–153.
Haddad, Robert. *Syrian Christians in Muslim Society: An Interpretation.* Westport and Princeton, 1970.
Hafez, Sabry. *The Genesis of Arabic Narrative Discourse: A Study in the Sociology of Modern Arabic Literature.* London, 1993.
Hakim-Dowek, Carol. *The Origins of the Lebanese National Idea 1840–1914.* D.Phil. dissertation, St. Antony's College, Oxford, 1997.
Hall, Stuart and Paul Du Gay (eds.). *Questions of Cultural Identity.* London, 1996.
Hanna, Faith M. *An American Mission: The Role of the American University of Beirut.* New York, 1979.
Harik, Iliya F. "The Impact of the Domestic Market on Rural-Urban Relations in the Middle East," in Richard Antoun and Iliya F. Harik (eds.). *Rural Politics and Social Change in the Middle East.* London, 1972, pp. 337–363.
——. *Politics and Change in a Traditional Society: Lebanon 1711–1845.* Princeton, 1968.
Haydar, Midhat A. *The Life of Midhat Pasha.* London, 1903.

Hitti, Philip K. *History of Syria—Including Lebanon and Palestine*. London, 1951.
——. "The Impact of the West on Syria and Lebanon in the Nineteenth Century," *Cahiers d'Histoire Mondial*, vol. 2 (1955), pp. 609–663.
Hobsbawm, Eric and Terence Ranger (eds.). *The Invention of Tradition*. London, 1983.
Hobsbawm, Eric. *On History*. London, 1997.
——. *Nations and Nationalism Since 1780, Programme, Myth, Reality*. 2nd ed., Cambridge, 1999.
Hourani, Albert. *Arabic Thought in the Liberal Age 1798–1939*. London, 1962.
——. "Historians of Lebanon," in Bernard Lewis and Peter M. Holt (eds.). *Historians of the Middle East*. London, 1962, pp. 226–245.
Howard, Harry N. *The King-Crane Commission*. Beirut, 1963.
Hurewitz, Jacob C. *The Middle East and North Africa in World Politics*. 2 vols., London, 1975.
Issawi, Charles. *The Economic History of the Middle East, 1800–1914*. Chicago, 1966.
Jandora, John W. "Butrus al-Bustani, Arab Consciousness and Arabic Revival," *Muslim World*, Vol. 74 (1984), pp. 77–84.
Johnson, Michael. *Class and Client in Beirut—the Sunni-Muslim Community and the Lebanese State, 1840–1985*. London, 1986.
Kandiyoti, Deniz. "Slave Girls, Temptresses, and Comrades: Images of Women in the Turkish Novel," *Feminist Issues*, Vol. 8 (1988), pp. 33–50.
Kaufman, Asher. "Phoenicianism: The Formation of an Identity in Lebanon in 1920," *Middle Eastern Studies*, Vol. 37 (2001), pp. 173–194.
——. *Reviving Phoenicia: The Search for Identity in Lebanon*. London, 2004.
Keddie, Nikki R. "Pan-Islam as Proto-Nationalism," *The Journal of Modern History*, Vol. 4 (1969), pp. 17–28.
Kedouri, Eli. "The American University of Beirut," *Middle Eastern Studies*, Vol. 3 (1966), pp. 74–90.
Khalaf, Samir. "New England Puritanism and Liberal Education in the Middle East: The American University of Beirut as a Cultural Transplant," in Şerif Mardin (ed.). *Cultural Transitions in the Middle East*. Leiden, 1994, pp. 50–85.
Khalidi, Rashid. *Palestinian Identity—The Construction of Modern National Consciousness*. New York, 1997.
Khoury, Ghada Y. *The Founding Fathers of the American University in Beirut—Biographies*. Beirut, 1992.
Kiraly, Bela. "Prussian Diplomatic Adventure with Poland and the Feudal Revolt in Hungary in 1790," *Polish Review*, Vol. 12 (1967), pp. 3–11.
Kontje, Todd C. *Women, the Novel and the German Nation 1771–1871—Domestic Fiction in the Fatherland*. Cambridge, 1998.
Krymskii, Agafangel E. *Istoria Novoi Arbskoi Literaturyi, XIX-Nachalo XX Beka* (History of New Arab Literature, XIX—Beginning of XX Century). Moscow, 1971.
Le Strange, Guy. *Palestine under the Moslems*. Beirut, 1965.
Lewis, Bernard. *The Emergence of Modern Turkey*. London, 1961.
Lindsay, Rao H. *Nineteenth-Century American Schools in the Levant: A Study of Purposes*. Ann Arbor, 1965.
Lynch Deidre and Warner William B. (eds.). *Cultural Institutions of the Novel*. London, 1996.
Makdisi, Ussama. *The Culture of Sectarianism—Community, History and Violence in Nineteenth-Century Ottoman Lebanon*. Berkeley and Los Angeles, 2000.
——. "Reclaiming the Land of the Bible: Missionaries, Secularism and Evangelical Modernity," *The American Historical Review*, Vol. 102 (1997), pp. 680–713.
Maʿoz, Moshe. *Ottoman Reform in Syria and Palestine, 1840–1861*. Oxford, 1968.
Mardin, Şerif. "Super Westernization in Urban Life in the Ottoman Empire in the Last Quarter of the Nineteenth Century," in Peter Benedict, Erol Tümertekin and Fatma Mansur (eds.). *Turkey: Geographic and Social Perspectives*. Leiden, 1974, pp. 403–446.

Masters, Bruce. *Christians and Jews in the Ottoman Arab World: The Roots of Sectarianism.* Cambridge, 2001.

Matti, Moosa. *The Origins of Modern Arabic Fiction.* Boulder, 1997.

McCarthy, Justin. "The Population of Ottoman Syria and Iraq 1878–1914," *Asian and African Studies,* Vol. 15 (1981), pp. 123–148.

Munro, John M., *A Mutual Concern: The Story of the American University of Beirut.* New York, 1977.

Naff, Alixa. *A Social History of Zahle, the Principal Market Town in Nineteenth Century Lebanon.* Ph.D. dissertation, University of California, 2 vols., Los Angeles, 1972.

Najamabadi, Afsaneh. "The Erotic Vatan [Homeland] as Beloved and Mother: To Love, To Possess, and To Protect," *Comparative Studies in Society and History,* Vol. 39 (1997), pp. 442–467.

Oddie, Geoffrey. *Missionaries, Rebellion and Proto-Nationalism—James Long of Bengal 1814–87.* London, 1999.

Owen, Roger. *The Middle East in the World Economy, 1800–1914.* London, 1982.

Özveren, Eyup Y. *The Making and Unmaking of an Ottoman Port City: Nineteenth Century Beirut, its Hinterland, and the World Economy.* Ph.D. dissertation, University of New York, 1990.

Pears, Edwin. *The Life of Abdul Hamid.* London, 1917.

Penrose, Stephen B. L. *That They May Have Life: The Story of the American University, 1866–1941.* Beirut, 1970.

Philipp, Thomas. *Acre: The Rise and the Fall of a Palestinian City, 1730–1831.* New York, 2001.

——. *The Syrians in Egypt.* Stuttgart, 1985.

Pipes, Daniel. *Greater Syria—The History of an Ambition.* Oxford, 1990.

Piterberg, Gabriel. "The Tropes of Stagnation and Awakening in Nationalist Historical Consciousness—The Egyptian Case," in James Jankowski and Israel Gershoni (eds.). *Rethinking Nationalism in the Arab Middle East.* New York, 1997, pp. 48–50.

Polk, William R. and Richard L. Chambers (eds.). *Beginnings of Modernization in the Middle East—The Nineteenth Century.* Chicago, 1966.

Polk, William R. *The Opening of South Lebanon, 1788–1840.* Cambridge, Mass., 1963.

Rabinovich, Itamar. "Syria and the Syrian Land: The 19th Century Roots of the 20th Century Development," in Philipp, Thomas (ed.), *The Syrian Land in the 18th and 19th Century,* Stuttgart, 1992, pp. 43–53.

Reilly, James A. "Damascus Merchants and Trade in the Transition to Capitalism," *Canadian Journal of History,* Vol. 27 (1992), pp. 1–27.

Roded, Ruth M. *Tradition and Change in Syria during the Last Decades of Ottoman Rule: The Urban Elite of Damascus, Aleppo, Homs and Hama, 1876–1918.* Ph.D. dissertation, University of Denver, 1984.

Rogan, Eugene L. *Frontiers of the State in the Late Ottoman Empire.* London, 1999.

Rosenthal, Franz. *A History of Muslim Historiography.* Leiden, 1968.

Said, Edward W. *Orientalism.* London, 1995.

——. *The World, the Text, and the Critic.* Cambridge, Mass., 1983.

Saliba, Najib E. "The Achievements of Midhat Pasha as Governor of the Province of Syria, 1788–1880," *International Journal of Middle East Studies,* Vol. 9 (1978), pp. 307–323.

——. *Wilayet Suriyya 1876–1909.* Ph.D. dissertation, University of Michigan, 1971.

Salibi, Kamal S. "The 1860 Upheaval in Damascus as Seen by al-Sayyid Muhammed Abu'l-Suʿud al-Hasibi, Notable and Later Naqib al-Ashraf of the City," in William R. Polk and Richard L. Chambers (eds.). *Beginnings of Modernization in the Middle East—The Nineteenth Century.* Chicago, 1966, pp. 185–202.

——. *The Modern History of Syria.* London, 1965.

——. "The Two Worlds of Asʿad Y. Kayat," in Benjamin Barude and Bernard Lewis (eds.). *Christians and Jews in the Ottoman Empire.* 2 vols., New York, 1982, pp. 135–155.

Schatkowski-Schilcher, Linda S. *Families in Politics: Damascus Factions and Estates of the 18th and 19th Centuries.* Stuttgart, 1985.
——. *The Islamic Maqased of Beirut—A Case Study of Modernization in Lebanon.* M.A. Thesis, American University of Beirut, 1969.
Schölch, Alexander. *Palestine in Transformation, 1822–1856.* trans. by William C. Young and Michael C. Gerrity, Washington DC, 1993.
Sethi, Rumina. *Myth of the Nation: National Identity and Literary Representation.* New York, 1999.
Shamir, Shimon. "Egyptian Rule (1832–1840) and the Beginning of the Modern Period in the History of Palestine," in Amnon Cohen (ed.). *Egypt and Palestine.* Jerusalem, 1984, pp. 214–231.
——. "Midhat Pasha and the Anti-Turkish Agitation in Syria," *Middle Eastern Studies,* Vol. 10 (1974), pp. 115–141.
——. "The Modernization of Syria—Problems and Solutions in the Early Period of Abdul Hamid," in William R. Polk, and Richard L. Chambers (eds.). *Beginnings of Modernization in the Middle East—The Nineteenth Century.* Chicago, 1966, pp. 351–381.
Sharabi, Hisham. *Arab Intellectuals and the West: The Formative Years. 1875–1914,* Baltimore, 1970.
Shaw, Stanford J. and Shaw, Ezel K. *History of the Ottoman Empire and Modern Turkey.* 2 vols., Cambridge, 1977.
Shehadeh, Lamia R. "The Name of Syria in Ancient and Modern Usage," *al Qantara,* Vol. 15 (1994), pp. 285–296.
Sheehi, Stephen P. *Foundations of Modern Arab Identity.* Gainesville, Florida, 2004.
——. "Inscribing the Arab Self: Butrus al-Bustani and Paradigms of Subjective Reform," *British Journal of Middle Eastern Studies,* Vol. 27 (2000), pp. 7–24.
Smilanskaya, Irena M. "From Subsistence to Market Economy—1850s" in Charles Issawi (ed.). *The Economic History of the Middle East, 1800–1914.* Chicago, 1961, pp. 226–247.
Smith, Anthony. *Myths and Memories of the Nation.* Oxford and New York, 1999.
Smith, R. W. "The American University of Beirut," *Middle Eastern Affairs,* Vol. 7 (1956), pp. 292–334.
Snir, Reuven. *Modern Arabic Literature: A Functional Dynamic Model.* Toronto, 2001.
Steppat, Fritz. "Eine Bewegung unter den Notabeln Syriens, 1877–1878," *Zeitschrift der Deutschen Morgenländischen Gesellschaft,* Sup. 1 (1968), pp. 631–649.
Strohmeier, Martin. *Crucial Images in the Presentation of the Kurdish National Identity: Heroes and Patriots, Traitors and Foes.* Leiden, 2003.
Stromquist, Shelton. "The Communist Uprising of 1926–1927 in Indonesia: A Re-Interpretation," *Journal of Southeast Asian History,* Vol. 7 (1967), pp. 189–200.
Taylor, Alan R. *The American Protestant Mission and the Awakening of Modern Syria 1820–1870.* unpublished Ph.D. dissertation, Georgetown University, 1957.
Tejirian, Eleanor H. and Reeva Simon S. (eds.) *Altruism and Imperialism: Western Religious and Cultural Missions to the Middle East.* New York, 2002.
Tibawi, Abdul Latif. *American Interests in Syria, 1800–1901.* Oxford, 1966.
——. "The American Missionaries in Beirut and Butrus al-Bustani," St. Antony's Papers, *Middle Eastern Affairs,* no. 16 (1963), p. 161.
——. "The Genesis and Early History of the Syrian Protestant College," in Fuad Sarruf and Suha Tamim (eds.). *American University of Beirut, Festival Book (Festschrift).* Beirut, 1967, pp. 257–294.
——. *A Modern History of Syria, Including Lebanon and Palestine.* London, 1969.
——. "Some Misconceptions about the Nahda," *Middle East Forum,* Vol. 47 (1971), pp. 15–22.
Tibi, Bassam. *Arab Nationalism: A Critical Inquiry.* London, 1981.
Tlass, Moustafa. *Zenobia, The Queen of Palmyra.* Damascus, 2000.
Van Leeuwen, Richard. "Monastic Estates and Agricultural Transformation in Mount

Lebanon in the 18th Century," *International Journal of Middle East Studies*, Vol. 23 (1991), pp. 601–617.

Weismann, Itzchak. *Taste of Modernity: Sufism, Salafiyya and Arabism in Late Ottoman Damascus*. Leiden, 2001.

White, Hayden V. *The Content of the Form: Narrative Discourse and Historical Representation.* Baltimore, 1987.

Wright, William. *An Account of Palmyra and Zenobia with Travels and Adventures in Bashan and the Desert.* London, 1895.

Yuval-Davis, Nira. *Gender and Nation.* London, 1997.

Zachs, Fruma. "Building a Cultural Identity: The Case of Khalil al-Khuri," in Thomas Philipp and Christoph Schumann (eds.), *From the Syrian Land to the States of Syria and Lebanon* (Beirut, 2004), pp. 27–39.

——. "'Novice' or 'Heaven-born' Diplomat? Lord Dufferin's Plan for a 'Province of Syria': Beirut, 1860–61," *Middle Eastern Studies*, Vol. 36, No. 3 (2000), pp. 160–176.

——. "Mīkhā'īl Mishāqa—The First Historian of Modern Syria," *British Journal of Middle Eastern Studies*, Vol. 28, no. 1 (2001), pp. 67–87.

——. "Toward a Proto-Nationalist Concept of Syria? Revisiting the American Presbyterian Missionaries in Nineteenth-Century Levant," *Die Welt des Islams*, Vol. 41 (2001), pp. 145–173.

Zeine, Zeine N. *The Emergence of Arab Nationalism, With a Background Study of Arab-Turkish Relations in the Near East.* New York, 1973.

INDEX